WRITING PHILOSOPHICAL AUTOETHNOGRAPHY

Writing Philosophical Autoethnography is the result of Alec Grant's vision of bringing the disciplines of philosophy and autoethnography together. This is the first volume of narrative autoethnographic work in which invited contributing authors were charged with exploring their issues, concerns, and topics about human society, culture, and the material world through an explicitly philosophical lens.

Each chapter, while written autoethnographically, showcases sustained engagement with philosophical arguments, ideas, concepts, theories, and corresponding ethical positions. Unlike much other autoethnographic work, within which philosophical ideas often appear to be "grafted on" or supplementary, the philosophical basis of the work in this volume is fundamental to its shifting content, focus, and context. The narratives in this book, from scholars working in a range of disciplines in the humanities and human sciences, function as narrative, conceptual, and analytical exemplars to act as a guide for autoethnographers in their own writing, and suggest future directions for making autoethnography more philosophically rigorous.

This book is suitable for students and scholars of autoethnography and qualitative methods in a range of disciplines, including the humanities, social and human sciences, communication studies, and education.

Alec Grant, PhD, is Visiting Professor in the Department of Psychology and Education, Faculty of Professional Studies, University of Bolton, UK.

Writing Lives

Ethnographic and Autoethnographic Narratives
Series Editors: Arthur P. Bochner, Carolyn Ellis and Tony E. Adams
University of South Florida and *Bradley University*

Writing Lives: Ethnographic and Autoethnographic Narratives publishes narrative representations of qualitative research projects. The series editors seek manuscripts that blur the boundaries between humanities and social sciences. We encourage novel and evocative forms of expressing concrete lived experience, including autoethnographic, literary, poetic, artistic, visual, performative, critical, multi-voiced, conversational, and co-constructed representations. We are interested in ethnographic narratives that depict local stories; employ literary modes of scene setting, dialogue, character development, and unfolding action; and include the author's critical reflections on the research and writing process, such as research ethics, alternative modes of inquiry and representation, reflexivity, and evocative storytelling. Proposals and manuscripts should be directed to abochner@usf.edu, cellis@usf.edu or tadams@bradley.edu

An Autoethnography of Letter Writing and Relationships Through Time
Finding our Perfect Moon
Jennifer L. Adams

A Performative Autoethnography of Five Black American Men
Stefan Battle

Writing Philosophical Autoethnography
Edited by Alec Grant

For more information about this series, please visit: www.routledge.com/Writing-Lives-Ethnographic-Narratives/book-series/WLEN

WRITING PHILOSOPHICAL AUTOETHNOGRAPHY

Edited by Alec Grant

Routledge
Taylor & Francis Group

NEW YORK AND LONDON

Designed cover image: Birth of a Dancing Star, painting by Alec Grant, 2022, acrylic on canvas

First published 2024
by Routledge
605 Third Avenue, New York, NY 10158

and by Routledge
4 Park Square, Milton Park, Abingdon, Oxon OX14 4RN

Routledge is an imprint of the Taylor & Francis Group, an informa business

British Library Cataloguing-in-Publication Data
A catalogue record for this book is available from the British Library

ISBN: 978-1-032-22911-9 (hbk)
ISBN: 978-1-032-22912-6 (pbk)
ISBN: 978-1-003-27472-8 (ebk)

DOI: 10.4324/9781003274728

Typeset in Optima
by Apex CoVantage, LLC

For two dear friends: Professor Jerome Carson who always enables me, and Dr Susan Young who always gets me.

CONTENTS

FOREWORD

Philosophy in Autoethnography: A Reflection on Quality in Qualitative Research

In the introduction to this book, editor Alec Grant makes a case for contextualizing autoethnographic work within philosophical frameworks and theories that will ensure a critical analysis of one's narrative work. He also names a central and very human reason why such "quality control" in the form of critical feedback and dialogue might be undermined by the good intentions of a community that has served to make room for minority, marginalized, and often stigmatized voices:

> criticism coming from within a family can be anathema, to the extent that it breaks tacitly held loyalty rules. But meanwhile, hard-headed criticality is regularly sacrificed at the altar of what to my mind amounts to an infantilising form of "inclusivity."
>
> *(Introductory chapter, pp. 3–4)*

It is clear that this book is a call to courage and an invitation to remember that peer critique of one's work is not a critique of one's person. It holds the fruitful possibility of telling one's story in ways that are stronger, thereby developing one's self, the community, and the field.

Autoethnographers, new or not so new to the work, are invited here to keep this vibrant research methodology alive and to benefit personally from its generative possibilities. Without frameworks to examine and conceptualize "the self" in "auto," or describe and analyze the social, historical, and cultural in "ethno," or play with and become aware of our form, genre, and writing choices in "graphy," we are destined to dumb down our stories and risk damaging the confidence in the method.

Indeed, we may be faced with having to defend the approach once more. Except this time, for reasons much more worrisome than when pioneers like Ellis, Bochner, Etherington, Richardson, and Denzin first stood for the value of this kind of qualitative research and made fundamental strides in the field. Ironically the earliest accusations about the work being navel-gazing or "not real research" could become true if we as autoethnographers aren't willing to engage in philosophically sophisticated self-reflection and peer review.

The idea that theory is an add-on in creating an autoethnographic narrative is a ridiculous notion, though not necessarily self-evident. The reason for this textbook is to argue for and show that theories (that is, the lenses by which we situate, free, and know ourselves to be contextualized and not infrequently stigmatized) are precursors as well as developmental lenses. They clarify what we see, can see, and will see. Indeed, unless we make explicit how we are and will be situating ourselves, and examine our assumptions of how our stories came to be, we will not be able to escape (or even realize the depths of) our narrative entrapment.

Despite the book's call to renewed rigour, don't be concerned that it will be difficult or painful to read – or if it at first feels that way, let it be an inspiration: a lesson in contrasts where creative failure is allowed and even welcomed as part of our knowledge building. It is okay to say, "I now see that what I want to accomplish intellectually is at odds with what I am hitherto accomplishing." This book offers important questions, and its chapters are rich and evocative (dare I use the word!) examples of how to develop philosophical criticality. One might see the book as a refresher course or intellectual knife sharpener that not only serves as a checklist and tuning fork for better work, but resists the risk of our writing becoming marginalized or discounted, or even worse, devolving into pathetic personal laments.

True to form, editor Alec Grant is self-critical and questions whether some of his critiques are motivated by his own "perfectionism" – however, I see no evidence of this in this volume. The message rather is "that good autoethnography demands diligence, sustained effort, and significant personal struggles on the part of writers and readers who have real 'skin in the game'" (Intro p. 5), and this book fulfils this promise.

Art Bochner's chapter does this in his analysis of what it means to write autoethnography in response to a comment that the material covered by autoethnographers is often unhappy. He explores what it means to be happy, drawing on many sources – both historical and popular – and shows how he leads his students to think beyond their simplistic notions and hopes. As a "founding father" of autoethnography, Bochner is willing as ever to examine this argument levelled against the method, reminding the reader why we need narrative to untangle and examine difficulty.

His treatise reminded me of expressive writing researcher James Pennebaker's observation that when good things happen they don't require integration, while difficulty leads humans to storying and re-storying (2011). That is why autoethnography will always include life's difficulties while at the same time being a method of writing for well-being, as it seeks to make (valuable) meaning of suffering.

Alex Brostoff's chapter is a well-designed and facetious exploration of the book "I love Dick" by filmmaker and academic Chris Krause. Brostoff demonstrates how in using what I will call "a metaform," one can analyse a piece of work using its own aesthetic properties (in this case, letters) to increasingly unpeel layers of meaning yet have the courage to not resolve the questions that are generated. At its core, this chapter is an exploration of the nature of voice and how it is represented in textual form: how it can be used (and misused) to challenge our assumptions about reality. For many this chapter will be a challenging read; the need to park one's assumptions about form and to read about Krause's work beforehand will make it more accessible.

Betsy Ettorre tells the compelling story of her academic career as a researcher, describing the often-toxic contexts she worked in because of being an out lesbian in the seventies and eighties in the UK. Now in retirement, she reflects on a lifetime of work as a sociologist in the field of women and addiction and she speaks of the "need to be rigorously self-aware, to be meticulously humble and most importantly, to be cognizant of the complex connections between the socially coded categories of race, gender, age, able-bodiedness, class and sex." (p. 62) She uses various concepts and theories to situate and examine her narrative; for instance, the concept of "la mestiza" by Gloria Anzaldua (1987), which allows Ettorre to explore the "ambiguity of personal and social relationships."

Renata Ferdinand's chapter explores the concept of "standing in a crooked room" as a Black woman mangling herself to fit the stereotype of the respectable "white woman" (therefore inadvertently also falling into Black women stereotypes). A racist remark made by a white male professor triggers the split in the author's identification with "Renata" (i.e., the respectable one) and her alter ego "Pinkie," representing legitimate anger at being demeaned again and again. She conceptualizes the need for recognition using Hegel's concept of *Anerkennung*. Her story reminded me of the concepts "suture and stigma" in a textbook on writing and healing by

Anderson and MacCurdy (2000), which shows that the narratives we have internalized not only risk contorting us but annihilating us.

As a white woman academic writing the midlife journey, I recognized the narrative entrapment of this "good girl" stereotype in my own life. The scene she sketches of herself as "Pinkie" on the hunt for the white male professor is riveting and took me with her on this fierce walk of visceral anger. I believe many non-tenured faculty at the hands of our current neo-liberal academy will also relate to this anger at being discredited and thus disenfranchised.

Mark Freeman makes the case that there is "no 'thinking' per se. There is only thinking-with," (p. 96) and this brings home acutely the message of this book. We need to ponder how we came to "be" as we are – that is, which theoretical and conceptual lenses we are looking through, even if those lenses have become such a part of us that we will inevitably "plagia-rize" and will struggle to discern the origin of each strand. This is further complicated by the notion of "distanciation": that we interpret the past through a present lens which will always alter what we see and render every self-narrative a fiction, and therefore – shockingly perhaps – every *self* as well. However, paradoxically, this fictionalizing can bring us closer to "deeper truths" as metaphorical language does in poetry.

Freeman's chapter radiates a gratitude for the thinkers who have influ-enced and "colonized" his way of being in the world, as well as humour as Freeman reflects on his chance as a young man to study with Paul Ricœur: "Even the name seemed magical. *Ricœur*. Like a cassoulet, accompanied by a rich Bordeaux. Or something like that. ("Fuckin' A!")" He even receives a typed letter from Ricœur in response to his fledging philosophical work, which is included in the chapter.

Alec Grant's chapter takes three distinct memories, salient in his life, to explore his identification with an "effectively trickster-carnivalesque" character. Using inspiration from Freeman's work, Grant distinguishes between historical truth and narrative truth, the latter ever changing and necessarily "open-ended, unfinalized, partial and provisional." (p. 118) The memories – which he uses to describe the evolution of his "nar-rative character" – are deeply engaging and are described in painfully funny ways. An encounter with one of two English folk music club "characters" is described as a kind of torture (i.e., "Nietzschean eternal recurrence"). The atmosphere of the clubs that in his younger years had nurtured Grant now seem to him to have become caricatures of them-selves. He argues that our retelling is not only a way to make mean-ing but that we also tell to self-protect, an idea he borrows from the American philosopher, Daniel Dennett.

In addition to Grant's thorough analysis of the personal and cultural implications of identifying with the "trickster" in service of disrupting cultural scripts and norms, he offers autoethnographers useful space to explore and pinpoint multiple motives for narrating: "I understand my life story to be comprised of constantly revised and re-embellished personal memories" (p. 121), and "I've found myself needing to make my self-culture mismatch feel less embarrassing by rescuing my remembered self from moral disgrace in more sophisticated ways." (p. 124).

This chapter affirms that critical reflection is part of having an ethical compass as we do this work, but that our work as autoethnographers is *not* to spare feelings but rather to undo cultural and personal "en-strangle-ments," to coin a term with Grant's own carnivalesque wit.

Andrew Herrmann takes readers into phenomenological existentialism, which cannot be – and should not be, he argues – precisely defined but explains in part the "inhospitality . . . queasy nauseousness . . . angst" we experience as humans. In this chapter, Herrmann honors and describes the work of theorist Karl E. Weick and his influence on many terrains, but especially organizational development and the complex processes of sensemaking within these. Through this philosophical lens, Herrmann explains how communication cycles are needed to engage in sensemaking, and how sensemaking influences our identity development. He explains that ruptures in expected patterns alert us to our relationship to things, and this disorientation in organizations leads to multiple (that is, equivocal) interpretations that need to be made sense of and reduced into useful meaning.

This chapter is valuable in bringing to light how narrative is the way in which we make use of relevant data to shape identity, recognizing that the importance of the "I" within organizations could help enact sensemaking more fully, as individual identity is always affected within organizational difficulties and change processes.

Christopher N. Poulos takes us on a journey that is both heartfelt and intellectually stimulating. He describes the reason he has been writing autoethnography and describes a key human problem: being – always – aware of our inevitable ending. His theoretical – mostly existential – frameworks include the works of Buber, Kierkegaard, Percy, Sartre, Tillich, and Camus's take on the tale of Sisyphus from Greek mythology. One of the central ideas in Poulos's chapter is that we survive mentally by imagining and reaching for possibility, without which we would be lost. He illustrates his own relationship to these ideas with the story of the death of his father and the unresolved feelings he had around their relationship.

This part of his story was particularly recognizable for me, having myself written an autoethnographic book on bereavement (Lengelle, 2021) and writing about unfinished business with my spouse. The illusion that conflict dies when a beloved does is a raw awakening that leaves us extra vulnerable in grief. Regardless of circumstances, it's clear that many bereaved people find themselves reaching for more solid ground and possibility through places, objects, memories, and telling stories. Poulos does this when he finds a baseball his father seems to have placed in full view – as if signaling to his son that he acknowledged their connection.

The chapter ends with a fantastic(al) dialogue between the author and Sisyphus, reminding us that, as Camus explains, we have time to do something useful on our way down the slope (that is, the moment of rest between all our striving).

Menah Pratt leads us through the evolution of her identity by observing and reflecting on the influence other Black women philosophers and feminists like Dotson, James, Gines, and Allen had on her thinking. She shares important moments when those theories and philosophies intersected with her lived experience and how those came to shape her identity as a "critical Blackgirl feminist scholar-activist." Like Rawlins in the next chapter, Pratt points out that the self we talk about is never a thing that exists in isolation:

> This self-defined voice is a voice that is often a relational identity influenced and informed by family, community, and diasporic realities. It is an individual and collective voice impacted by the intertwined identities of generations, gender, sexuality, race, religion, and class (Collins, 2000).
>
> *(p. 170)*

Her poetry is clear and to the point, and as a researcher of writing for well-being (and co-editor of a recent book that includes a powerful chapter by Pratt on how writing helped her heal), I could see its direct application for poetry therapy practice – for instance, using the following lines and asking students "what can't you ask . . ." and "when do you touch on a subject that is so hard, when you know it will be turned back on you . . . ?"

> When you're Black
> and things don't work out
> You wonder, sometimes
> "Is it me, my skin, or them?"
> One can't ask (p. 173)

Shelley Rawlins reminds us, like Pratt, that our "selves" are created and shaped within dialogical relationships, and that autoethnographic work done with the proper cultural support of philosophy can counter critiques by some who have called it too self-centered. She uses the story of attending a transgender rally to support its members (as a cisgendered white woman) to reflect on the act of public protest, as this "exemplifies embodied existential stakes and shared vulnerabilities that both beckon and challenge sophisticated autoethnographic exploration by individual authors." (p. 190) She uses phenomenology and existential phenomenology and the thinking of Husserl, Heidegger, and Sartre to analyze her experience, and:

> In doing so I locate existential hammers from these thinkers and demonstrate their conceptual utility for conducting qualitative research about individuals' experiences of communal activities. Then I (re)consider my story about what it means to (dis)engage in collective protest with others.
>
> *(p. 191)*

Not having encountered his work in any detail (yet), I was struck by the clear way in which Rawlins explains Husserl's thinking and associated steps to engage with experience. This is the kind of writing that makes a professor sing because it makes accessible the philosophies, how they may be applied, and in a way that students will be able to engage with that does not reduce the need for intellectual muscle-stretching.

Julie-Ann Scott-Pollock's chapter begins with a long poem, storying the embodied disablement of her son and herself. She juxtaposes her life as a full professor – with advantages of being a white, cisgendered professional with good health insurance – with the reality of having a disabled body, and being reminded of that in the gaze of the other; that is, by others with "normal" (i.e., socially accepted) bodies. Her memories of childhood show this perpetual struggle as well as the effort required to advocate for her son at school when the school nurse misdiagnoses his seizures. She uses existential phenomenology to create narratives that "not only uncover marginalization, stigma, and prejudice in our personal stories, but also look towards means to resist it." (p. 221).

This chapter's poignant message reminded me that, as Scott-Pollock says, "Our bodies 'know' when a moment matters" (p. 221). Her chapter also provided insight into the reasons for frustrated impatience and fierceness when a marginalized person speaks up and advocates for herself and others. It also points to the deep-seated fear the narrative of ableism is based on, perpetuating the split in the way the "able-bodied" view and receive the disabled. The feeling this chapter left me with was the reflected exhaustion of striving to alter the reality of being a recipient of an abiding, othering cultural script.

Georgina Tuari Stewart's chapter offers an identity analysis of being Māori when, by outward appearances, Māori people "may not look distinct" from white people, although strong binary conceptualizations remain. This chapter usefully reminds readers that "Colonisation by assimilation aims for Māori becoming the same as non-Māori, thereby deleting distinct Māori identity." This also applies to Canadian First Nations people. Indigenous students in Canada, one of whom co-authored a book chapter with me, speak of cultural genocide and the resulting illness-producing identity story that this can cause (Lengelle et al., 2018). Stewart's stories of ceremony, reflections on ethnicity, and revisiting historical protests, help explore the answer to the question "What is a Māori, really?" (p. 242), and illustrate why it's important to develop a response, which the author does: "While I am certain of the answer, it is not a formula. It is a question that defies succinct definition, but rather invites an holistic or experiential response, which narrative and autoethnographic writing seek to invite." (p. 242).

This chapter is a wake-up call and an invitation to decolonize together, but not in a way that makes it the ongoing task of the colonized to educate. Indeed, one of the final paragraphs of this chapter caught me off-guard, and the surprise of that emphasized for me the need to really hear that:

> One of the hardest concepts for non-Māori people at all levels of education to understand is that Māori people have their own interests that lie beyond the equity obsession with "closing the gaps" – most Māori academics are not interested in being career cultural advisors for their non-Māori colleagues.

Alec Grant brings this volume to an end with a creative and philosophical meander that revisits all the chapters and offers new questions about where autoethnography is headed. It's time to include non-Western philosophy. It's time to consider what a "non-self" in autoethnography might look like, and to watch for the next generation of autoethnographers who will show and tell their stories in film, art, music, and mixed media forms. We must be ready for unexpected forms and dialogues, and we need surprises to learn. For example, Grant puts Virginia Woolf and Renata Ferdinand (this volume) in the same sentence, as if to say we are all in conversation simultaneously, whether wearing time-period (or non-binary) appropriate attire or not.

I believe we can anticipate that future dialogues within autoethnography will also be made more complex by our "conversation" with AI text generators, and will require deepened emotional competencies (for example, we cannot get beyond racism without tolerating and making good use of ugly emotions like shame; we cannot really construct and deconstruct the self without humour).

Reinekke Lengelle, Scheveningen, The Netherlands

Author of "Writing the Self in Bereavement: A story of love, spousal loss, and resilience" (Routledge, 2021)

Qualitative Inquiry Book Award 2022

Best Book Award for Ethnography 2021

Reinekke Lengelle

References

Anderson, C. and MacCurdy, M. (2000). *Writing and Healing: Toward an Informed Practice*. Urbana, IL: National Council of Teachers of English.

Anzaldua, G. (1987). *Borderlands, La Frontera: The New Mestiza*. San Francisco, CA: Aunt Lute Books.

Lengelle, R. (2021). *Writing the Self in Bereavement: A Story of Love, Spousal Loss and Resilience*. New York and London: Routledge.

Lengelle, R., Jardine, C. and Bonnar, C. (2018). 'Writing the Self for Reconciliation and Global Citizenship: The Inner Dialogue and Creative Voices for Cultural Healing'. In Meijers, F. and Hermans, H.J.M. (eds.) *The Dialogical Self in Education: A Multicultural Perspective*. pp. 81–96. New York: Springer.

Pennebaker, J. (2011). *The Secret Life of Pronouns: What Our Words Say About Us*. London: Bloomsbury Press.

FOREWORD

Decades ago, an intense young man attended a seminar that I conducted on psychoanalytic theory and practice. At the time, he was a recovering cognitive-behavioral therapist looking to expand his scope, and I was a keen, if not somewhat fanatical, advocate of psychoanalysis. That young man was Alec Grant, the editor of this volume. Many years later, the magic of social media brought us together again. We had both changed over the intervening years, become both more open-minded and more critical of the psychotherapy profession.

It was through Alec that I first came across the term "autoethnography." I had never heard the word before, and so, flummoxed, I googled it to get at least a rough idea of what autoethnography is all about. Further down the road, when Alec invited me to write a preface for this groundbreaking collection, I thought I'd better up my game by digging deeper and thinking harder. In consequence, autoethnography captured my imagination, and – given that I am a professor of philosophy – the notion of *philosophical* autoethnography captured it all the more.

To explain why we should care about philosophical autoethnography, allow me to take you on a brief excursion into the history of philosophy. In 1739–1740, Alec's countryman David Hume published his great *Treatise of Human Nature*, a book that Hume described on the title page as "an Attempt to introduce the experimental Method of Reasoning into moral Subjects" (Hume, 2007). What did Hume mean by this? In Hume's day, a distinction was made between "natural" philosophy and "moral" phi-losophy. The former was more or less equivalent to what today we call "science," albeit more expansive in scope, and the latter was more or less equivalent to what we nowadays call philosophy. Many scholars agree that in citing the experimental method of reasoning, Hume was probably referring to the advances made by Newton, whose *Principia* had been published some four decades earlier, and the work of the Irish natural philosopher Robert Boyle, among other pioneers of the scientific revolution.

Newton and Boyle did real experiments, but there is not the slightest whiff of this sort of experimentation in the *Treatise*. Notice, though, that Hume was concerned with experimental *reasoning*, rather than experiments as such. By "experimental reasoning" he meant putting human experience front and center in one's investigations. As he explains in the 1751 *Enquiry Concerning Understanding* (Hume, 2000), the chief use of the study of history is:

> to discover the constant and universal principles of human nature, by showing men in all varieties of circumstances and situations, and furnishing us with materials from which we may form our observations and become acquainted with the regular springs of human action and behaviour.

Hume goes on to remark:

> These records of wars, intrigues, factions, and revolutions, are so many collections of experiments, by which the politician or moral philosopher fixes the principles of his science, in the same manner as the physician or natural philosopher becomes acquainted with the nature of plants, minerals, and other external objects, by the experiments which he forms concerning them.

Ever the empiricist, Hume believed that philosophical enquiry should be rooted in experience, either one's own, first-person experience, or the testimony of others, such as the historiographers alluded to in the earlier passage. Philosophical engagement should be based on matters of fact, rather than armchair speculation, and it is abundantly clear from Hume's philosophical writings that this includes drawing upon and generalizing from one's own experiences.

This strategy of using one's own experiences as the basis for generalizable claims that transcend those experiences is alien to an impoverished conception of objectivity that is all too often unreflectively embraced as gospel by present-day psychologists. This notion of objectivity decried by the philosopher Thomas Nagel, who described it as "the view from nowhere" (Nagel, 1986) – a position deemed to be independent of any individual human being's perspective. This is an impossible ideal, a wild goose chase, not just in the social and behavioral sciences, but in the natural sciences, too. As the philosopher Hans Reichenbach (one of the original logical empiricists and, interestingly, a founding member of the Los Angeles Psychoanalytic Association) pointed out, scientific work, and indeed all systematic enquiry, consists of two components. He called them the "context of discovery" and the "context of justification" (Reichenbach, 1938). The context of justification – the laborious, quantitative process of hypothesis testing – is probably the picture that most people have in mind when they think of science. But, as Reichenbach made clear, such procedures, vital as they are, must be grounded in the context of discovery – the process of generating hypotheses that one goes on to test. And guess what, there are no rules for doing this. The hypothesis might come in a dream, as in the case of Kekulé's discovery of the structure of the benzine molecule, or by free-associating on dreams, as in the case of Freud's hypothesis of a wish-fulfilling unconscious mind, or in a million other ways. There are no rules in the context of discovery. Anything goes, and that's a feature, not a glitch.

This may seem suspect to some because enquiry should be wholly "objective." But whatever "objectivity" amounts to (and surely *some* notion of objectivity is crucial for understanding the world around us), it cannot be unmoored from our first-person experiences, and our reflections upon and generalizations from those experiences. In the real world, objectivity and subjectivity intertwined rather than being antagonistic to one another, and it is nonsense to think that the latter can reasonably be renounced or demoted in favor of the former. Of course, autoethnography can be executed well or poorly, sloppily or in a disciplined, scholarly manner. So, the methodological challenge is to find ways to manage the interface between the subjective and objective domains – and, with the help of a philosophical toolkit, develop strategies for rigorously anchoring our research in our own subjectivity as a prelude and indispensable basis for extending it more broadly. The present volume is a philosophically sophisticated and pragmatically admirable effort in this direction.

David Livingstone Smith
David Livingstone Smith, Professor of
Philosophy, University of New England

References

Collins, P.H. (2000 [1990]). *Black Feminist Thought: Knowledge, Consciousness, and the Politics of Empowerment.* 2nd Edition. New York: Routledge.
Hume, D. (2000). *An Enquiry Concerning Human Understanding.* Edited by Beauchamp, T.L. Oxford: Clarendon Press.

Hume, D. (2007). *Treatise of Human Nature*. 2nd vols. Edited by Norton, D.F. and Norton, M.J. Oxford: Clarendon Press.

Nagel, T. (1986). *The View from Nowhere*. Oxford: Oxford University Press.

Reichenbach, H. (1938). *Experience and Prediction. An Analysis of the Foundations and the Structure of Knowledge*. Chicago: University of Chicago Press.

ACKNOWLEDGEMENTS

I can't adequately express how grateful I am for the support I've received for this book project from Tony Adams and his fellow "Writing Lives: Ethnographic Narratives" series editors, Carolyn Ellis and Art Bochner. I'm also of course equally grateful – as always – for the enthusiasm and editorial help of the lovely, indefatigable Hannah Shakespeare, and Lucy Kennedy and all the other good folks at Routledge.

Several other friends gave me helpful feedback along the way. Thank you, Zsuzsanna Chappell, Trude Klevan, Reinekke Lengelle, Graham Lever, Nigel P. Short, Andrew Sparkes, Susan Young, and Chunyan Zhang, for critically reading and responding to Chapter 1, and Susan Young and Graham Lever for their feedback on Chapter 14.

Thanks also to Tony Adams, David Carless, Zsuzsanna Chappell, Trude Klevan, Reinekke Lengelle, Graham Lever, Lizzie Lloyd-Parkes, Jess Moriarty, Chris Williams, Nigel P. Short, Andrew Sparkes, and Susan Young, for all your helpful comments on my Chapter 7 in its development.

And I'd like to thank all the contributing authors in this volume. I think you've all made it a great and memorable book, and you've certainly taught me a lot about the scope and possibilities of philosophical autoethnography.

I'm indebted to David Livingstone Smith and Reinekke Lengelle for their forewords, and to Andy West and Andrew Sparkes for their endorsements.

Last but by no means least, my dear family – Mary, Anna, Graeme, Amy, Mark, Charlotte, and James – are always there for me. And where would I be without my four-legged pals, Mabel and Oakley?

EDITOR BIOGRAPHY

Alec Grant, PhD
Alec Grant is currently Visiting Professor in the Department of Education and Psychology, University of Bolton, UK. His academic background is in psychology, cultural studies, psychotherapy, qualitative, and narrative inquiry – subsuming ethnography, autoethnography, and philosophy. He was the recipient in 2020 of the International Conference of Autoethnography (ICAE) Inaugural Lifetime Contribution Award, "in recognition of making a significant contribution to the development and nurturance of the field of autoethnography and those working within it." Extensively published in autoethnographic journal articles and book chapters, he is on the international editorial board of the *Journal of Autoethnography*. He co-edited *Contemporary British Autoethnography* (2013, Sense Publishers), and *International Perspectives on Autoethnographic Research and Practice* (2018, Routledge). His most recent text, co-written with Trude Klevan, is *An Autoethnography of Becoming a Qualitative Researcher: A Dialogic View of Academic Development* (2022, Routledge).

CHAPTER AUTHOR BIOGRAPHIES

Arthur P. Bochner, PhD
Arthur P. Bochner is a distinguished university professor emeritus, University of South Florida, and a distinguished scholar of the National Communication Association. He has established an international and interdisciplinary reputation for his theoretical, critical, and empirical contributions to the study of narrative and autoethnographic inquiry, including narrative identity, narrative truth, illness narratives, and memory work. An originator and developer of reflexive social science methodologies that bring emotions, subjectivity, and storytelling into research in the social sciences, his influential monographs and books have introduced new concepts such as institutional (organizational) depression, vulnerable medicine, relational dialectics, and genre-bending forms of representing lived experiences that have helped shape the work of three generations of qualitative researchers. His 2014 book *Coming to Narrative: A Personal History of Paradigm Change in the Human Sciences* (Left Coast Press) received the Best Book award from The International Congress of Qualitative Inquiry and the Ethnography Division of the National Communication Association. His current work focuses on living an autoethnographic life with his life partner, Carolyn Ellis, and their adorable rat terrier pal, Malee.

Alex Brostoff, PhD
Alex Brostoff is a writer, translator, and assistant professor of English at Kenyon College. Their research and pedagogy converge at the crossroads of critical theory and queer and transfeminist cultural production in twentieth

and twenty-first century hemispheric American studies. They are the guest co-editor of a special issue of *ASAP/Journal* on "autotheory," and their scholarship, translations, and public writing have appeared in journals including *Critical Times: Interventions in Global Critical Theory, Synthesis: An Anglophone Journal of Comparative Literary Studies, Assay: A Journal of Nonfiction Studies*, and *Hyperallergic*, among others.

Elizabeth Ettorre, PhD

Elizabeth Ettorre is an internationally known feminist scholar in the areas of substance misuse, genetics, reproduction, and autoethnography. She was born in Connecticut, did her BA in Sociology at Fordham University, New York, and completed her PhD at the London School of Economics, England. Her working life was mainly conducted in the UK. Now retired, she is Emerita Professor of Sociology, University of Liverpool, Honorary Professor, Aarhuus University, and Docent in Sociology, Helsinki and Åbo Akademi University. Besides publishing in a number of international journals, her scholarly books include *Health, Culture & Society; Autoethnography as Feminist Method; Gendering Addiction: The Politics of Drug Treatment in a Neurochemical World* (with Nancy Campbell); *Culture, Bodies and the Sociology of Health; Revisioning Women and drug use: gender, power and the body; Making Lesbians visible in the Substance Use Field; Reproductive genetics, gender and the body; Before Birth: Understanding Prenatal Screening; Women and Alcohol: From a private pleasure to a public problem?; Society, the Body and Well-Being* (with K. Suolinna and E. Lahelma); *Gendered Moods: Psychotropics and Society* (with Elianne Riska); *Women and Substance Use; Drug Services in England and the Impact of the Central Funding Initiative* (with S. MacGregor, R. Coomber, and A. Crosier), and *Lesbians, Women and Society*. Currently, she lives in Helsinki, Finland with her Finnish partner of 39 years. She was President of the American Women's Club, Finland (2018–9) and an active member of Democrats Abroad, Finland.

Renata Ferdinand, PhD

Renata Ferdinand is Professor and Chair of the Department of African American Studies at New York City College of Technology in Brooklyn, NY. She writes autoethnographies that explore the complexities of the lived experiences of Black women and girls, from how race and gender impact experiences within the healthcare system, to colorism, racial stereotypes, and Black women's identity. Her work has been featured in several outlets, including *Girlhood Studies, Cultural Studies + Critical Methodologies, Journal of Health Psychology, The Popular Culture Studies Journal*, to name a few, and within several edited volumes, including *International*

Perspectives of Autoethnographic Research and Practice, Blacklove: The Intimacies and Intricacies of Romantic Love in Black Relationships, and *Space and Culture: The Journal*. She has given several talks on Black Motherhood Studies and Black Girlhood Studies and was recently featured as a literary expert for the article, "Reblazing Saddles: Who Shapes the Wild West Lit Canon?" for *Bitch: Feminist Response to Pop Culture*. She is the recipient of the 2018 Ellis-Bochner Autoethnography and Personal Narrative Research Award from The Society for the Study of Symbolic Interaction (SSSI) of the National Communication Association for best published essay. She serves as an expert reviewer for several publications, and is currently an editorial board member of the *Journal of Autoethnography* and *The Autoethnographer: A Literary & Arts Magazine*. She is the author of the book *An Autoethnography of African American Motherhood: Things I Tell My Daughter* (Routledge, 2021).

Mark Freeman, PhD

Mark Freeman is Distinguished Professor of Ethics and Society in the Department of Psychology at the College of the Holy Cross, and is the author of numerous works, including *Rewriting the Self: History, Memory, Narrative* (Routledge, 1993); *Hindsight: The Promise and Peril of Looking Backward* (Oxford, 2010); *The Priority of the Other: Thinking and Living Beyond the Self* (Oxford, 2014); and, most recently, *Do I Look at You with Love? Reimaging the Story of Dementia* (Brill | Sense, 2021). Winner of the Theodore R. Sarbin Award from the Society for Theoretical and Philosophical Psychology, the Joseph B. Gittler Award from the American Psychological Foundation, and the Art Bochner and Carolyn Ellis Resonance Award from the International Association of Autoethnography and Narrative Inquiry, Freeman is a Fellow in the American Psychological Association and also serves as editor for the Oxford University Press series "Explorations in Narrative Psychology."

Andrew F. Herrmann, PhD

Andrew F. Herrmann (PhD, University of South Florida) is Associate Professor of Communication Studies at East Tennessee State University, where he teaches critical organizational communication courses. He studies identity, narrative, and power at the intersections of organizational, occupational, and popular culture contexts. He is a founding co-editor of the *Journal of Autoethnography*. He edited the award-winning *Routledge International Handbook of Organizational Autoethnography* and the authored *Organizational Communication Approaches to the Works of Joss Whedon*. He is also the co-editor of the *Communication Perspectives on Popular Culture* book series. He drinks too much coffee, collects too many comic books, and binge-watches too much television.

Christopher N. Poulos, PhD

Christopher N. Poulos is Professor of Communication Studies at the University of North Carolina, Greensboro. An autoethnographer and philosopher of communication, his scholarship focuses on ethnographic and narrative inquiry/methodology; communication in close personal relationships; stories, lies, and secrets; the impacts of trauma, violence, and loss on memory and communication; and communication ethics. He teaches courses in friendship and family communication, ethics, ethnography, dialogue, and film. He is the author of two books: *Essentials of Autoethnography* (2021) and *Accidental Ethnography: An Inquiry into Family Secrecy* (2099). His work has appeared in *Qualitative Inquiry, Communication Theory, Cultural Studies – Critical Methodologies, Southern Communication Journal, International Review of Qualitative Research, Qualitative Communication Research*, and in many edited books.

Menah Pratt, PhD

Menah Pratt is Vice President for Strategic Affairs and Diversity at Virginia Tech. She is also Professor of Education in the School of Education in the College of Liberal Arts and Human Sciences, with affiliations in Africana Studies, Women's and Gender Studies, and the Department of Sociology. Author of four books, she has a bachelor's degree from the University of Iowa with a major in English and minors in philosophy and African American studies. She received her master's degree in literary studies from the University of Iowa and a master's degree in sociology from Vanderbilt University. In addition, she earned her PhD and JD from Vanderbilt University.

Shelley Rawlins, PhD

Dr. Rawlins is Assistant Professor in the Department of Communication at Utah Tech University in St. George, Utah. Her research explores public and private relational contexts of fellowship and estrangement, currently through the lens of people participating in collective protest. She is also interested in legal and political relationships and identity (self-other) facets inscribed within law and policies, and how people pursue freedom and agency together through activism, allyship, and leadership. In her work, Dr. Rawlins employs qualitative methods and incorporates theories and insights from relational/interpersonal communication, existentialism, feminist and critical theory, and phenomenology. Dr. Rawlins has published articles in *Women & Language, Departures in Critical Qualitative Research, Kaleidoscope*, and *Health Communication*.

Julie-Ann Scott-Pollock, PhD

Julie-Ann Scott-Pollock is a Professor of Communication Studies and Performance Studies at the University of North Carolina, Wilmington. Her research and performance work focus on personal narrative, critical ethnography, and stigmatized embodiment. Her book, *Embodied Performance as Applied Research, Art and Pedagogy* was published by Palgrave MacMillan.

Georgina Tuari Stewart, PhD
Georgina Tuari Stewart (Ngāpuhi-nui-tonu, Pare Hauraki) is Professor of Māori Philosophy of Education in Te Ara Poutama, Auckland University of Technology, Aotearoa, New Zealand. She is the author of the successful book *Māori Philosophy: Indigenous thinking from Aotearoa* (Bloomsbury, 2021), the lead editor of *Writing for Publication: Liminal reflections for academics* (Springer, 2021), deputy editor of *Educational Philosophy and Theory* (EPAT), and co-editor of the *New Zealand Journal of Educational Studies* (NZJES). As principal investigator of a Marsden-funded research project (2022–2025), she is currently investigating how Flexible Learning Spaces (FLS) can support Māori aspirations in education.

Links: https://academics.aut.ac.nz/georgina.stewart, www.maoriphilosophy.com/maorifls

1

THE PHILOSOPHICAL AUTOETHNOGRAPHER

Alec Grant

Introduction

The aim of this edited volume is to promote the idea of *philosophical autoethnography* as a basis for writing lives, across the autoethnographic and related communities. Accordingly, this is the first collection of narrative autoethnographic work, in which:

> Authors autoethnographically explore their issues, concerns and topics about human society, cultures, and the nonhuman and material worlds through an explicitly philosophical lens. In specific terms, this means that each chapter – while written as first-person autoethnography (not precluding the use of second- and third-person narrative, as relevant) – will showcase sustained engagement with philosophical arguments, ideas, concepts, theories, and corresponding ethical positions. This philosophical basis will be fundamental to the content, topic, focus, and context of each autoethnography chapter, rather than supplementary.

This is the working definition of "philosophical autoethnography," which first appeared in the Routledge book proposal preceding the publication of this volume. The proposal itself emerged from an extended conversation I had with Tony Adams at the inception of the *Journal of Autoethnography* in 2020. As a member of the international editorial board, I expressed an interest in editing a special issue of the journal devoted to philosophical autoethnography. In the spring of 2021, after more discussion, Tony – co-editor of the journal – suggested I think instead about an edited volume

DOI: 10.4324/9781003274728-1

with the same focus. I'm immensely grateful to him for planting this seed of an idea, given my longstanding concerns about narrative autoethnography, and my wish for it to become more philosophically sophisticated.

My Issues with "Narrative Autoethnography"

> [O]rientation is a matter of how we reside in space . . . (shaping) not only how we inhabit space, but how we apprehend this world of shared inhabitance.
>
> (Ahmed, 2006, pp. 1–3, my brackets)

I've often found myself preoccupied over the years with the meaning and range of convenience of the term "narrative autoethnography." Accepting that *all* forms of autoethnographies tell stories, by this descriptor I specifically mean written work of the sort found in journal articles and books, as distinct from arts-based autoethnographic modality work (for example, documentary film, animation, or other forms of image- and performance-based autoethnography – the need for a future text exploring the philosophical basis of which I'll mention in my concluding chapter).

Accepting its default status as blurred genre, I also find myself in sympathy with Craig Gingrich-Philbrook's assertion that narrative autoethnography "(is) . . . more . . . a broad orientation towards scholarship than a specific procedure" (2005, p. 298, my brackets), if "writing" is substituted for "scholarship." At the risk of courting disapproval from among my more liberal-minded autoethnographic friends, colleagues, and associates, my problem is that in my experience too many unscholarly autoethnographies successfully reach the public domain.

I'm uncomfortably aware that this assertion puts me at odds with the frontstage image and promotion of the orientation. However, I believe that what "autoethnography" is *supposed* to be, according to contemporary definitive texts (which I think is what it *should* be; I've contributed to some of them) amounts to *platonization*. This concept best captures a troubling incoherence evident within the orientation: autoethnography is described in definitive texts in ideal terms, while some work of dubious quality – falling far short of these ideals – finds a home in a journal or as a conference presentation. In my view, as will hopefully become clear in this introductory chapter, this incoherence would happen less if autoethnographic writing became more philosophically rigorous.

The integrity of autoethnographic texts resting on deeper levels of philosophical sophistication rather than surface taxonomies might also result in less of a need to categorize autoethnography according to a growing proliferation of subtypes, including the old "evocative" and "analytical" favourites (Hernandez et al., 2022, pp. 4–5). While classifying autoethnography in subtype categorical terms can be useful, it also comes with a set of related problems. First, any autoethnography explicitly aligned to a single category will, as Hernandez and her colleagues argue, display assumptions and styles from other category subtypes. Categories, like standpoints and people, are always intersectional.

Second, the category label "evocative autoethnography" can function to defend and justify the very work of questionable quality that I have problems with. People identifying as evocative writers may take the following assumption for granted: that it's unnecessary to "formally analyze the study findings beyond what is expressed in storytelling" since "analysis takes place as the researcher makes meaning and engages in storying of the experience" (Hernandez et al., p. 4). Now, there's no doubting that such implicit analysis occurs in stories written by skilled autoethnographers, and that the ideal promise of evocative autoethnography is morally sound (Bocher and Ellis, 2022). However, I believe that among the less adept and analytically astute, this stock assumption can function as an unconvincing rationalization; a cop-out to avoid the hard work needed to improve on solipsistic and naïve realist work.

Lastly, there's the problem of where to draw the boundaries around what constitutes "evocative autoethnography." Hernandez and her colleagues rightly assert that this subtype encompasses work in the performing arts, and in prose and the spoken word – work that refuses explicit inclusion as social and human science writing. That being the case, it seems to me that much of what is not normally regarded as autoethnographic could arguably be incorporated into the ranks of evocative autoethnography. Plucking two names arbitrarily, the work of Devin the Dude and Dostoevsky, for example, proceeds from their personal experiences and speaks to their respective cultures. However, accepting that solipsism and cultural insularity often masquerade as critical cultural reflexivity, the calibre of implicit analysis in the work of the former compared with the latter must be questioned. I think this is an important issue as it speaks to my "quality" beef more generally.

You might think – especially if you know me personally – that I'm simply projecting purist and perfectionist tendencies. While I concede some truth to this, in line with my character I regard it a moral duty to engage in institutional critique whenever I think this is warranted (see Grant in this volume, pp. 114–132). I believe that a disturbing consequence of the autoethnographic world being too unconditionally inclusive is that its members often seem selectively blind and mute when it comes to publicly calling out unscholarly work. Denial that this happens is understandable; criticism coming from within a family can be anathema, to the extent that it breaks tacitly held loyalty rules. But meanwhile, hard-headed critical-ity is regularly sacrificed at the altar of what to my mind amounts to an infantilizing form of "inclusivity." A striking symptom of this for me is how unscholarly work – unscholarly in being solipsistically high in *auto* but deficient in *ethno* (critically addressing wider cultures and social groups), graphy (in its sophisticated analysis, in addition to representational, sense), depth, and critical reflexivity – is often responded to in conferences and on social media. Vacuous happy talk superlatives of our time – "brilliant," "awesome" – drown out critical dialogue.

But you may also have spotted an irony: making the – already difficult if done well – autoethnographic orientation even more demanding by charging it to become more explicitly philosophical threatens inclusivity. In this regard, there are some who might feel that I'm simply advancing a version of old-white-male-scholar normative discourse: new skin for tradi-tional, reactionary, ceremony. Others might foresee a "risk of autoethnog-raphy becoming a closed, unfriendly field, only available to the worthy and chosen ones." (Klevan, 2021). My response to this is that the laudable need for inclusivity – if "inclusivity" is understood in a grown-up rather than infantilizing sense – doesn't preclude the need for autoethnographers to become more philosophically sophisticated. I rest this response on the assumption that autoethnographers always remain part of the broader aca-demic/scholarly community. This holds true irrespective of the inclusion of non-academics in work reaching the public domain, and the ideal of mak-ing this, and autoethnographic work more generally, accessible to wider non-specialist audiences (Adams et al., 2017).

I should stress that my implied distinction between poor and good autoethnography is gradational, not categorical. When I imagine moving along the autoethnographic texts towards the "poor" end of my evalua-tive continuum, the necessary, fundamental concept (hereafter "FC") of autoethnography – comprised of the "auto" (self), "ethno" (social/culture/ wider communities), and "graphy" (analytical representation) elements – seems to increasingly function as irrelevant ideological background. This happens despite laudable attempts to demarcate and celebrate autoethnog-raphy in terms of a necessary balance between these constituent elements (see Herrmann, 2022). That the FC often seems more sleeping (perhaps comatose) than active partner doesn't in my experience appear to trouble the autoethnographic community at large – at least publicly. The way I make sense of this – what might be called – "FC drift" is by imagining that the FC always remains safely mothballed in genre-defining autoethnographic work. Functioning as a periodic multidirectional ideological reminder – to the world, to the orientation's detractors, to the qualitative inquiry com-munity in general, and to actual and potential autoethnographers – makes it a handy rhetorical resource to be pulled out whenever methodological justification is required.

At my most uncharitable I often wonder if what I see as the gap between the FC and poor practice is most evident in "autoethnographies" that could have been written the night before being uploaded onto a journal website or presented at a conference – one-shot drafts done with minimal and inadequate proofreading. In such work, I often read shallow, self-serving "quirkiness" substituting for depth and substance, in marked neglect of serious analysis, and reflexive cultural and self-interrogation (Klevan and Grant, 2022, pp. 90–126; Sparkes, 2020). In my view, this strongly signals a need for better, broader, and more rigorous educational preparation. I think it crucial that this should incorporate philosophical strands as well as related autoethnography-crafting supervision and mentoring (Klevan and Grant, 2022; Short, 2021).

Unfortunately, autoethnography is often regarded as an easy approach that can be carried off with minimal effort, background research, or thought. That this happens is understandable in the context of what Herrmann (2022) describes as the taming of autoethnography in the neoliberal academy. You may dismiss the term 'neoliberal' as a threadbare cliché. Or overused. Or, as with 'critical autoethnography,' simply a meaningless 'invented' term (Etherington, 2022). I disagree. It's palpable. Real. Feelable. And, as both process and product, it results in autoethnography being trivialized, or methodologically, aesthetically, and representationally debased to the level of technical-rational exercise. This is often done to fit with neoliberal publication, training, audit, and ethical – as opposed to critical scholarship – agendas (Grant, 2016, 2019, 2021; Grant and Young, 2022; Klevan and Grant, 2022; Sparkes, 2007, 2021).

To combat such onto-epistemological degradation, I hold that good autoethnography demands diligence, sustained effort, and significant personal struggles on the part of writers and readers who have real "skin in the game." In this regard, I believe that greater levels of philosophical sophistication among better educated, engaged, and passionate autoethnographic writers would help them to both recognize the centripetal pull of neoliberal training, practice, and publication norms, and more effectively resist and work against those (Grant, 2021). Good autoethnography emerges from an act of love, not a marriage of convenience.

Eschewing autoethnography on the grounds of poor scholarship relates directly to my personal impetus for editing this volume. As an experienced autoethnographer with an academic background in theoretical and applied social science, cultural studies, and the humanities, scholarly rigour and thorough preparation matter greatly to me. Equally personally important and relevant, because of my longstanding interest in the area, is my successful completion of an MA in Philosophy a few years back. I undertook this degree out of a desire to add philosophical depth to my autoethnographic writing, expressly because I thought it deficient in this regard. I also had the ambition to play some part in increasing the philosophical sophistication of the autoethnographic orientation. As a volume of work which I hope will push forward the drive to make autoethnography more explicitly philosophical, this text constitutes a logical culmination of these desires.

Philosophy and Philosophical Autoethnography

But at this point, if you're unfamiliar with philosophy you might reasonably ask for some clarification about it, and justification as to its importance and relevance for autoethnography. It's useful to begin with the proposition that in general terms, *doing* philosophy amounts to thinking for yourself about things that matter, especially around the appearance and reality of these things. Added to this, as an insider to the discipline, my understanding of philosophy coincides with and extends on those of a range of contemporary philosophers (Edmonds and Warburton, 2010, pp. xiii–xxiv; Haslanger, 2012, pp. 16–19): For me, philosophy is:

- always trying to better understand the nature of the narrative and cultural self, in philosophical terms;
- the attempt to bring the highest possible degree of analytic clarity to research;
- the process of reflection on the deepest, most fundamental concepts used in making sense of the world;
- the act of being as critically reflective, and as clear as possible, about presuppositions, premises, concepts, claims, and assumptions that people in general take for granted;
- the need to employ new concepts if existing ones are inadequate for the task at hand;
- the reflexive or second-order task of rigorously and uncompromisingly thinking about thinking;
- the use and development of ideas from existing philosophical work already in the public domain.

In distilling these for my own writing, my answer to the "what is philosophical autoethnography?" question is:

Thinking as clearly, critically, independently, and deeply as I'm able to about every aspect of my autoethnographic work, and never being satisfied with how well I've done in this regard; not resting on my pre-suppositional and conceptual laurels; thinking as nondefensively as I possibly can about the way I think; respecting, using, and developing extant philosophical work in my own writing

(or thinking with philosophy).

I therefore regard "Philosophical Autoethnography" as **autoethnography with philosophical depth**.

"What do I/you *think* about the way I/you think?" has perhaps been the most pertinent, discomfort-evoking question I've asked of myself and my colleagues, students, and readers over the years (Grant, 2013, 2018, 2020a, 2020b; Klevan and Grant, 2022). A few other, related questions arise from this one, including: "what do I/you *feel* about the way I/you think?" and "what led me/you to think about being, knowing, and the way the world works in the way I/you do?"

I believe I'm crafting philosophical autoethnography when, to borrow from and extend on a phrase from Herrmann (2022, p. 127), I'm "burrowing down" as far as I can, to uncover and interrogate how and what I'm writing about myself in the name of experiences I've lived through. From a philosophical perspective, this necessitates confronting what I'm taking for granted about:

being, or my own existence, and the existence of other – human, nonhuman, material, and cultural – entities

(ontology);

knowing, and what it means to know, about these existences

(epistemology);

and – subsuming ontology and epistemology – what grounds my knowledge of the world and how it "works," in terms of what I assume to be its universal, unchanging features and principles? How did I come to acquire this knowledge, and how and in what ways might it be limited?

(metaphysics).

Therefore, the crucial overarching metaphysical question for me in this regard is:

What are my assumptions about how the world works, specifically related to being in and knowing about it, and how might these assumptions be flawed?

The Case for and Against Making Autoethnography More Philosophically Sophisticated

With my metaphysical question in mind, I find the idea of plotting *all* narrative autoethnographic texts in the public domain on a continuum from *weak*- to *strong-sense* philosophical autoethnography to be a productive thought experiment. Every autoethnographic piece on this continuum will be *minimally philosophical* to the extent that each inevitably proceeds from more or less explicitly held metaphysical and onto-epistemological root metaphor standpoint positions. To put this another way, every autoethnographic text will be minimally philosophical in containing displayed assumptions, presuppositions, and concepts relating to how the world works and what counts as *being* in it and *knowing* about it.

I see *weak-sense philosophical* (synonymous with poor, and with minimally philosophical) autoethnographies displaying discursively-restricted, culturally-normative, and conventional assumptions, presuppositions, and concepts – all deployed in uncritical, unclear, confused, incoherent, and sometimes contradictory ways. I see *strong-sense* philosophical (conflated with good) autoethnographies doing the opposite.

I imagine that you might take issue with my weak-strong sense idea. You may think that my need to make autoethnography more explicitly philosophical is based on a "straw man" argument, on the grounds that, by my own lights, narrative autoethnography is always already minimally philosophical. If your objection is reasonable, then my expressed need to make autoethnography more strong-sense philosophical might amount to no more than a methodologically- and conceptually-irrelevant gripe.

My response to you is that "minimally philosophical" doesn't imply "sufficiently philosophical." To stretch a point, everything written by any human is minimally philosophical, containing as it does tacit assumptions about how the world works, but not every human is epistemically and reflexively aware of this. I hold by my contention that in becoming more explicitly philosophical, in terms of the level of rigour and clarity described in my **"Philosophy and Philosophical Autoethnography"** section,

autoethnographers will be better able to raise their autoethnographic game. Specifically, they will ideally be in a position to:

- increase their discursive – subsuming conceptual, interpretive, and analytic – range and sophistication. "Discursive" here refers to the ability to access, use, and socially transmit language in ways that can make a difference to how people comprehend their worlds and act in and on them (Haslanger, 2012; Purvis and Hunt, 1993). Minimally philosophical autoethnography is, by definition, likely to be discursively-limited;
- deepen and enrich their critically reflexive/second-order thinking abilities, by working against habitual tendencies to respond to themselves,

others and the world in incurious, unquestioning ways (see Archer (2010) for a useful resource text);

- combat their *naïve realism*, or the tendency to tacitly assume that how the world is perceived through their senses is how the world actually is, for themselves and for others (Crane and French, 2021);
- be wary of treating as timeless cultural concepts and ideas that may turn out to be evanescent or ephemeral. The philosopher Susan Stebbing (2022) describes this tendency as "potted thinking";
- challenge their received, insufficiently scrutinized assumptions about *self* and *culture* (which I will discuss extensively later);
- subject their ideological beliefs about how the world works, including the ideological basis of autoethnography, to critical scrutiny (I define "ideology/ideological" in this context after Haslanger (2012, p. 18), as "habits of thought, unconscious patterns of response, and inarticulate background assumptions . . . that we assimilate and enact in order to navigate our social world");
- Manage *equivocation* and *question* begging: In the philosophy discipline, "equivocation" refers to the phenomenon of concepts left vaguely or inadequately defined *and/or* treated in confused and contradictory ways in a single piece of work. "Question begging," sometimes called "arguing in a circle," occurs when an argument's premises assume the truth of its conclusion, instead of supporting or proving it (see Bennett, 2018);
- Deliberately and selectively engage theories and concepts from a variety of philosophical perspectives, in considering, questioning, and developing integrative – but often necessarily unresolved – narrative and dialogical perspectives on lived-through experience (see Klevan and Grant, 2022, for an exemplar).

But How Philosophically Credentialed and Informed Does an Autoethnographer Need to Be?

At this point in the chapter, your response to my developing position might be "With your postgraduate education in philosophy, it's easy for you to pontificate!" Point taken, but I should stress that I'm never satisfied with how well I write philosophical autoethnography. This chapter, and indeed the entire volume, is to my mind an aspirational work-in-progress.

Moreover, Sara Ahmed writes in defense of non-philosopher writers using philosophy in their work while being formally under-credentialed to do so, despite the risks:

> When we don't have the resources to read certain texts, we risk getting things wrong by not returning them to the fullness of the intellectual

histories from which they emerge. And yet, we read. The promise of interdisciplinary scholarship is that the failure to return texts to their histories will do something.

(Ahmed, 2006, p. 22)

I read Ahmed's words "will do something" as signalling the benefits of *creative failure*. This is a vital concept. You don't have to self-identify as a philosopher to add philosophical depth to your autoethnographic work. Good examples of this include the work of Gale (2018, 2023) and Gale and Wyatt (2009), which is influenced by Deleuzian and related philosophical work, the need to think with philosophical concepts in the process of autoethnographic inquiry (Jackson and Mazzei, 2012), and using Kierkegaard's journals to support the autoethnographic writing process (Woodley, 2022). Nor do you have to reach an ideal pinnacle of philosophical autoethnographic expertise (whatever that might be!). Aspiring to philosophical depth will, I believe, enable you to enhance your abilities to work creatively with new ideas and perspectives, and address established topics in fresh ways from a broader discursive platform. Despite my postgraduate degree in the discipline, like Ahmed, I don't consider that I reside comfortably and exclusively within philosophy. My writing home is narrative autoethnography, and my primary allegiance is to this orientation.

Autoethnography and Philosophy: Overlapping Characteristics and Concerns

That said, with a foot in each camp, I see philosophy co-existing with autoethnography in a state of mutual but uneasy overlap. Both orientations exemplify open-ended *dialogue*, or conversation, without which each would amount to dogma. Picking up on a point I made earlier, at the level of reflexive or second-order cognition, each claims an investment in *thinking about thinking*. Each is concerned about *criticality*: philosophy can be conceived as the elucidative exploration of fundamental aspects of life that people in general take for granted, while autoethnography is associated with selves engaged in critical cultural exploration. Philosophy and autoethnography therefore claim to champion the overarching idea of *the examined life*.

However, notwithstanding these overlapping characteristics and concerns, I believe that, in the interests of raising their onto-epistemological game, autoethnographers need to embrace philosophy more seriously in several respects. Extending on the critical points I've already made it seems starkly evident to me that in many cases what passes for "autoethnography" falls far short of the rigorous degree to which philosophy tackles each aspect of the examined life. In this regard, the latter orientation constitutes a much-needed exemplary role model for the former.

Particularly, I see a rigour gap evident in the tacit premises displayed in much poor, weak-sense philosophical autoethnographic work. While purporting to produce critical writing, autoethnographers – in line with lay population tendencies – can exhibit conceptual and cultural complacency, solipsism, naïve realism, and insufficient levels of critical reflexivity. Many appear to live in epistemically and morally "gated communities of inquiry" (Chetty, 2018), within which what they take for granted as both known and reasonable about self and culture is too narrow and insufficiently analytically scrutinised. This allows life-limiting cultural worlds to get away unscathed (Ferner, 2021). In displaying complacency through unreflexively presupposing that contingent (current time- and place-bound) cultural life, and their own selves within this, is more or less how it should be, weak-sense philosophical autoethnographers are always in danger of barely scraping the surface of rigorous critical inquiry.

With the elements of the FC – self, culture, and analysis – to the forefront, I now turn to consider how I think this state of affairs might be further improved upon.

Narrative Selfhood

First, narrative autoethnographers would do well to make more explicit their philosophical premises about the nature, ethics, and politics of the *self* they represent, and subject those premises to adequate levels of critical exploration. A premise held by many philosophers (and many autoethnographers) is that autonomy entails a capacity for self-constitution – "a capacity, that is, to define or invent or create oneself" (Velleman, 2020, p. 277). If this premise is accepted, one way of considering the narrative representation of the self is in terms of either *abstract* or *embodied* storytelling (Menary, 2008).

In distinguishing between the human organism and the "self," Dennett (1991, 1992) conceives the latter as a disembodied fictional abstraction. In Dennett's terms, as a "centre of narrative gravity" (hereafter CNG), the self maintains the illusion of a coherent identity governed by a tacitly assumed central controller. This illusion is sustained by the retrospective and prospective, creative, and continual re-embellishment of stories. In this regard, Dennett (1992, p. 114) regards us humans as:

virtuoso novelists, who find ourselves engaged in all sorts of behaviour, more or less unified, but sometimes disunified, and we try to make all of our material cohere into a single good story . . . our autobiography. The chief fictional character at the centre of that autobiography is one's *self*.

Although largely agreeing with Dennett, Velleman (2020, p. 280) regards this "fictive" self as real in an important sense. He argues that although we invent ourselves, "we really are the characters whom we invent." The abstract narrative self is fictive in inventing her or his – storied – role, but factually real in enacting that role. In this regard, the maxims "real but not true; true but not real" apply. Role enactment of a fictive story constitutes an act of unified autonomous agency, or in Velleman's terms (p. 302) "narrative intelligence." This is achieved through coherence between a person's retrospective and prospective stories, motives, and behaviour, where stories have ontological precedence and priority over embodiment.

In contrast, *embodied narrative construction* is premised on a particular self whose reality and autonomous agency, contra Dennett, are taken for granted as beyond question. Embodied experiences are tacitly regarded as having ontological precedence and are thus prior to the stories told about these experiences (Schechtman, 1996). Autoethnographers proceeding from this standpoint may explicitly employ narratives to clarify and represent embodied social experiences after the fact of their occurrence. From an embodied perspective, narrative self-representation is vitally concerned with embodied feeling, and with conveying a sense of oneself as a persisting subject with a valued body and bodily experiences (Menary, 2008).

You may now be wondering about my take on the kinds of ethical and political implications that might arise for the autoethnographic self, storied in either abstract disembodied or fleshly embodied terms. When in my own work I privilege my creative storytelling over representing my embodiment and the embodiment of others, I'm not overly concerned about conventional ethical representational norms. This is because I believe that stories held as having greater salience than embodied experiences allow abstract narrative autoethnographers a greater degree of latitude over decisions about what counts as useful "truth." This is an important issue when, for example, autoethnography is expressly used for therapeutic and social justice purposes in satirizing and lampooning events and people. Indeed, in this regard, deliberately trying to avoid embellishment in abstract storytelling is arguably unethical. Given the creative and dynamic function of the CNG, and the inevitability of failing memory, embellishment emerges an ethical and onto-epistemological necessity: imaginative flesh needs to be put on knowing, but not always reliable, narrative bone.

However, the pursuit of creative self-storying in autoethnography is not without the danger of committing moral violations. The path between writing to right and writing to retaliate, for example, is a difficult one to tread – or at least I've found this to be the case. My own work reflects my belief that satirical and lampooning representations can be justified if used in the service of broader cultural critique. However, it equally seems to me that virtue signalling achieved through traducing others constitutes a moral problem when this is done with insufficient degrees of reflexively held charity, compassion, discursive wisdom, and temperate emotion. Feeding into this problem includes tendencies such as: epistemically unjust stereotyping (Puddifoot, 2021); anger-fuelled fear, ignorance, and ressentiment – which is sometimes unconsciously held (Allen, 2021) and which may result in justified anger being managed inappropriately (Cherry, 2021); and, to recapitulate, "gated community" or habitual, discursively-restricted representational styles (Chetty, 2018). Following Haslanger (2020), Holroyd et al. (2016), Kahneman (2011), and Pinker (2021), acting on these tendencies as if they are *always* justified undermines social justice by blinding us to the implicit cognitive biases at play in our representations of others and, by ironic extension, ourselves.

Turning to the ethical implications of using narrative in the service of embodiment, the politics of the contested ownership of bodies starkly emerge when important aspects of a person's life – central to her or his embodied narrative character – are challenged. When this happens, the emphasis of philosophical autoethnographies may necessarily turn to writers' responsibility, survival, concern, and compensation for their negative lived-though experiences (Schechtman, 1996). So, should embodied autoethnographic self and other representations be stripped to the narrative bone, in the sense that unnecessary embellishment violates the corporeality of autoethnographers, and of others storied in their work? You might think that story over-embellishment can trivialize and obscure the power imbalances and social injustices at play. I partly agree, while also believing that as a function of its dramatic creative impact, embellishment might sometimes make these imbalances and injustices more memorable.

A question arises for me: is a fleshly CNG a viable concept or an oxymoron? It seems to me that autoethnographies often display abstract representation and embodied assumptions simultaneously; it's not an either-or issue. Can this lend itself to incoherence and ethical quagmires around represented identity? I might want to write an autoethnography in which I faithfully represent my embodiment while honouring my commitment to creative narrative embellishment. I may have no choice in the latter, in the face of my memories fading over time. If my need to honour both my embodiment and the creativity of my CNG storytelling are equally important to me, should I take accusations of self-representational incoherence seriously? Or should I simply ignore them, while conceding that related ethical problems may emerge which I'll need to deal with at the appropriate time?

Nonnarrative Selfhood

The narrative self-constitution standpoint of human lives and personhood status experienced as, and achieved through long lasting, more or less linear and coherent stories, although clearly held by many is rejected by others. Galen Strawson (2004, 2009, 2014, 2018, 2019a, 2019b, 2020) in particular has through the years consistently argued against what he has come to call the "Psychological Narrativity Thesis" and the "Ethical Narrativity Thesis" (hereafter PNT and ENT) (Strawson, 2018, pp. 45–46). Those who subscribe to the PNT (including, at a tacit level, many from the autoethnographic communities) make the *empirical* claim that human beings experience their lives as an extended story. They are likely to support the corresponding – *normative* and *ethical* – ENT claim that a "richly narrative outlook on one's life is a good thing, essential to living well, to true or full 'personhood.'" Strawson numbers himself as one person among others who, based on their lived-through experiences, reject both the PNT and ENT. In Strawson's ethico-political terms, those who are "nonnarrative" (2018, p. 46) can have perfectly rich lives in the absence of both experiencing themselves in terms of an unfolding story and believing that they should.

I think this has clear implications for writing philosophical autoethnography, whether the "self" is understood more in abstract narrative, or in embodied narrative terms, or in some permutation or combination of both. For example, abstract storying might represent selves who retrospectively experience and write about their past identities as disconnected and non-enduring over time. Equally, in embodied nonnarrative writing, people might concede enduring intercorporeality – embodiment among other bodies – while endorsing their non-enduring and disparate self identities.

It often makes political and ethical sense to write about oneself as biologically, but not ontologically, enduring. Among many other possible examples, this might be true for those writing about past identities which are analogous to past – unwanted and rejected – incarnations, or for those writing autoethnographies of changed sexual orientation, where past identities no longer feel a good intercorporeal, and by implication, cultural fit. Ahmed (2006, pp. 19–20) writes:

> In the "middle" of my life . . . I left the "world" of heterosexuality, and became a lesbian . . . this . . . meant leaving the well trodden paths . . . Inhabiting a body that is not extended by the skin of the social means the world acquires a new shape and makes new impressions.

Liberal-Humanist Selfhood

Ahmed's account speaks directly to the issue of *choice* over identity and cultural meaning and location. Although a key valued principle for those espousing an autoethnographic orientation, this viewpoint is not without its problems. This brings more into critical focus the tacit influence of political philosophy on autoethnographies of narrative selfhood. I see the Eurocentric model of the liberal-humanist self – deriving historically from writers such as Locke, Kant, Mill, and more recently John Rawls and Charles Taylor – as taken too much for granted in autoethnographic work. The assumption and representation of an ontologically and epistemologically secure, freely choosing, coherent, fully, and transparently aware self, who is fair and balanced regarding race and gender, and who self-identifies with a continuously flowing past, present, and anticipated future, is often insufficiently critically scrutinized. This is in spite of classical and contemporary philosophical and related psychological work that robustly challenges the premises of each element in this model of selfhood (e.g. Hume, 1969, p. 676; Mills, 2017; Strawson, 2009, 2018, 2019a, 2019b, 2020; Wilson, 2002).

With insufficient critical reflexivity about the liberal-humanist model of selfhood, work that's too invested in the idea of agentic autonomy may often seem unconvincing to more philosophically sophisticated readers. It's not difficult to imagine them posing uncomfortable questions about the possibility of writers' implicitly biased, positive narrative impression management of their identities, mediated by self-deception and wish fulfillment, having been projected onto their texts. This self-representational problem is compounded when writers neglect or misrecognise the role of culture and the social in shaping their identities.

Cultural Selfhood

The fish is the last to discover water.

I find this proverb useful. Sometimes we're aware of our cultural contexts, but oftentimes we're not. Sometimes we imagine we're in specific cultural contexts when we're not. Some of the cultural contexts that have shaped us, and continue to do so, will always elude us. "Culture flows through self and self flows through culture" is a compelling slogan for us autoethnographers. But resting one's FC cultural laurels on it renders it facile, saving the bother of burrowing down.

Phillips (2010, pp. 57–68) cautions against being seduced too much into the "catch-all" coherence, salience, and range of convenience of the "culture" concept. She contends that it is often used too carelessly, when – for example – contingent (time- and place-bound) social conventions are mistakenly taken to signify the palpable existence of cultural groupings. Phillips also sees the careless over-usage of the concept evident in simplistic assumptions about the existence of standalone cultures and cultural determinism.

For example, "single-axis" thinking (Ruiz, 2018, p. 342) occurs when narrated identities are written as if they were shaped by a narrow, one-to-one correspondence with cultures presumed to be discrete. At the other extreme is the issue of intersectional theoretical positions adopted in philosophically unsophisticated ways. An example of this is narrative identities represented as if they existed within the nexus of discrete cultural groupings, which have somehow come together in an "additive" sense (Ruiz, 2018, p. 338): culture A + culture B + culture C resulting in identity D. In this regard, I understand Chanter's (2006, p. 51, and pp. 23–55) argument to be that this is likely to reify a conceptually and ontologically artificial separation of cultures in what might be termed "naïve intersectionality." In contrast, Chanter, Mills (2017), and Freeman (2010) all seem to agree that historically-embedded cultural strands – such as gender, race, and sexuality – co-evolve, co-develop, co-shape, and co-constitute one another over a long time span. Such intercultural bleeding greatly exceeds, and thus eludes, individual memory and conscious awareness. This makes thinking through the intersection of race, gender, and sexuality an always necessary but always "impossible task" (Ahmed, 2006, p. 5).

All that said, my difficulty is that I've never actually felt too confident about what counts as "culture" in my own work. Textual definitions of the concept prove useful only up to a point. While I understand the words, reading them fails to result in me feeling on more secure ground. I find the idea of "queering culture" (Ahmed, 2006) more profitable. My reading of Ahmed is that the conventional and normative consensus around what being securely in the middle of "culture" is supposed to *be* and *feel* like is the very thing that needs to be looked past, disattended to, and imaginatively re-invented and re-framed in creative ways. Actively attempting to be on the cultural look-out in this sense will, I believe, help us to better grasp the critical implications of our banal socio-material immersion, and its potential or actual life-limiting impact, and – conversely – how we can turn this around in life-affirming ways.

Culture as the "space of the familiar" (Ahmed, p. 34) – when we feel ourselves to be *in* culture – invites the critical philosophical autoethnographer to exercise the *queering gaze*. If we imagine culture as "the skin of the social" (p. 9), then culture acquires a functional snug fit through how bodies, and by extension stories, inhabit and shape it (p. 12). Equally, bodies and stories acquire coherence through being inhabited and shaped by culture. Self thus flows through culture and culture flows through self, where "culture," understood in this sense, is co-constructed and reified through habit and repetition (pp. 13–14). By implication, some cultural habits are bad, and beg to be broken. Ahmed (pp. 1–8) speaks to the benefits of profitably capitalizing on times of cultural disorientation. Such "queer moments" occur when you don't feel at home in the familiar. You may have experienced those – sometimes epiphanic – moments, when there's a gap between the familiar and unfamiliar, when either your body or your stories, or both, no longer fit? When "big soft bufferings come . . . sideways . . . And catch the heart off guard and blow it open" (Heaney, 1996, p. 70).

What and why do we so often overlook, and fail to call out in the name of autoethnographic cultural critique, when we **don't** queer our cultural lived-through experiences? It seems to me that, among other possibilities, what we frequently disattend to and are too forgiving towards include culture's absurdities, craziness, pomposity, selective social judgementalism, stupidity, and assumed ownership of and colonising claims on bodies (which I'll particularly focus on in my conclusion to this volume). Why do we so often overlook these interrelated issues? We are habituated to culture, immersed in its flow like fish in water. In the light of my argument so far, because of familiarity and repetition, we see what we are conditioned, want, and expect to see, and fail to notice other – important – things. Our failure to notice is mediated by the cognitive biases discussed earlier. It's also the case that, in a more insidiously political sense, cultural familiarity, and repetition are often difficult to step back from, even with the greatest of reflexive effort. The centripetal pulling into the "straight line" of cultural normativity is a tricky one to resist; cultural groups are formed and sustained as a function of shared orientation and consensus (Ahmed, 2006, pp. 70–73). Cultural familiarity and repetition tighten the skin of the social, and our entanglement and entrapment within this.

So, when the culture concept is employed, even with consensually compelling levels of precision, in "questioning, critiquing, and interrogating one's culture and/or cultural discourses" (Herrmann, 2022, p. 127), I think that much more is demanded than the kind of lightweight "trip advisor" cultural tourist critique apparent in some autoethnographies. In such kinds of critique, I think that cultures are found lacking in conventional terms *precisely because they are regarded in conventional terms rather than queered.* Cultural complacency masquerades as cultural critique, and although cultures are challenged on a superficial level, their legacy, legitimacy, and internal logics are all implicitly accepted and supported.

In combating this tendency in the service of queering culture, I believe that autoethnographers would do well to follow Haslanger's (2012) idea of identifying and reflexively critiquing the hidden ideological bases of culture. To recapitulate, Haslanger (p. 18, my brackets) regards ideology as "habits of thought, unconscious patterns of response, and inarticulate background assumptions . . . that we assimilate and enact (through familiarity and repetition) in order to navigate our social world." In this regard, it's useful to consider "culture" as conflated with the social and with ideology. Murakami (2009, p. 68) writes:

> processes often don't allow for variation. If you have to be part of that process, all you can do is transform – or perhaps distort – yourself through . . . persistent repetition, and make that process a part of your own personality.

If cultural (social) ideologies vary from one social circumstance to another, then it becomes a necessary reflexive task to notice how we "become expert at a kind of social code-switching" (Haslanger, 2012, pp. 18–19), in terms of how we talk, present and reveal ourselves, across shifting contexts and shifting ideological norms.

Through taking pains to notice how different cultural (/social/ideological) circumstances make situated demands on us through shaping our perceptions and responses in these circumstances, including what we disattend to, we can engage in *cultural disruption*, rather than *cultural reproduction and reification*. In this regard, a necessary step in cultural critical analysis in autoethnography is making those cultural demands apparent, since "the crucial task of ideology critique is to reveal ideology as such" (Haslanger, 2012, p. 19). Queered culture is then achieved through writing ourselves against the culturally conventional and ideological. In thus re-shaping it and ourselves, we loosen the skin of the social.

Contributing Authors

Having read the proposal and the working definition mentioned at the beginning of this chapter, the authors represented in this volume were invited to join the project because of their willingness to shape and construct their contributions according to philosophical concerns. They might not all agree with some of the issues I've critically discussed, nor with aspects of my take on "philosophical autoethnography." However, in my opinion their chapters are high-quality examples of the central importance and relevance of philosophy to autoethnographic writing.

Because these philosophical autoethnographic chapters stand on their own merit, I've deliberately resisted the usual convention of (over-)introducing them. In terms of broad topic, they are wide-ranging, fascinating, and thought-provoking. In chapters ordered alphabetically according to author surname, you will traverse: happiness as an autoethnographic ethical commitment (Bochner); the autotheoretical textual aesthetics of Kraus's *I Love Dick* (Brostoff); the developing feminist body in challenging traditional philosophical binaries (Ettorre); race- and gender-driven affronts to the identity of an academic black woman (Ferdinand); thinking with Ricoeur in the formative development of an academic (Freeman); hindsight and character development deriving from key memories (Grant); the existential basis of organizational sensemaking (Herrmann), and liminal awakenings (Poulos); the evolution of a critical BlackGirl feminist scholar-activist identity (Pratt); how existential phenomenology informs dialogic being and activism (Rawlins); existential phenomenology and storytelling through disabled bodies (Scott-Pollock); finally, Māori cultural assimilation and difference in the face of continuing Western colonization (Georgina Tuari Stewart).

My minimal request is that you consider reading each chapter against the standpoint position I've set out in this introduction. For my part, I'll endeavour in my conclusion chapter to make some integrative sense of my reading of the contributors' chapters in relation to the concepts of *self* and *culture*, comprehensively discussed earlier. This will of course all amount to *my* reading and *my* philosophical autoethnographic sensemaking, which I hope you will add to, argue against, reject. The conversation, as always, needs to go on.

Final Statement

I write this chapter, my own autoethnographic chapter in the volume, and its conclusion as an elderly white, privileged, cisgendered, heterosexual, politically left-wing, European, hopefully cosmopolitan man. In socio-philosophical terms, starting off with low expectations as a working-class lad from the Scottish Highlands, I revel in the cultural and intellectual capital that has come to shape my existential purpose in life through the years. All this no doubt leaves me blinkered by my accrued and residual, more or less conscious, unscrutinised assumptions, and biases. While over the course of this book project I've consciously tried to exercise epistemic humility in my role as author and very "light touch" editor, these assumptions, biases, and other possible blind spots will be implicit in my writing and may irritate some of you readers. That's inevitable. You can't please everyone. All knowledge is situated, partial, flawed.

All that said, I hope that the impressive range of high-quality work provided in this volume effectively counterbalances my limitations as its editor and contributing author.

References

Adams, T.E., Ellis, C. and Holman Jones, S. (2017). 'Autoethnography'. In Matthes, J. (ed.) Davies, C.S. and Potter, R.E. (Associate eds.) *The International Encyclopedia of Communication Research Methods*. pp. 1–11. Chichester: John Wiley & Sons, Inc. https://doi.org/10.1002/9781118901731

Ahmed, S. (2006). *Queer Phenomenology: Orientations, Objects, Others*. Durham and London: Duke University Press.

Allen, A. (2021). 'Why Psychoanalysis?' *The Philosopher*. 109(2): pp. 63–68. www.philsoceng.uk

Archer, M.S. (ed.) (2010). *Conversations About Reflexivity*. London and New York: Routledge.

Bennett, B. (2018). *Logically Fallacious: The Ultimate Collection of Over 300 Logical Fallacies*. Sudbury, MA: Archieboy Holdings, LLC. www.LogicallyFallacious.com

Bocher, A. and Ellis, C. (2022). 'Why Autoethnography'. *Social Work & Social Sciences Review*. 23(2): pp. 8–18.

Chanter, T. (2006). *Gender: Key Concepts in Philosophy*. New York: Continuum.

Cherry, M. (2021). *The Case for Rage: Why Anger Is Essential to Anti-Racist Struggle*. New York: Oxford University Press.

Chetty, D. (2018). 'Racism as "Reasonableness": Philosophy for Children and The Gated Community of Inquiry'. *Ethics and Education*. 13(1): pp. 39–54. https://doi.org/10.1080/17449642.2018.1430933

Crane, T. and French, C. (2021). 'The Problem of Perception'. In Edward, N. (ed.) *The Stanford Encyclopedia of Philosophy*. Zalta, Fall. https://plato.stanford.edu/archives/fall2021/entries/perception-problem/

Dennett, D. (1991). *Consciousness Explained*. London: Allen Lane.

Dennett, D. (1992). 'The Self as a Center of Narrative Gravity'. In Kessel, F.S., Cole, P.M. and Johnson, D.L. (eds.) *Self and Consciousness: Multiple Perspectives*. pp. 103–115. Hillsdale, NJ: Erlbaum Associates.

Edmonds, D. and Warburton, N. (2010). *Philosophy Bites*. New York: Oxford University Press.

Etherington, K. (2022). Personal communication to Grant. 5 December 2022.

Ferner, A. (2021). 'Philosophy in the Real World: Reasonable People'. *The Philosopher*. 109(3): pp. 122–127. www.philsoceng.uk

Freeman, M. (2010). *Hindsight: The Promise and Peril of Looking Backward*. New York: Oxford University Press.

Gale, K. (2018). *Madness as Methodology: Bringing Concepts to Life in Contemporary Theorising and Inquiry*. London and New York: Routledge.

Gale, K. (2023). *Writing and Immanence: Concept Making and the Reorientation of Thought in Pedagogy and Inquiry*. London and New York: Routledge.

Gale, K. and Wyatt, J. (2009). *Between the Two: A Nomadic Inquiry into Collaborative Writing and Subjectivity*. Newcastle upon Tyne: Cambridge Scholars Publishing.

Gingrich-Philbrook, C. (2005). 'Autoethnography's Family Values: Easy Access to Compulsory Experiences'. *Text and Performance Quarterly*. 25(4): pp. 297–314. https://doi.org/10.1080/10462930500362445

Grant, A. (2013). 'Writing Teaching and Survival in Mental Health: A Discordant Quintet for One'. In Short, N.P., Turner, L. and Grant, A. (eds.) *Contemporary British Autoethnography*. pp. 33–48. Rotterdam: Sense Publishers.

Grant, A. (2016). 'Researching Outside the Box: Welcoming Innovative Qualitative Inquiry to Nurse Education Today'. *Nurse Education Today*. 45: pp. 55–56. http://dx.doi.org/10.1016/j.nedt.2016.06.018

Grant, A. (2018). 'Voice, Ethics, and the Best of Autoethnographic Intentions (or Writers, Readers, and the Spaces in-between'. In Turner, L., Short, N.P., Grant, A.

and Adams, T.E. (eds.) *International Perspectives on Autoethnographic Research and Practice*. pp. 107–122. London and New York: Routledge.

Grant, A. (2019). 'Dare to Be a Wolf: Embracing Autoethnography in Nurse Educational Research'. *Nurse Education Today*. 82: pp. 88–92. https://doi.org/10.1016/j.nedt.2019.07.006

Grant, A. (2020a). 'Autoethnography'. In Aranda, K. (ed.) *Critical Qualitative Research in Healthcare: Exploring the Philosophies, Politics and Practices*. pp. 159–176. London and New York: Routledge.

Grant, A. (2020b). 'The Reflexive Autoethnographer'. In Aranda, K. (ed.) *Critical Qualitative Research in Healthcare: Exploring the Philosophies, Politics and Practices*. pp. 196–213. London and New York: Routledge: Routledge.

Grant, A. (2021). 'Publishing'. In Grant, A., Short, N. and Turner, L. 'Publishing Autoethnography: A Thrice-Told Tale'. In Adams, T., Ellis, C. and Holman Jones, S. (eds.) *Handbook of Autoethnography*. 2nd Edition. pp. 249–261. London and New York: Routledge.

Grant, A. and Young, S. (2022). 'Troubling Tolichism in Several Voices: Resisting Epistemic Violence in Creative Analytical and Critical Autoethnographic Practice'. *Journal of Autoethnography*. 3(1): pp. 103–117. https://doi.org/10.1525/joae.2022.3.1.103

Haslanger, S. (2012). *Resisting Reality: Social Construction and Social Critique*. New York: Oxford University Press.

Haslanger, S. (2020). 'Social Structure, Narrative and Explanation'. *Canadian Journal of Philosophy*. 45(1): pp. 1–15. https://doi.org/10.1080/00455091.2015.10 19176

Heaney, S. (1996). *The Spirit Level*. London: Faber and Faber.

Hernandez, K-A.C., Chang, H. and Bilgen, W.A. (2022). *Transformative Autoethnography for Practitioners*. Gorham, ME: Myers Education Press.

Herrmann, A. (2022). 'The Future of Autoethnographic Criteria'. *International Review of Qualitative Research*. 15(1): pp. 125–135. https://doi.org/10.1177/19408447211049513

Holroyd, J., Scaife, R. and Stafford, T. (2016). 'Responsibility for Implicit Bias'. *Philosophy Compass*. 12(2): e12410, pp. 1–13. https://doi.org/10.1111/phc3.12410

Hume, D. (1969 [1739–40]). 'Appendix'. In Mossner, E.C. (ed.) *A Treatise of Human Nature*. pp. 671–678. London: Penguin Books.

Jackson, A.Y. and Mazzei, L.A. (2012). *Thinking with Theory in Qualitative Research: Viewing Data Across Multiple Perspectives*. Abingdon and New York: Routledge.

Kahneman, D. (2011). *Thinking, Fast and Slow*. London: Allen Lane.

Klevan, T. (2021). 'Email to Alec Grant'. 5 December.

Klevan, T. and Grant, A. (2022). *An Autoethnography of Becoming a Qualitative Researcher: A Dialogic View of Academic Development*. London and New York: Routledge.

Menary, R. (2008). 'Embodied Narratives'. *Journal of Consciousness Studies*. 15(6): pp. 64–84. Richard Menary, Embodied narratives – PhilPapers

Mills, C.W. (2017). *Black Rights/White Wrongs: The Critique of Racial Liberalism*. New York: Oxford University Press.

Murakami, H. (2009). *What I Talk About When I Talk About Running*. London: Vintage Books.

Phillips, A. (2010). *Gender & Culture*. Cambridge: Polity Press.

Pinker, S. (2021). *Rationality: What It Is, Why It Seems Scarce, Why It Matters*. New York: Viking.

Puddifoot, K. (2021). *How Stereotypes Deceive Us*. Oxford: Oxford University Press.

Purvis, R. and Hunt, A. (1993). 'Discourse, Ideology, Discourse, Ideology, Discourse, Ideology . . .'. *The British Journal of Sociology*. 44(3): pp. 473–499. https://doi.org/10.2307/591813

Ruiz, E. (2018). 'Framing Intersectionality'. In Tayor, P.C., Martin Alcoff, L. and Anderson, L. (eds.) *The Routledge Companion to Philosophy of Race*. pp. 335–348. New York and London: Routledge.

Schechtman, M. (1996). *The Constitution of Selves*. New York: Cornell University Press.

Short, N. (2021). 'Email to Alec Grant'. 16 November.

Sparkes, A.C. (2007). 'Embodiment, Academics, and the Audit Culture: A Story Seeking Consideration'. *Qualitative Research*. 7(4): pp. 521–550. https://doi.org/10.1177%2F1468794107082306

Sparkes, A. (2020). 'Autoethnography: Accept, Revise, Reject? Reflections of An Evaluative Self'. *Qualitative Research in Sport, Exercise and Health*. 12(2): pp. 289–302. https://doi.org/10.1080/2159676X.2020.1732453

Sparkes, A. (2021). 'Making a Spectacle of Oneself in the Academy Using the H-Index: From Becoming an Artificial Person to Laughing at Absurdities'. *Qualitative Inquiry*. 27(8–9): pp. 1027–1039. https://doi.org/10.1177/10778004211003519

Stebbing, S. (2022). *Thinking to Some Purpose*. Abingdon and New York: Routledge.

Strawson, G. (2004). 'Against Narrativity'. *Ratio*. 17(4): pp. 428–452. https://doi.org/10.1111/j.1467-9329.2004.00264.x

Strawson, G. (2009). *Selves: An Essay in Revisionary Metaphysics*. Oxford: Clarendon Press.

Strawson, G. (2014). 'The Sense of Self'. In Edmonds, D. and Warburton, N. (eds.) *Philosophy Bites Again*. pp. 105–114. Oxford: Oxford University Press.

Strawson, G. (2018). *Things That Bother Me: Death, Freedom, the Self, Etc*. New York: New York Review Books.

Strawson, G. (2019a). 'We Live Beyond . . . Any Tale That We Happen to Enact'. In Strawson, G. (ed.) *The Subject of Experience*. pp. 206–122. Oxford: Oxford University Press.

Strawson, G. (2019b). 'Introduction'. In Strawson, G. (ed.) *The Subject of Experience*. pp. 1–15. Oxford: Oxford University Press.

Strawson, G. (2020). 'Hume on Personal Identity'. In Russell, P. (ed.) *The Oxford Handbook of Hume*. pp. 269–292. New York: Oxford University Press.

Velleman, J.D. (2020). 'The Self as Narrator'. In Velleman, J.D. (ed.) *Self to Self: Selected Essays*. 2nd Edition. pp. 277–303. Michigan: Michigan Publishing.

Wilson, T.D. (2002). *Strangers to Ourselves: Discovering the Adaptive Unconscious*. Cambridge, MA: The Belknap Press of Harvard University Press.

Woodley, H. (2022). 'The Use of Kierkegaard as a Stimulus for Autoethnographical Journal Writing'. *Journal of Autoethnography*. 3(4): pp. 459–474. e-ISSN 2637–5192. https://doi.org/10.1525/joae.2022.3.4.459

2

SUFFERING HAPPINESS

On Autoethnography's Ethical Calling

Art Bochner

This chapter was originally published as: Bochner, A. (2012). 'Suffering Happiness: On Autoethnography's Ethical Calling.' *Qualitative Communication Research*. 1(2): pp. 209–229.
   http://dx.doi.org/10.1525/qcr.2012.1.2.209

> The question of happiness is not merely one among many questions we could ask about a life. For a finite being, the question of happiness *is* the question of its life.
>
> Vivasvan Soni (2010, p. 75)

"Do you know a fellow named Ben Myers?" I ask Carolyn as I sit down at the breakfast bar in our kitchen to join her for lunch.

"Yes. Don't you remember meeting him at the Qualitative Congress meetings?" she asks.

"The name sounds familiar, but I can't place him."

"We were on our way back from lunch. Mitch Allen introduced us. Last week I listened to a podcast he did with Norman Denzin, and he's supposed to do another one soon with Tony Adams," she replies, handing me the cheese and mushroom frittatas she has warmed in the toaster oven.

"Do you recall the conversation?" I ask.

"Not in any detail."

"What do you remember?"

"He talked about feeling emotionally drained after attending the autoethnography session on father-son narratives on which you gave a paper

DOI: 10.4324/9781003274728-2

(Bochner, 2010; published Bochner, 2012) – something to the effect that the presentations were electrifying but also terrifying."

"Oh, now I can place him. It all makes sense."

"What makes sense?" Carolyn asks, taking the seat next to me.

"The podcasts you mentioned are loaded onto a site called *Critical Lede*. They focus on new books and research publications within the qualitative research community in communication studies. I'm not sure, but I figure he must be turning a critical lens on autoethnography now."

"What makes you say that?"

"I received an e-mail from him this morning, asking me to contribute to a program on writing autoethnographies of happiness and joy at next year's Congress meetings," I say, pausing to take a bite of the frittata.

"Oh, that's hysterical," Carolyn interrupts. "Ummm, these are good." We sit in silence for a few moments, inhaling the aroma and savoring the tastes. Then Carolyn continues, "So he wants you to write about happiness and joy. Ha, he must have you confused with someone else."

"Very funny. Just because you see me as tragically happy doesn't mean everyone else does," I kid.

"You're not tragically happy, you're happily tragic," Carolyn replies in a mocking yet affirming tone.

"But no, he doesn't have me confused with somebody else, funny girl," I reply sarcastically.

"You mean he knows our work?"

"Well, that's just the thing. He reminded me that he had attended that awesome program on father-son narratives. That was his word, 'awesome.' Apparently, he went to several autoethnography panels, including the one on writing relationships that you were on."

"Then what are you concerned about? Sounds to me like he appreciates what we do."

"Yes and no. In one breath, he tells me how evocative and powerful autoethnography can be; then in the next breath, he talks about autoethnography as heavy, grim, and morose. He cites how critics say autoethnography is only cathartic for the author, implying that there may be something to that critique."

"Are you serious?" Carolyn says, sounding irritated at the direction of the conversation. "He doesn't identify with that foolishness, does he? He must realize that most of the critics of autoethnography are defending social science orthodoxy. They're afraid of vulnerable writing and mostly concerned about protecting their turf." (Ellis and Bochner, 1996).

"I can't say, since I don't really know Ben. However, his e-mail divides the possible content of autoethnography into two different categories: pain and suffering on the one hand; joy and happiness on the other. Apparently, he hasn't thought about the dialectical connection between suffering and happiness. He wants to open a space for autoethnographic work in which there is no attempt to seek catharsis."

"Then tell him to look at Ron Pelias's story about his relationship with his son (Pelias, 2002). There is a lot of pain and no catharsis in that story. Besides, he seems to be missing one of the main points of good autoethnography: The stories we write convey an affirming attitude toward life; they avow moral commitments and attempt to erase obstacles to living a good and meaningful life. What makes Ben so sure that the good life is happy?" Carolyn asks.

"Oh, I like that question! A meaningful life doesn't necessarily include protracted periods of joy. For me it's about finding a vital connection to something of value, a striving for excellence, something akin to Nietzsche's (Kaufman, 1974; Nietzsche, 2000) idea of a self-overcoming."

"If you decide to join that panel, you ought to point out that happiness may be purchased at too high a cost such as a depletion of the self," Carolyn suggests.

"That reminds me of the question Charles Guignon posed to our narrative class. He asked the class to imagine that a drug had been invented that would give you positive feelings for the rest of your life, but the side effect would be that you would become a mindless slave to society's conventions. 'Would you be willing to take that drug for the rest of your life?' he asked (see Guignon, 2004)."

"Oh, that's wonderful a way to get to the heart of the issue. I can see your mind churning. Sounds to me like this panel could provide a good opportunity for you to show some of the connections between pain and pleasure that we've talked about before," Carolyn says, a mischievous grin on her face.

"Yes, endlessly."

"Seriously, it looks as if we still need to clarify how autoethnography, at least the way we practice it, is all about what it means to live a good life. The best autoethnographies weave a sense of the good into an unfolding story of a life that points backward into the past and forward into the future. The autoethnographer wants to use the wreckage of the past to make a better future possible."

"I would like to do that, but I get so tired of being put on the defensive by scholars who have their own agendas," I reply.

"Do you think Benjamin has such an agenda?" Carolyn asks.

"I don't know. I think he is attracted to autoethnography, but at the same time scared of it. They may not say it, but I think autoethnography frightens many academics. They need the protection of distance. They have not been exposed to vulnerable scholarship (Behar, 1996; Bochner and Ellis, 2002;

Ellis and Bochner, 1996) in their educational histories. They've learned to hide or avoid showing the vulnerable parts of themselves that bring them to the work they are doing. There's safety in *standing apart from* rather than *becoming a part of* what you study. I can understand that fear. After all, autoethnography is an embodied form of scholarship, and that can be intimidating in the university, which tends to focus on everything from the neck up. What I don't appreciate is turning that fear into attacks on autoethnography, like the ones you wrote about in *Revision* (2009) – that it's self-indulgent navel-gazing, or it's not sufficiently analytical, or it's too realist, or the writing isn't up to the standards to which we hold other narrativists, poets, or novelists. Now, Ben adds yet another complaint – it's too morose and unhappy."

"But that seems only partially true in Ben's case," Carolyn corrects. "I mean if he's going to write joyful autoethnography, he's going to have to journey into very personal and private areas, forbidden areas, quite possibly areas of sexual pleasure or taboo."

"Yeah, I wonder whether Ben's talked himself into thinking that pleasure is somehow more public than pain. I could bring up something akin to what Adam Phillips (2005) writes about under the heading 'maps of happiness.' He says that happiness is all about what we want, but that the things we are most conscious of wanting get obscured by keener satisfactions that remain unconscious and beyond our awareness. What we really want is usually located in the realm of what is forbidden or repressed. But I don't think that's what Benjamin has in mind. He mentions writing about birth instead of death and weddings instead of funerals. He wants to celebrate the joyful moments of life."

"Maybe he just needs to get out more. You know, go to the movies or something. Get entertained," Carolyn jokes.

"I don't think Ben would appreciate my saying something like that," I continue. "Besides, this is not about Ben. Now that you talked me into joining this panel, I am feeling grateful to him for pressing his point. He made me think of a host of questions well worth addressing in this presentation. Should autoethnography make us feel good? Is happiness always light and comforting or does it have a dark side? What is the connection between happiness and mortality? Is there an important difference between a good life and a happy life, or are these one and the same? Is happiness a feeling, an experience, or a judgment?"

"Whew, that's a load," Carolyn says. "Are you planning to write a book or a conference paper?" she jabs. "I do agree, though, that the question of happiness Ben is raising can move us off the beaten track toward issues we haven't addressed. It is too easy to be stuck rephrasing the same old arguments as if you are addicted to one view of reality. And Ben is not alone.

There are plenty of other people who hold the view that autoethnographers are sad and traumatized individuals who can't find anything joyful in their lives to write about."

"I suspect other contributors will have something to say about the joys per se of writing and performing autoethnography," I say. "But that's not what I want to do. I want to focus on the links between happiness and narrative as well as how contingency and mortality connect to judgments about happiness. I have my doubts about whether happiness can be expressed in a story."

"I know every time I try to write a story about happiness it turns out dull and hackneyed. I end up throwing it in the trash," Carolyn moans.

"Right. And my point is that there is a good reason for that. Happiness defies narrativization. I'm going to try to defend that premise in my paper."

"So you've talked yourself into another project, eh," Carolyn smiles.

"No, I'd say *we* talked me into it. But I do so appreciate your indulgence," I say, acknowledging Carolyn's helpfulness and signaling that I am ready to go back to work.

"My pleasure, darling. These talks are what keep us sane," Carolyn reciprocates.

"Oh, no, let's not get off on sanity and madness. Not now, anyway. Let's save that one for later."

"Oh, you're impossible," Carolyn replies tongue-in-cheek, as she dashes off to her office on the opposite side of our house.

***

Happiness, Love, and Suffering

I retreat to my office sanctuary and begin to think about happiness. Oddly enough, the first image to enter my mind is a distant memory of the cornball bandleader, clarinetist, and singer Ted Lewis of the Big Band era who brought his show to the old vaudeville theatre, The Stanley Theatre, in Pittsburgh in the 1950s and 60s, when I was a teenager. Lewis would run out onto the stage in his trademark battered top hat and shout his tag question at the audience.

"Is evvvvvverybody happy?" Lewis hollered. "Yes!" the crowd roared back. Everybody in the audience was happy, or at least they said they were, though the prime period of Lewis's career spanned the Great Depression (Yanow, 2001).

In retrospect, I imagine that Lewis realized the importance of connecting to a deep cultural assumption circulating through the nervous system of most Americans – we are supposed to be happy, hopeful, cheerful, and optimistic! You've heard the tunes: *Put on a Happy Face, Walk on the Sunny Side of the Street, Have a Song in your Heart, Make Someone Happy*. It is not good, healthy, or even moral to be unhappy. If unhappiness is not an illness, it may be the cause of one (Sontag, 2001). Some religions conceive of unhappiness as a transgression (McMahon, 2010). The Gospels command God's children to "rejoice and be glad," turning sadness into a sin. The unhappy person, warns McMahon (2010, p. 476) is doubly damned, cursed in this life as in the hereafter.

In his e-mail, Ben (Myers, personal communication, June 4, 2010) insinuated that autoethnographers are preoccupied with damaged lives. He bemoaned the sadness and tragic qualities of so much autoethnographic storytelling, expressing a longing for more love stories and fewer accounts of broken or abusive relationships. He implies that stories of fractured relationships expose the hurt and suffering of shattered dreams, whereas love stories display pure joy and the divine repose of intimacy. However, one thing historians, poets, philosophers, novelists, and filmmakers have shown convincingly is that human love is not divine love. We should not confuse Eros with Agape (May, 2011; Nygren, 1955). Human love is conditional, self-interested, unstable, and risky (Frankfurt, 2006). Moreover, stories of broken relationships can teach us a great deal about love and human vulnerability as well as happiness. Beginning with Shakespeare, some of the world's greatest literature has depicted the inextricable connection between love and suffering. These archetypal love stories show that the destiny of lovers is distress, suffering, and loss. As Denis de Rougemont (1940, rev. 1956) curtly remarked in *Love in the Western World*, "Happy love has no history – in European literature" (1956, p. 52). Our vocabulary of passionate love reveals that in the thick of love, a person is fallen, fevered, frenetic, and frenzied. We talk about being *lovesick, out of our minds in love, love-crazed*. Some popular music depicts love as a disease, as "the drug," and as a toxic narcotic that can debase and degrade a person. Award-winning films warn us about "dangerous liaisons" and "fatal attractions." Clearly, the language of love is not a vocabulary confined to pleasure. Does this lexicon of love make lovers sound happy?

Still, Ben may have a point. Love is one of the most precious features of human nature. Most of us believe that we cannot be happy if we do not love or feel loved. Loving is one of the things we think desirable to do. Harry Frankfurt (2006, pp. 55–56) construes love as "the original source of terminal value" and "the ultimate ground of practical rationality." Love is important to us, Frankfurt observes (2006, p. 40), because "it is love that accounts for the value to us of life itself." However, writing love is not necessarily writing happiness or joy. When students in my undergraduate course Love and Communication write their "love autobiographies," they invariably choose to write about broken relationships. They express a great deal of pain and suffering, but many of them still hold on to these experiences as a valuable source of learning. Frequently they express how difficult they find it to let go of the "feelings" of love they have attached to the experiences they depict. They see their happiness and sadness as dialectically connected and many of them express a strong desire to take on the challenging task of fixing a damaged identity through narrative repair (Nelson, 2001).

Woody Allen's darkly comic depictions of love come to mind. You may recall his famous joke about love and suffering:

> To love is to suffer. To avoid suffering, one must not love. Then, one suffers from not loving. Therefore, to love is to suffer; not to love is to suffer; to suffer is to suffer. To be happy is to love. To be happy, then, is to suffer, but suffering makes one unhappy. Therefore, to be happy, one must love, or love to suffer, or suffer from too much happiness.
>
> *(Silet, 2006, p. 39)*

In *Annie Hall*, Allen provided a comic depiction of our sadistic yearning for love. Musing about the meaning of love, Alvie Singer says that he sees relationships in the same way he views life – "full of loneliness and misery and suffering and unhappiness, and it's all over much too quickly" (Shumway, 2003, p. 160). In my course on love, I showed the hilarious scene that takes place right after Annie dumps Alvie. Walking glumly down the street, Alvie interviews people about the status of their love relationships. Stopping one couple in their tracks, he asks, "Here you look like a very happy couple . . . um, are you?" "Yes," they reply in unison. "How do you account for it?" Alvie asks in a mystified tone. "I'm very shallow and empty and I have no ideas and nothing interesting to say," the woman replies. "And I'm the exact same way," mimics her partner (Conrad and Skoble, 2004, p. 141). The scene proposes that boredom is a recipe for happiness in love. We should be careful what we wish for.

The trade book market dispenses oodles of advice about happiness. There are books on happiness as an art form (Dalai Lama, 1998), the pursuit of happiness (Myers, 1993), authentic happiness (Seligman, 2002), habits to maximize happiness (Leonhardt, 2001), gateways to happiness (Lou Retton, 2000), and stumbling on happiness (Gilbert, 2007). Still, some question remains about whether one can be taught to be happy, as well as whether such "knowledge of happiness" might turn out to be a source of misery. Should we leave well enough alone? As Charles Schulz, the creator of the comic strip *Peanuts*, said, "My life has no purpose, no direction, no aim, no meaning, and yet I'm happy. I can't figure it out. What am I doing right?" (Baggini, 2004, p. 159).

The refrain that happiness is boring has a long history in literature. Tolstoy opens his epic novel *Anna Karenina* (1995) by declaring: "Happy families are all alike; every unhappy family is unhappy in its own way." Tolstoy believed there was nothing profound to say about "happily ever after." As undergrads might say, "BORING!"

Autoethnographers are in the business of storying lives. As storytellers, we are preoccupied with plots, and it is misadventures, reversals of fortune, blows of fate and lives spinning out of control that drive plots. Trouble is the "engine" of narrative that drives plot (Bruner, 1990; Burke, 1945; White, 1981). "Narrative, in a word," write Bruner and Kalmar (1998, p. 324), "organizes the travails of jeopardy. Trouble, in this sense, may be not only the engine of narrative, but also the impetus for its elaboration." A storyline free of discontent has nowhere to go, no place to move, no complication to uncomplicate. How can such a story be interesting or evocative? Moreover, the tragic circumstances of evocative autoethnographies invite the reader or viewer to relate and respond to the situation of the other. Soni (2010, p. 307) calls this tragedy's "ethics of happiness." In this sense, tragic autoethnography can (and should) produce an ethical connection to the other's narrative situation, a desire on the part of the reader or viewer to transform the material conditions of the other's tragic situation, increasing the possibility of happiness and a good life.

Embracing Edginess

I went through several years of analytic psychotherapy at two different times in my life. Both of my therapists made a point of disabusing me of the notion that a life free of conflict would be either possible or desirable. They encouraged me to embrace conflict, learn from it, and give up the myths of harmony, consistency, and redemption. I am not sure how successful I have been in putting my analysts' advice into practice, but I did learn a great deal about desire. I suppose most of us who turn to therapy voluntarily are seeking some "happy" outcome. We want to feel better, and that usually means we need a better grasp of the sources of our personal suffering. Even if we are not suffering at the moment, we want to learn how to make our lives better. It is quite possible that many of us are hopelessly confused about the terms "happier life" and "better life."

In therapy, I was encouraged to focus on events and feelings that might reveal insights about the deeper desires provoking my actions and decisions. Of course, my deepest desires were stubbornly unconscious and out of awareness. For me, participating in therapy was like taking a graduate seminar on myself. The painstaking and protracted work of analysis required me to turn off the censors and drop my defenses in order to produce unconscious material for analysis and interpretation. This would take time. There would be homework, and it was never clear when the course would end. At first, I remained disengaged, shielding my most revealing thoughts and feelings. Then I slowly began to trust the process. I was in the presence of someone who was showing I mattered to him and that he would support me no matter what I said. What did I have to lose?

Gradually, I lowered my guard, quit posturing, and allowed myself to express without evaluation whatever came into my mind. As the sessions probed deeper, I found myself increasingly eager to focus on some of the choices I had made over the course of my life, especially ones made long ago that continued to plague me. I am not talking here about just any old choices, but rather the choices on which a life turns in one direction or another. These are life's toughest decisions, those in which whatever you decide leaves undone something you feel you should have done (Bochner, 2010, 2012). In other words, you never feel released completely from the claims upon you of the other option (MacIntyre, 1984). As I looked back on these decisive moments of my life, I came face to face with the contingency and fatefulness of my life. I saw how given over to chance my life had been, and how much the contingencies on which my life rested had depended on the care and commitments of the people and communities in which I had lived, worked, and loved (Bochner, 2014). At this point, the more I delved into the analytic material that was coming to the surface, the more frightened I became. I began to question whether I really understood what happiness meant. Out of a fog of uncertainty, I began to understand that a person never does all he or she wants to do, nor all he or she ought to do. In the face of the tragic dilemmas and fatefulness of a mortal life, how can a person truly be happy?

Looking back on my life, I realized that I had never pursued the conventional ideal of happiness. As the son of a Jewish immigrant – a "greenhorn" raised in abject poverty and in an environment of discrimination and denial of basic needs – I had internalized a strong work ethic and a belief that suffering was an inescapable part of life. The fact that we human beings must live in and with a conditional and unforeseeable future is itself a potential source of suffering that can deaden our capacity to exercise our creativity and passion, draining us of the desire for all-out experience. Indeed, as the Athenian sage Solon observed, "the living can never be happy because a mortal life is full of suffering. Only in death is there any possibility of happiness" (Soni, 2010, p. 27). No matter how good my life may feel at a given moment in time, my momentary happiness hangs unsteadily in the balance, precariously haunted by the many possible blows of fate that can enter into my mortal life.

In therapy, I learned that a desire for happiness was not the governing principle of my life. I feared that if I were truly happy, whatever that might mean, I would have to renounce the very sources of desire that drive me. My writing and teaching were edgy. Happiness and contentment might take that edge away. What would I do then? Don't the best autoethnographers have an edginess to them that reveals itself in the stories they write?

During one memorable session, I complained to my analyst about my neuroses. "Why can't I just stop being so neurotic about these things?" I moaned. He countered by questioning how well I would function as an academic without my neuroses. "Thirty-some years of building relationships with neurotic intellectuals have taught me that neurosis is a muse and a source of inspiration for creative people," he quipped. Then he quoted a line he said was from Aristotle, one I assume he reserved for just such situations, something to the effect that "all of the outstanding philosophers, statesman, poets, and artists are by nature melancholic." He offered the same advice as Woody Allen: *Be careful what you wish for.* Not only is happiness usually a boring subject to write about, but it can also stifle the creative impulses that make a writer's work meaningful.

Happiness as an Existential Question

My mother used to say to me, "I want only that my children be happy. Are you happy, Arthur?" I knew Mother wanted me to say yes. An affirmative response would provide the validation she needed, so I complied with Mother's request, but I did not know whether happiness was what I was truly experiencing. Now I find myself intrigued by the depth and complexity of what happiness denotes. What did my mother's question mean? Would it be sufficient for me to say in reply, "I feel good; I'm happy"? Shouldn't some moral starting point exist for making such an assessment? After all, feeling good is not necessarily being good, is it? Serial killers have testified that they feel good when they crush their victims. Murdering makes them happy.

Each semester, I began my course on love by asking the students to respond to one question. "What do you want?" I ask. After they get over their hesitation and curiosity about the question, on which I refuse to elaborate further, they usually come up with some version of the statement "I want to be happy." Then I ask them, "How? How can you achieve happiness? What would make you happy?" The question apparently compels them to commodify the banal rewards they seek in their lives, and thus I typically get responses such as these: "to be rich," "to have a big house," "to own a sports car," "to have great sex." One student blurted out that she would achieve ultimate pleasure if I could guarantee she would receive every new Apple product as soon as it came on the market!

As the students rattled off the list of things that would make them happy, I played secretary, writing their items on the whiteboard. Looking over the whole list, I would turn suddenly to the class and encourage them to skip ahead in their lives. "Assume now that you possess these things and are looking back on your life in, say, 30 or 40 years. Would having these things be sufficient for you to say your life has been good and worthwhile?" Many of the students said my question stunned them, bringing into focus the possibility that what they really want is a good life and that their desire for a virtuous life requires something different from the momentary pleasures associated with feeling happy. They begin to understand that they have taken for granted a reward-centered conception that "thing-ifies" happiness.

The students' responses to this exercise reinforced my retrospective recognition that my mother's question was more complicated than I had imagined. Her concern for my happiness was not exclusively momentary. She wanted my happiness to be enduring. She wanted me to be happy over the course of my whole life. When my mother asked me, "Are you happy, Arthur?" I assumed she wanted to know how I felt at that moment, that is, to judge how I was feeling. Living a happy life over the course of *my whole life* is something quite different from the question of how I am feeling today, at this moment, instantly. Thus, my mother's question can evoke two categorically different responses requiring two distinctly different forms of appraisal. The question of whether I'm having a good time – whether I am enjoying myself, feeling good, or experiencing pleasurable sensations – does not invite a narrative depiction. It asks what I am experiencing or feeling without reference to how that experience is lived or made through narrative. Happiness, accordingly, becomes an experience that is private and subjective, not public or communal. Neither the narrative history giving rise to my pleasure nor the consequences of my pleasure going forward into the future are typically at issue. It is enough simply to say, "I'm happy; I feel good." Feeling good or experiencing happiness becomes a virtue in its own right.

Nor are there any ethical principles applicable to assessing one's own subjective experience of happiness. As we used to say in the 1960s and 70s, "Whatever turns you on." The question of the price at which one purchases happiness does not ordinarily come into play. Nor does the context in which one's happiness occurs. Take a pill, buy a car, win the lottery, write a book, eat an ice cream cone, have a wedding, give birth, throw a party – whatever makes you feel good at the time. One way of rewarding oneself is as good as any other. As my students' responses show, this affective conception of happiness is de-narrativized and decontextualized; it is a product, a reward, or a commodity directly accessible to experience; and, as a product, it stands apart from narrative (Soni, 2010). Thought of in this fashion – as a reward – happiness is almost impossible to make present. How can one narrate such a "thing"? Some people think of the moments of their greatest joy as peak or orgasmic instances, at once momentary and infinite. In this modernist conception, "happiness [is] not perceived to be a *narrative* problem at all" (Soni, 2010, p. 12). It is not an activity but a state of mind, and thus the study and understanding of happiness has been assigned to (or appropriated by) the disciplines of psychology, neuroscience, and economics. Without a robust temporality centered on past and future, "moments" of happiness resist even the most heartfelt attempts to narrate them. Rather than an activity, something lived over time, what we get is the kind of happiness that McMahon (2006) referred to as "a trivial pursuit," and Soni (2010) denounced as neither ethical nor political.

Living a happy life is an entirely different matter. A life is not a single moment or experience. It has a past, a present, and a future. And every life has a limit. We can be certain we will die, but we do not know when. As Jules Henry (1971, p. 11) observed, "We bleed time." We cannot see or know the future, but we must make plans. Typically, our plans connect a "known" past to an invisible future, charting a course that can lead to a happy life. We want to be able someday to look back on life and pronounce it happy, which is to say something about the worth or goodness of a person's whole life, a life completed with what Mark Freeman called "narrative integrity" (2010). In *After Virtue*, Macintyre (1984, p. 205) observed that the "unity of a virtue in someone's life is intelligible only as a characteristic of a unitary life, a life that can be conceived and evaluated as a whole." Accordingly, this "unity resides in the unity of a narrative which links birth to life to death as narrative beginning to middle to end." The question of whether a life is a happy one is inextricably tied to narrative. A life is always incomplete until it ends. Every life ends in death, but we do not know the ending, neither the how nor the when. The quality of a life, then, is always contingent on future events which one cannot anticipate and over which one has no control. A life that moves forward can be full of surprises.

Here is where things get messy. If a life is always in motion until one dies, how could one ever judge whether the life was happy until the life is over? If that is the case, then, one can never judge the happiness of his or her own life.

Can a person judge the happiness of his or her life as a whole? This is the important question about happiness that Vivasvan Soni develops in *Mourning Happiness* (2010), a marvelous and challenging book in which he develops the case for "a hermeneutics of happiness" modeled after the Athenian idea of happiness. Soni (2010) urges a return to the classical conception of happiness eclipsed by the narrative form of the 18th century "trial novels," which reduced happiness to an emotional and subjective state, privatizing and individualizing happiness, severing its connection to narrative and extinguishing the ethical, communal, and political content of happiness.

Soni (2010) argues that transforming happiness into a hopelessly affective experience severed the link between happiness and narrative. What we need, he argues, is a "hermeneutics of happiness" that mourns happiness and recovers its dependence on narrative. He insists, "Happiness is not an experience. Rather it is something we live and make in the course of a narrative" (Soni, 2010, p. 403).

Celebrating Solon's proverb – "Call no man happy until he is dead" – Soni (2010) emphasizes that the manner in which a person dies is part of the person's whole life, and every moment of a life is important. "According to the Solonian view," writes Soni (2010, p. 15), "happiness cannot be an uncontaminated positive experience, because it must take account of human finitude." The question of happiness is *the* question of every life, in many respects a tragic question because life is finite. Soni (2010) wants us to take human finitude and the "radical contingency" of life seriously. In light of the contingency and chance on which a life turns, it is never safe to assume that a life will continue on more or less the same course until it expires.

Solon's proverb does not claim that it is only in death that one can be happy – not at all. What he means, instead, is that happiness ought to be an *ethical judgment* of the whole of one's life, the unity of a life, in Alistaire MacIntyre's (1984) terms. Under the classical ideal, happiness is a judgment, not an experience; it is an assessment of the whole of one's life made only after one's life has ended. Given the tragic fatefulness and contingency of every life, Soni (1010) concludes that judgments about happiness can only be biographical; that is, told by another, not by one's self. A Solonian judgment of happiness also rests on the person's relation to community. As Soni (2010, p. 64) observes, "by its death, every finite being entrusts the question of its happiness to a community of others, whether it wants to or not."

Soni (2010) shifts the ground of happiness. He wants us to quit thinking of happiness as a thing we desire or pursue – a fleeting emotion, an object, a reward. Instead, we should regard the question of happiness as a serious question, even a tragic one, considering the condition of human finitude, and understand that we cannot make a judgment about happiness without a narrative. There is no specifiable content to happiness and no set of standards by which to judge it. Happiness is radically indeterminate, but unthinkable without responsibility (Soni, 2010). In the realm of Solonian happiness, the community wants to do everything it can to make a happy life possible, which includes working to provide the material conditions necessary for happiness. In other words, the community bears an ethical responsibility to demand and labor for justice. Happiness thus turns away from the epistemic (Are you happy? How do you know?) and toward the existential and ethical (an encounter with the existence of the other, with barriers to the fullness of living, and a concern for the material conditions of social justice).

Happiness and Existential Autoethnography

I turn finally to autoethnography's relation to happiness. "Instead of pain, let's write happiness," Ben announced when he invited me to contribute to this conversation (B. Myers, personal communication, June 4, 2010). Lamenting the "heaviness" of autoethnography, Ben challenged the participants to consider how autoethnography works "when removed from pain." To be fair, Ben actually expressed an approach-avoidance reaction to autoethnographies of suffering. "That father panel was brutal," he remarked, but he also referred to these autoethnographies as "awesome" and "amazing." I am not bringing up these competing responses to pick on Ben. His candid expression of how he responded to these "father stories" of loss and grief is immensely helpful in formulating an agenda for extending autoethnography's usefulness. In the literature on autoethnography, most of the attention goes to the writer or performer. Now we need to consider the question of how to read and listen to autoethnography and how to react to it; that is, what to do. What are we asking of our readers or listeners? I argue that autoethnography builds an ethical relation to the 'other' that is paramount. In light of our socialization into a modernist understanding of happiness, we may need to evoke an affective identification with the other, but our overriding concern should be producing a narrative that invites and encourages a responsiveness *to* the other and a responsibility *for* the other, what Levinas called an "ethics of alterity" (Hand, 1989). In Soni's (2010, p. 311) terms, it is not enough simply to produce an imaginative identification with the plight of the protagonist; one must instead evoke "an ethical connection to the narrative situation of the other."

In these remarks, I have tried to make a case for a dialectical conception of happiness, a suffering happiness that would reduce the confusion about autoethnography's existential convictions and ethical commitments. In practice, autoethnography is not so much a methodology as "a way of life." It is a way of life that acknowledges contingency, finitude, embeddedness in storied being, encounters with Otherness, an appraisal of ethical and moral commitments, and a desire to keep conversation going. Autoethnography focuses on the fullness of living and, accordingly, autoethnographers want to ask, *how can we make life better?* We autoethnographers are reluctant to commit to removing pain from our work because as Soni (2010, p. 15) observed, "the idea of happiness is a tragic one, inseparable from the experience of mourning." We believe that this does not make us heavy, depressing, or pain-obsessed individuals. On the contrary, the question of happiness is the most urgent calling of autoethnography. Our work as autoethnographers invites others to become involved with a life, engaged with it, and responsible for doing something about what its tragic qualities may signal or foreshadow, to commit to alleviate the narrative situation; in short, to make happiness more probable. Readers or listeners who take up this calling, accepting the responsibility, can show concern for the other's life, what Frankfurt (2006) calls "caring" and Hyde (2006) calls "the life-giving gift of acknowledgment," even when they share little or nothing with the other.

Ben is right to say that autoethnography does not seek to produce a momentary feeling of happiness in the reader or viewer. Autoethnography does not question the vital importance most people assign to their own happiness, only the grounds for making such a judgment. Our concern is with broader and deeper questions about the possibilities and meanings of happiness appropriate for mortal beings like us. The troubled lives autoethnographers depict usually resist simplification and raise moral and political questions about the possibilities of living a good life, a life of decency, kindness, integrity, and righteousness. Autoethnography thus inevitably and unambiguously draws the reader's attention to the urgent question of happiness and the ethical and social justice issues provoked by the tragic and fated circumstances of human life.

Initially, when I read Ben's e-mail, I felt discouraged. I was certain I had failed in my objective. My autoethnographic story of personal suffering, which Ben had witnessed at the Congress, had not gotten through to him (Bochner, 2010, 2012). If what made it "awesome" was its tragic and heavy quality, and it frightened or terrified Ben, then I had failed to evoke the kind of sympathy for which I had aimed. I do not deny the tragic quality of the story I told, but tragedy, as Aristotle suggested, is supposed to evoke the listener's capacity to be concerned for the happiness of the other, what some writers call "an ethics of sympathy," which may be indistinguishable from an ethics of happiness and alterity. In this respect, every autoethnographic narrative of suffering refuses to be an end in itself; it anticipates and seeks something beyond suffering, something to which an ethics of happiness and alterity applies. I wanted Benjamin and others in the audience that day to see that there was meaning and value in my suffering and that I was affirming life, my life and my father's. I wanted witnesses to the narrative context of my suffering, to feel their own lives implicated and to want to correct the injustice depicted.

We do not need autoethnographies of happiness, because every meaningful autoethnography addresses the question of happiness. Of course, most of us socialized into the post-Enlightenment formulation of happiness do not see, experience, or relate to autoethnography this way. That is why we need a richer, deeper, fuller grasp of the connection between suffering and happiness. We know that suffering is an inevitable part of every life story and that autoethnography is a powerful and evocative means of bringing vivid and resonant frames of understanding to one's suffering and trauma. Unfortunately, the forms of telling and showing suffering and happiness have created the impression they are oppositional or antithetical. My argument is that happiness is at stake in every narrative of suffering, and thus the question of the possibility of happiness in the presence of suffering is central to the whole project of autoethnography. Is there love without suffering? Is there happiness devoid of conflict, anxiety, or trouble?

What about sexual pleasure? you might ask. Isn't that the perfect image of orgasmic happiness? Isn't sexual pleasure an unrivaled blessing in our lives? This is a good note on which to end this conversation. In autoethnography, our project is the work of making, questioning, and engaging with meanings, values, and storylines. What is the meaning of sexual pleasure? Set in contrast to all other life experiences, doesn't sexual pleasure amount to unfettered joy? Isn't sex a story devoid of suffering or tragedy? Hardly. As Bataille (1994) observed:

in truth this [sexual] activity consumes our reserves of energy so dangerously that we contemplate it with anguish. It enraptures and frightens us. It frightens us because it enraptures us and it enraptures us all the more profoundly because it frightens us.

So, for those of you insistent on fulfilling your desire to write joy and happiness in whatever form, I leave you with these words: *Writing pleasure is a pleasure that can only anticipate its own failure.* As for me, I shall continue to write in the spirit of Ruth Behar's (1996, p. 177) words: "call it sentimental, call it Victorian and 19th century – or, Benjamin, call it heavy and painful – but I say that [social science] that doesn't break your heart just isn't worth doing anymore."

References

Baggini, J. (2004). *What's It All About? Philosophy and the Meaning of Life*. New York: Oxford University Press.
Bataille, G. (1994). *The Absence of Myth: Writings on Surrealism*. Translated by Richardson, M. New York: Verso.

Behar, R. (1996). *The Vulnerable Observer: Anthropology That Breaks Your Heart*. New York: Beacon Press.

Bochner, A. (2010). 'Bird on a Wire: Freeing the Father within Me'. Paper presented at the Sixth International Congress of Qualitative Inquiry, University of Illinois, Urbana-Champaign.

Bochner, A. (2012). 'Bird on the Wire: Freeing the Father within Me'. *Qualitative Inquiry*. 18: pp. 168–173. https://doi.org/10.1177%2F1077800411429094

Bochner, A. (2014). *Coming to Narrative: A Personal History of Paradigm Change in the Human Sciences*. Walnut Creek, CA: Left Coast Press.

Bochner, A. and Ellis, C. (2002). *Ethnographically Speaking: Autoethnography, Literature, Aesthetics*. Walnut Creek, CA: AltaMira Press.

Bruner, J. (1990). *Acts of Meaning*. Cambridge, MA: Harvard University Press.

Bruner, J. and Kalmar, D. (1998). 'Narrative and Metanarrative in the Construction of Self'. In Ferrari, M. and Sternberg, R. (eds.) *Self-awareness: Its Nature and Development*. pp. 308–331. New York: Guilford.

Burke, K. (1945). *A Grammar of Motives*. Englewood Cliffs, NJ: Prentice Hall.

Conrad, M.T. and Skoble, A.J. (eds.) (2004). *Woody Allen and Philosophy: You Mean My Whole Fallacy is Wrong?* Peru, IL: Carus.

De Rougemont, D. (1956). *Love in the Western World*. Princeton, NJ: Princeton University Press.

Ellis, C. (2009). *Revision: Autoethnographic Reflections on Life and Work*. Walnut Creek, CA: Left Coast Press, Inc.

Ellis, C. and Bochner, A. (eds.) (1996). *Composing Ethnography: Alternative Forms of Qualitative Writing*. Walnut Creek, CA: AltaMira Press.

Frankfurt, H. (2006). *The Reasons of Love*. Princeton, NJ: Princeton University Press.

Freeman, M. (2010). *Hindsight: The Promise and Peril of Looking Backward*. New York: Oxford University Press.

Gilbert, D. (2007). *Stumbling on Happiness*. New York: Vintage Books.

Guignon, C. (2004). *On Being Authentic*. New York: Routledge.

Hand, S. (ed.) (1989). *The Levinas Reader*. Malden, MA: Blackwell.

Henry, J. (1971). *Pathways to Madness*. New York: Random House.

Hyde, M. (2006). *The Life-Giving Gift of Acknowledgment*. West Lafayette, IN: Purdue University Press.

Kaufmann, W. (1974). *Nietzsche: Philosopher, Psychologist, Antichrist*. Princeton, NJ: Princeton University Press.

Lama, D. (1998). *The Art of Happiness: A Handbook for Living*. New York: Riverhead Books.

Leonhardt, D. (2001). *Climb Your Stairway to Heaven. The 9 Habits to Maximize Happiness*. Lincoln, NE: Writer's Showcase.

MacIntyre, A. (1984). *After Virtue*. Notre Dame, IN: Notre Dame University Press.

May, S. (2011). *Love: A history*. New Haven, CT: Yale University Press.

McMahon, D.M. (2006). *Happiness: A History*. New York: Grove Press.

McMahon, D.M. (2010). 'What Does the Ideal of Happiness Mean?' *Social Research*. 77: pp. 469–490. www.jstor.org/stable/40972226

Myers, D.G. (1993). *The Pursuit of Happiness: Discovering the Path to Fulfillment, Well-Being, and Enduring Personal Joy*. New York: HarperCollins.

Nelson, H.L. (2001). *Damaged Identities, Narrative Repair*. Ithaca, NY: Cornell University Press.

Nietzsche, F. (2000). *Basic Writings of Nietzsche*. Translated by Kaufmann, W. and Gay, P. New York: Modern Library.

Nygren, A. (1955). *Agape and Eros*. Translated by Watson, P. Philadelphia: Westminster Press.

Pelias, R.J. (2002) 'For Father and Son: An Ethnodrama with No Catharsis'. In Bochner, A.P. and Ellis, C. (eds.) *Ethnographically Speaking: Autoethnography, Literature, and Aesthetics*. pp. 35–43. Walnut Creek, CA: AltaMira Press.

Phillips, A. (2005). *Going Sane: Maps of Happiness*. New York: HarperCollins.

Retton, M.L. (2000). *Gateways to Happiness: Seven Ways to a More Peaceful, More Prosperous, More Satisfying Life*. Colorado Springs, CO: Waterbrook Press.

Seligman, M. (2002). *Authentic Happiness: Using the New Positive Psychology to Realize Your Potential for Lasting Fulfillment*. New York: The Free Press.

Shumway, D.R. (2003). *Modern Love: Romance, Intimacy, and the Marriage Crisis*. New York: New York University Press.

Silet, C. (ed.) (2006). *The Films of Woody Allen: Critical Essays*. Lanham, MD: Scarecrow Press.

Soni, V. (2010). *Mourning Happiness: Narrative and the Politics of Modernity*. Ithaca, NY: Cornell University Press.

Sontag, S. (2001). *Illness as Metaphor* and *AIDS and its Metaphors*. New York: Anchor Books.

Tolstoy, L. (1995). *Anna Karenina*. Translated by Tolstoy, L. and Maud, A. New York: Oxford World's Classics.

White, H. (1981). 'The Value of Narrativity in the Representation of Reality'. In Mitchell, W.J.T. (ed.) *On Narrative*. pp. 1–23. Chicago: University of Chicago Press.

Yanow, S. (2001). *Classic Jazz*. San Francisco: Backbeat Books.

3

DO *I LOVE DICK*? AN EPISTOLARY ADDRESS TO AUTOTHEORY'S TRANSITIONAL AESTHETIC OBJECTS

Alex Brostoff

I. Pushing the Envelope

Dear Editor,

Does a letter always arrive at its destination? To what extent is genre a symbolic solution to an ideological problem? And might my epistolary frame contribute to kindling a critique of mimesis as ideological?

In case it was unclear, the rhetorical question lodged in my title is facetious. Contrary to its titular confession, Chris Kraus's epistolary *I Love Dick* (1997)[1] does not love Dick, dick, or any other variation of the proverbial phallus and its host of psychoanalytic substitutes. "Chris Kraus, a 39-year-old experimental filmmaker, and Sylvère Lotringer, a 56-year-old college professor from New York, have dinner with Dick ____," the text begins (p. 19). What follows is frenzy: a fetish forms, a marriage unravels, letters proliferate. Chris writes to Dick. Sylvère – Chris's husband and co-conspirator; a prominent poststructuralist, a professor – writes to Dick. Chris and Sylvère inform Dick of their intention to hang 180 pages of letters from the cactuses in Dick's front yard and film his reaction to finding them. They invite him to write an introduction to a book called *I Love Dick*. The letters fantasize, rhapsodize, satirize; the letters theorize. Splicing creative nonfiction and critical theory, Kraus considers Kierkegaard's third remove, *Madame Bovary*, conceptual art, schizophrenia, sadomasochism, cyborgs, and more. And Dick, you ask? "Dick?" Kraus echoes in one interview. "Dick is every Dick, Dick is Uber Dick, Dick is a transitional object."[2] "Dear Dick,"

DOI: 10.4324/9781003274728-3

she writes, "I guess in a sense I've killed you" (1997, p. 74). More on this soon.

November 17, 1997: A headline in *New York Magazine* runs: "See Dick Sue: A Very Phallic Novel Gets a Rise out of a Beloved Professor." The "beloved professor," none other than British sociologist Dick Hebdige, author of *Subculture: The Meaning of Style* (1979), calls *I Love Dick* "beneath contempt." "This book was like a bad review of my presence in the world," Hebdige remarks, "if someone's writing gets read only because it exploits a recognizable figure, then it really is a despicable exercise."[3] In spite, or perhaps because she had already obscured identifying details – "everything short of the first name, which I needed for my title" – Kraus shoots back, "the whole book is about how to make privacy a feminist issue."[4] "A feminist issue?" Hebdige snarls, "Tell her to take it up with Princess Diana."[5] This from a Birmingham School cultural critic who wrote a book with the subtitle "The Meaning of Style."

Twenty years later, amid murmurs of gossip flanked by massive book sales and a 2016 adaptation into an Amazon Prime Video series,[6] the "meaning" of Kraus's style remains the subject of considerable controversy. A polarizing presence with a cult following, Kraus has been called "a spirited heroine, a trollish underground woman, a feminist social critic, and a phenomenologist of romantic longing" (Blair, 2016). Almost exclusively vilifying or idolizing, critical reception has fallen into two camps. I will call them the antiheroic exhibition camp and the abject vindication camp. The former ridicules Kraus as an obscene, confessional female antihero (Blair, 2016); the latter exalts her as "marching boldly into self-abasement and self-advertisement" (Myles, 2006, p. 13) and reclaiming abjection (Fisher, 2012, p. 224).

Both positions, however, are predicated on an oversight: namely, that *I Love Dick* anticipates and preemptively deconstructs its own reception, which is part and parcel of how Kraus pushes the epistolary envelope. To those who would demean her as an antiheroic exhibitionist, Kraus might quip, "Why does everybody think that women are debasing themselves when we expose the conditions of our debasement?" (p. 211) To those who would exalt her for reclaiming female abjection, she might cite institutionalized sexism, shrug off a satire of "The Dumb Cunt's Tale" (Kraus, 1997, p. 11), and top it off with recourse to the Deleuzian quip, "Life is not personal."[7] In short, both critical camps fail to meet and move with the politics *I Love Dick* performs, a shortcoming I intend to rectify in this epistolary inquiry.

Impersonally,

Alex

II. Playing with Contradicktion

Dear Editor,

"So what was Chris performing?" Kraus asks in one letter (1997, p. 177). "Reading delivers on the promise that sex raises but hardly ever can fulfill – getting larger 'cause you're entering another person's language, cadence, heart and mind" (p. 207). *"Fuck her once and she'll write a book about it,* you or anybody else might say" (Kraus, p. 254, italics in original). Dear Editor, she wrote a book about it. And if we agree that "reading delivers" on this intersubjective promise, as Kraus promises, then to what effect? "Getting larger" gets larger if and when we enter "another person's language, cadence, heart and mind." Isn't that the epistolary method of delivery in particular?

Enter *The Political Unconscious: Narrative as a Socially Symbolic Act* (1981), in which Fredric Jameson frames narrative "as a symbolic resolution or solution" to "a dilemma, contradiction, or subtext" (p. 42). For Jameson, "the ideology of form . . . in the area of literary genre" is ideological insofar as it distorts, dissimulates, and reproduces "allegorically articulated" conditions of capitalism (pp. 99–100). *"Does the Epistolary Genre Mark the Advent of the Bourgeois Novel?"* Kraus jests in an epistle (p. 68, emphasis in original). Jameson might reply that the semi-autonomy of the aesthetic underwrites the bourgeois illusion of the autonomy of the subject, while the critical distance of the aesthetic from social reality opens up utopian potential. Much like Terry Eagleton's *The Ideology of the Aesthetic*, *The Political Unconscious* conceives of the aesthetic as a vehicle of ideological interpellation that simultaneously performs ideology-critique.

One could, I suppose, fill in the blanks and like some kind of Marxist Mad Libs,[8] conclude that in *I Love Dick*, the epistolary operates as a symbolic, feminist resolution to the predicaments of cisheteropatriarchal, capitalist ideology. As such, one could say that Kraus at once lulls the reader into bourgeois illusions of progress while also providing the potentiality for emancipatory critique. The problem with this formula, however, is that if we map the logic of *The Political Unconscious* or *The Ideology of the Aesthetic* onto *I Love Dick*, we wind up back at square one: in the realm of the reclamation of female abjection and antiheroism – illusions of progress that arguably reproduce conditions of cisheterosexism and then some.[9] Unsurprisingly, neither Jameson nor Eagleton seem to feel friction (other than a touch of psychoanalytic universalizing on Eagleton's end) when they rub Marxism up against feminism.[10]

"Can the aesthetic be reclaimed for radical thought?" Isobel Armstrong asks. "Can it be reclaimed for feminist thought and praxis?" (2000, p. 28). Following a curt critique of Eagleton's "worst-case reading" of "the aesthetic as that which stands over and against the political as disinterested Beauty, called in nevertheless to assuage the violence of a system it leaves untouched" (p. 30), Armstrong's *The Radical Aesthetic* (2000) offers a reparative reading.[11] "Pivotal and transitional objects," Armstrong proposes, "establish the category of the aesthetic as *play*, with all its cognitive and representational potential, its specific cultural space, its interactive possibilities" (p. 40, emphasis in original). Understanding play as transitional and epistemological, cognitive, and cultural, Armstrong argues that the aesthetic enables play with contradiction. By this reckoning, the aesthetic performs neither the work of ideology nor ideology-critique.

If what characterizes play is its dialectical incorporation of invention and injunction, then play, I'd argue, is precisely what *I Love Dick* does with the contradictions inlaid in the gendering of the epistolary genre. Kraus's playfulness, to use Armstrong's language, might be said to take place in a "rule-bound," "imaginary situation" to the extent that the "transformation of categories" becomes the "prerequisite of political change". The categories with which I will be concerned are those produced by the gendering of genre. "Dick" is doubly transitional in this way: as an epistolary invocation, he serves as what I will describe as Chris's transitional aesthetic object, and as an autotheoretical text, *I Love Dick* can likewise be read as a transitional aesthetic object.

"It is surely our present task to play with contradictions," writes Armstrong (2000, p. 42), and that is surely my present task in this epistolary framework. But to what extent is it productive to locate the aesthetic outside of ideology? Will play prevent genre from capitulating to symbolic resolution? If I may take the liberty of foreshadowing, *Dick*'s end is staggering, but I'll save that for my own ending.

For now, let's begin,

Alex

III. The Gendering of Genre

Dear Editor,

Fredric Jameson excels at breaking the laws of composition we attempt to instill in our undergrads, don't you think? The oft-quoted preface to *The Political Unconscious* not only deploys superlative adverbs of frequency ("*Always* historicize!", "*all* dialectical thought") but makes a massive "transhistorical" sweep that ends up moralizing its own message (Jameson, 2014, p. 9). "*Always* historicize?" Eve Sedgwick (2006) retorts. "What could have less to do with historicizing than the commanding, atemporal adverb 'always'?" Indeed, "The imperative framing will do funny things to a hermeneutics of suspicion" (p. 125).[12] Despite my suspicion of the hermeneutics of suspicion, despite Jameson's and my irreconcilable differences when it comes to matters of genre and its etymological twin, gender, I will now perform a couple of acts of epistolary historicizing to set the stage for aesthetic play.

I've suggested that the ways Jameson historicizes genre leads us into territory that *I Love Dick* deterritorializes, a critical maneuver which its critics overlook. "A genre," Jameson professes:

> is essentially a socio-symbolic message, or in other terms, that form is immanently and intrinsically an ideology in its own right. When such forms are reappropriated and refashioned in quite different social and cultural contexts, this message persists and must be functionally reckoned into the new form.
>
> *(p. 141)*

By this reckoning, form and sociocultural context may shift, but the ideology of genre remains: an atemporal reification masquerading as a resolution to social contradiction. Drawing from Jameson, in "Special Topic: Remapping Genre," Bruce Robbins underscores the ideological work of genre as an appendage of the social institutions that uphold it. "Genre is seen as complicit with the larger culture," he writes, "it is a social institution, burdened with the weight of social interests and constituencies and relaying that unwelcome burden to literature" (2007, p. 1646). Conceived as such, genre kindles the critique of mimesis as ideological; that is, by Robbins's reckoning, genre serves the social interests of "the larger culture" by reproducing distorted approximations of reality which mask the conditions of (aesthetic) production. Yet more explicitly, in *The Ideology of Genre: A Comparative Study of Generic Instability*, Tomas O. Beebee (1994) likewise calls on a Marx to argue that "what makes genre ideological is our practice of speaking of it as a 'thing' rather than as the expression of a relationship between user and a text, a practice similar to that identified by Marx as 'commodity fetishism'" (p. 18). Indeed, ideology that reifies genre obscures the relationship between text and reader in the service of "social interests," much like ideology that reifies cisheterosexism obscures the social relations that produce it.

This is not to suggest that gender and genre are co-extensive, but it is to interrogate them on the grounds of shared social effects; namely, the ideological prescription and proscription of modes of being and doing. Gender and genre describe systems of norms that classify persons and texts, respectively; and yet, paradoxically, when read as performative practices, gender and genre construct and transgress the very boundaries that they justify and complicate with their exceptions. Dialectical though Jameson,

Robbins, and Beebee's approaches are, overlooked is the fact that even though genre, like gender, produces and/or critiques the ideological illusion of a norm, texts, like bodies, *play* into contradictions inlaid in the arbitrary divisions of multiple genres/genders.

As an oft-acknowledge precursor to the modern novel, the epistolary genre has long staged the social relationship between text and reader, playing into and with the very ideology that may appear to govern it. Formally speaking, that is, in narratively conjuring its absent correspondent (as I now conjure you), the epistle aestheticizes how the writing-subject corresponds to and with the illusion of a reader. In *Clarissa's Ciphers: Meaning and Disruption in Richardson's Clarissa*, Terry Castle (1982) expounds on this effect when she explains how the epistolary:

> creates the illusion of a palimpsest of reading. There are at once decipherers within the fiction – the myriad correspondents who, through the medium of the letter, swerve together, argue, flirt, cajole, and torment each other – and decipherers without, real readers.
>
> *(p. 16)*

In this way, as Castle explains, "letters preserve interpretations of previous texts" and "a *writing*" becomes, "paradoxically, a *reading*" (p. 19, emphasis in original).[13] "Acts of textual exegesis," from those of the author to the characters to the readers, are fictionalized as private correspondence but read openly, as you now read this. The absent addressee thus becomes present, and what was private is read as public.

And yet, even before its popularization in the eighteenth century, the gendering of the epistolary had made it subject to contradiction. At once deemed a feminized pastime but recurrently co-opted by male authorship, at once relegated to the realm of feminized sentimentalism but concurrently complicit in the ideology of their abjection,[14] epistolarity is less a resolution to and more a stage on which to play with the social contradictions of these categorizations. In "Female Trouble," Elizabeth Gumport (2012) notes, "The invention of what Katharine Ann Jensen calls the 'Epistolary Woman' effectively excluded all women from the sphere of serious male conversation," while still others argue that the epistolary genre was a gateway into the public sphere for women. Whether "as critics have suggested, the epistolary novel was the crucible of modern consciousness – of third-person narration in fiction," the genre has clearly played host to contradictions produced by a binary matrix and its host of aligned coordinates: male and female, present and absence, public and private.

Unequivocally conscious of this, Kraus's self-referential and intertextual epistles deconstruct the ideology of genre. Within the opening pages, in fact, she reveals that because Chris and Sylvère "are no longer having sex, the two maintain their intimacy via deconstruction: i.e., they tell each other everything" (1997, p. 5). That Kraus parodies deconstruction as concomitant with confession in a sexless marriage signals how acts of exegesis play the intersubjective role denied by sex in this text. In the midst of an early, unsent letter to Dick, Chris complains:

> Sylvère, who's typing this, says this letter lacks a point. What reaction am I looking for? He thinks this letter is too literary, too Baudrillardian. He says I'm squashing out all the trembly little things he found so touching. It's not the Dumb Cunt Exegesis he expected. But Dick, I know that as you read this, you'll know these things are true. You understand this game is *real*, or even better than, reality, and better than is what it's all about . . . It's about not giving a fuck, or seeing all the consequences looming and doing something anyway . . . I love you Dick.
>
> *(p. 28, emphasis in original)*

In addressing the absent Dick, Chris portrays his, and our, act of reading – a game as real as hyperreality, as real as the willing suspension of disbelief.[15] What's not to love? As we know, "Reading delivers on the promise that sex raises but hardly ever can fulfill – getting larger 'cause you're entering another person's language, cadence, heart and mind" (p. 207).

Insofar as gender and genre are concerned, this would seem to suggest that *I Love Dick* operates ideology-critique. And as I've noted, Kraus's reception is all about the reclamation of female abjection and antiheroism, which I've called counter-productive illusions of progress that reinforce cisheterosexism; that is, to say Kraus reclaims abjection and antiheroism depends on those genderings of genre Kraus is critiquing. But there's a more radical reading to be performed, with more significant stakes to be claimed.

Significantly,

Alex

IV. Transitional Aesthetic Object I: Dick

Dear Editor,

Marxist Mad Libs are only fun while the structure of the story holds. But what if we wanted to rewrite the story entirely, not just plug in choice figures of speech? What if we wanted to write a new story altogether? The aim of Isobel Armstrong's "The Aesthetic and the Polis: Marxist Deconstruction" (Armstrong, 2000) is just that. She begins by ridiculing Terry Eagleton's reading of Kant's aesthetic for two reasons. First, according to Eagleton

(1990, pp. 1–3), the aesthetic is the henchman of hegemony, personified: that is, the aesthetic *is* the ideology by which hegemony wields its powers of coercion and oppression. Second, ideology "requires a scene of seduction" to masquerade as such, and so, essentially, the aesthetic is personified as a "woman" (p. 31). Obviously, as Armstrong notes, this doesn't sit well for the left or for feminism (2000).

Dear Editor, I'm writing you letters about an epistolary work entitled *I Love Dick*. Neither the genre nor the title sounds particularly favorable to radicalizing the aesthetic for feminist praxis, now does it? Let's begin with "Dick" and work backward until we hit the "I." You'll remember that Dick is a proper noun, a name, but that the surname never appears in the text. Dick is the man to whom Chris and Sylvère's letters are addressed. Initially, the married couple's *billets doux* reconstructs and deconstructs events that have passed between themselves and Dick: dinner, drinks, homosocial networking between the two men,[16] a "Conceptual Fuck" (Kraus, 1997, p. 5) and later a physical one between Dick and Chris, and so forth. But Dick is never just Dick. To purloin a few letters from Castle's title *Clarissa's Ciphers*, Dick is but a cipher, and a not-so-secret one at that. Just try reading this book, its title blazing, on the subway.

Does it go without saying that to call someone a "dick" refers, variously, to misogyny, chauvinism, and sexism? Now I've said it: Dick is a dick. Dick is a cipher for "centuries of male supremacy and dickdom" (p. 110). He is Robert Lovelace. He is Vicomte Sébastien de Valmont. He is the notorious and nefarious "Dick" of the eighteenth century epistolary. He is a perpetrator of "the utter worthlessness of women . . . all orbiting around the big Dicks" (p. 96). And because *I Love Dick* is entangled in the politics of gender/genre in academia and the art world, he is intellectual fascism to boot, the author of Chris's marginalia in Sylvère's copy of Heidegger's *La question de la technique*, which she re-entitles, "*La technique de Dick*" (p. 113); however, he's also "The Dumb Dick" (p. 51) and "the absent Dick" (p. 51), he's "the whole sex/Dick thing" (p. 83). Alas, Dick is "a bit disturbed that dicks could be the butt of jokes" (p. 255). From here on out, I will use "Dick" in quotation marks to call forth this chain of signifiers. While this may make it appear as if *I Love Dick* were some kind of misandrous performance of phallogocentric castration,[17] how, then, would we account for the "love" of its title? This "love" is a great love; I will need to go on something of a digression to explain just how great.

When Isobel Armstrong (2000) reclaims the aesthetic for feminist praxis, she does so by proposing *play* as "cognate with aesthetic production" (p. 37). Instead of indoctrinating or inducting us into ideology, aesthetic play's rule-bound imaginary creates cultural space for epistemological experimentation.[18] According to Armstrong, play engenders a transitional stage in which a pivotal object (Lev Vygotsky's term) or a transitional object (Donald Winnicott's term) enables one thing to stand for another. Vygotsky's example registers all too crudely when mapped onto "Dick;" that is, when "a stick becomes a horse," the stick does not cease to be a stick, but becomes "a pivot for severing the meaning of a horse from a real horse" (Armstrong quoting Vygotsky, p. 38). Functionally similar, Winnicott's transitional object "opens up and contains" such contradiction, interiority, and indeterminacy (p. 39). Unlike a substitute, abstraction, or metaphor, however, pivotal and transitional objects act as material pivots for "remaking categories and for discovering new perceptions," creating "a space which redefines one's relationship to the world" (p. 38).[19] Unlike the hermeneutics of suspicion, which enlist practices of paranoid reading to expose, Armstrong's radical aesthetic is decidedly reparative in its playful imagining; "confer[ring] plenitude on an object that will then have resources to offer to an inchoate self" (Sedgwick, 2006, p. 149). With this understanding of reparative reading in mind, I'd like to play on a pivotal parenthetic question that Armstrong raises:

> Vygotsky does make play intrinsic to cognitive experience: the function of the essentially double-sided pivotal object (the aesthetic object?), acting within the constraints of material experience yet able to envisage new categories, emancipates us from the tyranny of the one and the primal ooze of the imaginary. And it is in itself emancipatory.
>
> *(p. 39)*

Dear Editor, I am contending that Kraus emancipate "(the aesthetic object?)" from its questionable, parenthetical frame by "loving" "Dick" as a pivotal and transitional object. Taking Armstrong's reading of Vygotsky and Winnicott in stride, I'd propose the phrase "transitional aesthetic object" to describe the two ways, one diegetic and one extra-diegetic, that *I Love Dick* plays into "the transformation of categories, which constitutes a change in the structure of thought itself . . . the prerequisite of political change" (Armstrong, 2000, p. 41).

You must be wondering which categories. What political change? This is the pivot of my epistolary argument: "Dick" is no stick-horse, but he serves the function of a transitional, aesthetic one, and this makes all the difference. "These letters included you," Chris writes to "Dick," "both as yourself and as some sort of object" (Kraus, 1997, p. 32). By her epistolary invocation, "Dick" becomes a pivot for "severing" the meaning of "Dick" from a/ the real one. This is not a metaphor for castration, but a transitional stage for deconstructing and redefining categories and relations of gender and genre. The letters may be addressed to "Dick" and its host of corollary con-notations, but as Chris observes, Dick becomes "a blank screen onto which we can project our fantasies" (p. 29); thus, as Sylvère observes, "In a sense Dick isn't necessary. He has more to say by not saying anything" (p. 59). By remaining a silent, "Dick" serves as a transition into the cognitive experi-ence of aesthetic play; and that is Chris's great "love." What she comes to understand, and the analytic system by which she comes to understand it will be the subject of my next letter.

For now, suffice it to say that Chris leaves Sylvère, and becomes the sole writer of the letters. She sleeps with Dick a few times, but it doesn't measure up to the epistolary "Dick," whom she likewise "maintains as an entity to write to" (p. 130). The letters transition.[20] As Kraus explains in *The Guard-ian Books Podcast*, "beyond the first flush of the infatuation and trying to be clever about the infatuation, once I got into the vein of letter writing, the letter writing turned into essay writing" (2016). Dear Editor, when does a letter become an essay? Is this one?

Yours in "the vein of letter writing . . . turned into essay writing,"
Alex

V. An Interlude

Dear Editor,

Lodged between two transitional aesthetic objects is this interlude about who gets to speak and why, about Kraus's aesthetic play, about the educa-tion it might enable. In this letter, education is what will get us from the diegetic exegetes (Chris and "Dick") to the extra-diegetic ones (Kraus, Heb-dige, readers), from thinking about "Dick" to thinking about *I Love Dick* as a transitional aesthetic object.

"WHO GETS TO SPEAK AND WHY?, I wrote last week, IS THE ONLY QUESTION," Chris writes to Dick (1997, p. 175). Kraus doesn't just rhetorically raise the question of who speaks and why in a genre that has traditionally repre-sented the silencing and abjection of women; she answers it:

> Because most 'serious' fiction, still, involves the fullest possible expres-sion of a single person's subjectivity, it's considered crass and amateurish not to 'fictionalize' the supporting cast of characters, changing names and insignificant features of their identities. The 'serious' contemporary hetero-male novel is a thinly veiled Story of Me, as voraciously con-sumptive as all of patriarchy. While the hero/anti-hero explicitly *is* the author, everybody else is reduced to 'characters' . . . When women try to pierce this false conceit by naming names because our 'I's' are changing

as we meet other 'I's, we're called bitches, libelers, pornographers, and amateurs.

(pp. 71–72)

An anticipatory description of its own reception, *I Love Dick* is the story of an "I" changing as it meets other "I"s, an "I" who refuses to "fictionalize the supporting cast of character," who tried "to piece this false conceit by naming names." Kraus names the "false conceit" that enables the "hetero-male . . . Story of Me" to gain public prestige in contrast to the vilification women, including Kraus herself, face when they do the same.

In a 2016 episode of *The Guardian Books Podcast*, Chris Kraus and Maggie Nelson have a chat in which Kraus speculates, "This tendency to describe female writing, female artists, visual arts [is] always prefaced by gender in a way that male work is never prefaced by gender . . . the same thing happens with descriptors of race." Deviation from the universalization of cisheterosexual, white, male subjectivity, as Kraus implies, necessitates identity markers to qualify and patronize the production of knowledge. The gendering of genre subjugates textual bodies as if they were extensions of human bodies. It's as if Barthes had never declared the author dead, as if Foucault had never given us the author function. Chris explains to Dick:

This problem's bigger and more cultural . . . To be female still means being trapped within the purely psychological. No matter how dispassionate or large a vision of the world a woman formulates, whenever it includes her own experience and emotion, the telescope's turned back on her. Because emotion's just so terrifying the world refuses to believe that it can be pursued as discipline, as form. Dear Dick, I want to make the world more interesting than my problems. Therefore, I have to make my problems social.

(Kraus, 1997, p. 155, p. 180)

I Love Dick, as my next letter will explain, pursues "experience and emotion . . . as discipline, as form," making genre a mode of aesthetic production that is inextricably linked to the social – not as ideological interpellation or ideology-critique, but as a transitional aesthetic object.

I've said that *I Love Dick* is a transitional aesthetic object in two ways. We've discussed the first of the two; that is, the diegetic "Dick" as epistolary invocation. This interlude has considered how textual bodies are read as ideological extensions of human ones. To think of *I Love Dick* as autotheory is the second, extra-diegetic way that it might conceived of as a transitional aesthetic object.

Transitioning now,
Alex

VI. Transitional Aesthetic Object II: Autotheory

Dear Editor,

We've been corresponding about how play prompts the transformation of categories, with the transitional aesthetic object at its fulcrum. In the opening sentence of *Clarissa's Ciphers*, Terry Castle (1982) suggests that "one might imagine the present book as a gloss for a single line of *Clarissa*. 'I am but a *cypher*, to give *him* significance, and myself pain'" (Castle quoting Richardson, p. 15, her emphasis). But *I Love Dick*, I'd argue, enacts an inversion of these categories, and thus, an intervention into contradictions endemic to the genre. Castle positions Clarissa "as an exemplary victim of hermeneutic violence" (p. 22), one whose voice is repeatedly objectified and silenced. Kraus, by contrast, positions herself as an artist of hermeneutic repair. "Dick" – precisely because "Dick is every Dick, Dick is Uber Dick, Dick is a transitional object" (Intra quoting Kraus) – is but a *cipher*, to give *Chris* significance and himself pain.[21] "I've fused my silence and repression with the entire female gender's silence and repression," Chris writes (p. 210, my emphasis). To fuse a singular "silence and repression" with that of the so-called "entire female gender," to contentiously take up the self as a site of cultural study, to publicly play at dismantling the categories and conventions that would otherwise hem a self in: Kraus is describing a critical maneuver that anticipates the aesthetics of what critics have recently referred to as "autotheory."

Dear Editor, why turn to autotheory in a volume on autoethnography? In his forthcoming work "That Obscure Object of Embodiment. On Autotheory and Disciplinary Knowledge," Jan Grue offers a disciplinary distinction that affiliates autoethnography with qualitative social science methodology in contrast to autotheory's humanistic approach to theorizing the relationship between subjectivity and sociality:

[T]here is also a distinction between autoethnography and autotheory in terms of their orientation, or *direction of fit*. I borrow this term from speech act theory, where direction of fit concerns the difference between fitting "word to world", i.e., describing an independently existing state of affairs, and fitting "world to word", i.e. changing the world through utterances. Conceived as a spectrum, autoethnographical investigations would tend toward the former; autotheoretical investigations towards the latter.[22]

Grue's delineation, in which autotheory fits "world to word" by virtue of performative utterances, in fact conjures *Changing the Wor(l)d: Discourse, Politics, and the Feminist Movement*, the work in which Stacey Young (1997) introduces the adjective "autotheoretical" to describe texts that embody:

> a discursive type of political action, which decenter the hegemonic subject of feminism . . . and as such, they offer sustained discussions of the politics of discourse and of identity and subjectivity in relation to gender, class, race, sexuality, and other major social divisions.
>
> *(pp. 61–62)*

Drawing from multi-genre anthologies published by small feminist presses in the eighties and nineties, Young emphasizes autotheory's counter-hegemonic project of theorizing how the self is subject to the structural forces that produce it. Since the publication of Maggie Nelson's autotheoretical *The Argonauts* (2015), a flurry of feminist scholarship has theorized autotheory as a merger of autobiography and theory, a critical-creative hybrid that theorizes from and about embodied experience as feminist praxis.[23]

I Love Dick conscientiously anticipates and aligns itself with autotheoretical aesthetics.[24] In a letter that alternates between her trip to Guatemala (with Jennifer Harbury's hunger strike in mind) and the moments leading up to her and Dick's first sexual encounter, Chris ponders, "Don't you think it's possible to do something and simultaneously study it? If the project had a name it'd be *I Love Dick: A Case Study*" (p. 153). Alternating between a satire "The Dumb Cunt's Tale" (p. 27) and "centuries of male supremacy and dickdom" (p. 110), between private correspondence and the public reading of it, *I Love Dick* autotheoretically plays with the contradictions that run streaking through the history of the epistolary. Speaking of the kinship between Kraus's work and her own, Maggie Nelson explains:

> We see ourselves as part of a very long history whether it's like Roland Barthes or Montaigne or *The Pillow Book* . . . to me it feels like part of a lineage and I wouldn't call that lineage confessional per se . . . Chris Kraus has been very good on this point . . . the notion of confession obviously presumes a certain kind of relationship of the private and if you are not someone who is accepting a certain kind of partition . . . or if you're not conceiving of your relation to the reader as one that is a metaphor for . . . therapeutic or theological space – the word [confession] just doesn't have a lot of traction, because as Chris has said . . . you presume a flow

between what you can learn about the culture by writing about the self and what you can learn about the self by writing about the culture.

(Armitstead et al., 2016)

Neither therapeutic nor theological, Kraus's epistolary relation to the reader, mediated by "Dick," refuses to recognize the partition that ideologically elevates a patriarchal public over a femininized private sphere. Under the auspices of autotheory, this epistolary frame "presumes a flow between what you can learn about the culture by writing about the self and what you can learn about the self by writing about the culture." "It all happened," Kraus concedes in *The Guardian Books Podcast*, and it all happens in the epistolary.

The second, extra-diegetic way that I will conceive of *I Love Dick* as a transitional aesthetic object is thus as part of a burgeoning autotheorical corpus. Read as autotheory, the book, published by a feminist press (i.e., Semiotext(e) Native Agents, which was founded by Kraus herself) with social interests and investments, is a transitional aesthetic object for writer and reader alike:

It is not me *and* part of me; it is neither subject nor object; it is neither inner psychic reality nor external reality . . . moving from continuity to contiguity to non-omnipotent relations and to the renegotiation of boundaries, the transitional object mediates a life-creating, culture-modifying space which is at once transgressive and communal.

(Armstrong pp. 39–40)

While "not me and part of me . . . neither subject nor object" sounds suspiciously like the abjection Kraus's critical reception attributes to the text, autotheory mediates, theorizes, and plays with as opposed to desecrates life. Introducing a "a life-creating, culture-modifying space," it plays with the reality of contradiction as a precondition of social change. This epistolary essay, dear editor, is an academic and educational reality, a material reality like "Dick" and like the stick-horse, but it also "opens up and contains" its own "interiority and indeterminacy" (Armstrong, 2000, p. 39). If the aesthetic is aligned with utopian space in which we can play out possibilities of narrative identification, then epistolary play has enabled that. Aesthetic play does critical work; it is the sphere in which we cultivate critical capacities, the condition of being serious about reality.

Seriously,

Alex

VII. Dick Writes Back

Dear Editor,

The final chapter of *I Love Dick* is entitled "Dick Writes Back." "Dick" writes back and at first, I hated it. I hated it like I hate arguments about psychoanalytic lack. But hatred doesn't erase a history of theoretical erasure. The final pages of Chris Krauss's *I Love Dick*, all save the last few paragraphs, are Dick's. Dick Fedexes a package to Sylvère and Chris. Inside are two white envelopes, not unlike the ones from which I imagine you extracting this chapter. One is addressed to Chris, the other to Sylvère. She opens Sylvère's first. After an academic preamble pertaining to shared research interests, Dick writes to Sylvère:

> *I can only say that being taken as the object of such obsessive attention . . . was, indeed still is, utterly incomprehensible to me. I found the situation initially perplexing, then disturbing and my major regret now is that I didn't find the courage at the time to communicate to you and Kris how uncomfortable I felt being the unwitting object of what you described to me . . . as some kind of bizarre game . . . .it may be that, for now at least, too much damage has been done on all sides for the kind of negotiated rapprochement that would be needed if we were to restore the trust in which real friendship thrives. That said, I still have immense respect for your work; I still enjoy your company and conversation when we meet and believe, as you do, that Kris has talent as a writer. I can only reiterate what I have said before whenever the topic has been raised in conversation with you or Chris: that I do not share your conviction that my right to privacy has to be sacrificed for the sake of that talent.*
>
> *(Kraus, 1997, p. 244)*

"Dick Writes Back," in numbers: he manages to misspell Chris's name twice, and then, third time's the charm, he spells it correctly. He recognizes how he's been positioned as an "object" twice. He (correctly) anticipates that his "right to privacy" is about to be sacrificed at the altar of Chris's aesthetic play, and he appeals to Sylvère, one masculinist academic to another, to control his wife so that they might *"restore the trust in which real friendship thrives."* But what is "the right to privacy" here? "Yes, it all happened," Kraus affirms in *The Guardian Books Podcast*, but "Dick outed himself in order to condemn the book. That's how his surname entered the public record of the book – it was never my intent." "Dick's" letter in "Dick Writes Back" anticipates Hebdige's legal action, which, as Elizabeth Gumport suggests, "is called on to conceal" the taxonomizing of male over female, political over personal, public over private.

Worse yet, Chris then opens the letter addressed to her. Are you sure you want to read what I'm about to unseal? Chris opens the letter addressed to her – and finds a Xerox of Dick's letter to Sylvère.

Dear Editor, one may find it difficult not to succumb to a reading of erasure here – that even if Chris metaphorically "killed" Dick (Kraus, 1997, p. 74), his Xerox erases her, an erasure that has been morphologically mapped onto genitalia (p. 267). "*Eraser, Erase-her* –" (p. 218). But such a reading depends on psychoanalytic lack, on a paranoid hermeneutics of suspicion, ideology all over again. Jameson writes that "texts come before us as the always-already-read; we apprehend them through sedimented layers of previous interpretations" (2014, p. 9). A reading of erasure succumbs to "sedimented layers" of psychoanalytic history, as does the reception of *I Love Dick* as either exhibition or abjection.

I see something different. "The text invites us, insistently and radically," writes Castle of *Clarissa*, "not simply to read, but to read our own reading – to turn it back on itself" (1982, p. 186). So, in turn, does the epistle, which is, variously, a reading of reading, a writing of reading, a rewriting, a rereading, a palimpsest. "(Dear Dick, Dear Marshall, Dear Sylvère, What is semiotics?)" Chris wonders, "Love and sex both cause mutation, just like I think desire isn't lack, it's surplus energy" (p. 239). Dick's Xerox speaks only insofar as it manifests his speechlessness. He recognizes that Chris has stripped him of his speaking-subjecthood. He cannot break out of his role as addressed object, a transitional aesthetic thing with which she, and we, play. And so he commits an act of self-sabotage. Instead of writing an introduction to the book *I Love Dick*, as Chris and Sylvère invite him to (p. 41), instead of joining in the game that is "even better than reality" (p. 28), Dick Fedexes the photocopy that seals his fate. *I Love Dick* is not a book about erasure or absence or castration or the fetish as penis-substitute. Rather, as a transitional aesthetic object freed from the confines of a parenthetical clause, it is a book about aesthetic play with false taxonomies, a book that plays with contradiction as a precondition of social change.

Dear Editor, I could go on writing these letters indefinitely. I'd write a letter about genre as a mode of aesthetic production, a letter that more explicitly differentiates between the act of playing with contradiction, the act of deconstruction, and the act of ideology-critique. I'd write another engaging with Derrida's *The Postcard: From Socrates to Freud and Beyond* (1987), another reading *I Love Dick* through the genealogy of psychoanalytic readings of the epistolary in *The Purloined Poe: Lacan, Derrida & Psychoanalytic Reading* (Muller et al., 1988). Unfortunately, I'm writing a letter than can never be finished, and thus a conclusion is itself a contradiction. Indeed, the cost of an ending is the foreclosure of alternate possibilities. For now, the question of future posts remains.

"The Editor Writes Back" has yet to be written. But the "I" characterizing this "I" imagines. "Dear Alex," I imagine it might begin.

One must imagine their addressee,

Alex

Notes

1 Chris Kraus is the author of *I Love Dick*. She is also a character in *I Love Dick* and the diegetic author of the majority of its epistles. Diegetically speaking, I will refer to Chris. Extra-diegetically speaking, I will refer to Kraus, but always with this critical conflation in mind.

2 Intra, Giovanni. "A Fusion of Gossip and Theory." Artnet.com Magazine. November 13, 1997.

3 Zembla, Nic. "See Dick Sue: a very phallic novel gets a rise out of a beloved professor." *New York* magazine. 17 November 1997.

4 Ibid.

5 Ibid.

6 Fourteen thousand copies of the book sold in 2016 alone. The Amazon adaptation was co-created by Joey Soloway and Sarah Gubbins, but was discontinued after a single season.

7 Intra quoting Kraus quoting Deleuze.

8 A riff on the word game booklets originating in 1958, in which one player prompts others to fill in the blanks of a pre-written narrative templates to create a new story.

9 Kraus's second novel, *Aliens & Anorexia* (published in 2000, three years after *I Love Dick*), addresses this problem explicitly.

10 Jameson calls radical feminism "perfectly consistent with an expanded Marxian framework" (p. 100). Isobel Armstrong responds, "Not only does he [Eagleton] retain without questioning . . . the insistently denigrating Enlightenment connection of the aesthetic and the feminine, but in invoking Lacanian and Althusserian parallels he manages to ontologize these psychoanalytical structures as universals" (p. 29).

11 Eve Kosofsky Sedgwick proposes reparative reading as an alternative to paranoid critical practices that are "anticipatory," "reflexive and mimetic," and which "places faith in exposure" (p. 130). Reparative reading, by contrast, hinges on amelioration and aesthetics; that is, the reparative stance does not aim to expose ideology, but rather, to "assemble and confer plenitude on an object that will then have resources to offer to an inchoate self" (p. 149). See "Paranoid Reading and Reparative Reading, or, You're so Paranoid You Probably Think this Essay is about You" (2006).

12 Sedgwick suggests what Paul Ricoeur calls "hermeneutics of suspicion" (with reference to critical practices of revealing that which is concealed in Marx, Freud, and Nietzsche) is now virtually synonymous with criticism itself. For a detailed discussion of the "hermeneutics of suspicion," see Ricoeur's *Freud and Philosophy: An Essay on Interpretation* (1970).

13 Another post, which I will one day write, will bring these matters into conversation with *Derrida's The Postcard: From Socrates to Freud and Beyond* (1987).

14 "Doesn't witnessing contain complicity?" Chris asks Dick, "Cause shame was what we always felt, me and all my girlfriends, for expecting sex to breed complicity. ('Complicity is like a girl's name,' writes Dodie Bellamy.)" (p. 155, p. 169).

15 Ralph Clare's "Becoming Autotheory" reads this game as a textual nod and challenge to the poststructural legacy that Sylvère (who studied with Roland Barthes) represents (2020, pp. 92–93). Whereas for Clare, this game pertains to the play of textuality and reality, my epistolary argument proposes playing with contradiction as a precondition of social change.

16 While it ranges beyond the scope of this letter, another might take up the queerness streaking through this marriage; and/or the homosocial desire that draws Sylvère and Dick together.

17 For a reading of "the castrating force of writing" through the lens of Derrida's "emajusculation," see Anna Watkins Fisher's "Manic Impositions: The Parasitical Art of Chris Kraus and Sophie Calle" (2012).

18 "This game is *real*, or even better than, reality . . . I love you Dick" Chris writes (p. 28, emphasis in original).

19 My reparative turn to Winnicott may come as a surprise for a text that appears to lend itself to a more Freudian or Lacanian reading, which would, no doubt, depend on a paranoid reading. For a take on *I Love Dick* that draws on Luce Irigaray's challenge to Freud and Lacan, see Lauren Fournier's "From Philosopher's Wife to Feminist Autotheorist: Performing Phallic Mimesis as Parody in Chris Kraus's *I Love Dick*" (2019).

20 Clare suggests that in this transition, Sylvère "remains trapped within the poststructuralist text/textuality, even as he realizes that 'these letters seem to open up a new genre, something between criticism and fiction'" (2020, p. 92; citing Kraus, 1997, p. 43). In "Dicktation: Autotheory in the Coupled Voice," Annamarie Jagose and Lee Wallace extend this observation with a discussion of how "Kraus's work is not so much a theory of the self but a theory of the couple as a limit-test of the social" (2020, p. 123).

21 My final letter discusses how Dick Hebdige ostensibly felt the "pain" of silencing and objectification that Clarissa attributes to herself, otherwise he wouldn't have taken legal action predicated on cisheteropatriarchal genderings of private and public.

22 Grue's "That Obscure Object of Embodiment. On Autotheory and Disciplinary Knowledge" is forthcoming in an edited volume title *Autotheories: Transdisciplinary Experiments in Self-Theorizing*, which I have co-edited with Vilashini Cooppan.

23 See, for example, Robyn Wiegman's "Autotheory Theory" (2020), Lauren Fournier's *Autotheory as Feminist Practice in Art, Writing, and Criticism* (2021), and "Autotheory ASAP! Academia, Decoloniality, and 'I'" (2021), which I co-wrote with Fournier.

24 Sylvère notes, "these letters seem to open up a new genre, something between criticism and fiction" (p. 43), while Chris playfully drops the neologism "Performative Philosophy" (p. 211). In her afterword to the text, Joan Hawkins calls it "theoretical fiction" (p. 272).

References

Armitstead, C., Cain, S. and Barnard, S. (2016). 'Maggie Nelson and Chris Kraus on Confessional Writing –Books Podcast'. *The Guardian*. Maggie Nelson and Chris Kraus on confessional writing – books podcast | Books | The Guardian.

Armstrong, I. (2000). *The Radical Aesthetic*. Oxford: Blackwell.

Beebee, T.O. (1994). *The Ideology of Genre: A Comparative Study of Generic Instability*. University Park: The Pennsylvania State University Press.

Blair, E. (2016). 'Chris Kraus, Female Antihero'. *The New Yorker*. www.newyorker. com/magazine/2016/11/21/chris-kraus-female-antihero

Castle, T. (1982). *Clarissa's Cyphers: Meaning and Disruption in Richardson's Clarissa*. Ithica, NY: Cornell University Press.

Clare, R., (2020). 'Becoming Autotheory'. *Arizona Quarterly: A Journal of American Literature, Culture, and Theory*. 76(1): pp. 85–107.

Derrida, J. (1987). *The Postcard: From Socrates to Freud and Beyond*. Translated by AlanBass. Chicago and London: The University of Chicago Press.

Eagleton, T. (1990). *The Ideology of the Aesthetic*. Oxford, UK: Blackwell.

Fisher, A. (2012). 'Manic Impositions: The Parasitical Art of Chris Kraus and Sophie Calle'. *WSQ: Women's Studies Quarterly*, 40(1–2): pp. 223–235.

Fournier, L. (2021). *Autotheory as Feminist Practice in Art, Writing, and Criticism*. Cambridge, MA: The MIT Press.

Gumport, E. (2012). 'Female Trouble'. *n+1 13: Machine Politics*. http://nplusonemag. com/issue-13/reviews/female-trouble/

Jagose, A. and Wallace, L. (2020). 'Dicktation: Autotheory in the Coupled Voice'. *Arizona Quarterly: A Journal of American Literature, Culture, and Theory*. 76(1): pp. 109–139.

Jameson, F. (2014). *The Political Unconscious Narrative as a Socially Symbolic Act*. Ithaca: Cornell University Press.

Kraus, C. (1997). *I Love Dick*. Los Angeles, CA: Semiotext(e).

Muller, J.P. and Richardson, W.J. (1988). *The Purloined Poe: Lacan, Derrida & Psychoanalytic Reading*. Baltimore: Johns Hopkins U Press.

Myles, E. (2006). 'Afterword: What About Chris?' In Kraus, C. (ed.) *I Love Dick*. South Pasadena, CA: Semiotext(e).

Nelson, M. (2015). *The Argonauts*. Minneapolis: Greywolf Press.

Robbins, B. (2007). 'Afterword'. *PMLA/Publications of the Modern Language Association of America*. 122(5): pp. 1644–1651.

Sedgwick, E.K. (2006). *Touching Feeling: Affect, Pedagogy, Performativity*. Durham, NC: Duke University Press.

Wiegman, R. (2020). 'Introduction: Autotheory Theory'. *Arizona Quarterly: A Journal of American Literature, Culture, and Theory*. 76(1): pp. 1–14.

Young, S. (1997). *Changing the Wor(l)d: Discourse, Politics, and the Feminist Movement*. New York: Routledge.

Zembla, N. (1997). 'See Dick Sue: A Very Phallic Novel Gets a Rise out of a Beloved Professor'. *New York Magazine*. 30(44).

4

THE DEVELOPING FEMINIST, PHILOSOPHICAL BODY

An Autoethnography of the Studious, Researching, Working, and Retiring Lesbian Body

Elizabeth Ettorre

Autoethnographers are aware that several philosophical movements contributed to the development of autoethnography. Adams and Herrmann (2020, p. 2) argue that these progressions include:

> the recognition of the ways personal/cultural identities shape perception and experience (e.g., "the personal is political"); the importance of narrative and storytelling; the "crisis of representation," particularly how . . . ethnography, is never neutral or objective; the increased attention to emotion; the need to address . . . ethical violations in research; the call for more accessible academic texts; and the understanding that discourse, power, and being "made subject" are interrelated phenomena.

Autoethnography demands breaking away from specific positivistic research techniques, toward a desire to listen more intently to 'my' researching body as the researcher becomes both object and subject (Daly, 2022).

In this autoethnography, I challenge the tendency of traditional philosophy to embrace different forms of binaries such as mind *versus* body, nature *versus* culture, reason *versus* emotion, public *versus* private, man *versus* woman, heterosexual *versus* homosexual, public *versus* private, production *versus* reproduction, etc. Studying the body provides me with an important philosophical challenge – confronting these entanglements throughout my academic life.

Pitts-Taylor (2003) highlights the entanglements of nature and culture by exploring the embodied mind and the "embrained" body.[1] An embodiment perspective allows me to examine the bodily roots of subjectivity without

DOI: 10.4324/9781003274728-4

the need for those dualistic assumptions. Bodies provide me with a way of examining a classical sociological concern, based on another dualistic assumption – the tension between structure and agency. In the social sciences, structure *versus* agency is an ongoing debate where traditionally clear distinctions are made between *agency* as the capacity of individual selves to act with intentionality, independence, or free choice without constraints imposed from the larger *social structure* viewed as the networks of statuses and relative power which influence or limit the choices and opportunities available to us.[2] Within a body perspective, *agency* (or the agentic body) refers to the individual practices and strategies used within existing social conventions, values, and sanctions in the struggle for social resources, while *structures* can be seen as the embodied spaces where social relations are reproduced as an outcome of power relations. This sort of embodiment perspective tends to break down the traditional dualism between structure and agency by emphasizing *agentic corporality*. Establishing agentic corporality is a key strategy in Judith Butler's work (1990, 1993). Her ideas on how gender is artificially constructed and performed are instructive. She contends that 'performance or parodic practices' (i.e., cross-dressing, etc.), 'existing from within gender essentialist culture expose and subvert that culture and its belief in a true gender identity' (Bordo, 1993, p. 255). My autoethnography employs *agentic corporality*, while acknowledging that feminist embodiment philosophy is all about rejecting "false universalisms" because no philosophy is universally binding and applicable to all.

Doing autoethnography makes me acutely aware that I am doing a method which allows for the formation of critical, interpretative space. I give way to an intimate, intermediate space, which includes ambiguity, uncertainty, and equivocality. Ruth Behar (1996, p. 174) talks about what happens when academics challenge methodologically or theoretically the orthodoxies of the academy. She envisages that when we make these challenges we create 'a borderland between passion and intellect, analysis and subjectivity ethnography and autobiography, art and life'. Often quoted, Behar's words concerning entanglements were conceived initially in dialogue with the works of Gloria Anzaldua (1987) in *Borderlands, La Frontera: the new mestiza*. Anzaldua talks about *la mestiza*, who walks in one culture and out of another but is in all cultures at the same time (p. 99). *La mestiza* is in the state of being beyond binary ("either-or") conceptions. *La mestiza* is the state of being 'both' and 'and'. *La mestiza* has a tolerance for ambiguity and contradictions (p. 101). Inhabiting the crossroads forms the *mestiza* consciousness. *La mestiza* must live without borders and be a cross between an insider and an outsider. She must be herself a crossroads (p. 217). (See also Ettorre, 2017; Henningham, 2021).

As a feminist autoethnographer familiar with *la mestiza*, I am an embodied crossroads in my agentic corporality. Occupying this *in between space*, I craft a transitional space of understanding between me, myself, and the other. Often, the boundaries between us become blurred. Writing in my first-person voice, I learn how to identify the ambiguity of personal and social relationships. All my interpretations are created in relationship, in between and on the borders of connections – in agentic corporality. To do this work I need to be rigorously self-aware, to be meticulously humble, and most importantly, to be cognizant of the complex connections between the socially coded categories of race, gender, age, able-bodiedness, class, and sex (Boylorn and Orbe, 2020) and how as 'enforced differences'[3] these factors come to be embedded in power relations. This work needs to be performed in that borderland space – of 'in betweenness' where complex relational subjects are framed by embodiment, sexuality, affectivity, empathy, and desire as core qualities (see Braidotti, 2013, p. 26). This space is unstable, ever-changing and always already shifting, yet full of discovery and hope.

My aim in this chapter is to discuss my developing feminist body as a philosophical tool in this borderland space. This body I have inhabited throughout my life to signify as well as understand the strangeness as well as familiarity of the others with whom I encounter in my embodied existence. Through incarnate thought and agentic corporality over the four distinct phases of my life, I hope to produce feminist, embodied narratives that transform not just myself but also the maleness of the planes of immanence that I inhabit. These phases include leaving my country of birth to come out as a lesbian in the 1970s; activating lesbian feminism in my work in the late 1970s-1980s; embodying a lesbian perspective in academia in the 1990s-2010s, and choosing feminist retirement from 2011-present. These four phases correspond to my studious, researching, working, and retiring lesbian body.

The Studious Lesbian Body: Leaving the US to Study in England and Coming Out

September 1972

As I wave goodbye to my mother at JFK Airport, I say, "Take care of yourself." She is crying. I feel somewhat lost and confused. I have a sense that I am free to be myself – but feel unsure of what that means. I smile at John and as the plane takes off for London, I murmur, "Goodbye, Big Apple" and my sad memories . . . I recall that a year earlier, I left the Sisters of Mercy, a Catholic order of nuns (see Ettorre, 2010).

The next few years in England have their ups and downs. I feel my sexuality, my identity, my embodied core is shifting. I marry, I divorce, I leave the Catholic Church, come out as a lesbian, and embark on doing a sociology Ph.D. on lesbians. In October 1973, I am a postgraduate student at the London School of Economics. The intellectual atmosphere is buzzing. I am in David Downe's and Paul Rock's thought-provoking seminar 'Criminology and Deviancy Theory', which meets every Thursday. I have many student colleagues who will become well-known sociologists.[4] While enjoying deviance theory, I am interested in feminist sociology, which is developing at a fast pace both in the UK and USA. I sense that feminist sociology will help me figure out some of the pressing theoretical issues related to my research, especially my ideas on lesbian identity, female sexuality, lesbian social organization, reproduction, and labor power – key concepts for my Ph.D.

November 1974

My supervisor, Professor Terry Morris, meets me every three months – much to the envy of my student colleagues who see their supervisors once a year. Terry encourages me with stories of his own Ph.D. study of juvenile delinquency. Terry loves talking about his observational work and is very inspiring. He gives me hints about good ethnographic practice: 'Betsy, why don't you do observational work on lesbians in London? I am sure it will be fruitful, and you will learn how to become a good empirical sociologist. The key is to watch and listen'. I say, 'OK, Terry. It is a big challenge, but I am up for it!' I begin my study of the London lesbian community. I survive by using my embodied difference and privilege (i.e., American, white, lesbian, etc.) as a way of placing myself within various ethnographic sites.

April 1978

I defend my dissertation, "The Sociology of Lesbianism: female sexuality and female 'deviance' " (Ettorre, 1978), the first sociology PhD on lesbianism in the UK. Not surprisingly, I am unable to get a job teaching gender or lesbian studies. I am aware that it will take a while for the academic fields of gender/women's/lesbian studies to become institutionalized in the UK. "Women's Studies develops through the Women's Liberation Movement" in campaigns, study groups, workshops, and adult educational organizations. "In the mid-1980s, some institutions begin to offer first postgraduate, later undergraduate courses in Women's Studies, beginning with an M.A. at the University of Kent". Gender studies follow some five to ten years later.[5]

The Researching Lesbian Body: Activating Lesbian Feminism in the Research World

December 1978

Terry Morris phones me . . . quite excited, he says, "Betsy, have you seen the job advertised at the Addiction Research Unit (ARU) at the Institute of Psychiatry? You must apply for it. They are looking for a research sociologist and it's just for you." "Are they looking for someone to do research on lesbians?" I ask. "No," he replies, "they want someone familiar with deviance theory. I am sure you have a chance of getting it." Terry is acutely aware that since getting my PhD I have been applying for academic posts with no luck. I have felt for some time that I embody depression. He continues, "Betsy, you're going to have to emphasize your knowledge of deviance theory. I'll give you a good reference. At least it's a step up the ladder." "OK, Terry, I'll apply," I say, feeling anxiety rising through my body. I think, "At least I'll share being 'deviant' with the people I research." I am offered the post and stay for seven years. It is an important time in my intellectual development. I work on many interesting projects in the alcohol and other drugs field.[6] It is not easy, as I have been totally out as a lesbian for three years already. Weekly, if not daily, I am the brunt of gay jokes and insults.[7] This hurts. I feel deep disappointment in my lesbian body and know that being an alcohol and drugs researcher puts me at the bottom of the academic hierarchy. I am aware that sociology colleagues outside of the ARU have a noticeable dislike for my research. I begin to realize that the reason is both political and academic. It is political because before my time, there was a well-known ARU strike instigated there by a group of critical social researchers who are fired (see Triesman, 1977). Since that time, colleagues outside the ARU believe that no critical work could come out of my unit and good sociological work would be suppressed.

January 1979

I arrive at work after being hurt by an air gun shot by someone hiding near where I live. A secretary asks, "Why do you have a bandage on your temple?" "Oh, someone shot me on Lupus Street," I reply hesitantly, "and I went to my doctor, who put it there." An ARU psychiatrist in the office turns toward me and says with derision, "What do you expect, writing a book about perverts?"[8] I walk out of the office hurt and disgusted, feeling as if I am kicked in my heart. I go quietly back to my office, sobbing, and ensure that my door is locked. Working on a national study of ATUs, I interview a consultant psychiatrist who says, "I don't allow any violent men to become patients, but if they beat their wives, it is not proper violence.

I'll admit them." I feel horrified and think, "A real misogynist." In feeling his undervaluing of women, my feminist sensibilities are heightened. I am enraged at his antipathy toward women and feel this stupid man insults me. I wonder how many other women, colleagues, or patients he undervalues. I am also aware that his way of thinking is supported by an overwhelming, misogynist structure in psychiatry and in the UK as a patriarchal society that condones his sickening antipathy. I am aware that the National Women's Aid Federation, which "enabled women and children experiencing violence and fear in the home to travel across the country to a place of safety", is only five years old, founded in 1974.[9]

While I do not experience sexual violence at the ARU, I experience sexual harassment, although I was not aware of it at that time. ('Sexual harassment' was not the term we used then.) Every day a colleague grabs my backside while we are alone. It makes me feel angry and my body invaded. While I don't know that this is "against lesbian" sexual harassment, I discover it when feminist friends tell me at a consciousness raising session. "It's not your fault. You should make a complaint against him," they say to me. I feel too vulnerable to do that. The next time it happens, I smack his hand hard. I know I hurt him as his hand caught my rings. I am somewhat satisfied. Nevertheless, his harassment continues for years until I leave the ARU. The situation makes me feel ashamed and marginalized. I think, "Yes, I guess this may be what my female respondents feel confronting an unwelcoming yet invasive treatment system." My consciousness raising group helps me to resist the sexual harassment which surrounds me. I refuse to normalize that behavior. I feel that my experiences are generating a deep passion for resisting the masculinist ways of thinking surrounding me not only at the ARU but also at my research sites. This time in my career is less than easy as my identity politics lead to my personal life, work, and activism becoming "sites of political expression".[10]

June 1980

I reflect, "I have an excellent opportunity to contribute to a field which is resistant both theoretically and methodologically to an approach sensitive to the needs of women." But I have no time to carry out this desire. I embody deep disappointment and frustration. When I visit a ward round with a Maudsley psychiatrist, he instructs his staff to give ECT to a woman patient, a self-confessed alcoholic. "She is obviously very depressed." "Why ECT?" I ask myself. "She's a real embodiment of a disposable woman – messy, sullen, and extremely sad." I sit on an easy chair across from her. I want to reach out to her but know I can't. It breaks my heart to look at her, a sufferer of this oppressive treatment system.

June 1981

I finish the study of all 30 ATUs in the UK, after having visited every single one of them. For at least a year, I travel on trains (very often late to their destinations) the length and width of the UK – every major city has an ATU. I am exhausted after speaking with staff – nurses, social workers, and consultant psychiatrists. ATUs are populated by male patients. I see only one female patient in my travels, and I am disappointed. But I also think, "As a woman, I wouldn't want to go to an ATU. They are all male-focused. Women are marginalized in this treatment system as I am at the ARU." This is a depressing fact of my life and theirs. I just wish these women could be helped and there could be women-only services available all over the UK.

June 1982–March 1984

My work at the ARU becomes extremely difficult as I write up the ATU project after having a preliminary article published earlier with my co-worker before he left in 1981 (Robinson and Ettorre, 1980). I am being accused of 'intransigency' and that my writing is lacking. I feel I am being de-skilled and forced to write draft after draft. Words like "WOT!" (Meaning 'What!') are written in my paper's margins. I feel some comments are personal attacks and I am being bullied, isolated, and misunderstood. No one supports me. One day, I am in my office feeling glum and twiddling my hair. The phone rings. A man with a deep voice says, "Dr. Ettorre, this is Professor White. Please, can you come to see me? Are you free at the moment?" I ask myself, "Is this the Head of the Institute of Psychiatry?" I feel terrified. "Am I being fired?" I ask myself. Immediately I say, "Yes, of course, I'll be right there." I run through the corridors to Professor White's office. Terrified, I knock on the door. He opens it and greets me warmly. "Hello, Dr. Ettorre, thank you for coming to see me at such short notice." I feel as if I am being treated with respect and it feels good. "You're welcome," I say. At the same time, I hand him a 300-page report of the ATU study (Ettorre, 1982) and say, "This is for you." He takes it, looks astonished, and says, "I was told that you have not written up the ATU study and thus have not fulfilled your contract to the Institute." As he is speaking, I see his face register that this is untrue. I guess I didn't write the report the way it was wanted. "Am I being misunderstood?" I ask myself.

What transpires is a truce between my boss and me. A well-known LSE social psychologist, Berry, a close friend of Terry, my PhD supervisor, is asked to work with me on writing up the ATU study in a series of published articles (see Ettorre, 1984, 1985a, 1985b, 1985c). I find that Berry is great fun, and we make swift progress. However, during and after that time, my boss is distant and hardly speaks with me. I don't meet him again face to face until April 1985. Happily, I supervise myself and without any contact with him, complete other studies (Ettorre, 1986b, 1988a, 1988b, 1988c, 1987a, 1987b). After observing women coming forward for help in both projects, I begin to write feminist pieces (Ettorre, 1985e, 1986a) in my spare time. While I feel relieved, I also feel that my being ignored at the ARU is a form of bullying. Of course, women are made invisible.

March 1984

I work on a survey on women in alcohol and other drugs agencies in London for DAWN (Drugs Alcohol and Women Nationally – London), a non-statutory drugs and alcohol agency funded by the Department of Health. We complete it in December. It is published in January 1985. It has a positive impact at the funders (see DAWN with assistance from Dr. E. M. Ettorre, 1985), and our DOH contact is pleased with the results. The survey reveals that alcohol and other drugs service providers are willing to treat women, but want more knowledge on how to do this effectively. Because of this success, the DAWN workers and I do a smaller survey on race and ethnicity in treatment agencies. I say to them, "You are doing great work for women users." While the DAWN survey on race and ethnicity is not reported publicly except to the management committee, it reveals that many agencies do not have the resources or the will to consider race and ethnicity as important treatment issues. I feel empowered by publicly showing my and DAWN's commitment to women and marginalized users.

April 1985

I am working in my office. There is a knock on my door. I say, "Come in." My boss looks in. As I look up, I am astonished and reticent at the same time. He has not talked to me for ages. "What have I done?" My boss does not sit down, leaving the door ajar as he stands between it and my room, saying:

> I found out this morning that the Medical Research Council is lowering ARU funding in our next grant. I have had to do some thinking. Although you have been here since 1978, you'll be the first to go. [I think, "It's usually 'last in, first out' – but not according to his logic"]. It's probably best that way.

Then he stops talking, looks at me severely, leaves my room, and shuts the door quickly. "It's almost as if he is afraid," I think. I feel overwhelmed but hopeful that I'll get a new job. Immediately, I spread the word around to various sociologists, feminists, and drugs researchers. I sigh, "It will be a relief to leave here."

March 1986

Jo Campling from Macmillan Publishing phones me. "Betsy, I want you to do a book on women and substance use." I respond excitedly, "How fantastic. I would love to, Jo. The experiences of women substance users need to be recognized and valued. I can create a critical framework in which the production of feminist knowledge becomes a real possibility." While I am looking for a new job, I know that whatever job I am offered will be better than my current one, in which I have no support for writing about my feminist ideas.

August 1986

Susanne MacGregor, a well-known drugs researcher, invites me to Birkbeck College to take up a Senior Researcher post on an evaluation of the Department of Health's Central Funding Initiative (see MacGregor et al., 1990). I agree to take up this post. This work demonstrates that government support of statutory and non-statutory drug services is crucial given the mounting visibility of HIV/AIDS. We find that these services respond in an effective way to stem the spread of HIV/AIDS in the UK. Birkbeck enables me to work in a supportive intellectual environment, open to me as an 'out lesbian'. I feel a free lesbian body for the first time in my academic career. I find many women drug users who have gained hope from CFI agencies, although they are still stigmatized in society. I stay at Birkbeck until September 1989 and publish feminist texts on my work (see Ettorre, 1989a, 1989b).

September 1989

I become Drugs Co-ordinator at the Terence Higgins Trust (THT), a large London organization for those (mainly gay men) with HIV/AIDS. (This role involves management of a small three-person team of drug workers.) While it is easy to be in this safe, lesbian, and gay environment, it is not easy from the point of view of being a woman in a predominantly male environment. Campaigning for drug users, especially women drug users, in an organization with 'an anti-female bias' was difficult.[11]

March 1990

After six months, I leave THT to go back to drugs research at the Centre for Research on Drugs and Health Behaviour, Charing Cross and Westminster

Hospital Medical School, University of London. My boss at the time is Gerry Stimson, whom I know from my ARU days, although we did not work there at the same time. I work on a study of HIV and drug users in London which is part of an international comparative study (see Stimson et al., 1991; Ettorre et al., 1991a, 1991b; Rhodes et al., 1993). At the same time, I am completing a book, *Women and Substance Use.* I am relatively happy. I discover most of the women drug users I interview for the study of HIV and drug use in London are sex workers.[12] While they are very clued in about HIV/AIDS prevention, they have a hard time being on the streets. Structural patriarchy works against them, and me, too, as I feel undervalued working in the drugs field.

The Working Lesbian Body: Embodying a Lesbian Feminist Perspective in the Academy

August 1991

I move to Helsinki, Finland to be with my life partner, Irmeli, and embark on a study of tranquilizer use with a well-known medical sociologist, Elianne Riska, at Åbo Academy University. The full study is published in book form (Ettorre and Riska, 1995). This is a fun study and feminist-oriented. I love working with Elianne, who treats me as an equal. After that study, I do some teaching around Finland – from Helsinki to Utsjoki, the northeast village in Lapland – as well as manage to visit the specialized treatment centers for women drug users in or near Helsinki. At that time, the Finnish priority is alcohol research, which historically is a male preserve. Illicit drug users are highly stigmatized, and women, who are seen as potential mothers, are seen as 'polluted'. I visit the first residential treatment facility for women drug users based at a hospital. It is a locked ward. I feel trapped before I leave the building. Feeling marginal as a lesbian feminist, I publish an article on women and drug use in Finland (Ettorre, 1994, 1992b). During my seven years in Finland, I apply at least fifteen times for Academy of Finland research monies on women drug users, but I am told by a leading alcohol researcher, "There is no illegal drug use in Finland," and, even if there is, "No one is interested in women drug users – they betray their roles as mothers." I also feel my lesbian body has marked me in Finland.

Gradually, I find that by centering on men (the most socially visible participants within drug-using cultures), scientific research in the addiction field tends to uphold traditional, patriarchal images of men and women. A distorted view of women is presented. I attempt to challenge these ideas in *Women and Substance Use* (Ettorre, 1992a) and *Women and alcohol: a private pleasure or a public problem?* (Ettorre, 1997) In both texts, I show how pleasure for women is a taboo subject in the addiction field.

March 1998 – October 2006

Because I feel unfulfilled academically and somewhat depressed, I move back to the UK to take up a Readership and then Professorship (Personal Chair) at the University of Plymouth. My partner, Irmeli, embarks on a Ph.D. on women and depression, which is apropos after my feeling depressed in Finland.[13] I help her for it to be a success. In Plymouth, I contact the Harbour Centre, a local voluntary agency for drug users. I become a member of their Board of Trustees and learn about what is happening to drug users. It is refreshing – the centre has a special women's worker. Immediately we become colleagues and she helps me to do a study of women drug users (Ettorre, 2013). With great care, I write *Revisioning Women and Drug Use: Gender, Power, and the Body* (Ettorre, 2007), linking the notion of dependence to my related, earlier notion of the hierarchy of drugs and, in turn, pollution. In January 2006, my partner and I have a civil ceremony at the magistrate's office in Truro. Eventually, this will be transferred to a UK marriage in 2016. My body, my self, feels free from discrimination. The following June, I am asked to apply for a named Chair (Professor of Sociology and Social Policy) at the University of Liverpool. In August 2006, I attend an interview. I feel excited. The spacious room on the top floor of a new administration building is filled with seven people seated in a circle – six men and one woman. I am seated at the head of the table. All glare at me. The Deputy Vice Chancellor, who I learn is a famous veterinarian, asked me bluntly, "Why have you done research on drug users?" I look him straight in the eyes and say, "Because I want to help those whom I research." Immediately, he laughs out loud. I continue, "It is important that as researchers we think about why we do research, and my aim has always been that I want my research to have a positive impact on those I research. I am aware that some academics want to do research to further their own careers." "Oh dear," I think, "Have I gone too far?" "But I am not that kind of academic." I stop and notice the external examiner on the interview panel is smiling at me as I am speaking. I am offered the job two hours later.

November 2009

I give my inaugural lecture at the University of Liverpool. My research on gender and drugs is central to my lecture. "I did not plan on embodying pride as a feminist drugs researcher, but I am. It's about time."

November 2010

I decide to retire from the academy. I was made Head of School and asked to fire "sub-standard" academics. This upsets me and I don't want to do it. My partner had already left to work in Helsinki. I am tired of full-time academic life and the increasing burden of administrative work. When I tell my colleagues, some are shocked. But it feels good . . . I feel a sense of fulfillment with my academic work and happy to be a free woman with my own rights and independence.

The Retiring Lesbian Body: Getting Used to Feminist Retirement

January 2011

I leave Liverpool to retire and live in two cities – Helsinki, Finland and Truro, UK. My research on women and drugs continues. I am asked to be an Honorary Professor at the Centre for Alcohol and Drug Research, Aarhus University. I accept gladly. "Gendering addiction: the politics of drug treatment in a neurochemical world" (Campbell and Ettorre, 2011) is published, a collaboration on the history of gender-specific drug treatment between two feminists across generations and continents. We adopt feminist philosopher Nancy Tuana's notion of "epistemologies of ignorance" to demonstrate how strategies of not knowing are embedded in the alcohol and other drugs field. Tuana (2004, 2006) contends that we must also account for practices that result in a 'group unlearning of what was once a realm of knowledge' (Campbell and Ettorre, 2011, p. 2). I realize that this 'unlearning or forgetting' is exactly what feminist autoethnography is written to prevent.

September 2013

I am the recipient of the prestigious Emeritus Leverhulme Fellowship, which means I will go abroad to do research on autoethnography. I am absolutely delighted. All my ideas emerge from my thinking as a feminist working in this field. Over time, I find that boundaries between 'deviant bodies' (i.e., lesbian bodies and drug-using bodies) finally break down in my mind as I theorize my own embodiment (Ettorre, 2014).

March 2014

My three-month trip to the USA, Sweden, and the UK is successful, and I meet inspiring academics in the field of autoethnography, including

Carolyn Ellis and Arthur Bochner. I decide to write a book on autoethnography and feminism and get a Routledge contract in September 2014.

January 2016

I am sad at leaving England, my home for 37 years. I go to Finland, where my partner and I bought a holiday home in Lapland. We both enjoy skiing, and we both relax.

Up to the Present . . .

The next years in Finland have their ups and downs. I feel that as an older lesbian, my body is shifting, getting older and slower but still skiing. We register our marriage in Finland. It is a freeing experience. A dear friend of mine, Deborah Steinberg, dies in February 2017. I experience deep bodily grieving. In March 2020, we decide to get a Finnish Lapphund, Ruusa, and have many wonderful moments with her. The next year we get Sampo, another Finnish Lapphund, and feel as if our family is complete. In October 2021, I have an operation on my thyroid gland as a large, benign tumor obstructs my throat. Although I have been a member of Democrats Abroad for 20 years, I become active and start a Seniors Caucus in January 2022. While enjoying retirement with my partner and dogs, I am still interested in feminist sociology. I no longer need feminist sociology to help me figure out pressing theoretical issues of the day. I no longer need to put my body through the rigors of academic work. However, I keep in touch with feminist friends and continue to publish work that I see as relevant in today's world . . . In a real sense, my life has come full circle. I started my young life in a convent in Connecticut in a remote place where silence and solitude were all around me. Now I live most of the time in a remote place in Finland, Luosto, with 100 other inhabitants. While I lived in New York and London with millions of people, I liked these cities very much. My body could adjust easily, but my agentic corporality is happiest in a calm place. AND my circle is complete as I meet my ex-nun friends from the 1960s in Zoom meetings every month!

Feminism, Philosophy, and Autoethnography

In this chapter, I have placed autoethnography firmly within the tradition of feminist narrative writing and the literary turn within ethnography. I see autoethnography as just one way of doing feminism and, as many of us are aware, there are many ways of doing feminism. Narrative methods generate useful ways of creating embodied knowledge about individuals, collective agency and the interior language of emotional vulnerability and wounding, which to me is at the heart of good autoethnography. When using my body as a philosophical tool, I try to entangle my incarnate knowledge with my agentic corporality. Nevertheless, my researching and working lesbian body wounds in confrontation with prejudice, discrimination, and bullying.

In this context, the philosopher Hannah Arendt's impact on narrative and autoethnography is instructive. Arendt (1998, p. 184) says 'stories (or narratives) are living realities' and it is through 'action and speech that we insert ourselves in the world'. For her, we are 'not the authors or producers' of our own life stories; rather, there are many 'actors, speakers and sufferers' who exist in the 'web of human relationships' wherever men (sic) live together – but 'no authors' (p. 184). This is because stories (i.e., narratives) 'pre-exist every individual, set the context for their activities, and shape the way actors are understood, responded to and remembered' (Bowring, 2013, p. 18). The fact that Arendt understood her political and philosophical theorizing as storytelling is instructive to us as autoethnographers. As storytellers, we too perceive the theorizing of our stories as political. Think about the stories of my studious and working lesbian body – I was making politics in the academy. On the one hand, with Arendt, we see the redemptive power of narrative (Benhabib, 1990). On the other hand, as with my autoethnography, we see the embodied power of 'writing the self', transforming personal stories into political, philosophical realities. By revealing power inequalities inherent in human relationships, we see the complex cultures of emotions embedded in these unequal relationships. At the ARU early in my career, my researching lesbian body was trapped in a web of sexual harassment, bullying, and depression; my agentic corporality was battered and shaped by unequal human relationships.

While doing my autoethnography in my borderland spaces, I treat identities and experiences as uncertain, fluid, open to interpretation, and able to be revised (Adams and Jones, 2011, p. 110). My working lesbian body is molded by my environment, but also an uplift occurs often when I meet kindness, openness, and understanding, leading to transitional spaces. These fluid spaces create for me a sense of empathy with those I study (Ellis, 2007), especially women alcohol and drug users and with my partner's work on depressed women. I realize that when telling an autoethnographic story, the story is not only mine – it is co-owned with those in my story, sharing this borderland space. I am telling a story without borders. Yet I am an insider and an outsider – a living, embodied crossroads of words, flesh, emotions, interpretations, and humanity. As this insider and outsider, I represent those people in my stories in the most compassionate ways possible – with care, humility, and honesty, and most importantly, with political and ethical sensitivity. At a crossroads and embodying one, I have the responsibility to show the way ahead, to make passage to understanding available and to allow stories to unfold with scrupulousness and honor. Autoethnography exposes the numerous possibilities I have in borderland spaces and how in these liberatory spaces I make sense of my flexible and multiple embodiments, whether they be studious, researching, working, or retiring bodies.

The strength of my autoethnography is that not only does it 'successfully represent in another medium – such as oral interview into scholarly writing' (Clarke, 2005, p. 34) – but also as an authentic method, it locates research experience in the changing ebb of emotional, embodied life, allowing interpretations of personal 'truths' and speaking about oneself to transform into narrative representations of political responsibility (Ettorre, 2010) – an important issue for us as feminists who often function as cultural mediators.

In conclusion, my autoethnographic stories of different forms of embodiment and borderland spaces exposed me in a matrix of always and already political activities as I passed through my life experiences. Furthermore, in asking the epistemological question, 'How do I know what I know?' I demonstrate that autoethnography is very versatile as it reveals several levels of consciousness which link the personal to the cultural (Ellis and Bochner, 2000, p. 739). Simply, knowledge comes from political understandings of my social positioning as well as experiences of the cultural freedoms and constraints I encounter. Hopefully, this became clear when my studious lesbian body was unemployed after doing a 'deviant' Ph.D. or when living in Finland in the 1990s, I found it difficult to face the discrimination against my work on women drug users and additionally, against my lesbian body. I hope I demonstrated that my knowing as an autoethnographer is always embodied and that my incarnate knowledge along with my agentic corporality help me 'to practice embodied perspectives, allowing for distinctive points of encounter' (Briadotti, 2022, p. 38) without me being co-opted into the male academy. In the end, I hope you can see that allowing my body to become a philosophical tool has empowered me as a feminist autoethnographer.

Notes

1 See also Campbell and Ettorre (2011).
2 For a discussion of the co-constitutive nature of structure and agency with special reference to health, see Maller (2015).
3 Rosi Braidotti (2013, p. 27) talks about how within 'an intersectional analysis', we need to look at 'the methodological parallelisms of these factors . . . without flattening out any differences between them but rather investing politically in the question of their complex interaction'. See footnote 4.
4 Including Eva Garmonikow, Pat O'Malley, Ken Plummer, to name a few.

5 See: www.bl.uk/sisterhood/articles/education-and-the-womens-liberation-movement#sthash.6TeCS2CY.dpuf; accessed April 4, 2022.
6 A national study of Alcohol Treatment Units (ATUs) (Robinson and Ettorre, 1980; Ettorre, 1982, 1984, 1985a, 1985b, 1985c); an ATU follow-up study (Ettorre, 1988d); DAIGE (Drug Agency Information Gathering Exercise) A study of London based Drugs Agencies (Ettorre, 1988a, 1988b, 1988c, 1987a, 1987b); A Case Study of TRANX (the first UK voluntary agency for tranquilizer users) (Ettorre, 1986b) and a brief study of the Society for the Study of Addiction (Ettorre, 1985d).
7 I recollect, *"This was 1978 – Harvey Milk has just been assassinated in the US."*
8 See Ettorre (1980). Soon to be republished in 2022.
9 See www.womensaid.org.uk/about-us/history/; accessed April 4, 2022.
10 See Taylor and Raeburn (1995, p. 254).
11 See also Mold and Berridge's (2010, p. 108) account of my involvement at THT.
12 These women referred to themselves as "prostitutes."
13 See Laitinen et al. (2007, 2006); Laitinen and Ettorre (2007, 2004).

References

Adams, T.E. and Herrmann, A.F. (2020). 'Expanding Our Autoethnographic Future'. *Journal of Autoethnography*. 1(1): pp. 1–8. https://doi.org/10.1525/joae.2020.1.1.1
Adams, T.E. and Holman Jones, S. (2011). 'Telling Stories: Reflexivity, Queer Theory, and Autoethnography'. *Cultural Studies – Critical Methodologies*. 11(2): pp. 108–116. https://doi.org/10.1177/1532708611401329
Anzaldua, G. (1987). *Borderlands, La Frontera: The New Mestiza*. San Francisco: Aunt Lute Books.
Arendt, H. (1998). *The Human Condition*. 2nd Edition. Chicago: The University of Chicago Press.
Behar, R. (1996). *The Vulnerable Observer: Anthropology That Breaks Your Heart*. Boston: Beacon Press.
Benhabib, S. (1990). 'Hannah Arendt and the Redemptive Power of Narrative'. *Social Research*. 57(1): pp. 167–196. www.jstor.org/stable/40970582
Bordo, S. (1993). 'Feminism, Foucault, and the Politics of the Body'. In Ramazanoglu, C. (ed.) *Up against Foucault: Explorations of Some Tensions between Foucault and Feminism*. pp. 179–202. London: Routledge.
Bowring, F. (2013). *Hannah Arendt: A Critical Introduction (Modern European Thinkers)*. London: Pluto Press. Kindle Edition.
Boylorn, R.M. and Orbe, M.P. (eds.) (2020). *Critical Autoethnography: Intersecting Cultural Identities in Everyday Life*. New York and London: Routledge.
Braidotti, R. (2013). *The Posthuman*. Cambridge: Polity Press.
Braidotti, R. (2022). *Posthuman Feminism*. Cambridge: Polity Press.
Butler, J. (1990). *Gender Trouble: Feminism and the Subversion of Identity*. London and New York: Routledge.
Butler, J. (1993). *Bodies that Matter: On the Discursive Limits of 'Sex'*. New York and London: Routledge.
Campbell, D. and Ettorre, E. (2011). *Gendering Addiction: The Politics of Drug Treatment in a Neurochemical World*. Houndsmills Basingstoke: Palgrave Macmillan.

Clarke, A.E. (2005). *Situational Analysis: Grounded Theory after the Postmodern Turn*. London: Sage Publications.

Daly, D.K. (2022). 'Playing with the Past: An Autoethnography'. *Qualitative Inquiry*. 28(3–4): pp. 353–364. https://doi.org/10.1177/10778004211026897

DAWN with assistance from Dr. E. M. Ettorre. (1985). *A Survey of Facilities for Women Using Drugs (Including Alcohol)*. London: DAWN.

Ellis, C. (2007). 'Telling Secrets, Revealing Lives: Relational Ethics in Research with Intimate Others'. *Qualitative Inquiry*. 13:(1): pp. 3–29. https://doi.org/10.1177/1077800406294947

Ellis, C. and Bochner, A. (2000). 'Autoethnography, Personal Narrative, Reflexivity: Researcher as Subject'. In Denzin, N. and Lincoln, Y. (eds.) *Handbook of Qualitative Research*. pp. 733–768. Thousand Oaks, CA: Sage Publications.

Ettorre, E.M. (1978). 'The Sociology of Lesbianism: Female Sexuality and female "Deviance."' Unpublished Ph.D., London School of Economics, University of London, April.

Ettorre, E.M. (1980). *Lesbians, Women and Society*. London: Routledge.

Ettorre, E.M. (1982). *The History and Development of Alcohol Treatment Units (ATUs) in England and Wales*. London: Institute of Psychiatry.

Ettorre, E.M. (1984). 'A Study of Alcohol Treatment Units – I. Treatment Activities and the Institutional Response'. *Alcohol and Alcoholism*. 19(3): pp. 243–255. https://doi.org/10.1093/oxfordjournals.alcalc.a044441

Ettorre, E.M. (1985a) 'A Study of Alcoholism Treatment Units: Some Findings on Unit and Staff'. *Alcohol and Alcoholism*. 20(4): pp. 371–378. https://doi.org/10.1093/oxfordjournals.alcalc.a044559

Ettorre, E.M. (1985b) 'A Study of Alcoholism Treatment Units: Some Findings on Patients'. *Alcohol and Alcoholism*. 20(4): pp. 361–369. https://doi.org/10.1093/oxfordjournals.alcalc.a044558

Ettorre, E.M. (1985c) 'A Study of Alcoholism Treatment Units: Some Findings on Links with Community Agencies'. *British Journal of Addiction*. 80(2): pp. 181–189. https://doi.org/10.1111/j.1360-0443.1985.tb03269.x

Ettorre, E.M. (1985d) 'The Society for the Study of Addiction: Temperance, Treatment and Tolerance? (1930–1961)'. *Drug and Alcohol Dependence*. 16(1): pp. 51–60. https://doi.org/10.1016/0376-8716(85)90081-x

Ettorre, E.M. (1985e). 'Compulsory Heterosexuality and Psych/Atrophy: Some Thoughts on Lesbian Feminist Theory'. *Women's Studies International Forum*. 8(5): pp. 421–428. https://doi.org/10.1016/0277-5395(85)90074-3

Ettorre, E.M. (1986a). 'Women and Drunken Sociology: Developing a Feminist Analysis'. *Women's Studies International Forum*. 9(5–6): pp. 515–520. https://doi.org/10.1016/0277-5395(86)90043-9

Ettorre, E.M. (1986b). 'Self-Help Groups as An Alternative to Benzodiazepine Use'. In Williams, P. and Gabe, J. (eds.) *Tranquillisers: Social, Psychological and Clinical Perspectives*. pp. 180–193. London: Tavistock Press.

Ettorre, E.M. (1987a). 'A Study of Voluntary Drug Agencies: Their Roles in the Rehabilitation Field'. *British Journal of Addiction*. 82(6): pp. 681–689. https://psycnet.apa.org/doi/10.1111/j.1360-0443.1987.tb01531.x

Ettorre, E.M. (1987b). 'Drug Problems and the Voluntary Sector of Care in the UK: Identifying Key Issues'. *British Journal of Addiction*. 82(5): pp. 469–476. https://doi.org/10.1111/j.1360-0443.1987.tb01503.x

Ettorre, E.M. (1988a). 'London's Voluntary Drug Agencies. III. A "Snapshot" View of Residential and Nonresidential Clients'. *International Journal of the Addictions*. 23(12): pp. 1255–1269. https://doi.org/10.3109/10826088809058856

Ettorre, E.M. (1988b). 'London's Voluntary Drug Agencies.II: Staffing'. *The International Journal of the Addictions*. 23(11): pp. 1157–1170. https://doi.org/10.3109/10826088809056192

Ettorre, E.M. (1988c). 'London's Voluntary Drug Agencies. I. Funding and Organisational Management'. *The International Journal of the Addictions*. 23(10): pp. 1041–1056. https://doi.org/10.3109/10826088809056184

Ettorre, E.M. (1988d). 'A Follow-Up Study of Alcoholism Treatment Units: Exploring Consolidation and Change'. *British Journal of Addictions*. 83(1): pp. 57–65. https://doi.org/10.1111/j.1360-0443.1988.tb00453.x

Ettorre, E.M. (1989a). 'Women and Substance Use/Abuse: Towards a Feminist Perspective or How to Make Dust Fly'. *Women's Studies International Forum*. 12(6): pp. 593–602. https://doi.org/10.1016/0277-5395(89)90003-4

Ettorre, E.M. (1989b). 'Women, Substance Abuse and Self-Help'. In MacGregor, S. (ed.) *Drugs and British Society*. pp. 101–115. London: Tavistock Press.

Ettorre, E.M. (1992a). *Women and Substance use*. New Brunswick, NJ: Rutgers University Press and London: Macmillan.

Ettorre, E.M. (1992b). 'Kung alkohol och utbolingen narkotika (King Alcohol or foreigner Narcotics)'. *Nordisk Alkohol Tidskrift (Nordic Alcohol Journal)*. 9(3): pp. 121–122. https://doi.org/10.1177/145507259200900312

Ettorre, E.M. (1994). 'Women and Drug Abuse with Special Reference to Finland: Needing the "Courage to See"'. *Women's Studies International Forum*. 17(1): pp. 83–94.

Ettorre, E.M. (1997). *Women and Alcohol: From a Private Pleasure to a Public Problem?* London: Women's Press.

Ettorre, E.M. (2007). *Revisioning Women and Drug Use: Gender, Power, and the Body*. Gordonsville, VA and Basingstoke, UK: Palgrave Macmillan.

Ettorre, E.M. (2010). 'Nuns, Dykes, Drugs, and Gendered Bodies: An Autoethnography of a Lesbian Feminist's Journey Through "Good Time" Sociology'. *Sexualities*.13(3): pp. 295–315. https://doi.org/10.1177/1363460709363137

Ettorre, E.M. (2013). 'Drug User Researchers as Autoethnographers: "Doing Reflexivity" with Women Drug Users'. *Substance Use and Misuse*. 48: pp. 1377–1385. https://doi.org/10.3109/10826084.2013.814999

Ettorre, E.M. (2014). 'Embodied Deviance, Gender, and Epistemologies of Ignorance: Re-Visioning Drugs Use in a Neurochemical, Unjust World'. *Substance Use and Misuse*. 50(6): pp. 794–805. https://doi.org/10.3109/10826084.2015.978649

Ettorre, E.M. (2017). *Autoethnography as Feminist Method: Sensitising the Feminist "I."* London: Routledge.

Ettorre, E.M. and Riska, E. (1995). *Gendered Moods: Psychotropics and Society*. London: Routledge.

Ettorre, E.M., Crosier, A., Stephens, S. and Stimson, G. (1991a). *Prevalence Study of HIV and Injecting Drug Misuser in EC and Coast Countries: A Report from the London Centre*. London: Centre for Research on Drugs and Health Behaviour.

Ettorre, E.M., Stimson, G., Crosier, A. and Stephens, S. (1991b). *Trends in HIV Infection among Drug Injectors in London*. London: Centre for Research on Drugs and Health Behaviour, Executive Summary No. 5.

Henningham, M. (2021). 'Blak, bi+ and Borderlands: An Autoethnography on Multiplicities of Indigenous Queer Identities Using Borderland Theory'. *Social Inclusion*. 9(2): pp. 7–17. https://doi.org/10.17645/si.v9i2.3821

Laitinen, I. and Ettorre, E.M. (2004). 'The Women and Depression Project: Feminist Action Research and Guided Self-Help Groups Emerging from the Finnish Women's Movement'. *Women's Studies International Forum*. 27(3): pp. 203–221. https://doi.org/10.1016/j.wsif.2004.04.002

Laitinen, I. and Ettorre, E.M. (2007). 'Writing of Sadness and Pain: Diary Work with Depressed Women in Finland'. *Journal of Poetry Therapy*. 20(1): pp. 1–18. https://doi.org/10.1080/08893670701254636

Laitinen, I., Ettorre, E.M. and Sutton, C. (2006). 'Empowering Depressed Women: Changes in "Individual" and "Social" Feelings in Guided Self-Help Groups in Finland'. *European Journal of Psychotherapy and Counselling*. 8(30): pp. 305–320. https://doi.org/10.1080/13642530600878238

Laitinen, I., Ettorre, E.M. and Sutton, C. (2007). 'Gaining Agency Through Healthy Embodiment in Groups for Depressed Women'. *European Journal of Counselling & Psychotherapy*. 9(2): pp. 209–226. https://doi.org/10.1080/1364253070 1363577

MacGregor, S., Ettorre, B., Coomber, R. and Crosier, A. (1990). *Drug Services in England and the Impact of the Central Funding Initiative*. London: Institute for the Study of Drug Dependence.

Maller, C.J. (2015). 'Understanding Health Through Social Practices: Performance and Materiality in Everyday Life'. *Sociology of Health & Illness*. 37(1): 52–66. https://doi.org/10.1111/1467-9566.12178

Mold, A. and Berridge, V. (2010). *Voluntary Action and Illegal Drugs: Health and Society in Britain since the 1960s*. Houndmills, Basingstoke: Palgrave Macmillan.

Pitts-Taylor, V. (2003). *In the Flesh: The Cultural Politics of Body Modification*. Basingstoke: Palgrave Macmillan.

Rhodes, T.J., Bloor, M.J., Donoghoes, M., Haw, S. Ettorre, Elizabeth., Platt, S. Rischer, M., Hunter, G.M., Taylor, A. Finlay, A. Crosier, A., Stephens, S., Covell, R., Stimson, G., Goldberg, D.J., Green, S.T., Mckeganey, N.P. and Parry, J. (1993). 'HIV Prevalence and HIV Risk Behaviour among Injecting Drug Users in London and Glasgow'. *AIDS CARE*. 5(4): pp. 413–425. https://doi.org/10.1080/09540129308258011

Robinson, D. and Ettorre, B. (1980). 'Special Units for Common Problems: Alcoholism Treatment Units in England and Wales'. In Edwards, G. and Grant, M. (eds.) *Alcohol Treatment in Transition*. pp. 234–247. London: Croom Helm.

Stimson, G., Ettorre, B., Crosier, A. and Stephens, S. (1991). *Serial Period Prevalence Study of HIV Related Risk Behaviour among Injecting Drug Users in London: A Report of the First Year*. London: Centre for Research on Drugs and Health Behaviour.

Taylor, V. and Raeburn, N. (1995). 'Identity Politics as High-Risk Activism: Career Consequences for Lesbian, Gay, and Bisexual Sociologists'. *Social Problems*. 42(2): pp. 252–273. https://doi.org/10.2307/3096904

Triesman, D. (1977). 'Institute of Psychiatry Sackings'. *Radical Science*. 5: pp. 9–36. (no DOI available).

Tuana, N. (2004). 'Coming to Understand: Orgasm and the Epistemology of Igno-rance'. *Hypatia*. 19(1): pp. 194–232. https://doi.org/10.1111/j.1527-2001.2004.tb01275.x

Tuana, N. (2006). 'The Speculum of Ignorance: The Women's Health Move-ment and Epistemologies of Ignorance'. *Hypatia*. 21(3): pp. 1–19. https://doi.org/10.1111/j.1527-2001.2006.tb01110.x

5

WHICH WAY IS UP? A PHILOSOPHICAL AUTOETHNOGRAPHY OF TRYING TO STAND IN A "CROOKED ROOM"

Renata Ferdinand

The Hunt

I quietly sit cross-legged in my seat.

I think about Pinkie, my brash *I don't give a fuck* alter ego. She wouldn't sit for this. But Renata would. Renata would sit through this humiliating experience, if only to replay the events as they unfolded.

I am on my way to teach Modern African Literature. I confidently approach my classroom, only to find that my students are gathered in the hallway outside of the room.

"What's wrong?" I ask.

One of my students steps forward from the crowd, responding, "The door is locked."

"Okay. Give me a minute. I'll go and ask the secretary to call security to come and unlock the door."

I walk toward the departmental office to notify the secretary. After chatting with her, I return to the hallway to find my students slowly entering the room. However, I do not see any security guards. I enter the classroom after the students, walking toward the front of the room to place my bag on the desk. Then I approach the podium, casually holding my book and supplies.

"Who unlocked the door?" I ask.

Silence.

The students look uncomfortable. They uneasily squirm from side to side in their seats.

"Come on, tell me."

Silence.

DOI: 10.4324/9781003274728-5

"What's wrong?"

One of the students finally responds, "It was the White professor from across the hall. He said that if you were a real professor, you would have a key."

Silence.

Sweat begins to slowly drip from my head. I squirm at the podium, my body jolting from side to side. A mixture of different movements with my head, arms, and legs, each going in its own direction. My hands tremble. I watch helplessly as my fingers try to grip the pen, but refuse to hold it. The four corners of the small classroom close in on me. I am trapped.

"Give me a moment." I hurriedly leave the class.

I step out into the hallway. I can feel the anger rising in me, and Pinkie is almost displaying her head. I try to push her back down, to bury her within my body. Mouthing to myself, *fuck that! You can stay quiet, Renata. Let Pinkie handle it.*

And so, I do.

I go on a hunt for this man. Have you ever seen a lion hunt for a gazelle? The gazelle is usually caught off-guard. Maybe it is drinking from a stream. Sometimes the lion will appear to not be paying any attention to the gazelle. Or the lion may be hiding in the brush to prevent the gazelle from seeing it. Either way, by the time the lion begins to chase the gazelle, it is usually too late for the gazelle to escape. The lion pounces on the gazelle, clenching the gazelle's neck in its mouth. A disturbing, but wonderous sight. In this situation, I was the lion. And my prey, a silver-haired White male professor with a slick mouth from across the hall.

I start searching for him, reminding myself to be like the lion. Move cautiously. I tiptop into the adjacent classroom, scanning all corners of the room, but he is not there. I gently walk down the hallway to see if I can catch a glimpse of him, but to no avail. I go back into the departmental office and quietly ask the secretary if she has seen him, but she hasn't. I walk back down the hall, the balls of my feet slightly touching the ground as I walk. I stop halfway to look in both directions, determined to not miss my prey. My hair is in a bun today and I think about how I should maybe take it down, of how I should probably remove any jewelry (earrings and all) just in case this comes to a physical altercation. Tyler Perry (2006) says in *Don't Make a Black Woman Take off Her Earrings*, "Take your earrings off! This is the Black woman's national anthem. She's getting ready to fight" (p. 238). He is right; my intent is to cause this man due harm. If not physically, surely verbally. I am preparing to go into a tirade that would take him down several sizes. Between my academic jargon, I would lace my sentences with *fuck you fuck you fuck you,* followed by some concoction of verbs and nouns. Shit, I am not even opposed to talking about his momma, if it came to that.

I make my way back to the classroom, just long enough to peek my head in the doorway.

"Give me one minute. I'm coming."

I go back on my hunt.

It was on my second hunt for this man that I became bolder. I slip into his classroom and ask the students of his whereabouts. They don't know. Thinking quietly to myself, *"Don't try to protect him. I'm gonna fuck him up!"* But I move on. Again, back down the hallway, back to the departmental office, back in both directions, searching endlessly for this man. My gazelle. I finally arrive back to my classroom, unfortunately with no prey in my mouth. Just me, my students, and a suffocating classroom.

I walk back to the podium. It just so happens that today we are reviewing *The Joys of Motherhood*, a book that clearly demonstrates the powerlessness that Black women can feel in their relations to others. Here I am, a professor at this university for eight years, being stripped of my power (amongst other things). My hunt is an attempt to get my power back. I stand there for a moment, reveling in my desire for retribution, thinking about how good it will feel to clench him in my teeth. To watch him squirm, losing all bodily functions. Of how I will then slowly chew on his carcass, relishing each bite as if it is my last. And after quenching my thirst for revenge, I will throw his indigestible parts to the side. A diabolical smile comes over my face. I scan the room, looking at the solemn faces of my students. The normally talkative group sits quietly. Still, I stand motionless. I think about what this situation is costing me, what Pinkie's actions would cost me: my reputation, my relationship with my students, and ultimately my job. My smile slowly dissipates. I look around the small room, zooming in on the sullen faces meeting my eyes. I step away from the podium.

I quietly sit cross-legged in my seat.

The Crooked Room

In 2011, American writer, professor, television host, and political commentator Melissa Harris-Perry introduced the idea of the "crooked room" in her seminal book, *Sister Citizen: Shame, Stereotypes, and Black Women in America*. Harris-Perry borrows the idea of the crooked room from field dependency experiments, where subjects are asked to align themselves with a crooked room while sitting in a crooked chair. Some subjects are able to straighten themselves despite being in a crooked room; others unconsciously tilt themselves to align with the crooked surroundings. The aim of the experiment is to show how people will adjust and modify themselves to fit or relate to their surroundings, even if the surroundings are not based in reality. Harris-Perry aptly applies this concept to Black women in America by describing how gender and racial stereotypes cause Black women to bend and distort themselves. She writes:

> When they confront race and gender stereotypes, black women are standing in a crooked room, and they have to figure out which way is up. Bombarded with warped images of their humanity, some black women tilt and bend themselves to fit the distortion.
>
> *(Harris-Perry, 2011, p. 29)*

You would think I was a contortionist in the ways that I have bent myself into unimaginable and unnatural positions. I have had to navigate a world that has pitted me against the stereotypes that plague Black women: Sapphire, Mammy, Jezebel. This may sound strange, but at various times I have both played into the role of a stereotype and actively resisted it. Admittedly, it has been an arduous juggling act of sorts, one that I have felt compelled to repeatedly perform. But why? This leads to a pivotal question I intend to explore in this chapter:

What, historically and philosophically, has contributed to the inauthentic compliance that leads to me having to accept and resist social and environmental stereotyping pressures on me to fit the crooked room?

I intend to tackle this question by critically analyzing the binary identities that I have constructed in order to engage with the world. First, there's Renata, an identity I developed largely as a response to larger society's idea of ideal femininity. Framed as the "good girl," this is the identity that most strives to meet the stereotypical standards of White womanhood. A further exploration of this identity reveals how I, unfortunately, accept stereotypes of Black womanhood as well. Then there's Pinkie, my alter ego, who resists this ideal framing of femininity, yet is only revealed in moments of extreme distress. This chapter explores how and why she manifests in certain situations. Ultimately, both identities reveal a problem of recognition; hence, I will argue just how deep the problem lies, thereby exposing how the historical and philosophical forces are linked together.

To do this, this chapter engages in the idea of the "crooked room." As an autoethnography, it applies this concept to my life experiences and theorizes the ways that the concept can be used as a sensemaking technique for understanding complicated racialized and gendered experiences. Furthermore, it shows what happens when one tries to "stand" in a crooked room, with a particular emphasis on what it does to the physical body, but also the mental anguish that is largely due to having to bend oneself in the first place. Included in this discussion is an exploration of the ways that respectability politics (the idea that Black women will suffer from less degradation if they appear "respectable") have influenced my identity. Ultimately, this chapter reveals aspects of my own personality, yet also highlights the particular ways that a conglomeration of several other factors (including historical, societal, gender, racial, etc.) continue to influence the ways I move about in the world (and even how I perceive my world). The best way of understanding these moments is by critically examining how I negotiate these different identities while in specific situations. In the earlier example, I have given you a glimpse of Pinkie. However, let me tell you more about Renata, the "good girl."

The Good Girl

Renata is the safe one, the respectable one. The one who learned early that a "good girl" is one who does not use her voice. At home and at school, a "good girl" is rewarded for silence. I can even remember in elementary school always being assigned as the class name-taker to keep track of other students' silences when the teacher would momentarily leave the room. I would be given a golden sticker for my monitoring of silence, a clear marker of a "good girl." Other markers include excelling in areas approved by society, like school. Or religion. Or just generally following the rules. A "good girl" does not upset or challenge the status quo. Instead, she follows the path that is laid for her. I can apply Carter G. Woodson's (2006) idea from *The Miseducation of the Negro*, "If you control a man's [sic] thinking, you do not have to worry about his actions. When you determine what a man [sic] shall think, you do not have to concern yourself about what he [sic] will do" (p. 84). My actions were all in line with what society expects from a "good girl."

This indoctrination is intentional even though it is based on an ideal femininity that is centered around White womanhood. In fact, the characteristics mostly associated with appropriate femininity revolve around the stereotypical image of White women as being chaste, demure, and in need of protection. This leaves Black women and girls to try to live up to a feminine ideal that frames them in opposition to Whiteness. Hence, to thrive in a "crooked room" that is not based on reality. Puff (2014) writes:

> Because Black and White have been historically defined as binary opposites, the meaning of a Black female body is contingent on what it means to be a White woman. If the seventeenth-century Anglo Americans who colonized the New World used White womanhood to signify femininity, purity and chastity, then Black womanhood had to be defined as oppositional to those characteristics and thereby *Othered*.
>
> *(p. 225)*

I bend to try to fit the stereotypes of a "good girl"; unfortunately, in this effort, I also bend to not fit the stereotypes of Black womanhood. This is problematic on many levels, but ultimately speaks to the "problem of recognition" that Harris-Perry (2011, p. 35) describes. In her book, she leans on Georg Wilhelm Friedrich Hegel's philosophy of recognition, *Anerkennung*, which describes the value that citizens place on being recognized as equals in the social contract of the nation-state. She writes:

> An individual who is seen primarily as a part of a despised group loses the opportunity to experience the public recognition for which the human self strives. Further, if the group itself is misunderstood, then to the extent that one is seen as a part of this group, that 'seeing' is inaccurate.
>
> *(p. 38)*

To go further, let's take a brief look at Hegel's theory.

Anerkennung

Anerkennung is a German word that literally translates to mean "recognition." As a theory, it initially appeared in Hegel's widely discussed book, *Phenomenology of Spirit* (1977), where he examines the evolution of human consciousness. Within the chapter "The Truth of Self-Certainty," he explains that for one to achieve self-consciousness requires that he/she must be recognized by another self-conscious being. He writes, "Self-consciousness exists in itself and for itself, in that, and by the fact that it exists for another self-consciousness; that is to say, it *is* only by being acknowledged or 'recognized'" (p. 229). In other words, mutual recognition between subjects is required for both subjects to achieve self-consciousness, or to be more exact, freedom. McQueen (no date) writes, "For Hegel, recognition is the mechanism by which our existence as social beings is generated. Therefore, our successful integration as ethical and political subjects within a particular community is dependent upon receiving (and conferring) appropriate forms of recognition." So, in a way, I needed this professor's recognition *and* needed to give him my recognition as a way of sustaining my own reality. Referencing Hegel's idea, Stewart (2018) explains it simply:

> When I look into the eyes of another person, I can see the inwardness that I recognize from myself and my own inner life . . . I know who I am due to the fact that I can see myself from the outside as others see me.
>
> *(p. 475)*

However, this professor could not see me as a fellow colleague who, at a minimum, was deserving of professional courtesy and respect. Expanding on the benefits of Hegel's theory, Brownlee (2015) writes:

> Recognizing others as persons means ascribing to them a specific and equal standing, which, in turn, entails distinctive normative commitments . . . . Recognizing someone as a person means ascribing to her a set of rights, especially property rights, that it would be inappropriate to violate.
>
> *(p. 382)*

And yet, this professor did exactly that: he violated me. The implications of his remark speak to my lack of qualifications to be an effective teacher, simply because I lack the keys to the classroom. The keys to the classroom, therefore, are symbolic of my qualifications. A "real" professor has keys; and since I did not have any, I am not a "real" professor, whatever that means. He reduced me in one fell swoop. I was in the "Life and Death" struggle that Hegel (1977) describes as a clash between individuals who refuse to see each other as self-conscious beings. Sinnerbrink (2004) describes Hegel's "Life and Death" struggle as occurring when:

> Each individual proto-subject asserts its own self-identity by negating the other, where the other is taken to be a mere obstacle confronting the subject, rather than another intentional being with its own point of view . . . . The relation between the protagonists thereby becomes a violent conflict, with each staking its own life in seeking the death of the other.
>
> *(pp. 278–279)*

I was in a battle, one that I was quickly losing because, unfortunately, I could recognize him, but he refused to recognize me. And I hate that I even needed his recognition! Stewart (2018) writes, "Hegel's theory forces us to ask what it would mean not just to treat others as equals but to see them as necessary for our free existence" (p. 477). Clearly, I wasn't necessary. He did not need me.

And yet, I freely admit here that I could not see myself clearly either. How could I? I have been aligning in this "crooked room" all my life. No matter what I do, I am always positioned against the image of White womanhood. O'Grady (2003) writes, "White is what woman is; not-white (and the stereotypes not-white gathers in) is what she had better not be" (p. 174). Because it has been my normative script, I bought into it. Hence my quest to be a "good girl." Even though I am years removed from my earlier childhood socialization, I bring all of this into the academic classroom with me.

I also bring the stereotypes of Black womanhood with me, the ones that I too subconsciously accepted. Jacobs (2016) describes a study conducted by *Essence* magazine where they asked Black women readers to keep a journal of stereotypical images depicted of themselves in the media. She writes:

> Those images that appeared most frequently were of 'Gold Diggers,' 'Modern Jezebels,' 'Baby Mamas,' 'Uneducated Sisters,' 'Rachet Woman,' 'Angry Black Women,' 'Mean Black Girls,' 'Unhealthy Black Women,' and 'Black Barbies,' – images that collectively show Black women as uneducated, opportunistic, hypersexual, and unapproachable.
>
> *(p. 227)*

I believed this, too, to a certain extent. A "good girl" for me translated to the most approximate qualities of White femininity as possible. Sadly, I had aligned myself with the "crooked room." It was White femininity that was acceptable. The one that would keep me safe from harm. It was like wearing a cloak of protection. And as long as I stayed shrouded in it, I would be rewarded for my good behavior. I saw it clearly throughout my life: the casual opportunities that came to me because I was "different" from other Black women; the career advancements that easily landed in my lap due to my "agreeable behavior"; of how I was so "easy" to work with, never making my colleagues feel "uncomfortable to be White." Yet, they did not know I was tilting my body, forcing it to cave into the pressure. Of how I would stay awake at night, replaying the words they use to describe another Black female colleague as "difficult" and "not deserving" of a leadership position. Of how they often tried to pit us against each other, the only two Black females in the department. Of how I would sometimes, after a particularly exhausting situation of having to explain "why Black people complain so much," I would walk pass my own home without even recognizing a glimpse of it. And it would only occur to me after having walked several blocks that I had missed my turn. Yeah, society told me who I was. And I bent my body to accept it.

However, my own community contributed to this understanding as well. Harris-Perry (2011) describes the "politics of respectability" that Black women have engaged in to challenge the distorted images of Black women as hypersexual. The myth of promiscuity has had damaging effects on society: it was and has been widely believed that Black women are incapable of being raped or sexually assaulted, for their natural promiscuity prevents them from being victims. To counter this negative stereotype, prominent Black leaders adopted a "politics of respectability" that sought to prove Black women as being deserving of full citizenship. This meant that they would refrain from any behavior that did not conform to the idealized version of femininity. Harris-Perry (2011) writes, "If a claim to full citizenship rests on the assertion of a narrowly defined, sexually repressive respectability, then black women must adhere to a rigidly controlled public performance of themselves . . . . It forced them to wear a mask" (p. 62). Or, as I like to say, to be a "good girl." And oh, how I played the part! I occupied rooms like an apparition. Hell, if you blinked, you might have missed me. Truly, I was skilled at leaning into these positions while in the "crooked room," flexing my spine to accommodate the pressures of the bend. I aptly understand why when Harris-Perry (2011) describes the impact of myths, she also describes how "the myth also resonates in the hearts and minds of black women" (p. 69). However, the experience with the White male professor described earlier challenged this. I thought that presenting a sterling moral character would prevent me from experiencing racism. I was wrong. And that's why I needed Pinkie.

The Alter Ego

Pinkie is my alter ego. I have described her in my own research as "fierce, tattooed, facial piercings, gold teeth, and a bad attitude" (Ferdinand, 2021, p. 31). Over the years, I have come to realize that there is a clear distinction between Pinkie and Renata. Pinkie is my opposite. She is confident. She is bold. I position her as *not giving zero fucks*. When I tap into her, I feel powerful. Like nothing can get to me. My outward appearance reflects this as well. For example, when I am Pinkie, I am more likely to wear my hair down. I will wear earrings that say *Black Girls Rock!* or *Black Girl Magic*. I may wear something less formal, like jeans and a graphic tee shirt. This is very different from how I usually portray myself, as I typically dress to make my White colleagues feel comfortable and to assuage any negative feelings that they may have about me or Black people in general because it is "widely believed that black people cannot afford to be individualistic . . . . Every Black Man/Woman *is* the 'race'" (Spillers, 1996, p. 100). Feeling pressure to represent my entire race is just another "crooked room" I slant my body in. At any rate, as Renata, I am very cognizant of how I look, and this is reflected in my appearance: no wildly-colored clothes, no extreme Black hairstyles, no visibly Black anything (jewelry; hair accessories). And absolutely no race talk! But when I channel Pinkie, I stroll into work with a different attitude, one less compromising. My language adjusts, too. I will use more African American Vernacular English (AAVE), going between words so specific to my community that they can hardly be translated or written here. Whereas I would usually code-switch (going between Standard English and AAVE) while at work, when I'm Pinkie I feel less obligation to. In those moments, I care less what my White colleagues think.

I realize now that I resort to Pinkie in those moments of emotional difficulty. In fact, the times that I have summoned her, I was having extreme racial anxiety. And my racial anxiety typically manifests itself as anger. I need Pinkie because I need her anger. Like the time I describe in my book of how Pinkie showed up when I was angered at the lack of Black women representation in a local Barnes and Noble (Ferdinand, 2021, p. 31). Or how Pinkie emerged when I was angered at watching a mammy stereotype in the children's movie, *The Princess and the Frog* (Ferdinand, 2021, p. 35). Or the time my daughter's kindergarten teacher, Mrs. Nawarski, proceeded to proclaim my daughter a menace to her classroom, ending with a profound assertion: "I know how this may sound, but you can't expect our children to be ready for a Black child, and you can't force people to accept this" (Ferdinand, 2021, pp. 56–57). I had to visualize Pinkie's words just to process this moment. I have written extensively about this in my book, but it is only here that I am willing to further examine Pinkie and her purpose.

I look back at Harris-Perry's words and realize something significant: Pinkie is my Sapphire. Sapphire is a version of the Angry Black Woman, another stereotype created in opposition to White femininity. Harris-Perry (2011) writes, "Sapphire is one name for the myth, the angry black woman has many different shadings and representations: the bad black woman, the black 'bitch,' and the emasculating matriarch" (p. 88). The name Sapphire itself stems from a character from the 1930s comedy show, *Amos 'n' Andy*. Sapphire is described as loud, emasculating, brash, and hostile. Pictured as an angry, neck-rolling, finger-pointing, hip-swaying woman, she is confrontational and combative, particularly using anger as a weapon. Harris-Perry (2011) describes how this stereotype shows up in popular culture, from Omarosa from the reality show *The Apprentice*, to the news coverage of Black women politicians like Maxine Waters and Cynthia McKinney, who are often described as being "angry about something." This stereotype is just as damaging as the others, and in this case, particularly so because Black women's anger is trivialized as unimportant, thereby failing to "acknowledge black women's anger as a legitimate reaction to unequal circumstances" (Harris-Perry, 2011, p. 95).

So, yes, Pinkie is my Sapphire. I deploy her in instances where I feel threatened or vulnerable. Often, just as in this situation, it is a response to a feeling of powerlessness. West (2008) writes, "Although Black women perceive this image as powerful, they may be using an angry, self-protective posture to shield themselves from discrimination, victimization, and disappointment" (p. 296). The fact that I only use her when needed speaks to my awareness of the peculiarity of my social position. And it speaks to a significant epiphany: I keep Pinkie hidden because I am aware of the consequences of her behavior. This reveals a simple truth: a part of me must also see this anger as irrational. I ask myself, why does it take Pinkie to acknowledge my anger? Why is Renata incapable of expressing anger? Clearly, I have made a distinction between the two: there is the "well-mannered, well-dressed, palatable to White audiences" Renata, and there is the loud, angry, not-giving-a-fuck Pinkie. This is emblematic of W. E. B. DuBois' theory of double consciousness (2014), the twoness that develops as a result of Black people living in a country that despises them. He writes, "It is a peculiar sensation, this double-consciousness, this sense of always looking at one's self through the eyes of others, of measuring one's soul by the tape of a world that looks on in amused contempt and pity" (p. 3). I must admit that it bothers me that this professor was rejecting Renata, the safe identity that I had so carefully crafted for White audiences. Hence, this is a cruel reminder that he did not see the difference, or more likely, a difference did not matter. He saw a Black woman out of place.

This also shows the extent to which I have invested in the stereotypical images of Black women. I struggle in even writing this, but I must be honest: I have absorbed them. Morgan and Bennett (2006) describe the dangers of stereotypes, writing, "Stereotypes do not merely tell us how a culture 'sees' a group of people; they also tell us how a culture controls that group, how it bullies them into submitting to or evading the representations that haunt them" (p. 490). Consequently, I have done an injustice to myself by reducing myself to only two emotions – angry or not angry. I have painfully done just what society does to Black women: rob them of their ability to experience a range of human emotions. In this case I robbed myself, for there were other emotions I felt in this moment. Like humiliation. Embarrassment. And emotional pain and hurt. Yet, I did not readily lean on these emotions, although I tend to think that the anger is an expression of the other emotions. Still, I did not cry or express sadness. Instead, I went right to anger. It was anger that I had at my disposal. Harris-Perry (2011) writes:

> What is so dangerous about the Angry Black Woman stereotype: it holds Black women responsible for power they do not possess, power that is, in fact, being utilized in very real ways by members of other social groups who can claim emotional innocence as they hide behind, and persecute, the 'Black Bitches' of our cultural imaginations.
>
> *(p. 93)*

Kudos to this White male professor for strategically using his power. And I did not even have to be in his presence for his power to be enacted. What a way to exist in the world! Now that I have unpacked Pinkie and Renata, let's go back to the situation to further unpack the dynamics of it.

The Lion and the Gazelle

Who is the lion? And who is the gazelle? Because if the lion equates to having power, then surely I am not the lion. Imagine the situation: an older White-male professor unlocks the door to the classroom of a young Black woman professor. Already, the dynamics are unbalanced. Research has extensively shown that college students, both Black and White, regard White male professors as being more legitimate than others. West (2008) describes how "many Black women professors have been mistaken for clerical staff and even prostitutes" (p. 287). I have witnessed this firsthand! I have seen students refer to White male instructors as "Dr. suchandsuch," even when they have no doctorate. Meanwhile, I can hardly get students to stop calling me "Ms." Ferdinand. And I have been mistaken for quite a number of people. The librarian. The secretary of the department. Personnel in the Registrar's office. Just random bullshit. And when I correct them, I always get the same line: "You look so young to be a professor." And I always wish to respond with: "If I were working at McDonalds, would I look too young then? Or if I were cleaning your office or picking up your trash, would I look young then?" But I say nothing, choosing instead to turn my body at an angle in this "crooked room." But in this situation, his mere presence spoke power.

And if that was not enough, his accompanying words furthered his might. His exact wording: "If she were a real professor, she would have a key." Stop for a moment and take in the gravity of these words: "If she were a real professor, she would have a key." This statement is so loaded that I can hardly do justice to it in fully unpacking it. I even have a problem with the use of the word "she." "She" is so dismissive in this situation. It eerily reminds me of the word "boy" in reference to how Black men are insulted by it when a White person uses it in conversation with them. It makes them feel small; in this case, referring to me as "she" instead of as Dr. Ferdinand did the exact same thing. I taught English for several years, so bear with me here as I engage in a brief grammar lesson. Not only had he removed me as the subject of the sentence, choosing instead to replace me as a pronoun; he did so twice to prove a point. How ironic is it that his sentence is a conditional sentence – a sentence based on a condition. A conditional sentence, or if-clause, has a main clause and a conditional clause.

Main Clause: "She would have a key."
Conditional Clause: "If she were a real professor."

There are various types of if-clauses. The one he uses implies a condition of the past as influencing the present moment. Hence, something did not happen in the past – *I did not become a real professor* – is affecting the present moment – *I do not have a key*.

And in that, he blames me. It is my fault the door is locked. It is a failure upon me that I did not acquire the right amount of education that magically unlocks doors. It was not an error by the security office. It was not due to the department locking the door as a failsafe to keep the expensive piano from being removed from the room (I do not know how anyone would do this). It was not because the classroom was hardly used. No, this locked door was due to my lack of ambition. Images of the no-account, lazy, shiftless Welfare Queen come to my mind. Had I been more of a go-getter and taken advantage of the opportunities afforded me, I would now be in the position to open a door for my students; instead, my own lack of motivation had resulted in the door remaining locked, barring me from entering it without the help of a good ol' White savior. I fear that him unlocking the door cements the savior image in his mind, and maybe in the minds of my students.

This was a very public humiliation for me, like the one Harris-Perry describes about Chana Kai Lee, a tenured professor who was made to return to work after having a stroke because the University feared she would abuse her sick leave. Harris-Perry (2011) quotes Lee as saying:

> Ph.D or no Ph.D., tenure or no tenure, I was just like the rest of those lazy black folks: I'd do anything for a cheap ride. I'd take advantage of any situation. I'd exaggerate and manipulate good, responsible, white folks who played by the rules, all to avoid my responsibilities.
>
> *(p. 44)*

To him, I am responsible for the locked door. Harris-Perry would argue that what he actually did was shame me. She writes, "Though we seldom think of it this way, racism is the act of shaming others based on their identity. Blackness in America is marked by shame" (2011, p. 109). His tactic was just as stigmatizing as the others she describes as being used during Jim Crow, the Reagan administration, and in contemporary life.

And what about my students? This White male professor made this statement to young, impressionable students, age ranging from anywhere between 18 and 22. Mostly female and all students of color, reflecting a mixture of various ethnic and racial backgrounds (Black, Latinx, and Middle Eastern). It may be surprising to you that some of these students come from high schools with no Black teachers; in some cases, I am their first one. He disrespected them, too, in multiple ways. With both hands, he gave them his biases. He was making a judgment about the worth of a woman of color in front of a bunch of other women of color. Undoubtedly, I am sure it affected how they saw themselves. He also belittled their education, because if I am not a real professor, then their education is not real. The content of the course is not real. The things they are learning within the class are not real. He told these black and brown students, ultimately, that they are not real either. And he had no qualms about it, a clear indication of how he viewed them as well. It rolled easily off his tongue as if he were saying, "Have a nice day!" To this very moment, I wonder if he would have said this in front of White students, or if his verbiage would have been different. I do not know. I do not wish to find out. But his message to my students was clear. And his quest to discredit me clearly affected them, for I could tell by their hesitance in telling me what happened that they knew it was inappropriate, so much so that they did not want to repeat the words.

His words lingered in the air long after it happened. That day, we did not resume our discussion of *The Joys of Motherhood*. We did not get into a debate about cultural expectations and their effect on Black women. We did not get to explore the prominent themes of the book. Instead, we sat in silence, holding the words of the professor in our minds. My response still bothers me. I imagine him proceeding to teach an exhilarating course, something on communicating power, with his students in a raucous response to his passionate delivery. They would cling to his every word as if it were made of gold. And here sit my students, distraught and sullen, waiting for me to impart some special knowledge that could offer them some understanding, either of the book or an explanation of what just happened. But I do not. The fact that we were still stewing, lost in the moment, is just another indication of the power he exerted. So I ask again, who is the lion? And who is the gazelle?

The Bend or the Upright

I wish I was like Janie Crawford, the protagonist from *Their Eyes Were Watching God* (Hurston, 1998). Harris-Perry (2011) describes Janie's journey as "a model of the struggle many black women face," the struggle of not letting the opinions and expectations of others become a weight for them to carry (p. 28). Instead, by Janie choosing her own path, despite the objections of her grandmother, she "finds the upright" (p. 31). She chooses to escape the bonds of domesticity in exchange for travel and freedom. She did not let the stereotypes about Black women impede her life. I have read and reread this story what seems like a thousand times, and I certainly admire Janie, but I still cannot figure out how to apply it to my own life. I try to "stand," but honestly, standing in a "crooked room" is exhausting.

And so, I continue to bend. I tilt at work. I stretch at the grocery store. While I am at the bank. I distort myself at my children's school. I adjust my posture when walking on the sidewalk. While traveling on the train. Hell, while I am even on the bus. Why, just the other day, a random White woman approached me after having seen me interacting with my own kids to inquire on whether I would be willing to serve as a nanny to her well-behaved children. She proceeded to tell me how wonderful an opportunity this would be for me, as I would receive a generous salary that could certainly help my children get further in life. I would have said *fuck you fuck you fuck you*. But since we were in public, I chose a different response.

I quietly sat cross-legged in my seat.

References

Brownlee, T. (2015). 'Alienation and Recognition in Hegel's *Phenomenology of Spirit*'. *Philosophical Forum*. 46(4): pp. 377–396. https://doi.org/10.1111/phil.12084

Du Bois, W.E.B. (2014). *The Souls of Black Folk: The Oxford W. E. B. Du Bois*. Oxford, UK: Oxford University Press.

Ferdinand, R. (2021). *An Autoethnography of African American Motherhood: Things I Tell My Daughter*. New York: Routledge.

Harris-Perry, M. (2011). *Sister Citizen: Shame, Stereotypes, and Black Women in America*. New Haven: Yale University Press.

Hegel, G. (1977). *Phenomenology of Spirit*. Revised ed. Translated by Miller, A.V. New York: Oxford University Press.

Hurston, Z. (1998). *Their Eyes Were Watching God*. 2nd Edition. New York: Harper Perennial.

Jacobs, C. (2016). 'Developing the "Oppositional Gaze": Using Critical Media Pedagogy and Black Feminist Thought to Provoke Black Girls' Identity Development'. *The Journal of Negro Education*. 85(3): pp. 225–238. https://psycnet.apa.org/doi/10.7709/jnegroeducation.85.3.0225

McQueen, P. (no date). 'Social and Political Recognition'. In *The Internet Encyclopedia of Philosophy*. https://iep.utm.edu/recog_sp/#:~:text=For%20Hegel%2C%20recognition%20is%20the,conferring)%20appropriate%20forms%20of%20recognition (Accessed: 24 June 2022)

Morgan, M. and Bennett, D. (2006). 'Getting off of Black Women's Backs: Love Her or Leave Her Alone'. *Du Bois Review*. 3(2): pp. 485–502. https://doi.org/10.1017/S1742058X06060334

O'Grady, L. (2003). 'Olympia's Maid: Reclaiming Female Subjectivity'. In Jones, A. (ed.) *The Feminist and Visual Culture Reader*. pp. 174–187. New York: Routledge.

Perry, T. (2006). *Don't Make a Black Woman Take off Her Earrings: Medea's Uninhabited Commentaries on Love and Life*. New York: Riverhead Books.

Puff, S. (2014). 'Writing (about) the Black Female Body'. In Goldman, A. et al. (eds.) *Black Women and Popular Culture: The Conversation Continues*. pp. 225–246. Lanham, MD: Lexington Books.

Sinnerbrink, R. (2004). 'Recognitive Freedom: Hegel and the Problem of Recognition'. *Critical Horizons*. 5(1): pp. 271–295. https://doi.org/10.1163/1568516042653503

Spillers, H.J. (1996). 'All the Things You Could Be by Now, if Sigmund Freud's Wife Was Your Mother: Psychoanalysis and Race'. *Boundary 2*. 23(3): pp. 75–141. https://doi.org/10.2307/303639

Stewart, J. (2018). 'Hegel's Theory of Recognition and Philosophical Anthropology and the Ethical Challenges of a Globalized World'. *Philosophical Forum*. 49(4): pp. 467–481. No doi.

West, C. (2008). 'Mammy, Jezebel, Sapphire, and Their Homegirls: Developing an "Oppositional Gaze" Toward the Images of Black Women'. In Chrisler, J.C., Golden, C. and Rozee, P.D. (eds.) *Lectures on the Psychology of Women*. pp. 286–299. New York: McGraw-Hill.

Woodson, C. (2006). *The Mis-Education of the Negro*. 10th Edition. Trenton, NJ: Africa World Press.

6

THINKING-WITH

Paul Ricoeur Becomes Part of Mark Freeman

Mark Freeman

Introduction

Despite my having been a student of philosopher Paul Ricoeur in the 1980s and despite being profoundly affected by his courses, his mentorship, and his thinking, I rarely refer to him in much of the work I currently do. This isn't because his impact has diminished; on the contrary, his thinking – about time, narrative, and personal identity in particular – was, and remains, so significant that it has become part of the very fabric not only of my own thinking but my own way of being in the world. This means that much of what I think, and indeed much of who I am, is "derivative." Alongside Ricoeur is a whole host of others, all of whom have colonized me in one way or another: Martin Buber, William James, Emmanuel Levinas, Iris Murdoch, Simone Weil. Subtract them, and what is left? And what does this say about the nature of "originality" and selfhood? There is no getting around this colonization and appropriation, no getting around this inevitable plagiarism, no getting around the derivative nature of so much of our thinking and being, suffused as they are with the ideas and life-worlds and souls of others. But this is hardly reason for lamentation. On the contrary, it is reason for celebration and immense gratitude. There is no "thinking" per se. There is only thinking-with; and that, I think, is a quite beautiful thought, one I seek to explore in this humbling excursion into intellectual indebtedness and, by extension, the irrevocable otherness that exists within the boundaries of the self. Will I be able to determine, autoethnographically, the many and profound ways in which Paul Ricoeur has become part of me? Strictly speaking, no; that would require leaping out of myself and seeing myself

DOI: 10.4324/9781003274728-6

from afar, without his very influence. This caveat notwithstanding, I will do what I can to discern this influence and, in so doing, speak to the very nature of our originality, as thinkers and as persons.

The Beginning: Enchantment

I can remember strolling through a bookstore and seeing Paul Ricoeur's mammoth tome on Freud (1970). I can't remember how I stumbled upon his work 45 or so years ago. Nor can I recall whether I really had any idea what it was about. But having been introduced to phenomenology during my undergraduate years and having done some exploring of the field subsequently, I can recall the magic of seeing that magisterial work and, eventually, the magic of knowing I might be able to study with him at the University of Chicago, where I would be pursuing my doctorate in the Committee on Human Development. Relatively early during my time at Chicago, I came across the announcement of a two-semester seminar on "The Phenomenology of Time Consciousness" that Ricoeur would be teaching. I needed to apply, though, to get in. I so wish I could remember the plea I made; it may well have been pathetic, in a groveling sort of way. "Please! *Please!* My entire identity as a would-be phenomenological psychologist committed to probing the depths of being is at stake!" Whatever I said, I guess it worked because, not too long after, I was told I could enroll. What was my response at the time? I can't tell you for sure. But knowing my self of the time and my preferred vocabulary, it was probably something like, "Fuckin' A! I'm going to study with Paul Ricoeur!" What *was* all that? How did it come to acquire the magic it did? Why should I be so attracted to what he was doing? And his book covers? It just felt . . . large, like a kind of arrival, in a way: Whatever the reason, here was something I cared about, maybe more than anything else in the world of ideas I had ever cared about. Paul Ricoeur! Even the name seemed magical. *Ricoeur.* Like a cassoulet, accompanied by a rich Bordeaux. Or something like that. ("Fuckin' A!")

Ricoeur had joint appointments in the Department of Philosophy, in the Divinity School, and in the extraordinary Committee on Social Thought, which had been peopled by scholars ranging from T.S. Eliot to Saul Bellow to Hannah Arendt. I had actually thought about moving to the Committee at one point; it just seemed so much cooler than the (somewhat less cool) committee I was already on. But the reality was, I wasn't nearly as well-schooled in the history of ideas as the students in Social Thought were, and venturesome (and audacious) though I was, I really didn't know how I would fare in that program, whose requirements essentially consisted of students selecting and mastering some 15 classic texts of their choosing and then crafting a dissertation that would, ultimately, launch them into the coveted corridors of high-level academia. And so I stayed where I was. This must have been disappointing. Yes, I think it was. I didn't go for it. But between my somewhat frivolous ways (I turned out to be something of a model for grad students who wanted to be high achievers but also liked to party down) and the sheer inertia of my way of relating to the situation ("Should I take the time and energy required to convince these luminaries that I was worthy of their club? Nah."), I stayed the course.

But back to that seminar. It was a 12-student class, and all of the other students were either in Philosophy, the Divinity School, or the Committee on Social Thought. Fine, whatever. What exactly would we be reading? Plato. Plotinus. St. Augustine. Kant. I've heard of them! Good to be humbled now and then. I really didn't know shit about any of these. Which text did I want to do a presentation on? I can't help but think of one of our daughter's responses to occasional requests we made of her to do this or that. "How about no?" she would say. Part of me wanted to throttle her. And part of me wanted to gush with pride over the cynical little renegade we seemed to have spawned. Which text did I want to do a presentation on? How about none! Despite my New York Jewish background, I gravitated to that great, wicked bishop, St. Augustine, who seemed to be doing a deep dive into the muck of being. A psychologist is in our midst. They seem to know things about the mind – or at least think they do. I would have to discuss the justly famous Chapter 10 from *Confessions*, on the nature of memory. Can do! I just needed to know who St. Augustine was and why he had to confess. And Plato, Plotinus, Kant, and all the rest. Daunting. And exhilarating. If truth be told, I didn't really follow a lot of the material in that class, or at least I didn't "locate" it in the way that most others seemed able to do. But all things considered, it went well enough and paved the way to the next semester, when we would leap into modern continental philosophy, focusing on Husserl, Heidegger, and a bunch of other wordy sages. This time I would lead the seminar on Husserl's *Lectures on Internal Time Consciousness*. I thought this one went pretty well too, but I'm not sure, actually. It was high-level stuff, and although I was doing what I could to keep with Ricoeur and the budding philosophers and theologians in my midst, it's hard to say whether I really nailed it. How could I even know? This whole experience was good for me, not just because I got to study with Paul Ricoeur, learned a lot of stuff, and so on, but because I got a good, healthy dose of intellectual humility. Small fish in a big pond. Need to work harder. Need to hurl myself into these texts and ideas and allow them to speak to me. This was a different sphere of intellectual life, and for all the challenges it posed, I was indeed enchanted.

There was only one glitch that I can recall from around that time. The seminar met at night, and I stayed a bit later at one point to chat with Ricoeur about this and that. And then, generous and sycophantic person as I was at the time, I asked him whether he would like a lift home to his apartment a little ways away. Yes, he said, he would appreciate that. So there I was, cruising around Hyde Park with one of the preeminent intellectuals of our time, and we arrived at his street – which, unfortunately, I couldn't go down because it was one-way. "No worries!" he essentially said (before the term "No worries" existed). "It's just a little ways up the street. I'll be fine." Well, okay, I didn't want to be pushy, so I let him go. And as I let him go, I saw a car with a person inside, headlights off. *What do I do?!* He (she?) could be a killer, specializing in hermeneutic phenomenologists! (Fuck.) I went home. And of course, I couldn't help but fantasizing: *I just killed Paul Ricoeur.* Not a good night of sleep. Fortunately, I knew he was teaching a class in the morning (if he survived) and I raced to campus to see whether he was there. *He was! He's alive!* Have I ever felt such relief? Mainly, of course, because he had survived the walk home, but also because there wouldn't be the kinds of headlines I'd begun to imagine in my addled, semi-delirious mind: "Careless Grad Student Tragically Lures 20th Century Luminary to Untimely Demise." Or: "Couldn't Go Around the Block: Grad Student's Encounter with One-Way Street Leads to Horrific Dead End." And so on.

Audacity

Ricoeur survived, as did I – not just that dreadful, scary night but the two-semester seminar into the *aporias* (a favorite term of Ricoeur's) of temporality. *I can do this! What's next?!* Another two-semester course: *Historicity, History, and Narrative*, co-taught by Ricoeur, the philosopher Stephen Toulmin, and two theologians, David Tracy and Langdon Gilkey. Very different kind of course: classic historiography (e.g., Collingwood's *The Idea of History* [1946]), critical theory (e.g., Benjamin's "The Storyteller" [1968]), Holocaust memory and narrative (e.g., Emile Fackheim's *The Jewish Return into History* [1978]), and, not least, Freud (Why do I not remember what we read?). Phenomenal. And psychologist that I was (sort of), I would dig deep into psychoanalytic hermeneutics – so deep, in fact, that at one point I sent Ricoeur a lengthy piece on the development of his own thinking as well as a 69-page volcanic eruption of thought that included, among other things, some critical commentary on why I objected to his use of the word "proof" in his seminal article "The question of proof in Freud's psychoanalytic writing" (1977). *Wow.* I'll say it again: *Wow.* "Here you go, Paul. Take some of this!" *WTF?*

It's difficult to make sense of that phase. On the one hand, it absolutely reeks of audacity and presumptuousness. Mr. Intellectual! Mr. Big Word Writer! There had certainly been hints of some of this, but never in so bold and self-assured a way. Shocking, really. The more charitable version I might tell is that I was simply on fire with ideas, that something in me had awakened and, through the influence of Ricoeur and others, I had begun to come into my own as a thinker. Both of these versions seem right to me, and I could no doubt offer a few more too. Whatever it was, it was heady and amazing. What was also heady and amazing is that Ricoeur actually read these pieces and wrote back to me about them. Here is a copy of the letter.

Dear Mark,

I want to thank you for your two articles. You have done a fine job of interpreting my own "development"! Linking together the problematic of the text and that of action is certainly the best perspective on the present phase of my work. But I am much more interested in your suggestions concerning the theory of development itself. In this regard, Habermas's current work should be considered: for it is in the pragmatics of discourse that we find the key to the pragmatics...of action. One must then see how the distinction between syntax, semantics and pragmatics can be transferred into the field of action.

As for your paper on psychoanalytic hermeneutics, I was particularly interested in your discussion of Spence, Shafer, Habermas and myself and especially in your attempt to rectify the idea of life history by means of that of development, in order to find explanatory criteria lacking in the narrative version of psychoanalysis (pp. 51-9 or your article) As for my own use of the word "proof", I accept your criticism: I had in mind the notion of "vindication" rather than the demonstration of a truth claim. I am anxious to read the book you announce, History, Narrative and Life Span Developmental Knowledge. I wonder if it is possible to have a concept of development without a normative criteria of what human nature might be, in the sense of Freud's question Was ist Aufklärung? Should we not introduce a criteriology of the end of the state of puerility? Otherwise, the "marvelous plot of Oedipus" would not be the best plot to recount a certain phase of development. I wonder what you think of Kolberg in this respect.

Cordially,

Paul Ricoeur

FIGURE 6.1

May I say it again? *Wow*. If that doesn't send an academic pup into a swoon of ecstatic delight, I don't know what does. Me and Paul, besties. Not really. But still.

The piece on Ricoeur himself, titled "Paul Ricoeur on Interpretation: The Model of the Text and the Idea of Development," would find its way into the journal *Human Development* (Freeman, 1985a). That bloated piece on psychoanalytic hermeneutics would become "Psychoanalytic Narration and the Problem of Historical Knowledge," and would be published in *Psychoanalysis and Contemporary Thought* (Freeman, 1985b). Why do I mention this? Well, this is pretty shocking too. Both of these journals were top-of-the-line journals. I had already written one piece for *Human Development* (titled "History, Narrative, and Life-Span Developmental Knowledge" [Freeman, 1984], which Ricoeur had mistaken for a book), which the editor of the journal liked so much he asked me to do the piece on Ricoeur. As for the psychoanalysis article, I really do have to ask: What was it that possessed me to think that a (mere) grad student, with no direct experience of psychoanalysis at all, should share his thoughts with seasoned analysts and philosophers in one of the top journals in the field? Looking backward, it really seems kind of ridiculous and embarrassing. Audacity squared. But the fact is, people liked this stuff. *Paul Ricoeur* liked this stuff! I don't know where it all came from. I don't know where *I* came from! Was that who I actually was but didn't know it? Was I possessed, aloft on the wings of Large Ideas? Some of my fellow students on the Committee on Human Development at Chicago were taken aback by these achievements. They were mystified too. *How do you do this?* they wanted to know. I can't recall the tone with which I answered them, but the answer was essentially: I wrote it. And then I sent it. Freaky.

Lest the reader suppose I was just a cerebral egghead whose only fun was reading hermeneutic philosophy, I should note again that, alongside my burgeoning reputation as an audacious scholar, I had also acquired a reputation for being a work hard/play hard guy who somehow managed to fit a good deal of fun into his busy schedule. Through it all, I never took things too seriously and I liked to have a good time: played a lot of basketball, was a big fan of the Chicago Bears and Bulls, regularly hit the local blues bars, and loved to cut loose with some good food and drink. So there was that question again: *How do you do this?* they wanted to know. Well, I stop working. And then I go and do other stuff that's fun. That's how it was then, and that's how it is now.

Aporetic Labor

But I really haven't said anything about the substance of the ideas I was exploring. What was it that drew me to them in such a powerful, thoroughgoing way? There were several things, actually. In the Committee on Human Development, there had emerged a significant focus on interpretive issues, especially as they related to the idea of life history. There was even someone there at the time – a psychoanalyst named Bert Cohler – who had begun referring to narrative in his work in the early 1980s (e.g., Cohler, 1981). Alongside this focus on life history, the Committee also had a longstanding interest in and commitment to exploring the theory of development, especially in relation to the *telos* issue – that is, the issue of developmental ends. And so, at a relatively early stage in my time at Chicago, I found myself face to face with one of those *aporias* Ricoeur loved so well, which essentially had to do with reconciling, in some meaningful way, the backward movement of history with the forward movement of development (see Freeman, 1991, 1992, 1993; Freeman et al., 1986; Freeman and Robinson, 1990).

The first of these interests was founded on a relatively simple premise: As compared with the inchoate flux of immediate experience, looking backward gives us an after-the-fact, synoptic view of the past. "In the immediate moment," Georges Gusdorf (1980 [1956]) has written,

> the agitation of things ordinarily surrounds me too much for me to be able to see it in its entirety. Memory gives me a certain remove and allows me to take into consideration all the ins and outs of the matter, its context in time and space. As an aerial view sometimes reveals to an archeologist the direction of a road or a fortification or the map of a city invisible to someone on the ground, so the reconstruction in spirit of my destiny bares the major lines that I have failed to notice, the demands of the deepest values I hold that, without my being clearly aware of it, have determined my most decisive choices.
>
> *(p. 38)*

Memory, therefore:

> inverts the so-called natural order of time. By reading the end in the beginning and the beginning in the end, we learn also to read time itself backward, as the recapitulating of the initial conditions of a course of action in its terminal consequences.
>
> *(Ricoeur, 1981a, p. 176)*

Simple though this premise may be, its implications are anything but. Here, it may be useful to turn briefly to some of Ricoeur's work before his embrace of narrative in order to glean its philosophical foundations.

Consider in this context some passages from his seminal (1970) work on Freud. "Reflection," he writes, "must become interpretation because I cannot grasp the act of existing except in signs scattered in the world" (1970, p. 46). This marks Ricoeur's move from phenomenology to hermeneutics, the "prerogative" of reflection thus being displaced by the demand for interpretation. There is no "shortcut" to self-understanding through consciousness:

> There is no direct apprehension of the self by the self, no internal apperception or appropriation of the self's desire to exist through the shortcut of consciousness but only through the long road of the interpretation of signs.
>
> *(1974, p. 170)*

The Cartesian *cogito* thus emerges as a "wounded *cogito*, which posits but does not possess itself, which understands its originary truth only in and by the confession of the inadequation, the illusion, and the lie of existing consciousness" (p. 173).

There is more, though. For another related idea Ricoeur had been exploring, via Freud (e.g., 1962, 1966), is the idea that the meaning of a given incident or event is frequently *deferred* until some subsequent point in time. It's not only that self-understanding requires interpretation, therefore; it's that it requires "revisiting" the past and discerning meanings that may have been inaccessible in the immediate moment. It is precisely at this juncture that we can begin to see the seeds of Ricoeur's work on narrative. Strictly speaking, there is no revisiting the past, no returning to it "as it was," for the past can only be viewed, interpretively, from the vantage point of the present. What this in turn means is that self-understanding requires *narrative* interpretation, such that the events and experiences of times past become episodes in an evolving story.

Central to these ideas is "the positive and productive function of distanciation at the heart of the historicity of human experience" (1981b, pp. 131–132), that is, the process of stepping back from the ongoing flow of experience and discerning its movement and patterning – even, perhaps, its plot. Intriguing though this set of ideas is, it also opens the door to some problems that have bedeviled aspects of narrative inquiry. For, by virtue of the distanciation that is part and parcel of both memory and narrative, we are in fact a step removed from experience itself. Moreover, in discerning the movement and patterning of experience after the fact, we are inevitably engaging in a constructive – one might even say *fictive* – act. Here, then, we arrive at another *aporia*: the very distanciation that is the requisite condition for self-understanding would seem to lead, inevitably on some level, to the fictionalization of the past. As I put the matter several years ago in a piece on narrative hermeneutics:

> there is no wholly unvarnished narrative view but instead one that is always and irrevocably selective, partial, and, on some level, preconceived. Hence the aporia: the very condition of possibility for our discerning the contours of things from afar, via narrative, would seem to militate against this possibility due to the inevitable intrusion of the present upon the past. How can this be? And is there any way to move beyond this apparent, and very knotty, conundrum?
>
> *(Freeman, 2015, p. 238)*

There is a corollary to this conundrum as well. If in fact there is an inevitable intrusion of the present upon the past; if, moreover, this entails an inevitable element of narrative fictionalization; and if, finally, narratives are understood to be constitutive of self, does it not follow that the self is itself a fiction?

Consider once more the case of autobiographical understanding, a dialogical process wherein an "I" seeks to come to terms with its "me." We have already acknowledged that there is no view from nowhere, that there is an interpretive and perspectival dimension to any such encounter. As for the result, it's likely to be a narrative of one sort or another, a story that somehow binds together some set of life episodes in a more or less coherent way . . . And in regard to the notion that it might be considered a "text" of some sort, that may be fine – as long as we recognize that, unlike *actual* texts, of the sort we find on bookshelves, the ones that we interpret as we seek to come to terms with our own lives are in fact ones that, on some level, we ourselves have created (Freeman, 1997). The result, not surprisingly, is that not only are the stories we tell about ourselves best regarded (by some) as fictive constructions, or even outright fictions, but *so too are we*. How could it be otherwise? (Freeman, 2015, p. 238).

But we are not done yet. For, however fictive or even fictional the stories of our lives may be:

> it is patently the case that there are both utterly false life stories and utterly deluded selves, that is, people whose very sense of who and what they are flies in the face of what others know them to be. It is also the case that, occasionally, we selves seem to be able to move from a less truthful version of who and what we are to a more. That is, our self-interpretations don't merely change but somehow "progress"; there is insight, illumination, "development," perhaps even a movement in the direction of truth.
>
> *(pp. 238–239; see also Freeman, 2002a).*

Out of the fictive, it seems, there can be truth (Freeman, 2003). Indeed, it might plausibly be suggested that narrative fictionalization (or is it fictive narrativization?) is the requisite condition for the emergence of truth. How can this be?

Ricoeur's work (e.g., 1978, 1983) proved extremely helpful in this context. In his (1978) reflections on metaphor and poetic language, for instance, he acknowledges that, "At first glance poetry refers to nothing but itself." Appearances notwithstanding, however:

> Poetic language is no less about reality than any other use of language but refers to it by the means of a complex strategy which implies, as an essential component, a suspension and seemingly an abolition of the ordinary reference attached to descriptive language. This suspension, however, is only the negative condition of a second-order reference, of an indirect reference built on the ruins of the direct reference. This reference is called second-order reference only with respect to the primacy of the reference of ordinary language. For, in another respect, it constitutes the primordial reference to the extent that it suggests, reveals, unconceals – or whatever you say – the deep structures of reality to which we are related as mortals who are born into this world and who dwell in it for a while.
>
> *(p. 153)*

As Ricoeur goes on to suggest:

> In the same way as the self-abolition of literal sense is the negative condition for the emergence of the metaphorical sense, the suspension of the reference proper to ordinary descriptive language is the negative condition for the emergence of a more radical way of looking at things.
>
> *(pp. 153–154)*

In sum: metaphorical language, as it is found in poetry, fiction, and certain forms of nonfictional writing, can yield "deeper structures of reality" and deeper *truths* than the kind of ordinary descriptive language that is generally assumed to depict reality. One significant challenge of narrative inquiry, therefore, is precisely to tell these deeper truths in and through narrative *poiesis*. This struck me as especially fertile territory, and the result was a number of pieces (e.g., Freeman, 1999, 2000) in which I sought to explore it, which ultimately led what I would come to call "poetic science" (Freeman, 2007, 2011). But there was another challenge too, and it had to do with how these ideas might apply to my own life and writing. How might this notion of *poiesis* enter into the project of self-understanding?

Auto-Poiesis

As luck would have it, I was asked at one point to contribute a chapter to a volume that was to include life writing. It was to be a volume on fathers and sons, and we were asked to share a story about an event that involved the relationship between ourselves and either our father or our sons (if we had them). I had actually written about my relationship with my father once before, about ten years earlier, but it was in the context of a talk I gave at Holy Cross at the time I was appointed a class dean, an administrative position in which I followed the entering class across the four (or so) years of their time at the college. I was humbled by that appointment. And I also couldn't help but reflect on the fact that my father would never know I had come so far in my career and my life. He died back in 1975, the summer of my sophomore year at college, and although I had been a decent enough student, there was nary a hint at the time that I would find the path I did. It was shortly after his death that I began to truly connect to the world of ideas. In some ways, I think that world saved me, gave me the sort of energy and drive that had been missing. And so, I told the 600-plus students I was speaking to at the time, it can save you too. Would that my dad had been there to witness that event. He would have been shocked. And, of course, proud that his shaggy-maned, somewhat wild, lead-singer-in-a-band son would eventually amount to something.

When the invitation to write the aforementioned chapter arrived, I seized the moment and gladly accepted. But what would I write about? Certainly not the talk I gave; that would have been a little too gooey. The event I landed on was the four-hour ride he and I took from Binghamton to our home on Long Island following the end of my sophomore year. I couldn't claim that this ride home was some sort of extraordinary, watershed moment. It wasn't that; it was just a nice ride home during which we chatted, did some father-son sharing, and so on. The fact is, I hadn't spent four hours alone with him in years, maybe even ever, and I was glad for the opportunity. He seemed to be also. It was about a month later that he had a heart attack and left this earth. And me. So that ordinary ride home, which might scarcely have been remembered had he lived, became a kind of "monument," as I called it, something that had increased in value, so to speak, become precious.

As I had admitted in the piece, it is possible that I was projecting meaning onto this incident, perhaps as a way of reassuring myself that it was in fact monumental in its way. Here is how I put the matter:

> It could be that, in order for me to fend off the grim reality of my father having died without our ever really having the opportunity to make contact, I had to somehow convince myself that we did. After twenty

years, something had happened, a breakthrough; boy, was I lucky . . . .
Similarly, perhaps I have merely devised a means, through this yarn, to
assuage some of my guilt and shame over the fact that, at the time of his
death, I had done decidedly less than my brothers to make him proud.
Maybe I had to convince myself that he could see that I was finally getting it together, that I had some promise and potential. To admit that he
had seen nothing of the sort would have been too painful, too wasteful.
Each of these interpretations presume that I had somehow foisted meaning onto that car ride, using it as a means to ensure that there was – or
that there appeared to be – some redeeming value to our lives together.
I could have chosen any one of a number of things to serve in this role.
Not unlike the way dreams seem to work, according to Freud at any rate,
maybe I just latched onto to this particular scene because it somehow
allowed me to do what was necessary to carry on with some measure of
self-affirmation: I think I can make something of that car ride.

(Freeman, 2002b, pp. 172–173)

But there was another way to think about all this too, and it was at this juncture that I turned to the idea of *poiesis*. As I went on to write:

It is sometimes said that poetry seeks to make present what is absent in
our ordinary, everyday encounters with the world. Or, to put the matter
more philosophically, it is a making-present of the world in its absence.
It is thus seen to provide a kind of "supplement" to ordinary experience,
serving to draw out features of the world that would otherwise go unnoticed. But there is a kind of puzzle at work here. If it is assumed that
these features go totally unnoticed and that absence is essentially complete, then poetry can be nothing more than the fashioning of illusions,
replacing absence with presence . . . .
    But it could also be that absence is not complete and that the world of
ordinary experience bears within its absence a certain presence, a limited presence, which the poet, in turn, must try to bring to light.

(p. 173)

Seamus Heaney (1995) has written about the "redressing" effect of poetry
in this context, which "comes from its being a glimpsed alternative, a revelation of potential that is denied or constantly threatened by circumstances"
(p. 4). And so, I suggested, that's what seemed to have happened as I looked
back on that fateful day. "What my dad's death seemed to do," I wrote:

was activate the poetic function of memory, such that I would return to
that ride home and try to disclose what was there, waiting. The incident
itself, as a historical event, was filled with a kind of diffuse, unspecified

potential. It could have been played out in a wide variety of different ways, from the most ordinary and unmemorable all the way to the most extraordinary and memorable; it all depends on what follows. The reason the balance has in this case been tipped to the latter is clear enough. If only that ride could have remained in its ordinariness, pleasant and good, father and son, going home for the summer.

(Freeman, 2002b, p. 174)

Indeed.

I would actually revisit that incident some years later. Shortly before leaving for a conference on narrative down in Texas, my daughter Brenna was diagnosed with pneumonia. Admittedly:

> It's not as if I was a perpetual mess for the two days that followed the diagnosis. The doctor didn't seem too concerned and, by and large, it was life as usual – permeated by an extra load of worry (not to mention guilt over leaving my suffering family behind for the sake of "narrative," important though it is) but not radically different than most other days. The next night, as ever, my wife and I were watching the 10 o'clock news and we learned that a 10-year-old girl, from Boston (less than an hour away), had suddenly died. She had had flulike symptoms and been taken to the hospital just a day earlier – where nothing out of the ordinary had been diagnosed – and 24 hours later she was, mysteriously, especially given the speed with which her young body had been ravaged and destroyed, gone. Her beautiful smiling face was on a little box on the side of the TV screen as the newscaster reviewed her fate. It was probably one of those photos they take of kids in school where they wear their Sunday dresses or their clip-on ties . . . . Not a good piece of news to watch before leaving for the dry plains of Lubbock, Texas.

Brenna seemed to look a little better the morning I was to leave. Not unlike the way I had thought about the ride home with my dad, that morning wasn't particularly intense and I didn't want to make it seem any more dramatic than it was:

> Things changed, though, for a few moments, as I looked at my wife and Brenna standing in the doorway, looking at me presumably – though I actually didn't know if they could see me behind the smoky glass of the limo van. When I waved, they didn't wave back. There they were, the two of them, one taller and ruddy, the other shorter and pasty, soon to recede from view.

(Freeman, 2003, p. 122)

I was freaked. And as I thought more later on about what why I had been as freaked as I was, I had an insight:

> It could very well be, I realized, that there was some connection, that there *is* some connection . . . between how I had responded to her as I drove away in the van and what had happened that summer after my sophomore year: it could be, it can always be, the last time.

And it could very well be, I surmised, that "that earlier wound is fresher and more powerful than I sometimes assume and has created, on the fringes of consciousness, a certain fragility and uncertainty in how I think and feel about people I care for" (p. 124).

A story was in the making. Ricoeur (1991) speaks of the idea of "life as a story in its nascent state . . . *an activity and a passion in search of a narrative*" and thus seeks "to grant to experience as such a virtual narrativity which stems not from the projection of literature onto life, but which constitutes a genuine demand for narrative" (p. 29). Yes, here was exactly this sort of demand. As he goes on to ask, "are we not inclined to see in a chain of episodes in our own life something like *stories that have not yet been told*, stories that demand to be told, stories that offer points of anchorage for the narrative?" As against those who considered narrative to be some sort of fictive imposition on the past, Ricoeur was insisting here that experience and narrative were in fact organically related to one another. We are "entangled" in stories, as he put it; narrating is a secondary process "grafted" onto this entanglement. "Recounting, following, understanding stories is then simply the continuation of these unspoken stories" (p. 30).

Well, that's pretty much how I was thinking about all this too! And it had been that way from the get-go (e.g., Freeman, 1985b), which is why I had been critical of those who adopted the "imposition" thesis and essentially severed narrative from the fabric of experience itself. How, though, had I come to think this way? Was it that Ricoeur had essentially "taught" me to think this way? Was it that I *already* thought this way and that he gave me words that could help me articulate my own thinking? Why did I connect to his way of thinking about the world in the way that I did? Why not Derrida or Foucault or the many others I was reading at the time? Why did his work and his way of being as a philosopher "take" in the way it did? I don't really know. There's an aspect of it that seems almost . . . miraculous in a way – a gift, unsought and unbidden, one that gave me a whole world to inhabit. How curious that this ostensibly new world "fit" in the way it did.

Looking Backward and Moving Forward

There is still more, and it calls for one final story. The year was 2005, and I was invited to Israel to speak at the Institute for Advanced Studies at Hebrew University. The talk was titled "From Past to Future, From Self to Other: Rethinking the Idea of Development via Narrative." It began as follows:

> My main purpose in the paper was to try to relate two terms that, on the face of it, would seem either unrelated or, more severely, unrelatable. These two terms are *development* and *narrative*. The reason for the difficulty of relating these two terms is clear enough: while "development" generally connotes movement forward in time and would thus seem to be an essentially *prospective* concept, "narrative" generally connotes movement backward in time and would thus seem to be an essentially *retrospective* concept. As is often the case, though, that which initially seems clear enough turns out to be much more complicated.
>
> *(Freeman, 2005)*

I then proceeded to share a passage from the very first piece I published (Freeman, 1984), in which I had written:

> Although narration moves inescapably backward in its concern with the understanding of the past-in-the-present, the view of development that derives from it can retain a focus on the forward movement that is rendered in the texts provided. Thus, perhaps paradoxically, it is out of retrospection that a project, an approximation toward desired ends, can be revealed. The shape that emerges out of the past extends itself into the future.
>
> *(p. 17)*

This, I went on to say, was not unrelated to what Ricoeur, in his extraordinary book on Freud (1970), had referred to as the "dialectic of archeology and teleology."

Not unrelated, indeed. For what Ricoeur had essentially sought to do in that book was see in Freud's psychical archeology, wherein the buried fragments of the past might be excavated, a parallel movement forward, into the future, Hegel-style. I suppose one could say that I "took" this idea from Ricoeur. But that wouldn't be quite right. Instead, I see the connection here as one of those instances in which his own thinking seemed so compelling, and so *right*, that it became part of my thinking – and part of *me* – too.

When I arrived in Jerusalem early in the morning, I had some coffee and began reading the newspaper, only to learn that Ricoeur had died. I therefore added a brief preface to the paper I was to give later that week:

> It's strange – and somewhat coincidental – that I should be giving this particular talk just a few days after the death of the philosopher Paul Ricoeur, who was 92. As you will see, some of the issues I raise in the paper, early on especially, bring me back quite a number of years, to when I was a student of his, trying to think through some difficult issues. With this in mind, I'd like to offer the hope that the present paper, in some small way, honors his memory and is faithful to some of the ideas he found important.

This "coincidence" also seemed miraculous in its way. It had been some time since I had tried to work through the relationship between narrative and development. My concerns had taken me elsewhere for a time, but for this particular event, I found myself wanting to return to some of that earlier thinking – and to Ricoeur. And so I did. The only change I made to the paper I had prepared was the preface and the concluding paragraph, in which I wrote:

> Let me close by turning to some words that serve as a fitting epitaph to what I've been exploring here today. It's from the article about Paul Ricoeur's death I read in *The Jerusalem Post* the morning I arrived. The words are from an interview in *Le Monde* from last year: If I had to lay out my own vision of the world . . . I would say: Given the place where I was born, the culture I received, what I read, what I learned [and] what I thought about, there exists for me a result that constitutes, here and now, the best thing to do . . . . I call it 'the action that suits.' "

Need I say more?

References

Benjamin, W. (1968). *Illuminations*. New York: Harcourt, Brace & World.

Cohler, B.J. (1981). 'Personal Narrative and Life Course'. In Brim, O.G. and Kagan, J. (eds.) *Life-Span Development and Behavior*. Vol. 4. pp. 205–241. Cambridge, MA: Harvard University Press.

Collingood, R.G. (1946). *The Idea of History*. Oxford, UK: Oxford University Press.

Fackenheim, E. (1978). *The Jewish Return into History: Reflections in the Age of Auschwitz and a New Jerusalem*. New York: Schocken.

Freeman, M. (1984). 'History, Narrative, and Life-Span Developmental Knowledge'. *Human Development*. 27(1): pp. 1–19. https://doi.org/10.1159/000272899

Freeman, M. (1985a). 'Paul Ricoeur on Interpretation: The Model of the Text and the Idea of Development'. *Human Development*. 28: pp. 295–312. Paul Ricœur on Interpretation: The Model of the Text and the Idea of Development on JSTOR.

Freeman, M. (1985b). 'Psychoanalytic Narration and the Problem of Historical Knowledge'. *Psychoanalysis and Contemporary Thought*. 8(2): pp. 133–182.

Freeman, M. (1991). 'Rewriting the Self: Development as Moral Practice'. In Tappan, M.B. and Packer, M.J. (eds.) *Narrative Approaches to Moral Development. New Directions for Child Development*. 54: pp. 83–101. https://doi.org/10.1002/cd.23219915407

Freeman, M. (1992). 'Self as Narrative: The Place of Life History in Studying the Life-Span'. In Brinthaupt, T. and Lipka, R. (eds.) *The Self: Definitional and Methodological Issues*. pp. 15–43. Albany, NY: SUNY.

Freeman, M. (1993). *Rewriting the Self: History, Memory, Narrative*. London: Routledge.

Freeman, M. (1997). 'Death, Narrative Integrity, and the Radical Challenge of Self-Understanding: A Reading of Tolstoy's *Death of Ivan Ilych*'. *Ageing and Society*. 17(4): pp. 373–398. https://doi.org/10.1017/S0144686X97006508

Freeman, M. (1999). 'Life Narratives, the Poetics of Selfhood, and the Redefinition of Psychological Theory'. In Maiers, W.B., Bayer, B., Esgalhado, R. and Jorna, S.E. (eds.) *Challenges to Theoretical Psychology*. pp. 245–250. North York, ON: Captus.

Freeman, M. (2000). 'Theory Beyond Theory'. *Theory & Psychology*. 10(1): pp. 71–77. https://doi.org/10.1177/0959354300010001601

Freeman, M. (2002a). 'The Burden of Truth: Psychoanalytic *Poiesis* and Narrative Understanding'. In Patterson, W. (ed.) *Strategic Narrative: New Perspectives on the Power of Personal and Cultural Stories*. pp. 9–27. Lanham, MD: Lexington Books.

Freeman, M. (2002b). 'The Presence of What is Missing: Memory, Poetry, and the Ride Home'. In Pellegrini, R.J. and Sarbin, T.R. (eds.) *Between Fathers and Sons: Critical Incident Narratives in the Development of Men's Lives*. pp. 165–176. Binghamton, NY: Haworth.

Freeman, M. (2003). 'Rethinking the Fictive, Reclaiming the Real: Autobiography, Narrative Time, and the Burden of Truth'. In Fireman, G., McVay, T. and Flanagan, O. (eds.) *Narrative and Consciousness: Literature, Psychology, and the Brain*. pp. 115–128. New York: Oxford University Press.

Freeman, M. (2005). 'From Past to Future, from Self to Other: Rethinking the Idea of Development Via Narrative'. Presented at conference on The Narrative Turn in the Social Sciences: Implications and Promise for the 21st Century, Institute for Advanced Studies, Hebrew University, Israel.

Freeman, M. (2007). 'Psychoanalysis, Narrative Psychology, and the Meaning of "Science."' *Psychoanalytic Inquiry*. 27(5): pp. 583–601. http://dx.doi.org/10.1080/07351690701468124

Freeman, M. (2011). 'Toward Poetic Science'. *Integrative Psychological and Behavioral Science*. 45(4): pp. 389–396. https://doi.org/10.1007/s12124-011-9171-x

Freeman, M. (2015). 'Narrative Hermeneutics'. In Martin, J., Sugarman, J. and Slaney, K.L. (eds.) *The Wiley Handbook of Theoretical and Philosophical Psychology:*

Methods, Approaches, and New Directions for Social Sciences. pp. 234–247. Chichester, West Sussex, UK: Wiley Blackwell.

Freeman, M., Csikszentmihalyi, M. and Larson, R. (1986). 'Adolescence and Its Recollection: Toward an Interpretive Model of Development'. *Merrill-Palmer Quarterly*. 32(2): pp. 167–185. www.jstor.org/stable/23086182

Freeman, M. and Robinson, R. (1990). 'The Development within: An Alternative Approach to the Study of Lives'. *New Ideas in Psychology*. 8(1): pp. 53–72. https://doi.org/10.1016/0732-118X(90)90026-X

Freud, S. (1962). 'Further Remarks on the Neuro-Psychoses of Defense'. In *Standard Edition III*. London: Hogarth. (originally 1896).

Freud, S. (1966). 'Project for a Scientific Psychology'. In *Standard Edition 1*. London: Hogarth. (originally 1895).

Gusdorf, G. (1980). 'Conditions and Limits of Autobiography'. In Olney, J. (ed.) *Autobiography: Essays Theoretical and Critical*. pp. 28–48. Princeton, NJ: Princeton University Press.

Heaney, S. (1995). *The Redress of Poetry*. New York: The Noonday Press.

Ricoeur, P. (1970). *Freud and Philosophy: An Essay on Interpretation*. New Haven, CT: Yale University Press.

Ricoeur, P. (1974). *The Conflict of Interpretations*. Evanston, IL: Northwestern University Press.

Ricoeur, P. (1977). 'The Question of Proof in Freud's Psychoanalytic Writings'. *Journal of the American Psychoanalytic Association*. 25: pp. 835–872. https://doi.org/10.1177/000306517702500404

Ricoeur, P. (1978). 'The Metaphorical Process as Cognition, Imagination, and Feeling'. *Critical Inquiry*. 5(1): pp. 143–159. https://doi.org/10.1086/447977

Ricoeur, P. (1981a). 'Narrative Time'. In Mitchell, W.J.T. (ed.) *On Narrative*. pp. 165–186. Chicago, IL: University of Chicago Press.

Ricoeur, P. (1981b). *Hermeneutics and the Human Sciences*. Cambridge, UK: Cambridge University Press.

Ricoeur, P. (1983). 'Can Fictional Narratives Be True?' *Analecta Husserliana*. 14: pp. 3–19. https://doi.org/10.1007/978-94-009-6969-8_1

Ricoeur, P. (1991). 'Life in Quest of Narrative'. In Wood, D. (ed.) *On Paul Ricoeur: Narrative and Interpretation*. pp. 20–33. London: Routledge.

7

IN SEARCH OF MY NARRATIVE CHARACTER

A Philosophical Autoethnography

Alec Grant

Introduction

Engaging in hindsight work is a productive way of uncovering the nature of our individual characters over time. According to my understanding of Freeman (2010), the purpose of such work is to demystify the manifest content of seemingly disparate memories. This enables the reflexive discernment of how these may be connected, which in turn might point to deeper, increasingly sophisticated understandings about the meaning and moral significance of our individual lives. For the purposes of this chapter, I use the concept "character" to capture this – always provisional and flexible – end point in the process of narrative self-exploration.

Three memories have stood out in my consciousness over the years. As memories go, many would judge them unremarkable. However, thematically connected to other memories in my life in terms of my enduring dispositional and behavioural tendencies, they have punctuated the grammar of my existence in simultaneously disturbing and instructive ways. I'll present them in storied form, in boxed text sequence. Each story will be followed by a gradually developing discussion in which I'll address emerging philosophical issues. This will enable me to reach the provisional but personally compelling conclusion that my character is effectively "trickster-carnivalesque."

In closing my chapter, I'll critically evaluate its storied content against the relational ethical assumptions of mainstream qualitative inquiry informing naïve humanist-informed autoethnography. I'll then subject my discussion

DOI: 10.4324/9781003274728-7

to critical scrutiny from the philosophy of autobiography. Finally, I'll briefly evaluate the moral status of my trickster identity in the context of dominant cultural narratives.

Implied in this are my aims for crafting the chapter. Over the course of writing it, approaching, and reaching 70 years of age, I recognise more acutely than earlier in my life that narrative time is at the heart of my existence. Relatedly, I *feel* the stark existential need to use autoethnography purposefully before that time, my time, runs out (Adams et al., 2021; Améry, 1994). I've a pressing developmental motivation to sharpen and deepen my philosophical awareness of the person I present to myself and the world. In so doing, I also wish, as much as is possible, to cleanse my memories of their lingering negative residue – particularly embarrassment, anger, and toxic time-wasting. These feelings, implicit to varying degrees and permutations across all three of my storied memories are expressed most strongly in the first one here.

Committees and Non-Professing Professors: 1997–2017

With a newly minted PhD, I started my first university lecturer job in 1997. In retrospect, it was naïve of me to hope for debating societies, small tutorials, and enthusiastic students hungry to engage with knowledge for its own sake. It wasn't. It was mostly COMMITTEES – to my mind the neoliberal infrastructural mechanism dedicated to maintaining and concealing the deceit of training masquerading as critical higher education in UK healthcare. I quickly realised that I needed to add COMMITTEES to my list of pointless, irritating, and tedious events I was born never to belong in. By contrast, they seemed to have underwear-soaking orgasmic appeal among those for whom COMMITTEES functioned as ideal platforms for shameless, promotion-hungry narcissism. As a cynical and bored participant-observer cum forced-witness, such displays made me want to scream "WHY DON'T YOU ALL SHUT THE FUCK UP. YOU'RE TALKING FUCKING NONSENSE, YOU BUNCH OF PHONEY BASTARDS!"

And the years passed, with few stimulating ideas ever being discussed. Much of the time my boredom manifested as resentful sluggishness. I also found that, sadly – with some exceptions – I didn't have vast reserves of magnanimity for many of the students whose minds I was supposed to nurture. This wasn't really their fault as we were all – students and university staff alike – caught up in the neoliberal student recruitment agenda. At least in the UK, this is based more on money-generating "bums on seats" and discomfort-free student credentialism than intellectual promise and enthusiasm. Once, in a class I led to welcome new students, a young woman made the following disclosure: "I don't like reading books, but I love watching television." I was tempted to ask her what made her want to come to university as opposed to an undemanding horizontal life as a couch potato? Another lad asked me in a one-to-one tutorial, "what's the minimum amount of reading I need to do to pass this course?" I responded by telling him that at that moment I wanted to vomit all over his shoes.

As for the academic staff, it angered me that some greasy pole climbers who got their careerist rocks off on the COMMITTEES I loathed were being promoted to professor grades. In my estimation neoliberal educational technocrats rather than public intellectuals, they never seemed to *profess* anything – in the sense of passionately associating themselves with standpoint positions.

Despite all of this, along the way I fortunately managed to land the plum title of Reader (professor without a chair). This proved to be a coup as my non-professing professor colleagues were having to sit on even more COMMITTEES, while I found I could now mostly avoid them, which made me joyful. Since no one locally seemed to know what the role of a Reader was beyond its abstract conceptualisation, I took it upon myself to shape it in my own emerging image. I had long since made a home for myself in narrative inquiry, and had a developing international reputation, particularly in autoethnography. Nobody complained that I spent most of my time working from home, reading, writing, and mentoring up-and-coming autoethnographically-talented people across the world. Or perhaps they didn't notice or find this of interest. Serious scholarly activity, and how people went about this, was way down the scale of organisational importance. It seems to be the case that in many UK universities you can have the status of a medieval serf in your own institution and be an academic rock star outside of it.

Unfortunately, I was still called in to regular meetings with my insecure, micromanaging Head of School. A Gucci-accessorised, non-professing professor and enthusiastic COMMITTEE prima donna, with a predictably unreflexive stance on what constituted "professionalism," she often glowered disapprovingly at my earrings, tattoos, and choice of clothes. She had earlier made a point of advising me to return to conventional scholarship and research, as continuing with autoethnography was going to damage my career, apparently (she was really talking about *her* career, as she regarded having an autoethnographer in her school bad for her imagined professional image). In her blinkered eyes, "my career" should exclusively be focused on the former, which I'd long grown tired of. So, I immediately thought, "Yesssss! I'm going to write loads more autoethnography. Forever. Thank you for being such a wonderfully consistent negative role model!"

Self, Memory, Time, and Truth

In helpful feedback from Tony Adams on a very early draft of this chapter, I was alerted to Mark Freeman's excellent *Hindsight* text (Freeman, 2010). I connected with what I read as his sustained critique of the sovereign, liberal-humanist self. I've never felt that I've exactly coincided with myself; myriad forces have always shaped me, both preceding and exceeding me. Troubling popular contemporary cultural notions of personal choice and transparent self-invention, the nature, and origins of many of these forces will always elude me.

The moral philosopher Alasdair MacIntyre (1981) argues that we are all born into, and co-evolve with, culturally coherent storylines. In Freeman's terms, the narrative force of these craft me as an "historical self," or – echoing Bergson (2002) – a self in the flow of time, promising meaning for the moral significance of my life as far as I can apprehend this. I'm convinced by Freeman's argument that I've more chance of grasping the significance of relatively recent storylines in purposeful reflective hindsight afforded by the passage of time. In contrast, storylines increasingly temporally distant – forming part of, and exceeding, my narrative unconsciousness – will go unrecognised, despite being "silently" instrumental in my shaping.

Whenever I've brought my memories to mind over the years since the events on which they are based occurred, their meaning and significance have frequently qualitatively changed. These memories, although lacking detailed historical accuracy, do increasingly seem to me to be connected as my personal moral storyline, supporting Freeman's thesis. With "truth" as a significant background troubling issue in autoethnography (Tullis Owen et al., 2009), to clarify further the nature and significance of my personal memories and the importance of hindsight work in my moral development, I'm pointed in the direction of important differences between narrative and historical life, truth, and, by implication, time.

Freeman (2010, pp. 176–177) argues that:

> the narrated life is the examined life . . . one steps out from the flow of things and seeks to become more conscious of one's existence . . . auto-biographical narratives are not only about what happened when . . . but also about how to live, and whether the life is a good one.

In line with Freeman's thesis, I take *historical truth* to mean what happened over the course of my existence. In contrast, the *narrative truth* of my life is theoretically discernible through the process of looking back at past events, to recognise their possible connections and moral significance. This amounts to "demystification" of my historical past. However, because the moral significance of my past is always evolving, never closed, and determinate, the narrative truth of my life remains open-ended, unfinalised, partial, and provisional. Some aspects of it may be either deferred, refused, falsified, or denied.

In terms of historical truth, I did work at that university. I did attend those committees, while trying to avoid them as much as I possibly could. I did want to scream abusive profanities, while – mostly – restraining myself. I did (and still do) feel little respect for COMMITTEE, non-professing, professors. My views on this issue are in the public domain (Grant, 2017), which is testimony to my attempt to *live* an academic life autoethnographically in terms of what has been described as "feral pedagogy" (Holman Jones, 2021) (I understand this term to mean integrity-grounded, conscientious scholarship that frees itself from, and resists as much as is possible, the centripetal pull back into neoliberal academic normativity). The meeting with my Head of School who tried to dissuade me from writing autoethnography really happened. However, in line with Freeman's thesis, the way I've storied this memory, shifting it from historical to narrative truth, is necessarily creatively and imaginatively shaped.

This points to a personal social-psychological agenda which arguably has an evolutionary basis. I'll clarify both these points later, but for the moment my second story further illustrates the differences between dry historical and creative narrative truth.

Monumental Ineptitude and Historical Men: 1980–1985

At the turn of this present century, I sat on a train going through a familiar town in England. Images flooded back of playing my violin in a folk club there 20 years earlier, and shortly after, out of curiosity, I decided to pay the club a visit. The original members – the stalwarts – were still there. The idea of doing any one thing again and again for ever always fills me with dread. Doing this in a folk club adds for me a layer of nerdiness that might best be described as "drerdiness." Glued, as it were, to the floor of the club since 1980 were the same (mostly) men, who had morphed from long hair, slim bodies, and Levis into corpulent, clean-shaven, and smart-but-casual middle and old age. Earrings, once the symbol of the culturally rebellious male folky were mostly gone, but the need for an acoustic Neverland wasn't, despite this having become increasingly arthritic.

Back in the 1980s there was a short, self-satisfied man in the club, whose face always seemed switched to default smug. He kept buttonholing me to bring me up to speed with his life. I suppose he imagined, or hoped, that I was interested. Or perhaps he considered me a friend, although I had to focus hard to see him on account of his beigeness. I began to notice that he said "monumental ineptitude" a lot – for example, "The problem with my job is the monumental ineptitude of my manager." He said this phrase to me every week. He said it so much, in so many different contexts, that after a while his words lost all sensible meaning. The syllables in "monumental ineptitude" started to move around, shape-shift, morph and neologize, forming new brain-assaulting words and phrases. As a result, it sometimes sounded like he might be telling me about "mental neptune moments," or "peptidal mutant demons," or "attitudinal lamenting." Him speaking *at* me put me in mind of dripping water torture, except that it was a "monumental ineptitude" auditory and psychic assault instead of water drops regularly falling on one specific part of my head.

Over time I developed a deep hatred for him, although I never told him how I felt. This was partly because when I purposefully looked for him, he wasn't there. Perhaps I looked too hard and should have instead tried to catch him in my peripheral vision. Or maybe he really was there but had simply blended into the background in a kind of colourless, stick-insecty way. I began to believe that he wanted to destroy me by saying "monumental ineptitude" only to me and to no other sentient entity in the entire universe. Him and "monumental ineptitude" gradually came to be fused with folk clubs in my phenomenological world. Not just the folk club we both attended, but every folk club in England, and perhaps beyond. So, the hybrid phenomenon I came to fear and loathe was *folk clubs-monumental ineptitude*. This scared and frightened me because it signalled a horrible Nietzschean eternal recurrence – a personally calamitous Groundhog Day where traditional music met diminutive, psychologically tormenting bore.

The last straw came on the night I went to the club and spotted a young man with a very long beard. He was smoking a clay pipe and wearing velvet knee breeches and a pristine white, frilly, puffed-sleeve blouson, which looked as if it had lain untouched in a chest in an attic of a stately home for three centuries. All that was missing from his weird ensemble was a tricorn hat. I wanted to scream. I thought that maybe I was hallucinating, but he was real enough. As if *folk clubs-monumental ineptitude* wasn't an intolerable burden, I now had to carry *folk clubs-monumental ineptitude-early modern period man*. Strangely, I found myself desperately wanting to know him. What was his day job? Did he have one? Could anyone else see him, or just me? Did he dress and act like a seriously odd anachronism all the time or only on Friday nights? Did his partner, or mother, or father, or aunt, or friends worry about him? Did he embarrass them? Were they glad that he went to places they didn't? What was his name? Was it Jim, or Bill, or Mike, or Dave? Or was it

Jacob? Ichabod? Zacharia? Zephod? Jeremiah? Ezra? Elias? Gideon? Titus? Did he ever watch television? Did he own a television? Did he know what a television was? Did he know what electricity was? What were his opinions on football, dental hygiene, Indian food, zoos, or the promise of bicycle lanes on English roads? Did he have any opinions? Being asked these questions might have upset him in unpredictable ways, so I never did find out.

The Storied Self

Monumental ineptitude man and early modern period man really existed. However, on top of its lampooning satire, the layer of magical realism in this story distinguishes it from my undoubtedly more mundane times in English folk clubs. Relative to how I really experienced them 40 years ago, the picture of the characters I've presented naturally raises the question for me about the relationship between memory and the storied self.

From the perspective of narrative truth, Freeman argues that the moral awareness provided by hindsight aided by the imagination comes to out-weigh pedantic obsessing about how historically true memories are. Such is the nature of memory over time, that creative "autobiographical poiesis" becomes necessary for its narrative recounting (Freeman, 2010, p. 183). Historically accurate memories gradually weaken and drop out of con-sciousness. In keeping with the nature of the shaping of the individual nar-rative self in the flow of time, argued earlier, these are replaced by "short-hand" versions:

> The way we remember, and the way we tell, is suffused with conven-tions, with schematic, even stereotypical, renditions of the personal past, derived from countless sources, many of which are external to our own personal experience.
>
> *(p. 157)*

So, the default use of culturally and historically-shaped memory recounting might be described as a creative mixture of bespoke and off-the-peg *narra-tive tailoring* of individual memories.

Daniel Dennett (1993) argues, from an evolutionary philosophical stand-point, that there are good reasons behind our emergence as memory-based creative storytellers within the flow of history. He believes that human storied words are "potent elements of our environment that we (weave) like spiderwebs into self-protective strings of narrative" (p. 417). Comple-menting Freeman's creative hindsight thesis, Dennett asserts that – for each of us – at some point in this process our words take over and create us. I recount memories that were once grounded in events in my past. These have been co-shaped by extra layers of the historical storylines I've been born into, and the more contemporary ones to which I've been socialised (Freeman, 2010), all embellished in my own satirical and sardonic, magical realist style. In so recounting, I've effectively forgotten large chunks of my historical past and have re-written this as my working narrative truth. This functions in the service of my day-to-day positive self-presentation. Hopefully, through hindsight work, this can in principle, with increasing levels of sophistication, be at least partially transformed into inferences about my moral character.

Dennett argues that our success as a species has in large part been down to our ability to tell and share stories. At the level of the individual, these have the dual social-psychological function of *creation* and *protection*, whether in the banal day-to-day intra- and interactional sense of dialoguing with oneself and others, or in the more formal sense of doing autoethnography. Either way, my repeated telling of this inventively developing story over the years serves in the continual, self-protective crafting of the self that is me. This increases its interest value and the uniqueness of the storied personal and relational environment through which the self-as-me is constituted. To put this in a more concise way, to keep it fresh and distinct, my remembered and recounted past regularly receives a creative psychological makeover.

In this regard, like everyone else, I function in Dennett's words as my own "centre of narrative gravity," producing and performing my self as a subject position in an "infinite web of discourses" (pp. 410–411). Such *selfing*, put in terms of Freeman's thesis, draws and builds on innumerable storylines, and this is *all* that "my self" is, since "The limits of my stories are the limits of my world" (Loy, 2010, p. 5). To labour the point because it's an important one, like all other people, I build – spiderweb-like and defensively – *my self as storied environment* in the tales I tell about my past experiences in life. The trick for me, and by extension others with a methodological, theoretical, and personal investment in working with "lived experience," is in grasping the significance of these tales for individual moral development and character discernment.

To summarise my developing position at this point in the discussion, I understand my life story to be comprised of constantly revised and re-embellished personal memories. It functions like a porous narrative exoskeleton between the mutual flow, or two-way conduit, of my interior and external environmental worlds. Some of my stories are time-shared with other people. The origins of many of these stories are long lost in the flow of historical and narrative time. The accessible memories upon which my storied self is based need updating in narrative time, to creatively compensate for the specific details of past events dropping out of my consciousness and/or becoming schematised and stereotyped. In my case, the rewriting of my personal history is also psychologically motivated in positioning me apart from, and against, those whom I negatively and defensively lampoon and subject to magical realist representation. This last point is evident in the first two of my stories, and in this final one.

The Talking Tomcats of Totnes: 1968–1973

At the tail end of my adolescence, although the process of gradually ebbing credulity that comes with age and experience had kicked in, I was still sufficiently naïve to swallow a lot of 1960s countercultural nonsense. Temperamentally unsuited to it in just about every way, it was odd that I found myself in the British Royal Air Force in Germany, but I made this more bearable by performing in folk clubs there and reading esoterica.

A few of us military misfits approaching demob toyed with alternative futures. With the lack of discrimination that often characterises the bright and curious but insufficiently educated and mature, we were culturally primed to devour the magick of Aleister Crowley, the lightweight Tibetan Buddhism of Tuesday Lobsang Rampa, and the Zen of D.T. Suzuki and Alan Watts. However, I gradually came to believe over time that I was sorting out the respectable from the pap. My friend Ozzie on the other hand became seriously taken with the idea – from Lobsang Rampa – that tomcats can talk with humans, and that every tree comes with a complete set of tiny nature spirits. It would be several years before "Rampa" – real name Cyril Henry Hoskin, a nondescript plumber from Devon in the south-west of England – was exposed as a consummate bullshitter. I couldn't wait that long, so one day I devised a spectacular test of Ozzie's gullibility: I told him that the actual name of Del Shannon, the rock and country singer, was Arthur Puzzle. Not being very sophisticated on the social intelligence front, Ozzie, quietly nodding sagely while puffing on his pipe, accepted this as fact with the dignity and gravitas befitting his emerging New Age Dingbat persona.

A few months later, demobbed from the military, we were in the north of Scotland, in Aberdeen. The people there seemed much like their buildings – grey, dour, and stony-faced, miserable inside and out. It wasn't too clear to me why we were in Aberdeen as opposed to anywhere else, but we needed jobs – or at least I did. Having trained as a clerk in the military, that was what I thought I should continue to be. Ozzie had other ideas. When we got to the front of the queue in the Employment and Benefits Office, a scowling elderly official asked him what line of work he was in. "I'm an astrologer," proclaimed Ozzie proudly. "Not much call for that here, laddie," came the dismissive reply.

Despite this, determined to make a career out of finding meaning in the sky, Ozzie stuck to his guns, impressively managing to avoid any kind of proper job, and for the next half century getting by largely on benefits. Broke but seemingly content, he ended up as a practising astrologer in Totnes, England's epicentre of spectacularly unreliable star charts. I haven't seen him in decades but recently caught his website. He has a blog that appeals to the wide-eyed gullible. In it he writes his sage horoscopic musings – more precisely astrolobabble, given that his words constitute vacuous vapidity masquerading as arcane wisdom: "When a man gets to his late 60s, he feels a natural urge to slow down and take things a little easier." Wow, gee whiz, blimey, and I'll be damned! How about that! I start to make up new entries for his blog: "When you drink too much alcohol you fall over." "When you saw your arm off it drops to the ground." It's all in the stars!

The Trickster-Carnivalesque Self

The characters in *Monumental Ineptitude* and *Talking Tomcats* are the narrative equivalent of cartoon people, and in *Committees* they're not far off being so. My psychological need to defensively project sarcasm and ridicule onto others in these storied memories, and in many of my other accumulated memories to this point in my life, implicitly reflects my growing cultural alienation through time. Haruki Murakami (2021, p. 225) captures the existential subtext of my life memories well:

> that vague sense of unease . . . Like the contents didn't fit the container, like the integrity of it all had been lost . . . that somewhere I'd taken a wrong turn in life . . . it wasn't . . . like I was making a choice, but more like *the choice itself* chose *me*.

In engaging with the memories of poor fit choices that chose me, to make them feel less awful, I've tended over the years to treat them like therapeutic LEGO through the storied reconstruction of their component parts. In my historically distant past, I tended to regard my self as problematic in these memories, while unreflexively accepting the cultures I was inscribed within as neutral phenomena. This usually resulted in me trying to tidy up my remembered self so that it could pass cultural muster on culture's terms.

I did this to try to make my memories stop evoking the feeling I might have while wearing situationally inappropriate and tasteless garb – the phenomenological equivalent of going to a funeral of a close relative in a gorilla costume while carrying a balloon. However, over the years, highlighting the creative nature of defensive hindsight (Freeman, 2010), I've found myself needing to make my self-culture mismatch feel less embarrassing by rescuing my remembered self from moral disgrace in more sophisticated ways.

Grappling with the significance of those memories in recent years, culminating in the process of researching for and crafting this chapter, has resulted in me seeing more clearly how my demystified memories are interconnected. They seem to signal an important longstanding task for my moral character: calling out the carnivalesque nature of the life I've experienced. The Bakhtinian image of "Carnival" (Bakhtin, 1968, pp. 61–63) disrupts authoritative and conventional acceptance of cultural and social values. I read Mikhail Bakhtin's concept as simultaneously a state of mind, a performance, and – as a necessary philosophical antidote to conventional life – an opportunity to contest dominant cultural meanings. In this regard, the "carnivalesque" speaks to cultural reversal: the subversion and inversion of normative power relationships, and the refusal of stifling cultural stability and meaning closure in favour of constant liberating possibilities.

Laughter is central to Bakhtin's Carnivalesque concept (Bakhtin, 1968, pp. 58–144). A folk, or cultural underdog, form of catharsis, laughter emerges in Bakhtin's writing as a social-psychological defence and defiance vehicle with a long historical pedigree. Its purpose down the centuries has been to help people resist being tamed by institutional and organisational cultural conventions, whether externally imposed or individually internalised as "right and proper." More than this, according to Bakhtin, laughter has an important universal philosophical meaning, which is to see the world anew, more profoundly, and more coherently.

The absurdities of human society remain invisible when too much stifling solemnity is accorded to life's rituals, events, and relationships. According to Bakhtin, official spheres over the centuries have been sustained by hierarchically-imposed *seriousness* – at ideological, institutional, social, organisational, and cultural levels. This serves to simultaneously divert attention from, and normalise, inequitable cultural relations between people. From a philosophy of culture perspective, such inequities are sustained through the intergenerational transmission of cultural *tradition* (Allan, 1993). In this regard, Pierre Bourdieu's philosophical sociology helps me understand how seriousness gets to be inscribed within social groups as *habitus* (Lukes, 2005).

In line with and complementing Freeman's idea of the narrative unconscious, where history inevitably shapes the personal stories of individuals

(Freeman, 2010, pp. 95–123), the habitus concept refers to embodied dispositions. These are passed down through the generations as forms of unscrutinised and unnoticed social-psychological inheritance (Webb et al., 2002), manifesting in people in unreflexive and unselfconscious ways (Bourdieu, 1990). In Bourdieu's terms, habitus dispositions facilitate people's entry into the demarcated social spaces, or "fields," constitutive of their socially and symbolically structured conventional worlds. Subsuming "narrative habitus" (Frank, 2010, pp. 52–54) or communication styles, those dispositions determine and shape identity and interactional styles. At tacit, intuitive, and unconscious levels, they – as it were "naturally" – result in people fitting more or less neatly into their pre-supposedly appropriate places, within social, organisational, institutional, and cultural hierarchies and environmental settings.

The processes through which habitus socialisation occurs appear "natural," precisely because they are inscribed within, thus indistinguishable from, conventional and normative life socialisation processes. As a result, social structural positions give rise to interactions and cultural worlds which, although often life-limiting, are generally regarded as morally neutral reflections of the world as it is and *should* be. The cultural philosopher George Allan expresses this as "a part of the of the way things are: natural givens, brute facticities" (Allan, 1993, p. 24). Underwritten by hierarchical power and officialdom, however, such – contingent rather than necessary – manufactured worlds clearly further the interests of some groups and individuals at the expense of others. In this context, carnivalesque laughter serves as a psychological pressure-valve release in lampooning the worst and most absurd excesses of cultural life.

More profoundly, according to Bakhtin (1968, p. 75), carnivalesque laughter symbolises cultural degeneration and regeneration, gradually provoking cultural change for the better. Laughter challenges and undermines the power of taken-for-granted and insufficiently scrutinised cultural monoliths, when "Foolishness and folly" disrupts the business-as-usual of cultural pomposity. Knott (2014, p. 10) expresses this well:

> laughter is a reaction that bypasses reason and can potentially give momentum to freedom and sovereignty in the midst of the constraints of this world and all its buttoned-up social conventions.

In this regard, Lewis Hyde (2017) argues that the never-ending task of cultural regeneration – of forging the different from the old – falls naturally to the "trickster." Always resisting full and unproblematic cultural participation, the trickster belongs to the periphery, to the edges, never to the centre, and is constantly moving on. Being on the road between cultures is a necessary antidote to a chronic inability to feel at home in them. Having come to value my storied memories for their iconoclastic power to disrupt, call out, and lampoon from the edges, cultures which I've experienced as inhospitable and in lots of ways absurd, the narrative character descriptor of *cultural trickster* feels right for me. It demystifies and unites my otherwise disparate memories. It also relates to my second aim in crafting this chapter: to make the ways in which I story the world psychologically more endurable through purging my memories of their negative affect. This has been achieved – at least to a far more tolerable degree.

The trickster character descriptor squares well with the person I've seemed to be throughout my life. I've always experienced myself as in the margins of cultural and social groups, but with the passage of time have felt more of a sense of personal power that seems co-extensive with my maturation as scholar and the accrual of cultural capital. This has enabled me to occupy marginal positions more comfortably and successfully in my role as a critical autoethnographer working in the service of feral pedagogy. Regarding this role, Thomas Frentz (2008) captures my agenda well in his view that being a trickster amounts to learning the rules of the cultural game, then sidestepping and subverting those in the service of rescuing critical education from the dehumanising neoliberal agenda. In this context, I believe my trickster character to be morally and ethically justified. In Hyde's terms (2017, p. 9), the self as culturally antagonistic trickster fulfils a necessary and sacred duty:

> the origins, liveliness, and durability of cultures require that there be space for figures whose function is to uncover and disrupt the very things that cultures are based on.

Concluding Evaluation

In this final section of my chapter, a pressing question for me to consider is how it might be responded to by readers. Some will be socialised into, and conditioned by, the naïve humanist assumptions of mainstream qualitative inquiry, often apparent in conventional takes on autoethnography. For example, those who focus on my stories at the expense of seriously engaging with their contextualising philosophical discussion might accuse me of being in breach of relational ethics. From such a "Tolichist" perspective (Grant and Young, 2022), securing anticipated or retrospective consent from the characters mentioned in the stories will be assumed to have been an essential prerequisite. Readers motivated by a need for historical veracity might also discount the credibility of my stories from an equally narrow epistemic perspective.

However, if taken seriously, such objections beg an important question: who exactly would I have been attempting to secure consent from? Relative to their historical event originals, some of whom may no longer be alive, my storied characters are at a substantial epistemic remove. Cartoon characters are not the same as real flesh-and-blood people. By my philosophical lights the former, inevitably, are a product of my creative and imaginative narrative self. Because this product fits epistemically with my narrative, as opposed to historical, truth, the only person I need worry about seeking consent from is myself. And not surprisingly, I approve wholeheartedly and without reservation. Moreover, I anticipate that those still biologically alive might well experience the storied characters derived from them as offensive, even unrecognisable, and so consent would not be forthcoming, even if consent-seeking *was* relevant and possible. The compromises I'd have to make to secure approval would render the stories pointless on all levels. To draw on Laurel Richardson and Elizabeth St. Pierre (2018), *creative analytical practice*, subsuming dialogue-generating evocative storytelling, would be sacrificed for boring chronology.

All of this leads me to examine the conceptual and epistemic status of autobiographical "truth." From the perspective of the philosophy of autobiography, Garry Hagberg (2015) challenges as overly simplistic the conventional dualism between *truth*, or telling the world as it is or was, and *lying*, or fabrication. In so doing, Hagberg isn't invoking a banal "shades of grey in-between" argument. At more fundamental conceptual and epistemic levels, he's challenging the meaning of these key words. In arguing that "lying . . . is not one thing" (p. 61), Hagberg contends that it is reductive to conceive this word in the monodimensional dualistic context of "lying versus truth telling."

Ludwig Wittgenstein (2009) reminds us that in making coherent sense of them, all words need to be understood in their contextual fields of use. The original events on which my stories are based are long gone. As previously argued, the contextual fields of the words spoken during these events have mostly all fallen out of my memories or have changed through becoming schematised and conventionalised. I inevitably re-contextualise them from an increasingly mature *present*, informed down the years by a corresponding accrual of knowledge, reading, writing, thinking, and living. In short, I *fill in*. Jean-Jacques Rousseau (2011, p. 44) wrote:

> I never said less than the truth, but sometimes I said more than it, and this kind of lie was the result of my confused imagination rather than an act of will.

The idea of autobiography arriving at the truth via imagination rather than historical facticity unites Rousseau with Freeman. "Filling in" is both inevitable and necessary, given the memory gaps occurring over time which steadily widen the gulf between historical and narrative time. However, filling in amounts to perhaps more than an act of conceptual and epistemic necessity. From an aesthetic perspective, Hagberg (2015) contends that filled in content makes language real, giving it determinate significance. Through a philosophy of autobiography lens, the storied memories I've recounted should be judged on their own merit, for giving voice to aesthetically shaped critical cultural commentaries, rather than in the banal obsessive terms of their correspondence with original events.

What though are the implications of all of this for the autobiographical truth status of my storied memories, and the inferences I've made about my emerging character? My developing discussion led me to conclude that my character is "trickster-carnivalesque." I acknowledged that this conclusion must remain temporary and provisional given the nature of personal hindsight, which never, as it were, catches up with itself. In support of my conclusion, however, the critically satirical autoethnographic publications in which I've taken healthcare practice and academic organisational cultures to task in recent years seem to me to constitute reasonably adequate representational evidence (Grant, 2013, 2017, 2018).

However, the overlapping premises and motivations which led to my conclusion of my character as coherently trickster-carnivalesque need more adequate scrutiny. Regarding my own centre of narrative gravity, there's clearly always going to be a temptation to fabricate *too* wildly and defensively in the service of narrative self-manufacture. I may pretty-up my storied self via the rationalising tendencies of narrative-smoothing and narrative-retrofit, simply to conceal myself from myself and from the world, and refuse – when pressed – accusations of consciously or unconsciously held mendacity. At unconscious levels, this illustrates "hindsight bias" in action (Freeman, 2010, p. 22), where denial and resistance to look squarely at oneself substitute for authentic narrative truth.

I'm not sure about the extent to which I might reasonably be held to account for this. My motivation to "cleanse my memories of their lingering negative residue," expressed as an aim near the beginning of my chapter, might simply constitute a virtue-signalling rationalisation. If this is the case, its function might be to make me *feel* and hopefully *be* historically culturally vindicated; to render my presence in the past blame-free before my time share in life expires. In relation to this point, like most adult humans I'm not without enemies. Some of them might no doubt make counter claims about the narrative truth of my life, suggesting – sometimes reasonably from their perspectives – that my presence in the past has been far from virtuous.

And even if my moral rear-view vision is 20:20, whether or not I've discerned wrong or false truths about myself remains a moot point. Perhaps, linking to what Freeman (2010, pp. 67–94) describes as "moral lateness," I've taken a tourist rest break at too early a point on my memory journey to look back at a view that's obscure, misty, or partial? In this regard, my hindsight attempts might amount to a time-wasting philosophical detour. In related terms, I may well be committing the logical fallacies of *circular reasoning* and *question begging*, having started with a pre-supposition (premise) of myself as a cultural trickster, then mustering autoethnographic and philosophical arguments to support this, then confirming (conclusion) the truth of my trickster identity premise, and qualifying all of this with the disingenuous disclaimer that I'm making a provisional inference.

However, against this, Allan (1993, p. 25) brings me back down to earth by reminding me that – in the context of cultural traditions – my character "is a matter of dispositions; I am how I am likely to behave." Since I've always in my estimation tended to behave like a cultural trickster, did I really need all that arduous hindsight work to tell me what I knew all along? I suppose not; however, engaging in it has formally legitimised my trickster character, making it more solid, more historically extensive, and continuous rather than provisional. Ironically for me as someone who claims to be always passing through cultures, this places me squarely within the trickster cultural tradition – one I probably won't be leaving anytime soon.

Moving to what I see as a main strength of my argument, I believe that through demonstrating my engagement in hindsight work I've at least provided a thoroughgoing exemplar of according "lived experience" the sophisticated respect it begs and deserves. I've argued in press that this concept is often employed in autoethnography, and in qualitative inquiry more broadly, in insufficiently scrutinised clichéd and careless ways (Klevan and Grant, 2022, pp. 112–126), to add a veneer of superficial rhetorical respectability to work lacking adequate levels of critically reflexive depth.

However, in resting my case on Freeman's *Hindsight* thesis, I'm investing in a contemporary cultural theoretical position that's become an integral part of my hindsight horizon. If hindsight work is viewed as a contemporary culturally contingent – as opposed to a necessary and timeless – character discerning strategy, this could be regarded as a weakness in my overall argument. Conversely, it might be viewed as a strength from the standpoint that a serious hindsight orientation provides a necessary, more sober, and robust alternative to what seems to me to be the current widespread, facile, cultural investment in "McMindfulness" (Purser, 2019). Simplistic, one-dimensional, reductionist solutions to the messy complexities of life abound, and in my experience are sadly often apparent at the interface of autoethnography and therapy. If I am right in this estimation, in considering the broader moral significance of my identity, my hindsight-grounded critical orientation constantly calls accepted cultural values into question.

It seems important that I elaborate on this point, and so I'll now briefly address a deeper issue at the heart of my discussion so far. This is: *the moral status of my trickster self in the context of dominant cultural narratives.*

Those who exclusively value such narratives might view "trickster morality" as an oxymoron, given that it signals a breach of – normative – morality, or how a person *should* reasonably story themselves across multiple conventional cultural narrative fronts. However, the moral value of perpetuating, respecting, and transmitting cultural stories about oneself, unquestioningly and uncritically, needs to be set against the costs of this for creativity and life affirmation. This can be usefully responded to from – to my mind related – Nietzschean existential and queer phenomenological perspectives.

Reginster (2006) and Seigel (2005), sympathetic interpreters of Nietzsche, explain his *life-affirming morality* concept in abstract terms – as a commitment to standing against the crowd. This translates as resisting and overcoming the usually accepted and unchallenged limitations and boundaries of conventional cultural narratives of established social groups. Seigel (p. 538) argues in this context that "resistance" constitutes an act of self-overcoming, in the constant transformation of one's own being, or constant reinvention of oneself. I believe that this sits well with the viewpoint that conventional cultural narratives always invite "queering": making critical sense of them, rejecting them, playing with them, tweaking them, undermining their authoritative dominance. From this standpoint, Sara Ahmed (2006, pp. 1–8) describes the existentially fruitful moments of "disorientation" felt towards dominant cultural narratives, where the fit between normative cultural story (*this is who you should be*) and person (*this is who I am*) no longer works. At these moments the choice is between carrying on along the well-trodden paths of the culturally familiar or choosing the riskier, yet-to-be-explored, paths of the counterculturally unfamiliar, and in consequence and of necessity re-inventing personal identity.

In terms of my moral value as a human, I believe my contribution to life has been immeasurably better as a trickster than it ever would have been if I'd followed more conventional cultural directions and stayed loyal to pre-established social groups (even supposing I was cut out for and wanted to do this). This fits well with my scholarly orientation. Rejecting the centripetal pull of cultural belonging, embeddedness, and loyalty to conventional narratives in favour of the centrifugal push of cultural estrangement, dislocation, and robust, sustained cultural critique seems to me to be central to what good autoethnography is about.

And when my timeshare in life runs out, my "lived experiences" – like everyone else's – will have amounted to a farrago: a mixture of fact, creative fiction, and compressed interpersonal narrative memory. Freeman

(2010) convincingly maintains that this strengthens rather than weakens the epistemic status of the narrative self. For the time being, that's good enough for me.

References

Adams, T.E., Boylorn, R.M. and Tillmann, L.S. (2021). 'Righting and Writing (For) Our Lives: Turning Inward When the World Falls Apart'. In Adams, T.E., Boylorn, R.M. and Tillmann, L.S. (eds.) *Advances in Autoethnography and Narrative Inquiry: Reflections on the Legacy of Carolyn Ellis and Arthur Bochner*. pp. 1–11. London and New York: Routledge.

Ahmed, S. (2006). *Queer Phenomenology: Orientations, Objects, Others*. Durham and London: Duke University Press.

Allan, G. (1993). 'Traditions and Transitions'. In Cook, P. (ed.) *Philosophical Imagination and Cultural Memory: Appropriating Historical Traditions*. pp. 21–39. Durham and London: Duke University Press.

Améry, J. (1994). *On Aging: Revolt and Resignation*. Translated by Barlow, J.D. Bloomington and Indianapolis: Indiana University Press.

Bakhtin, M. (1968). *Rabelais and His World*. Translated by Iswolsky, H. Bloomington and Indianapolis: Indiana University Press.

Bergson, H. (2002). *Key Writings*. Edited by Ansell Pearson, K. and Maoilearca, J.O. London: Bloomsbury Academic.

Bourdieu, P. (1990). *The Logic of Practice*. Translated by Nice, R. Cambridge: Polity Press.

Dennett, D. (1993). *Consciousness Explained*. London: Penguin Books.

Frank, A.W. (2010). *Letting Stories Breathe: A Socio-Narratology*. Chicago and London: The University of Chicago Press.

Freeman, M. (2010). *Hindsight: The Promise and Peril of Looking Backward*. New York: Oxford University Press.

Frentz, T.S. (2008). *Trickster in Tweed: My Quest for Quality in Faculty Life*. London and New York: Routledge.

Grant, A. (2013). 'Writing Teaching and Survival in Mental Health: A Discordant Quintet for One'. In Short, N.P., Turner, L. and Grant, A. (eds.) *Contemporary British Autoethnography*. pp. 33–48. Rotterdam: Sense Publishers.

Grant, A. (2017). 'Toilets Are the Proper Place for "Outputs"! A Tale of Knowledge Production and Publishing with Students in Higher Education'. In Hayler, M. and Moriarty, J. (eds.) *Self-narrative and Pedagogy: Stories of Experience within Teaching and Learning*. pp. 45–57. Rotterdam: Sense Publishers.

Grant, A. (2018). 'Moving Around the Hyphens: A Critical Meta-Autoethnographic Performance'. in Bull, P., Gadsby, J. and Williams, S. (eds.) *Critical Mental Health Nursing: Observations from the Inside*. pp. 30–50. Monmouth: PCCS Books.

Grant, A. and Young, S. (2022). 'Troubling Tolichism in Several Voices: Resisting Epistemic Violence in Creative Analytical and Critical Autoethnographic Practice'. *Journal of Autoethnography*. 3(1): pp. 103–117. https://doi.org/10.1525/joae.2022.3.1.103

Hagberg, G. (2015). 'A Person's Words: Literary Characters and Autobiographical Understanding'. In Cowley, C. (ed.) *The Philosophy of Autobiography*. pp. 39–71. Chicago: The University of Chicago Press.

Holman Jones, S. (2021). 'Becoming Wild: Autoethnography as Feral Pedagogy'. In Adams, T.E., Boylorn, R.M. and Tillmann, L.S. (eds.) *Advances in Autoethnography and Narrative Inquiry: Reflections on the Legacu of Carolyn Ellis and Arthur Bochner*. pp. 35–40. London and New York: Routledge.

Hyde, L. (2017). *Trickster Makes This World: How Disruptive Imagination Creates Culture*. Edinburgh: Canongate Books Ltd.

Jean-Jacques Rousseau. (2011[1776–8]). *Reveries of the Solitary Walker*. Translated by Goulbourne, R. New York: Oxford University Press.

Klevan, T. and Grant, A. (2022). *An Autoethnography of Becoming a Qualitative Researcher: A Dialogic View of Academic Development*. London and New York: Routledge.

Knott, M.L. (2014). *Unlearning With Hannah Arendt*. London: Granta.

Loy, D. (2010). *The World is Made of Stories*. Boston: Wisdom Publications.

Lukes, S. (2005). *Power: A Radical View*. 2nd Edition. London: RED GLOBE PRESS.

MacIntyre, A. (1981). *After Virtue: A Study in Moral Theory*. Notre Dame, IN: University of Notre Dame Press.

Murakami, H. (2021). *First Person Singular: Stories*. Translated by Gabriel, P. London: Harvill Secker.

Purser, R. (2019). *McMindfulness: How Mindfulness Became the New Capitalist Spirituality*. London: Repeater Books.

Reginster, B. (2006). *The Affirmation of Life: Nietzsche on Overcoming Nihilism*. Cambridge, MA: Harvard University Press.

Richardson, L. and St. Pierre, E.A. (2018). 'Writing: A Method of Inquiry'. In Denzin, N.K. and Lincoln, Y.S. (eds.) *The SAGE Handbook of Qualitative Research*. 5th Edition. pp. 818–838. Thousand Oaks, CA: Sage.

Seigel, J. (2005). *The Idea of the Self: Thought and Experience in Western Europe since the Seventeenth Century*. New York: Cambridge University Press.

Tullis Owen, J.A., McRae, C., Adams, T.E. and Vitale, A. (2009). 'Truth Troubles'. *Qualitative Inquiry*. 15(1): pp. 178–200. http://dx.doi.org/10.1177/1077800408318316

Webb, J., Schirato, T. and Danaher, G. (2002). *Understanding Bourdieu*. London: SAGE Publications Ltd.

Wittgenstein, L. (2009). *Philosophical Investigations*. 4th Edition. Translated by Anscombe, E. Chichester: Wiley-Blackwell.

8

AN AUTOETHNOGRAPHIC EXAMINATION OF ORGANIZATIONAL SENSEMAKING

Andrew Herrmann

Introduction

To suggest that Karl E. Weick is an instrumental scholar and theorist would be akin to saying Neil Armstrong was instrumental to space flight. That would be a horrific underestimation of the deep and wide influence his research has had across a diversity of academic disciplines, including sociology, psychology, communication, and business (Eisenberg, 2006; Gioia, 2006; Tsoukas et al., 2020). In my own field, Weick's concepts of sensemaking, organizing, loose coupling, and mindfulness influenced crisis communication, financial communication, human resources, knowledge management, leadership, strategic management, and a variety of other organizational subdisciplines, including organizational behavior, organizational communication, organizational learning, organizational psychology, and organizational studies (Anderson, 2006; Czarniawska, 2005; Glynn and Watkiss, 2020; Sutcliffe et al., 2006). According to Google Scholar, his first book, *The Social Psychology of Organizing*, has been cited over 25,000 times. That's likely an undercount.

Weick's (1979, 1995) conception of organizing was a paradigm shift. He changed the way we think about organization by emphasizing the verb form of the term rather than the noun form. As a process, organizing is about making sense. Organizing is often chaotic and shambolic. Instead of merely examining organization as an entity or a product, Weick reminds us that organizing is a process and an activity. Organizing is sensemaking and sensemaking is messy.

DOI: 10.4324/9781003274728-8

Before moving forward to explain Weick's theory of organizing and how it is connected to autoethnography, it is worth exploring the philosophical foundations of both. As an activity, organizing lends itself to a particular philosophical underpinning that goes against the grain of empirical and foundational reductionism (Tsoukas, 2019; Weick, 1989, 2012). So does autoethnography and related personal narrative research (Adams and Herrmann, 2020; Bochner and Adams, 2020; Bochner and Herrmann, 2020; Ellis, 1991; Krizek, 2003). In order to explore the connections between organizational sensemaking and autoethnography, we need to explore the basic tenets of existential phenomenology. This might seem an odd choice, given that sensemaking is based on systems theory. However, in the end it will make sense.

Embedded Life in Action

Defining existential phenomenology is elusive, for the philosophical schools of thought from which it is derived are themselves ill-defined (Guignon and Pereboom, 2001). For example, existentialism developed through philosophical treatises, as well as novels, plays, and memoirs. The term itself was embraced and/or rejected by proponents of the philosophy, and appears in both atheistic and religious modes (Aho, 2014; Herrmann, 2021). A number of concepts that formed the base of existential philosophy began to develop in the 19th century, and most genealogies list Søren Kierkegaard as the first significant figure, who made ontology (the study of existence) and human experience its focal point (Guignon and Pereboom, 2001).

For existentialists, individuals are free to choose. This means that an individual has the power to become who they will be through the choices they make. Individuals therefore are "unforgivingly responsible for those choices" (Herrmann, 2015, p. 67). At its heart, existentialism is the study of human existence from an attached, interested, invested lived human standpoint. The trouble is, as Kierkegaard (1958) noted, "life in the temporal existence never becomes quite intelligible, precisely because at no moment can I find complete quiet to take the backward-looking position" (p. 111). Existentialist philosophy is primarily concerned with the subjective "I," with self-knowledge, and "the first choice confronting every person is the choice of being either a mere reflector of societal norms or becoming subjectively involved and choosing for oneself what kind of social individual one will be" (Herrmann, 2008, p. 79). Important to existential philosophy is the type of character *I* develop, how *I* maintain relationships, and how *I* come to understand living the good life. Moreover, our lives mean something. My life means something to my loved ones, to my friends, to my colleagues.

My life means something to me. Because it is so personal. Existentialism is not easily systematized.

Phenomenology also came to fruition in the 19th century. Husserl (1973) attempted to examine consciousness and the way in which things appear to it, rather than relying on preconceived notions of the way things seem to be. As such, phenomenology puts epistemology (the study of knowledge) before ontology.

> For Husserl, phenomenology was a discipline that attempts to describe what is given to us in experience without obscuring preconceptions or hypothetical speculations; his motto was 'to the things themselves' – rather than to the prefabricated conceptions we put in their place.
>
> *(Barrett, 1962, p. 190)*

To practice ideal phenomenology, one needs to abstract (or bracket out) existence, including all our preconceived notions of the world. The actual conditions of everyday existence are, for Husserl, problematic for the study of phenomena that appear to our consciousness – and how that appearance happens. What is important is that, just as in existential philosophy, our conscious experiences are uniquely ours. We, as individual subjects, experience them. Due to this, like existentialism, "a unique and final definition of phenomenology is dangerous and perhaps even paradoxical as it lacks a thematic focus" (Farina, 2014, p. 50).

Now take these two amorphous schools of philosophical thought and put them in a post-World War I blender with Heidegger, Sartre, Merleau-Ponty, and others. In Heidegger, "existentialism gave up its anti-scientific attitude. Phenomenology, on the other hand, enriched itself and developed into a philosophy of man by borrowing many topics from Kierkegaard's existentialism" (Luijpen and Koren, 1969, p. 21). According to Heidegger, we exist in a space of "unheimlich," which literally means "unhomelike," a place of "not-being-at-home" (1962, p. 237). We live in a condition of "thrownness" in the world by the simple facticity of our existence in time (Heidegger, 1962, p. 237). The past and present are hostile, moving continuously, while we are constantly being pushed forward by our existence. "It's what Sartre meant by the queasy nauseousness we feel, or the Kierkegaardian angst we have about our own existence" (Herrmann, 2016, p. 31). Our task is to live through the inhospitality where there is no sanctuary. This is what it means to be a human individual. What makes Heidegger's existential phenomenological project unique was his interest in our facticity, our everyday ways of being and doing.

Heidegger (1962) realized that to understand what being human is, the facticity of the world is a *necessary* backdrop for all human experience, and any examination of *Dasein* (the human individual) begins not through a subject-object dichotomy, but through the lens of embeddedness, our "Being-in-the-world." According to Heidegger, Husserl's bracketing out of existence was the wrong philosophical move. We are involved in a world of everyday activities and projects. In our contextually embedded activities, we overlook features of the world that are familiar to us, because in our everyday affairs, we encounter the world as "equipment" that has a practical purpose for tasks we are undertaking (Heidegger, 1962, p. 99). "That with which our everyday dealings proximally dwell is not the tools themselves. On the contrary that with which we concern ourselves primarily is the work – that which is to be produced at the time" (Heidegger, 1962, p. 99). Heidegger shows that "the world at the most basic level is initially and most fundamentally a meaning-filled context in which we carry out our practical lives" (Guignon and Pereboom, 2001, p. 192). Equipment – the items we use – are normally understood as part of a grander context through the labor that constitutes our projects.

An example may help. Let's say I am driving to my parents' house, something I do regularly. As part of this process, I use my Honda Civic. I use its steering wheel to stay in the correct lane. I use the blinkers to tell people I am changing lanes. I use my clutch to shift gears. I use my brakes to slow down, etc. As I drive, I encounter my car through the totality of relations organized around my purpose of driving. There is not a "car-thing" with certain "properties," but a purposeful relationship contextualized in the activity of driving to my parents' house. In Heidegger's terminology, when equipment is "ready-to-hand" in this way, these tools are normally unnoticed and unobtrusive (1962, p. 135).

I don't think of the "car-ness" of my Honda until something goes awry. The battery dies. My tire blows. The brakes start squealing. In other words, when "stuff happens." These experiences break the flow of what is normally encountered as part of the everydayness of driving. Suddenly, my Civic's "car-ness" captures my explicit attention as an object, becoming what Heidegger calls "present-at-hand" (Heidegger, 1962, p. 104). "The modes of conspicuousness, obtrusiveness, and obstinacy all have the function of bringing to the fore the characteristic of presence-at-hand in what is ready-to-hand" (Heidegger, 1962, p. 104). For Heidegger, this objective stance toward objects and the world is not our primordial, normal stance in everyday activity, but caused by a rupture in our everyday embeddedness. If you have ever stood on the side of the road staring dumbfounded at your malfunctioning car, you have experienced your car as "present-at-hand."

Heidegger also notes that in our everyday activity, we are not necessarily conscious of ourselves as discreet isolated subjects with objectified bodies, in a world "out there."

> For Heidegger, we are always *in situ*. We do not become ourselves by only making ourselves abstract subjects of self-reflection, but through what we *do* in our everyday experience and projecting that into the future. The world itself comes to appear – or discloses itself – through our everyday activities within it.
>
> *(Herrmann, 2015, p. 69)*

I do not consider myself as a "subject" who is driving a Civic. Rather, I am embedded in a web of significant relations in the process of driving, and I get lost in my driving activities. Or as Merleau-Ponty wrote: "the subject that I am, when taken concretely, is inseparable from this body and this world." (2012, p. 408). The context of the world helps define our agency (and the limits thereof) and our identity as we go about doing our everyday business. As Sartre noted, "Without facticity freedom would not exist" (2003, p. 517).

I've started a piece about organizational sensemaking and autoethnography with an overview of existential phenomenology. It might not seem as if these are connected, but they are. Historicity, facticity, and situated embeddedness help define the existential "I." While the connection between the first-person perspective and autoethnography is well developed, a brief review of organizational sensemaking is needed first.

Organizational Sensemaking

The theoretical underpinnings that form the foundation of Weick's (1974, 1979, 1995, 1998) concepts of organizing and sensemaking include systems theory, information processing, and sociocultural evolution. Despite the theoretical complexity, his conceptual frame for sensemaking and organizing can be considered a communicatively pragmatic socially constructed process. "When we say that meanings materialize, we mean that sensemaking is, importantly, an issue of language, talk, and communication. Situations, organizations, and environments are talked into existence" (Weick et al., 2005, p. 409). Sensemaking is the reduction of message equivocality. As Weick (1995) pointed out, the problem to be solved "is that there are too many meanings, not too few. The problem faced by the sensemaker is one of equivocality, not one of uncertainty. The problem is confusion, not ignorance" (p. 27). The possible meanings of messages need to be reduced through communicative action (Weick, 1979, 1995).

Weick (1979, 1995) introduced sensemaking as an activity that includes both individual and organizational behaviors. Not only do I have to make sense regarding my identity, I have to simultaneously make sense for the organization as well. Organizations exist in complicated and uncertain environments, and one purpose of organizing is to make sense of equivocal messages in their information environment (Weick, 1979). So how, according to Weick, do we make sense of equivocal information?

Weick's (1979) model of organizing consists of three distinct activities: enactment, selection, and retention. Enactment starts with the bracketing or framing of a datum in the environment by an individual. Through enactment, the individual assigns importance to the datum in the information environment. Accordingly, Weick (1988) wrote that enactment is a way to socially construct reality:

> The product of enactment is not an accident, an afterthought, or a byproduct. It is an orderly, material, social construction that is subject to multiple interpretations. Enacted environments contain real objects such as reactors, pipes, and valves. The existence of these objects is not questioned, but their significance, meaning, and content is.
>
> *(p. 307)*

Weick (1979) stressed that "reality is selectively perceived, rearranged cognitively, and negotiated interpersonally" (p. 164). Although often understated, important to the process of sensemaking is personal identity (Weick, 1995).

Sensemaking starts with the idea that some encountered data doesn't fit with what I know to be true or how I believe things should be. In other words, I need to make sense of this. As Eisenberg (2006) noted, "Struggles over meaning invariably have implications for identity . . . It is no accident that Weick lists identity as the first property of sensemaking" (pp. 1699–1700). The process begins with an individual trying to make sense of some information that is important to them. If it is important to them, they then enact it. They start sensemaking. Sensemaking is entwined with identity construction. Why? From an existential phenomenological standpoint, what I enact is based upon my positionality and facticity.

For example, if I am an employee taking orders at a hamburger shop and I hear about a computer virus attacking the servers in the corporate office of a competitor, I would likely ignore that information. It doesn't affect me or my job. However, if a health inspector comes into my shop telling me customers at my hamburger shop got botulism, I am likely to enact that information, because that information is important to me. It impacts me. Why? Because being an employee at that particular hamburger shop is part of my identity. Do I know those customers? How will this affect me? Will we have to shut down? Will the store go bankrupt? Will I be out of a job? And how the hell could we have given them botulism? Is it something I did? Uncertainty can present a challenge my identity. As Weick, Sutcliffe, and Obstfeld noted, "When people face an unsettling difference, that difference often translates into questions such as who are we, what are we doing, what matters, and why does it matter? These are not trivial questions" (p. 416). Answering these questions about identity is an important part of the process of sensemaking.

If an enacted message is substantially equivocal, organizational members select communication cycles, which consist of act-response-adjustment communicative interactions. As Weick (1979) explained:

> The unit of analysis in organizing is contingent response patterns, patterns in which an action by actor A evokes a specific response in actor B (so far this is an interact), which is then responded to by actor A (this complete sequence is a double interact).
>
> *(p. 89)*

The more equivocal a message is, the more communication cycles are required to reduce its equivocality. Individuals use communication to make sense of new datum and what steps an organization should take (if any) regarding it.

Sensemaking is about the enlargement of small cues. It is a search for contexts within which small details fit together and make sense. It is people interacting to flesh out hunches. It is a continuous alteration between particulars and explanations, with each cycle giving added form and substance to the other. It is about building confidence as the particulars begin to cohere and as the explanation allows increasingly accurate deductions (Weick, 1995, p. 133). If the communication cycles succeed in reducing message equivocality, organizations can retain this as an organizational rule for future use.

The primary advantage of Weick's model is the attention to communicative praxis (Magala, 1997). Meaning materializes via the use of communication cycles, reducing equivocality. However, as Weick et al. (2005) noted:

> Sensemaking is not about truth and getting it right. Instead, it is about continued redrafting of an emerging story so that it becomes more comprehensive, incorporates more of the observed data, and is more resilient in the face of criticism.
>
> *(p. 415)*

Sensemaking is an ongoing process. As shown in the imagined example of the hamburger joint employee, "making sense of 'something out there' is self-referential because what is sensed, and how it is seen, bears on the actor's identity" (Weber and Glynn, 2006, pp. 1645–1646). To put Weick's concept into existential phenomenological terms, I enact the data that I need to make sense of, because of its importance to my identity within the facticity of my life.

Narrative is an inherent part of the sensemaking process because data "are inconsequential until they are acted upon and then incorporated retrospectively into events, situations, and explanations" (Weick, 1988, p. 307). As I noted in research on narrative (Herrmann, 2011):

> Narratives are one process by which we organize and make sense of the world. In fact, narrative can be seen as an organizing process that constitutes an organization, organizational members' activities, and their identification with the organization itself. Since individuals create meaning based upon specific interests and frames of reference, identity is implicitly involved. Sensemaking is grounded in the process of narrating and re-storying one's identity simultaneously with one's social context.
>
> *(p. 246)*

In other words, data doesn't make sense until said data is storied, that is, made sense of through narrative. which brings us back to autoethnography. Autoethnography is a sensemaking activity, and the following includes organizational autoethnography as sensemaking in action.

Organizational Autoethnography

Unlike more objective forms of research, autoethnography is uncharacteristically existential-phenomenological in nature (Berry, 2011; Bochner, 2013; Esping, 2010; Herrmann, 2021; Ngunjir, 2020; Poulos, 2010; Rawlins, 2018). Autoethnographers regularly convey their appreciation for existential and phenomenological approaches to first-person research and it should come as no surprise that there's a deep connection between the two. Although autoethnography is a qualitative research method, it is also more than that. Autoethnography is writing about – or otherwise representing – one's lived experience (Boylorn, 2013; Ellis et al., 2011; Herrmann, 2020). It is both process and product (Ellis et al., 2011). Moreover, autoethnography has been called "a way of life" (Bochner, 2020, p. 84).

Autoethnographers use selfhood, subjectivity, and individual experience ("auto") to illustrate, depict, and portray ("graphy") the ideologies, customs, and identities of a group or culture ("ethno") (Adams and Herrmann, 2020).

In pursuing the "auto," authors dismiss the God-like objective view from nowhere, as there is always an author doing the research and writing the representation. Moreover, much of organizational autoethnography is a first-person account of sensemaking in action (Brommel, 2017; Herrmann, 2020; Hunniecutt, 2017; Khalifa and Briscoe, 2015; Townsend, 2019; Vickers, 2007). Autoethnographies expose the I, which is sometimes very vulnerable. The following vignette provides an example of the vulnerable (and exasperated) self:

> Now, it wasn't the first time that the IRB asked for clarification that a breaker flipped in Angela's head. Oh no. It wasn't the second time either. Or the third time. Or the fourth. It was the fifth time, right after Spring Break, when the IRB started arguing with Angela because she was using *gender inclusive neutral pronouns*. Apparently, the IRB had an issue with *gender inclusive neutral pronouns*. WTF? That finally pushed Angela over the edge, hurtling into a blind panic about how we would never have the time to actually do our consulting project. I was tethered tightly to Angela. And Jessica tightly to me. "You go, we go!" was not encouragement but the shrieking cries of three students banging headlong at 80 miles per hour into the stone wall.
>
> *(Townsend et al., 2020, p. 377)*

However, "while first person positionality is a necessary component of autoethnography, it is not sufficient" (Taylor et al., 2021). Personal experience alone does not an autoethnography make.

For autoethnographers, personal experience must be purposefully used to shed light on and critically examine beliefs, practices, and identities within the cultural milieu ("ethno"). As Herrmann and Adams noted, "autoethnographies move beyond oneself by connecting with the relationships we have with others and/or with cultural beliefs, norms, situations, structures, and institutions" (2022, p. 2). Similarly, since personal experience is permeated with social norms and expectations, autoethnographers engage in meticulous self-reflection.

As Allen-Collinson (2013) notes, "At the heart of autoethnography, for me, is that ever-shifting focus between levels: from the macro, wide sociological angle on socio-cultural framework, to the micro, zoom focus on the embedded self" (p. 296). Here's an example of the "ethno":

> I am the dumb girl bartender, a role I play with some consistency and plausibility. With my mouth closed or lips slightly parted in a smile or giggle I can pass. I can play the support role, the accessory, the too weak to pull a keg role. I am where they want me. I am needy. I am dependent,

meek, and easily confused. I am there for their support, their pleasure. I am making money off this mask, off my ability to deceive individuals. In this environment who I am (college educated), and what I want to be (further educated) is masked. When I am masked, I am ill.

(Denker, 2017, p. 32)

In this vignette about her gendered performance working in a dive bar, Kathy Denker shows the ethnographic aspects of autoethnography through both critical macro analysis and self-reflection.

Finally, there is the "graphy," where the thick descriptions of the "ethno" and the personal reflexivity of the "auto" engage with the art and the craft of representation. Autoethnographies often "showcase concrete action, dialogue, emotion, embodiment, spirituality, and self-consciousness" (Ellis, 2004, p. 38). Autoethnographers utilize a variety of literary techniques and differing writing styles, including vignettes, dialogues, poetry, flashbacks, conversations, foreshadowing, and short stories. For autoethnographers, it is important to both tell what happened and to "show" what happened (Adams, 2006). While telling is much like an objective chronology and critique, showing is "written like your favorite scene in a novel, with the writing so lush in detail that the reader can get lost within it" (Herrmann and Herbig, 2021, p. 111). As an example, Arnold (2020) shows us the anguish of having a stillbirth in an organization that is not interested in loss:

I'm helped into a wheelchair and transported past the nursery and the pink and blue decorated doors to the room where I will recover. *Recover?* I clutch my weak legs to my chest in the fetal position, burying my face and covering my ears. I cannot take the sensory overload of a mother/baby unit, the newborn cries and the "ohs and ahs" of enraptured grandparents. The nurse helps me into the bed and gives me a shot of some medication which instantly puts me into a deep sleep.

(p. 211)

As one can see from these vignettes, the three aspects of auto-ethno-graphy are intimately intertwined during the process of writing and the representation within the end product.

What's important to note is that within all three of the vignettes the authors are in the process of sensemaking. "Autoethnography foregrounds an author's ability to offer insight into sensemaking processes, even – and perhaps especially – how we grapple with experiences that generate discomfort or that do not feel right or make sense" (Adams et al., 2021, p. 4). Townsend et al. are trying to figure out the complexities and intricacies of their Institutional Review Board as they negotiate their identities as burgeoning researchers. Denker is trying to understand how she feels about the sexualized performance at that dive bar. Arnold is working out how to deal with the inane organizational attempts of dealing with a woman who had a stillbirth within its walls. Each is working through the contexts of their situations, as well as their identities within said situations. This is what makes organizational autoethnography such a fruitful area of research for organizational sensemaking.

Coda: A Warning and a Proposal

Critics of organizational sensemaking theory note that it is decidedly focused on cognition and discursive strategies to the detriment of aspects of embodiment and power (Cunliffe and Coupland, 2012; Sandberg and Tsoukas, 2015; Schildt et al., 2020). By bringing in the existential "I," organizational autoethnography can act as a corrective to both. Autoethnography includes the body, the performative, the sweat of work, motherhood and the workplace, work in academe, workplace bullying, the exhaustion of work-life imbalances, psychological pain, the suffering of the worker, the grief of losing a colleague and friend, the flesh of sex work, and more (Chaudhari and Jaggi, 2020; Herbig, 2021; Johnson, 1999; Kempny, 2021; Klevan and Grant, 2022; Sobre-Denton, 2012; Stern and Manning, 2020; Tigchelaar, 2019). This is becoming truer as autoethnographers explore more nontextual ways of representation (Herbig et al., 2015; Johnston, 2020; Kouhia, 2015).

One of the other big dilemmas with sensemaking is that it is often retrospective; that is, it is backward-looking. Remember that the last part of Weick's process is retention. Having "made sense," organizations retain it for future use (Weick, 1979). When we encounter some new data, we rely on and refer to what we already know to help us make sense of the present equivocality. Retrospective sensemaking can be a trap. Sometimes what we did before will not work in new circumstances. Sometimes clinging too tightly to our identity and identifying items has an outsized importance on our identity (Weick, 1993). This can lead to disaster and even death:

> In 1949, 13 firefighters lost their lives at Mann Gulch, and in 1994, 14 more firefighters lost their lives under similar conditions at South Canyon. In both cases, these 23 men and four women were overrun by exploding fires when their retreat was slowed because they failed to drop the heavy tools they were carrying. By keeping their tools, they lost valuable distance they could have covered more quickly if they had been lighter.
>
> *(Weick, 1996, p. 305)*

The firefighters who died did not drop tools. Why did they not drop their tools? They could not separate their identity from the tools of their profession. Their tools were integral to who they believed themselves to be. "Given the central role of tools in defining the essence of a firefighter, it is not surprising that dropping one's tools creates an existential crisis. Without my tools, who am I? A coward? A fool?" (Weick, 1996, p. 305) By relying on previous definitions and identifications of who they were, rather than making sense of their context and identities in new ways, they lost their lives. Analyses of other disasters have found that identity threats and confusions have muddled the activity of sensemaking. (Brown, 2004; Christianson and Barton, 2021; Mills and Weatherbee, 2006; Parrish et al., 2020; Weick, 1990, 2010). For Weick (1995), dropping one's tools became the metaphor for the imperative of reinterpreting a narrative, creating a new narrative, or redefining one's identity when faced with new information or data.

If confusions, ambiguity, and equivocality make identity one of the prime movers of the sensemaking process, then it would behoove organizational researchers to reengage the "I" in sensemaking studies. If information and data are based upon individual enactment, the what, why, and how questions might be best asked from the first person perspective. "What is this that has appeared to me?" "Why is this important to me?" "How might I make sense of this?" Since the process of sensemaking starts with the facticity of the existential "I," writing autoethnographies might help us to get a better understanding of the individual processes of sensemaking that lead to the organizational processes of sensemaking. If identity is one key to the puzzle of sensemaking, restorying via autoethnography is one way to turn the key to unlock the puzzle.

References

Adams, T.E. (2006). 'Seeking Father: Relationally Reframing a Troubled Love Story'. *Qualitative Inquiry*. 12(4): pp. 704–723. https://doi.org/10.1177/1077800406288607
Adams, T.E. and Herrmann, A.F. (2020). 'Expanding Our Autoethnographic Future'. *Journal of Autoethnography*. 1(1): pp. 1–8. https://doi.org/10.1525/joae.2020.1.1.1
Adams, T.E., Jones, S.H. and Ellis, C. (2021). 'Introduction: Making Sense and Taking Action: Creating a Caring Community of Autoethnographers'. In Adams, T.E., Jones, S.H. and Ellis, C. (eds.) *Handbook of Autoethnography*. 2nd Edition. pp. 1–19. New York and London: Routledge.
Aho, K. (2014). *Existentialism: An Introduction*. New York: John Wiley & Sons.
Allen-Collinson, J. (2013). 'Autoethnography as Engagement of Self/Other, Self/Culture, Self/Politics, Selves/Futures'. In Holman Jones, S., Adams, T.E. and Ellis, C. (eds.) *Handbook of Autoethnography*. pp. 281–299. Walnut Creek, CA: Left Coast Press.

Anderson, M.H. (2006). 'How Can We Know What We Think Until We See What We Said? A Citation and Citation Context Analysis of Karl Weick's the Social Psychology of Organizing'. *Organization Studies.* 27(11): pp. 1675–1692. https://doi.org/10.1177/0170840606068346

Arnold, A. (2020). 'Birthing Autoethnographic Philanthropy, Healing, and Organizational Change: That Baby's Name'. In Herrmann, A.F. (ed.) *The Routledge International Handbook of Organizational Autoethnography.* pp. 209–224. New York and London: Routledge.

Barrett, W. (1962). *Irrational Man: A Study in Existential Philosophy.* New York: Doubleday.

Berry, K. (2011). 'The Ethnographic Choice: Why Ethnographers Do Ethnography'. *Cultural Studies<=>Critical Methodologies.* 11(2): pp. 165–177.

Bochner, A. (2013). 'Putting Meanings into Motion: Autoethnography's Existential Calling'. In Holman Jones, S., Adams, T. and Ellis, C. (eds.) *Handbook of Autoethnography.* pp. 50–56. Walnut Creek: Left Coast Press.

Bochner, A.P. (2020). 'Autoethnography as a Way of Life: Listening to Tinnitus Teach'. *Journal of Autoethnography.* 1(1): pp. 81–92. https://doi.org/10.1525/joae.2020.1.1.81

Bochner, A.P. and Adams, T.E. (2020). 'Autoethnography as Applied Communication Research'. In O'Hair, D. and O'Hair, M. (eds.) *The Handbook of Applied Communication Research.* pp. 707–729. New York: John Wiley & Sons, Inc.

Bochner, A.P. and Herrmann, A. (2020). 'Practicing Narrative Inquiry II: Making Meanings Move'. In Leavy, P. (ed.) *The Oxford Handbook of Qualitative Inquiry.* 2nd Edition. pp. 285–328. Oxford: Oxford University Press.

Boylorn, R. (2013). *Sweetwater: Black Women and Narratives of Resilience.* New York: Peter Lang.

Brommel, B.J. (2017). 'Sensemaking in the Dialysis Clinic'. In Herrmann, A. (ed.) *Organizational Autoethnographies: Our Working Lives.* pp. 87–106. New York, NY: Routledge.

Brown, A. (2004). 'Authoritative Sensemaking in a Public Inquiry Report'. *Organization Studies.* 25(1): pp. 95–112. https://doi.org/10.1177/0170840604038182

Chaudhari, M. and Jaggi, R. (2020). 'Documenting Migrant Lives of Sugarcane Harvesting Labourers in Maharashtra – Autoethnographic Reflections'. *Rupkatha Journal on Interdisciplinary Studies in Humanities.* 12(5): pp. 1–7. http://dx.doi.org/10.21659/rupkatha.v12n5.rioc1s30n2

Christianson, M. and Barton, M. (2021). 'Sensemaking in the Time of COVID-19'. *Journal of Management Studies.* 58(2): pp. 572–576. https://doi.org/10.1111/joms.12658

Cunliffe, A. and Coupland, C. (2012). 'From Hero to Villain to Hero: Making Experience Sensible Through Embodied Narrative Sensemaking'. *Human Relations.* 65(1): pp. 63–88. https://doi.org/10.1177/0018726711424321

Czarniawska, B. (2005). 'Karl Weick: Concepts, Style and Reflection'. *The Sociological Review.* 53(1_suppl): pp. 267–278. https://doi.org/10.1111/j.1467-954X.2005.00554.x

Denker, K. (2017). 'Power, Emotional Labor, and Intersectional Identity at Work: I Would Not Kiss My Boss But I Did Not Speak Up'. In Herrmann, A. (ed.) *Organizational Autoethnographies: Power and Identity in Our Working Lives.* pp. 16–36. New York: Routledge.

Eisenberg, E.M. (2006). 'Karl Weick and the Aesthetics of Contingency'. *Organization Studies*. 27(11): pp. 1693–1707. https://doi.org/10.1177/0170840606068348

Ellis, C. (1991). 'Sociological Introspection and Emotional Experience'. *Symbolic Interaction*. 14(1): pp. 23–50. https://www.jstor.org/stable/10.1525/si.1991.14.1.23

Ellis, C. (2004). *The Ethnographic I: A Methodological Novel about Autoethnography*. Thousand Oaks, CA: AltaMira.

Ellis, C., Adams, T.E. and Bochner, A.P. (2011). 'Autoethnography: An Overview'. *Historical Social Research/Historische sozialforschung*. 12(10): Art 10. pp. 273–290. View of Autoethnography: An Overview | Forum Qualitative Sozialforschung/Forum: Qualitative Social Research (qualitative-research.net)

Esping, A. (2010). 'Autoethnography and Existentialism: The Conceptual Contributions of Viktor Frankl'. *Journal of Phenomenological Psychology*. 41(2): pp. 201–215. http://dx.doi.org/10.1163/156916210X532126

Farina, G. (2014). 'Some Reflections on the Phenomenological Method'. *Dialogues in Philosophy, Mental and Neuro Sciences*. 7(2): pp. 50–62. Gabriella Farina, Some reflections on the phenomenological method – PhilArchive

Glynn, M.A. and Watkiss, L. (2020). 'Of Organizing and Sensemaking: From Action to Meaning and Back Again in a Half-Century of Weick's Theorizing'. *Journal of Management Studies*. 57(7): pp. 1331–1354. https://doi.org/10.1111/joms.12613

Gioia, D.A. (2006). 'On Weick: An Appreciation'. *Organization Studies*. 27(11): pp. 1709–1721. https://doi.org/10.1177/0170840606068349

Guignon, C. and Pereboom, D. (eds.) (2001). *Existentialism: Basic Writings*. Indianapolis: Hackett Publishing Company.

Heidegger, M. (1962). *Being and Time*. Translated by John Macquarrie and Edward Robinson. London: SCM Press.

Herbig, A. (2021). 'Understanding Privilege in a Pandemic: The Small Systems that Perpetuate the Large Structures'. *Journal of Autoethnography*. 2(2): pp. 242–247. https://doi.org/10.1525/joae.2021.2.2.242

Herbig, A., Hess, A., Watson, A., producer Herbig, A. and Director. (2015). *Never Forget: Public Memory & 9/11*. [Motion Picture]. Fort Wayne, IN: Living Text Productions.

Herrmann, A.F. (2008). 'Kierkegaard and Dialogue: The Communication of Capability'. *Communication Theory*. 18: pp. 71–92. https://doi.org/10.1111/j.1468-2885.2007.00314.x

Herrmann, A.F. (2011). 'Narrative as an Organizing Process: Identity and Story in a New Nonprofit'. *Qualitative Research in Organizations and Management: An International Journal*. 6(3): pp. 246–264. http://dx.doi.org/10.1108/17465641111188411

Herrmann, A.F. (2015). 'Communicating, Sensemaking, and (dis)organizing: Theorizing the Complexity of Polymediation'. In Herbig, A., Herrmann, A.F. and Tyma, A.W. (eds.) *Beyond New Media: Discourse and Critique in a Polymediated Age*. pp. 61–82. Washington, DC: Lexington Books.

Herrmann, A.F. (2016). 'On Being a Homeless Work of Fiction: Narrative Quests and Questions'. *International Review of Qualitative Research*. 9(1): pp. 23–49. https://doi.org/10.1525/irqr.2016.9.1.29

Herrmann, A.F. (ed.) (2020). *The Routledge International Handbook of Organizational Autoethnography*. New York: Routledge.

Herrmann, A.F. (2021). 'Autoethnography as Acts of Love'. In Adams, T.E., Holman Jones, S. and Ellis, C. (eds.) *The Handbook of Autoethnography*. 2nd Edition. pp. 67–78. New York and Abingdon: Routledge.

Herrmann, A.F. and Adams, T.E. (2022). 'Autoethnography and the "So what?" Question'. *Journal of Autoethnography*. 3(1): pp. 1–3. e-ISSN 2637-5192

Herrmann, A.F. and Herbig, A. (2021). 'An Autoethnography of Working, Failing and Reworking Public Scholarship'. In Leavy, P. (ed.) *Popularizing Scholarly Research: Research Methods and Practices*. pp. 104–131. New York: Oxford University Press.

Hunniecutt, J. (2017). 'Stroking My Rifle Like the Body of a Woman: A Woman's Socialization into the U.S. Army'. In Herrmann, A.F. (ed.) *Organizational Autoethnographies: Our Working Lives*. pp. 37–58. New York, NY: Routledge.

Husserl, E. (1973). *The Idea of Phenomenology*. The Hague: Martinus Nijhoff.

Johnson, M. (1999). 'Pole Work: Autoethnography of a Strip Club'. In Barry, M., Dank, B. and Refinetti, R. (eds.) *Sex Work & Sex Workers*. pp. 149–158. New York: Routledge.

Johnston, B. (2020). 'Framing Stories from the Academic Margins: Documentary as Qualitative Inquiry and Critical Community Engagement'. In Herrmann, A.F. (ed.) *The Routledge International Handbook of Organizational Autoethnography*. pp. 437–456. New York: Routledge.

Kempny, M. (2021). '(Auto) Ethnography of Breastfeeding in Northern Ireland: Agency-Centered Approach'. *Journal of Autoethnography*. 2(4): pp. 405–420. https://doi.org/10.1525/joae.2021.2.4.405

Khalifa, M. and Briscoe, F. (2015). *Becoming Critical: The Emergence of Social Justice Scholars*. Albany: SUNY Press.

Kierkegaard, S. (1958). *The Journals of Kierkegaard*. New York: Harper.

Klevan, T. and Grant, A. (2022). *An Autoethnography of Becoming a Qualitative Researcher: A Dialogic View of Academic Development*. London and New York: Routledge.

Kouhia, A. (2015). 'The Making-of: An Autoethnographic Cinema on the Meanings of Con-temporary Craft Practicing for a Young Hobbyist'. *Textile*. 13(3): pp. 266–283. https://doi.org/10.1080/14759756.2015.1084788

Krizek, R. (2003). 'Ethnography as the Excavation of Personal Narrative'. In Clair, R. (ed.), *Expressions of Ethnography*. pp. 141–151. Albany: SUNY Press.

Luijpen, W. and Koren, H. (1969). *First Introduction to Existential Phenomenology*. Pittsburgh: Duquense University Press.

Magala, S. (1997). 'The Making and Unmaking of Sense'. *Organization Studies*. 18(2): pp. 317–329. http://dx.doi.org/10.1177/017084069701800206

Merleau-Ponty, M. (2012). *Phenomenology of Perception*. Translated by Landes, D.A. London: Routledge.

Mills, J. and Weatherbee, T. (2006). 'Hurricanes Hardly Happen: Sensemaking as a Framework for Understanding Organizational Disasters'. *Culture and Organization*. 12(3): pp. 265–279. https://doi.org/10.1080/14759550600871485

Ngunjiri, F. (2020). 'Existential Crisis in a Global Pandemic: Writing Autoethnography'. *Journal of Autoethnography*. 1(4): pp. 408–413. https://doi.org/10.1525/joae.2020.1.4.408

Parrish, D. Clark, T. and Holloway, S. (2020). 'The Collapse of Sensemaking at Yarnell Hill: The Effects of Endogenous Ecological Chaos on Enactment'. *European Journal of Management Studies*. 25(2): pp. 77–95. http://dx.doi.org/10.1108/EJMS-10-2020-005

Poulos, C. (2010). 'Spirited Accidents: An Autoethnography of Possibility'. *Qualitative Inquiry*. 16(1): pp. 49–56. http://dx.doi.org/10.1177/1077800409350063

Rawlins, L.S. (2018). 'Poetic Existential: A Lyrical Autoethnography of Self, Others, and World'. *Art/Research International: A Transdisciplinary Journal*. 3(1): pp. 155–177. http://dx.doi.org/10.18432/ari29208

Sandberg, J. and Tsoukas, H. (2015). 'Making Sense of the Sensemaking Perspective: Its Constituents, Limitations, and Opportunities for Further Development'. *Journal of Organizational Behavior*. 36(S1): pp. S6–S32. https://doi.org/10.1002/job.1937

Sartre, J-P. (2003 [1943]). *Being and Nothingness*. London: Routledge.

Schildt, H., Mantere, S. and Cornelissen, J. (2020). 'Power in Sensemaking Processes'. *Organization Studies*. 41(2): pp. 241–265. https://doi.org/10.1177/0170840619847718

Sobre-Denton, M. (2012). 'Stories from the Cage: Autoethnographic Sensemaking of Workplace Bullying, Gender Discrimination, and White Privilege'. *Journal of Contemporary Ethnography*. 41(2): pp. 220–250. https://doi.org/10.1177/0891241611429301

Stern, D.M. and Manning, L.D. (2020). 'Grieving Kathy: An Interactional Autoethnography of Cultivating Sustainable Organizations'. In *The Routledge International Handbook of Organizational Autoethnography*. pp. 271–286. New York: Routledge.

Sutcliffe, K., Brown, A. and Putnam, L. (2006). 'Introduction to the Special Issue: Making Sense of Organizing in Honor of Karl Weick'. *Organization Studies*. 27(11): pp. 1573–1578. https://doi.org/10.1177/0170840606068327

Taylor, B.C. et al. (2021). 'Revisiting Ethnography in Organizational Communication Studies'. *Management Communication Quarterly*. 35(4): pp. 623–652. https://doi.org/10.1177/08933189211026700

Tigchelaar, A. (2019). 'Sex Worker Resistance in the Neoliberal Creative City: An Auto/Ethnography'. *Anti-Trafficking Review*. 12: pp. 15–36. http://dx.doi.org/10.14197/atr.201219122

Townsend, T.W. (2019). 'A Groundhog Moment: Examination of a Pivotal Emotional Singularity'. *Qualitative Inquiry*. 25(2): 100–110. https://doi.org/10.1177/1077800417750678

Townsend, T.W. et al. (2020). 'The IRB's Stone Wall: Rollercoaster of Doom'. In Herrmann, A.F. (ed.) *The Routledge International Handbook of Organizational Autoethnography*. pp. 366–382. New York: Routledge.

Tsoukas, H. (2019). *Philosophical Organization Theory*. Oxford: Oxford University Press.

Tsoukas, H. et al. (2020). 'On the Way to Ithaka: Commemorating the 50th Anniversary of the Publication of Karl E. Weick's the Social Psychology of Organizing'. *Journal of Management Studies*. 57(7): pp. 1315–1330. https://doi.org/10.1111/joms.12616

Vickers, M.H. (2007). 'Autoethnography as Sensemaking: A Story of Bullying'. *Culture and Organization*. 13(3): pp. 223–237. https://doi.org/10.1080/1475955 0701486555

Weber, K. and Glynn, M.A. (2006). 'Making Sense with Institutions: Context, Thought and Action in Karl Weick's Theory'. *Organization Studies*. 27(11): pp. 1639–1660. https://doi.org/10.1177/0170840606068343

Weick, K.E. (1974). 'Amendments to Organizational Theorizing'. *Academy of Management Journal*. 17(3): pp. 487–502. https://doi.org/10.2307/254652

Weick, K.E. (1979). *The Social Psychology of Organizing*. 2nd Edition. Reading, MA: Addison-Wesley.

Weick, K.E. (1988). 'Enacted Sensemaking in Crisis Situations [1]'. *Journal of Management Studies*. 25(4): pp. 305–317. https://doi.org/10.1111/j.1467-6486.1988. tb00039.x

Weick, K.E. (1989). 'Organized Improvisation: 20 Years of Organizing'. *Communication Studies*. 40(4): pp. 241–248. Organized Improvisation: 20 Years of Organizing. | Semantic Scholar

Weick, K.E. (1990). 'The Vulnerable System: An Analysis of the Tenerife Air Disaster'. *Journal of Management*. 16(3): pp. 571–593. https://deepblue.lib. umich.edu/bitstream/handle/2027.42/68716/10.1177_014920639001600304. pdf?sequence=2&isAllowed=y

Weick, K.E. (1993). 'The Collapse of Sensemaking in Organizations: The Mann Gulch Disaster'. *Administrative Science Quarterly*. 38(4): pp. 628–652. https:// psycnet.apa.org/doi/10.2307/2393339

Weick, K.E. (1995). *Sensemaking in Organizations*. Vol. 3. Thousand Oaks, CA: Sage Publications.

Weick, K.E. (1996). 'Drop Your Tools: An Allegory for organizational Studies'. *Administrative Science Quarterly*. 41(9): pp. 301–313. https://doi.org/10.2307/2393722

Weick, K.E. (1998). 'Introductory Essay—Improvisation as a Mindset for Organizational Analysis'. *Organization Science*. 9(5): pp. 543–555. https://doi. org/10.1287/orsc.9.5.543

Weick, K.E. (2010). 'Reflections on Enacted Sensemaking in the Bhopal Disaster'. *Journal of Management Studies*. 47(3): pp. 537–550. https://doi. org/10.1111/j.1467-6486.2010.00900.x

Weick, K.E. (2012). *Making Sense of the Organization, Volume 2: The Impermanent Organization*. New York: John Wiley & Sons.

Weick, K.E., Sutcliffe, K.M. and Obstfeld, D. (2005). 'Organizing and the Process of Sensemaking'. *Organization Science*. 16: pp. 409–421. http://dx.doi. org/10.1287/orsc.1050.0133

9

A LIMINAL AWAKENING

Christopher N. Poulos

Introduction

As I get older, I find myself lingering in the liminal spaces of life, in the betwixt and between, on the thresholds. I *want* to linger here, embracing the mystery and take it all in before I act. And then I write, as always driven by the existentialist philosophy that spoke so deeply to me in my youth, and continues to speak to me across time and space and through memory and story. Existentialist philosophy animates and illuminates my autoethnography and my life, opens up a space of *possibility*, speaks into the gaps between finitude and action, between call and response, between memory and forgetting, between being and nothingness, between anxiety and creation . . . and infuses everything I do with a creative vitality, in ways I hope to show in this chapter.

Liminal Openings

I pause in the liminal spaces . . . between cry and echo, between dreaming and waking, between memory and forgetting. I hover between despair and hope, between fear and faith, between finitude and creation, between anxiety and courage, between joy and grief. And between speaking and being heard, between listening and understanding, between I and Thou, between reflecting and writing . . . I pause, engulfed in wonder, taking a breath, embracing the mystery of it all, and searching . . . searching . . .

Today, I find myself drawn inexorably back to my philosophical awakening some 40 years ago. I was a student in a course on existentialist

DOI: 10.4324/9781003274728-9

literature at the University of Colorado. One of our reading assignments was a book of essays by Albert Camus. In *The Myth of Sisyphus*, Camus recasts the ancient Greek tale of punishment and woe, wherein Sisyphus is condemned by the gods to roll a rock to the top of a mountain, only to have it roll back down, repeating his task over and over for eternity. Punished for *hubris* – for daring to defy the gods – Sisyphus labors in endless futility. His fate is, as Camus put it, absurd. He is bound by eternal suffering, with no chance of escape. But he does have moments of respite, as he walks back down the hill to retrieve his rock. Camus (re) reads the myth:

> It is during that return, that pause, that Sisyphus interests me. A face that toils so close to stones is already stone itself! I see that man going back down with a heavy yet measured step toward the torment of which he will never know the end. That hour like a breathing-space which returns as surely as his suffering, that is the hour of consciousness. At each of those moments when he leaves the heights and gradually sinks toward the lairs of the gods, he is superior to his fate. He is stronger than his rock.
>
> *(Camus, 1955, p. 89)*

This was his moment of *possibility* (Kierkegaard, 1980). I stumbled into this reading not long after a six-month stint working in a lumberyard, where I spent 10 hours a day performing repetitive, monotonous, exhausting manual labor, loading boards onto forklifts. Day after day, week after week, month after month, I faced my rock – or, rather, my board(s). One icy January day, I was standing, loading boards, and happened to pause and gaze down at my feet, which had gone numb. I noticed that the ice in the puddle I was standing in had coalesced around my boots. I was frozen in place. It was clearly a metaphor for my life. But I knew at that moment that I was stronger than that puddle; I was more than a stacker of boards. My eyes opened wide; I was on the threshold of epiphany. It was my Sisyphus-walking-down-the-hill moment.

So, I made my way to college and wandered into existentialism, which led me to story, which took me to theology, which pushed me toward communication, where I stumbled into autoethnography. In writing autoethnography, I find my *possibility*. I make my way across thresholds . . . into new worlds. In this essay, I will explore autoethnography as a way into and through the liminal moments of my life, driven by the muse-voices of existentialist philosopher-writers like Buber, Camus, Kierkegaard, Percy, Sartre, and Tillich.

The existentialist movement, which itself hovered on thresholds – between the search for God and the repudiation of God, between the 19th and 20th centuries, between the great World Wars, between literature and philosophy, between being and nothingness, between finitude and action, between absurdity and meaning, between suicide and affirmation of life – can be understood as a way of seeing the world in which human consciousness of our existence is a primary creative moment. Following Heidegger's notion that we are "thrown into being" (Heidegger, 1962), Sartre, in a talk titled *Existentialism is a Humanism*, puts it thus: "What do we mean by saying that existence precedes essence? We mean that man first of all exists, encounters himself, surges up in the world – and defines himself afterwards" (2007, p. 22).

Humans do not live out a predetermined pattern or essence. We humans are thrown into Being as free agents, exercising our creative will to construct our lives, and thus the meaning of our existence. Our fate may sometimes resemble that of Sisyphus – doomed to endless labor – but in those moments of respite, those pauses where we become *conscious* of our freedom, we can act. There is no "essence" of what it means to be a human being; instead, through the acts of our lives we craft a meaningful path. In Kierkegaard's terms, we seek *possibility*. Thus, in Sartre's way of thinking, *we create ourselves*, and we author our lives.

Living in Liminality

In my view, the biggest gift the existentialist movement gave us is this insistence that we can choose to live as free agents, in spite – no, in *defiance* – of our basic human finitude. But it is not happening while we are "sunk in everydayness" (Percy, 1960), nor is it happening when we are grinding through days of labor. But in our (rare?) moments of respite, in those liminal breathing spaces, we can find our way. It is in that liminal space, that pause, the return . . . that Sisyphus can find meaning in his struggle. Even Viktor Frankl (1959), as he walked through the grinding torture of Nazi work camps, found beauty – in the moment when he paused to gaze at a rainbow, or a sunset – in the *possibility* of something beyond his suffering. And so can we, as we go about our bounded lives, pause from our labors, from our trials and tribulations, and take our stand in liminality, in that threshold between struggling to learn and coming to know, between the call and the response, between meeting and relation. Engulfed in the mystery of being (Marcel, 1950), always *becoming*, always *on our way*, we can build a life that makes sense even in the face of the absurdity of a universe that condemns us to death. Of course, most existentialist writers put our predicament more bluntly:

Camus: There is only one really serious philosophical question, and that is suicide (1955, p. 3).

Kierkegaard: [We are] battling madly, if you will, for possibility, because possibility is the only salvation. When someone faints, we call for water, *eau de cologne*, smelling salts; but when someone wants to despair, then the word is: Get possibility, get possibility, possibility is the only salvation. A possibility – then the person in despair breathes again, he revives again, for without possibility a person seems unable to breathe.

(1980, pp. 38–39)

Percy: To become aware of the possibility of the search is to be onto something. Not to be onto something is to be in despair.

(1960, p. 13)

Sartre: Nothingness haunts being.

(1993, p. 3)

Tillich: Courage is the self-affirmation of being in spite of the fact of nonbeing.

(1952, p. 155)

These writers zeroed in on the raw fact of human finitude – that we are limited, that we can surely rebel against our finitude, but we cannot fully escape it – and that then we can craft a path for ourselves. Still, we all know that at some moment sooner or later, we will find ourselves in direct confrontation with our end. The stark realization that whatever we face here in this life – whatever we create, struggle with, overcome, whatever joys and sorrows we live through – all of it ends in the oblivion of death – is the jumping-off place, the beginning of existentialist philosophy. Can we find "possibility" in this moment of stark realization, and beyond it? Is there some way to wrest meaning out of an existence that appears to begin and end in oblivion, in nothingness?

For Camus, the answer lies in creative acts – in his case, writing. I have no quarrel with that. I've found it there myself, more times than I care to count. For Percy, it is in the *search* itself. For Buber, it is in that liminal space between I and Thou, that realm of "holy sparks" that is the opening to dialogue. For Kierkegaard and Tillich, it comes from a leap of faith, a kind of embracing of possibility beyond the possibility of possibility – or as Tillich puts it, in the God beyond God that appears after the Death of God* – where we land in the "courage to be" in spite of the clear and present reality of nonbeing (Tillich, 1952). I do not know much about faith, but I can follow Kierkegaard's methodology of doubt and see how it ends in a sort of leap beyond doubt into . . . *something*. You can't hang out in doubt forever. And like Tillich, I can hold on to at least the idea of courage. Or, as he puts it later, I can dwell in "ultimate concern" (Tillich, 1957).

Personally, I find possibility in the moments *before* I write, *before* I am in the act of creation, between life and death, between dream and story, between anxiety and courage, between despair and hope, between being frozen and acting.

Often, I find it while wandering through the forests that surround my North Carolina home. As I write this, we are on the threshold of spring. New leaves are sprouting from the slumbering limbs of the trees, the birds are coming to life, and my dogs are busy sniffing the newness of it all. I like to dwell on the threshold, in those liminal moments where, betwixt and between being and nonbeing, in the midst of becoming – yes, always *becoming*, I can sense that if nothing else, I can "stand in relation" (Buber, 1970, p. 55).

The Magic Hour

Cinematographers speak of the "magic hour" – those 20 minutes or so after the sun sets and before darkness descends in full, a liminal time of golden-blue light, in which we find ourselves wanting to hover, to feel fully alive on the cusp, on the threshold before we lose all light for another cycle and fall into slumber. It is in this magic hour that I want to dwell for a time, wandering and wondering, holding the mystery of it all close to my heart, anticipating what may come next. Of course, this body feels the weight of another day and senses the need for rest, and for dreams, and for the chance to rise again a few hours later, where dreams blend into waking, and slow waking wobbles into writing, and I begin the search once again.

It is here in the evening magic hour, and in its twin, that moment just before full dawn, when the songbirds begin to stir outside my North Carolina forest home and call out to each other: *A new day is upon us! It is time to rise, and rejoice, and seek sustenance.* And I follow their lead, embracing the new day and seeking sustenance, first in their presence as I wander the forest with our dogs Lucky and Finley and my partner Susan, and then at our table. And then at my keyboard – at least on the best of days. And as I sit down to write, fingers hovering, I find my way into the mystery of creation.

Dying

Those who have read my work know I've been visited often by Death (Poulos, 2006, 2014b). Oh, he wasn't knocking on my door directly, but . . . he has swept away many family members, friends, colleagues, and students over the years – often in big *bursts* of death (four in one year, seven in another, five in yet another). And with Death's every visit, I have tried to make some sense of my world without one or more of my people. I have grieved, I have cried, I have written, I have attended funerals and "celebrations of life," I have told stories about the deceased and listened to even more, I have wondered if I could carry on some beautiful quality of each lost person in my own life. I have even written hate mail to Death, demanding an explanation. I have ranted and I have raved and I have sobbed.

But the one that hit hardest was my father's death. That it hit so hard shook me a bit, given the conflicted nature of our relationship. On July 5, 2019, my father shuffled off "this mortal coil" (Shakespeare, 1992). He had been dying for months. Years, really. In some ways, it seemed that he died long before that day (Poulos, 2012, 2014a). But that day it was final, unavoidable. His body just broke down. And his spirit left the room. That day, the earth shifted under my feet.

I felt a big, gaping hole where my dad had been. For years, we had been locked in a battle of the wills. Rarely did we see eye to eye. It almost seemed we could not, or would not, ever give an inch. Tension filled the air between us. Too much was said. So much was left unsaid. But since his passing, I've been *leaning in* to my dad (Pelias, 2011). I do not know how to cope with losing him, a man whose approval I always desperately craved but rarely got, who left me with more questions than answers. Like him, I was not ready for the end.

My dad, who had been a "man of the cloth" (an Episcopal priest, to be precise) for decades, who had sat by many bedsides while his parishioners and friends and family members reached their expiration dates, was not persuaded that his time had come. He seemed surprised. Shocked, even. Death was for other people. He knew how to comfort *them*. But himself?

Really, though, it was no surprise to the rest of us. After all, he had been suffering for at least five years with multiple conditions: congestive heart failure, edema, COPD, rheumatoid arthritis, spinal stenosis, very high blood pressure, sleep apnea, and probably slowly progressing kidney failure.

For three long months, he hovered on the threshold, dying but not dying, searching for something. He spent his final months asking lots of questions, but his body was failing him, and he was, during the last three months in particular – when he spent most of his time being shuttled back and forth between the hospital and the nursing home – brimming over with questions. "*What could possibly be wrong?*" he wondered aloud more than once. He could barely move. It was painful to watch. He was clearly suffering. Nobody had the heart to tell him what he probably knew, somewhere deep inside. I don't know for sure, but he seemed puzzled that it could actually happen to *him*. I don't think he was ready.

On one trip to the hospital, he was having tremors. These were new. They would usually begin at his feet, and work their way up through his body, all the way to his neck. I was visiting one day as the doctor popped in.

"Doc, do you see that tremor?" he asked, somewhat plaintively. "What could be causing that?"

"I'm not sure, Mr. Poulos. We are running some tests."

The doctor looked at me. If it's possible for a look to communicate, this one said, pretty clearly, *"The tremors are the least of his problems. He's dying."*

"I know," my eyes shot back.

And my mind fell back to a short story by Leo Tolstoy, *The Death of Ivan Ilych*, which we read in that Existentialist Literature class so many years before. In the story, Ilych, a judge, trembles uncontrollably as he begins the process of what doctors now call "active dying" (Tolstoy, 1960). He can't shake the tremors. He cannot escape his fate; he cannot emerge from what he thinks of as the "black sack" that has taken him, and he cannot escape what truly haunts him: the idea that he's led an inauthentic life, that he's been a pretender, that he did most of what he did as a performance to ingratiate himself to others, that he was caught up in a terrible cycle of phoniness. This is what haunts him in his final hours. So, he descends into three days of shaking and screaming on his way into the final abyss. On the third day, while he is screaming, his body tremors mightily one last time, he lets out a long slow rattling breath, and he dies.

And it almost seems to me that my dad, who I doubt knew this story but who did not want to depart in the way of Ilych, decided on a different route. It seemed spontaneous, but I doubt it. My father was not a spontaneous man. He was methodical, a scientist at heart, a man who was a pharmacist before he was a priest, a man who loved procedure, then procedural ritual, more than he loved anything. He planned the timing of his exit, even as he hoped not to accept it.

While he was waiting, my dad took up a new hobby during our visits. He had never spent much time telling me stories of his childhood, but during those final months, he told me many. Every time I walked through the door, he started a new one.

It was as if he was working with me, trying to help me understand through the power of story how he became who he was, how he and I got to a place where our relationship was mostly conflicted. And I think he was hoping that we would lay all that to rest and look at our history with new eyes.

The first story he told me was, I think, born of his hope that I might understand how he saw father-son relationships, and why ours was the way it was:

When I was young – about eight, I think – Pop had a little general store. All I wanted to do on a Saturday was play baseball. But he made me work at the store. It was one of those stores that sold all kinds of things. Sometimes he had fresh fruit, sometimes clothes, all kinds of assorted stuff. You know, if you needed it, Pop would sell it. He had a big basket of socks up front with a sign that read: "Socks 10 cents a pair, two for a quarter." People would be confused by that sign. If they came up with one pair of socks, he would charge them a quarter. They would say, "Hey! I thought it was two for a quarter." He would reply, in his heaviest Greek accent, "Two socks. You have two socks. It's a quarter." But the insiders knew that two pairs of socks were also a quarter. Pop was a trickster.

> If someone came in asking for milk and he didn't have any, he'd tell them to wait. Then, he'd take me in the back, and give me a dollar, and tell me to run down to the grocery store as fast as I could and get some milk – but be sure to bring it in the back door so the customer couldn't see. So, I would run down the block as fast as I could and get the milk. Pop would be waiting for me, then he would sell it for at least a dime profit. In those days, that was money. A dime would buy you half a gallon of gas or a loaf of bread.
>
> Then he would send me out to the corner in front to sell oranges to passersby. I wasn't allowed to come back until I'd sold the whole basket. He was a tough taskmaster. If I failed to sell them all, he wouldn't pay me.
>
> I loved Pop, but boy, he was hard on me. We could never talk back to him; if we did, we were in for it. Jimmy was always in a lot of trouble because he had a smart mouth. I just kept mine shut. Pop was the boss more than he was my father. He ran the show.

And there, in the twilight of my father's life – in his magic hour – I got a glimmer of the golden light that animated his life. And that infused his own ways as a father. And I came to understand that the things I thought he'd done – the demands he made on me, the pushing, the insults, the tough-guy act – was him simply passing on his "narrative inheritance" (Goodall, 2006). This is what fathers do: They are hard on their sons – especially the ones with "potential." *The father is the boss.*

So, Dad was hard on me. Relentless, even. What I wanted from him was support. What I wanted was pure, unconditional love, given in a way that I could recognize. What I got instead was challenge and obstacle and suffering. What I got was my own hero's journey (Campbell, 1948).

On the evening before his death, he was home under hospice care. We visited him to say goodnight – my wife Susan, my son Eli and his wife Laura, and me. He seemed to be fading in and out of consciousness while he tried to tell one last story. He drifted off before he could finish. Later that evening, my sisters Mary and Sarah and my mom went in to tell him goodnight. They say he seemed animated, hopeful.

The next morning, at 7 a.m. sharp, my phone rings. I know what it is before I answer.

Mom says simply: "Your dad died. Sometime in the middle of the night."

"I know," I reply. "I'll be there in a few minutes."

Now, three years after his death, people who know our past ask me, "Do you have closure now?" Ha! I find myself thinking. *Closure? What the hell is that, anyway? Closure is a fantasy*. What I do have is a growing, ever-changing relationship with my dad. I know him now better than I did when he was alive. I see him in me, in my siblings, in my sons, and in the wider world he touched.

Someone who knew him for many years recently said to me, "I never noticed it before, but you look like your dad." In truth, I look a bit more like my maternal grandfather, I think. But I know what she meant. There is something of him in me. I have his voice, but sometimes people mistake that for something they can see. And I have come to accept all of it. I have come to *love* it. This is the gift of my father to me – a trace of his genetic legacy. And, of course, he gave me his final stories, which illuminated, if only dimly, that part of his life that preceded my existence, but that shaped how we were together, who my dad was as a father, how he approached relationships.

As I try to make sense of the earth-shattering feeling of losing him, I have come to know that he did love me in his own way, and that I of course loved him and still do. And that is *something*.

I wish he could tell me one more story.

The Search

In his breakout novel *The Moviegoer*, Walker Percy puts his existentialist antihero, Binx Bolling, in the driver's seat. But Binx is a wanderer, often lost in wonder and in the reverie that comes at the magic hour, just before he heads in to see another movie. Binx is on what he calls a *search*:

> What is the nature of the search? you ask. Really it is very simple, at least for a fellow like me, so simple that it is easily overlooked. The search is

what anyone would undertake if he were not sunk in the everydayness of his own life. This morning, for example, I felt as if I had come to myself on a strange island. And what does such a castaway do? Why, he pokes around the neighborhood, and he doesn't miss a trick.

(1960, p. 13)

So, soon after my dad's death, I decide to poke around the neighborhood in search of something that would re-solidify the ground under me. A week or so later, my mom and I are sorting some of his things in his bedroom. As I shuffle through some papers stored in a file box in his closet, searching for his Last Will and Testament, I look across the room at his bookcase. Perched atop a pile of books is a baseball.

Hmmm, I find myself thinking. *That's strange. What's that about?*

I walk over, pick up the baseball. As I examine it, I realize it's not just any baseball. It's a Spalding official Little League ball, signed by my teammates from the Gresham Park Twins the summer I was on the cusp of turning 13, the summer I had my one and only growth spurt, the summer my dad finally showed up to my baseball games because he volunteered to be an assistant coach. It was his attempt to bond with me. It was a point of contention between us, since he had never before shown up for any of my games, though I secretly appreciated the gesture. But for a boy nearly 13, it wasn't "cool" to take instruction from your dad. And I was probably about as gracious as your average 12-year-old, which is to say not at all.

But he held onto that baseball for all these years, and he put it in plain sight. And that is *something*.

What could it mean? Our baseball paths crossed only once or twice, really, and that was long ago. Nearly 50 years has passed. Why does the baseball show up now, at this moment so many years later? Why would he want me to find this baseball? What is this ball telling me? What is Dad telling me, from beyond the grave?

I fall into memory. I am nine years old. I have nothing to do and nobody to do it with, so I grab a baseball and my glove, and start throwing it at the side of our brick house, catching the ball on the rebound, playing pitch with myself. Inside, on the other side of that wall is my dad (ironically) watching a baseball game on TV. I don't have the patience to watch baseball, but I love playing it. Dad, on the other hand, seems to have no interest in playing pitch with me. But he will watch a ball game until he passes out in his chair. The ball obviously makes a noise every time it hits that wall.

Thok. Thok. Thok.

"Knock it off out there!"

Thok. Thok. Thok.

"I said knock it off! Don't make me come out there!"

I sigh, and start tossing the ball up in the air, catching fly balls. The sound of the glove is fainter, and soon my dad is dozing off in his chair.

And I'm back in the room, staring at this 50-year-old baseball.

"Mom, do you remember this baseball being here?"

"No, I can't say that I do."

"I wonder why Dad put it here, and when."

"It had to be recent. I don't remember seeing it before."

"OK."

As I head home, I find myself once again entering a swirl of long-ago memories. Baseball. The smell of dusty base paths. Sweat trickling down my brow. The sound of the ball hitting the bat, my glove snapping as I snag the line drive and quickly turn a double play, catching the runner on second off-guard. I was an All-Star shortstop that year. We even played an exhibition game in the US Penitentiary in Atlanta.

Dad did try to coach me. I have no doubt he could have helped me improve my hitting. Hitting was always my weak spot, at least until I stopped trying to hit for power and started place-hitting the ball.

Like everything else I tried before or since, I was only good if I relaxed. He tried to tell me to loosen up, but damn, that ball came fast. For some reason, the glove was easy for me – all smooth reflex – but the bat was awkward, tight, twitchy, and it didn't seem to offer the same kind of protection from that hard orb hurtling at me.

Dad, on the other hand, had been a pretty good hitter in his day. He could have helped. But I was 12. If you've ever met a 12-year-old boy, you know that each of them knows more than all the adults in the world combined. This standoff was one of many I had with my dad over the span of our lives. He wanted me to listen, to bow to his authority. I wasn't having it. *The man liked black-eyed peas, for God's sake, and tried to make me eat them. It was the worst culinary experience of my life.* All of this is to emphasize that we almost never saw eye to eye. But we shared a love of the game. And now, all these years later, he leaves me a baseball, of all things, in plain view.

I think it was his way of making amends. At least I like to think so. And the memories play on, dancing at that threshold between the basement of my brain and today's storied consciousness. I try to draw them up, but they are elusive. Many fragments and wisps of memory hover in that liminal space, and never make it to the surface. I am sure of this. And I am OK with this. They will come, if the time is right.

Memory and Forgetting

Memory is a tricky business. Sometimes it comes upon us unexpected. Sometimes it eludes us. It seems to have a mind of its own. The ancient

Greeks thought of memory as a dialectical relationship, a dynamic movement, between the two faces of the twin goddess Mnemosyne-Lesmosyne. Mnemosyne (memory) was the mother of the Muses. It is through a relationship with Mnemosyne that I can engage in acts of creation. For without the grounding of memory, I would not know where to begin. It is memory that calls me to create, to render my life as a story. But Lesmosyne, tender of the River Lethe, the great goddess of forgetting, is also always present. She protects me from the deeply traumatic, from the sharp pain of too much information. As existential psychiatrist Alan McGlashan puts it:

> Perhaps the two most moving chords that can be struck from the human heart are contained in these four words: I remember, I forget. For the unheard anthem of our whole existence is created out of the antiphonal movements of remembering and forgetting . . . perfect balance between this pair of opposites is the mark of maturity. Memory is, in fact, the mortar between all events, a veritable *glutinum mundi* . . . but if memory is a vital function, so also is forgetting. To forget is essential to sanity.
>
> *(1988, p. 6)*

And so, we find ourselves tacking back and forth between these two vital energies – the memory that holds us in a coherent life narrative and the forgetting that allows us to go on, to make meaning out of the raw material, the joyous and brutal realities of existence. But these days, I want to linger *between* memory and forgetting, engulfed in wonder, seeking the deeper meanings of the transition, of the betwixt and between. In the space between memory and forgetting, I find an opening to possibility that may be foreclosed by a surge of memory, or by the fog of forgetting. But here in this liminal space, I can choose. It's not what you think, though. It's not that I can choose to remember, or to forget. But I *can* choose the story I need to tell. I am the author of my fate and of my story. I write my life. I write it autoethnographically, to move me from liminality to storied meaning and back again.

This is why I have crafted *this* story of liminality. It is why I craft all the stories I write. It is also why I find affinity with existentialism. Existentialism, was, to be sure, a philosophical orientation, but more pointedly, it was a *literary* movement. Its best-known – and most widely-read – authors (Camus, Kafka, Sartre, Percy, et al.) wrote their philosophy as *fiction* more readily and just as purposefully as in philosophical tomes like *Being and Nothingness*. In this urge to turn a tale, to craft a narrative that shows forth the inner/outer life of a human being thrown into this world, existentialism and autoethnography share a common trajectory and a common purpose – what Alec Grant calls, in his introduction to this volume, an "uneasy overlap" (p. 10).

Anxiety

Rollo May, the existential psychotherapist, wrote the book on anxiety. Following in the footsteps of Kierkegaard's *Fear and Trembling* (1986) and *The Sickness unto Death* (1980), May's exhaustive study, *The Meaning of Anxiety* (1950), walks the reader carefully through the philosophical foundations that aid us in understanding anxiety, as well as biological, psychological, cultural, and clinical interpretations of the phenomenon. The aim here is to study anxiety as an admittedly pervasive phenomenon, one that is so extensive and compelling that it almost goes without saying that it has profound effects on society as a whole, even among those who deny feeling it:

> Every alert citizen of our society realizes, on the basis of his own experience as well as his observation of his fellow-men, that anxiety is a pervasive and profound phenomenon in the middle of the twentieth century. The alert citizen, we may assume, would be aware not only of the more obvious anxiety-creating situations in our day, such as the threats of war, of the uncontrolled atom bomb, and of radical political and economic upheaval; but also, of the less obvious, deeper, and more personal sources of anxiety in himself as well as in his fellow-men – namely the inner confusion, psychological disorientation, and uncertainty.
>
> *(p. 1)*

Today, more than 70 years after this book's publication, we find ourselves emerging (maybe haltingly) from two years of deadly pandemic, civil wars around the globe, social unrest in many countries, dark moves toward authoritarianism, and quite possibly teetering on the brink of World War III. Anxiety isn't going anywhere. If anything, we are suffering from a collective resurgence, a phenomenon I've taken to calling "panxiety" (pan-world-anxiety, pandemic-anxiety). You can feel it in the air if you're paying attention.

I could have told May all this from my own personal life experience. I have suffered anxiety since the day of my first memory. For me, it's almost always about what to do next, what action to take. It may be rooted in the absurd "duck and cover" drills we did in school, ostensibly (absurdly!) to protect us from nuclear annihilation. There, under my desk, I did not know whether to tremble in fear or laugh at the absurdity of it all.

What interests me is not the moment of anxiety gripping me, but the moments before it comes and after it passes. Where is the anxiety before it arrives? Where does it go when I'm done with it? And mostly, I'm fascinated by what sends it packing. For me, it's those small, concrete steps I take toward changing the world – by speaking, by writing, by teaching, by loving. By moving. And maybe, by moving others too.

Echoes

Echoes: Lately, I have been thinking a lot about echoes. But not just the echo, which I read as a trace, a reverberation of the presence of a voice, of a call into a void and a faint response. I'm also thinking about the brief pause, the moment between the voice calling out . . . and the trace of that voice making its return. What is happening during that pause? What shall we call the liminal moment, the threshold, between the call and the echo, and in dialogue, between call and response?

What happens during the pause between speaking and responding, between writing and writing back, between the words uttered and their traces returning, understood or not? What is the most important moment in communicative *praxis*, in dialogue, in what the ancient Jewish mystics thought of as "lighting holy sparks" between us (Hyde, 2006). What does Martin Buber mean when he claims that we humans take our stand in *relation*?

Whatever else might be going on, I see this pause, this liminal space between us, as a place of creation. Either of us can spoil it, with selfishness or defensiveness or vitriol. But just as possible – though perhaps less convenient – we can create something new. We can, as bell hooks claims, learn to *love* again: "I write of love to bear witness . . . to call for a return to love. Redeemed and restored, love returns us to the promise of everlasting life. When we love we can let our hearts speak" (2001, p. xi).

So I see this pause, this liminal space between us, as a crucible – a crucible wherein the alchemy of the word can spark the energy of love. And that is my own echo across time and space . . . lingering on the brink of love, I speak your name, and I call you into my circle. You are one of my people. And so, I will always *remember* you.

Acts of Creation: Liminality Revisited

I have a confession. (Perhaps this should be the first line of every autoethnography I write.) It's simple, really. When I started writing this chapter, I had no idea where it would take me. No, I am not one of those writers who plans everything, who maps out or outlines the story before beginning. There are no storyboards. Oh, sure, I knew it would be, like so much of my life, scholarly and otherwise, an ode to those moments in the classroom of Dr. Hazel Barnes, supreme teacher of existentialism and translator of *Being and Nothingness*, at the University of Colorado, now over forty years ago. She is always there in my memory, her voice ringing out, offering the most beautiful, thoughtful, compelling, passionate, brilliant teaching I have ever encountered.

My own act of creation always hovers for a time in that liminal space between wonder and possibility, between memory and forgetting, between openness and the unfolding of words, between staring at the screen and fingers hitting the keyboard. In fact, this particular chapter took many recursive loops into and out of the liminality that makes creation possible. I find myself, on any given day, poised to write, then falling back into reverie, stumbling into memory, hearing the echoes of voices, engulfed in wonder. And then, at some point, I sit down and I start. And the words pour out as my Muse takes over, as Lesmosyne and Mnemosyne pull into harmony, sometimes briefly, sometimes for a longer time, but always writing through me.

My hands are my instrument. This embodied experience of creation, of writing my way, or more accurately, of this writing *having its way* with me, has almost always surprised me. I have come to embrace the nature of this mysterious *praxis*. It is, above all, a *communicative praxis* wherein my consciousness and yours stumble into dialogue and thus create a world of meaning (Schrag, 1986).

This is the way of it: Like Sisyphus, in my moment betwixt and between my other labors, I find my way to freedom and meaning, and transcend my finitude by sitting down to write. While I am acutely aware that perhaps few will read these words, I know just the same that you are, right here in this moment, engaging with this text that is my story, my story of my liminal awakening, my Sisyphean autoethnography, my attempt to write in a way that shows forth the act of creation as a way forward into a meaningful life.

Coda

As we round our final corner, I find myself walking alongside Sisyphus, trudging down the hill of happy destiny. I like to think we would have a little talk.

Me:	"Hey."
Sisyphus:	"Hey yourself."
Me:	"So, what's going on here?"
Sisyphus:	"I don't know. That rock is a bitch. Man, I could use some help. Wanna give me a hand on the way back up?"
Me:	"Sure. Why not? But I have a question."
Sisyphus:	"Shoot."
Me:	"Well, I was just wondering what you're doing on the way back down. Since I read Camus, I've been curious."

Sisyphus:	"That guy? Well, he was a great writer. But damn. He's kinda dark. *The Stranger*? Whew. *Dark*. I mean, I love that existentialism shit. But I've never once thought of suicide. I mean, who has the time? Besides, the gods won't let me die. They want me to do this forever."
Me:	"Yeah. I wondered about that. So . . . what *are* you doing?"
Sisyphus:	"Oh. I've been writing my memoirs. In my head. It's all there. My story. And the philosophy that drives it."
Me:	"What's that?"
Sisyphus:	"Existentialism, of course. I can always find something here, in these moments heading down this hill of absurdity, to drive me. I'm a creative guy. That's how I got into this mess in the first place."
Me:	"Yeah, I heard you tried to rob the gods."
Sisyphus (sighing):	"My epic fail. Anyway, I'm writing about my experience, and about what it says about culture, and about the gods, and about *us*."
Me:	"And here you are, letting me interrupt your writing. Thanks. I think what you are writing, by the way, isn't a memoir. You're an autoethnographer."
Sisyphus:	"Cool. Is that what you are?"
Me:	"Yes."
Sisyphus:	"Cool. Well, shit. Here we are. That rock ain't gonna push itself."
Me:	"All right then. Here we go . . ."
Sisyphus:	"Do me a favor, will you?"
Me:	"What's that?"
Sisyphus:	"Write this story."
Me:	"Consider it done."

References

Buber, M. (1970). *I and Thou*. Translated by Kaufmann, W. New York: Touchstone/ Simon and Schuster.

Campbell, J. (1948). *The Hero with a Thousand Faces*. Princeton, NJ: Princeton University Press.

Camus, A. (1955). *The Myth of Sisyphus and Other Essays*. New York: Alfred A. Knopf, Inc.

Frankl, V. (1959). *Man's Search for Meaning*. New York: Washington Square Press.

Goodall, H.L., Jr. (2006). *A Need to Know: The Clandestine History of a CIA Family*. Walnut Creek, CA: Left Coast Press.

Heidegger, M. (1962). *Being and Time*. New York: Harper Collins.

hooks, b. (2001). *All About Love: New Visions*. New York: William Morrow.

Hyde, M.J. (2006). *The Life-Giving Gift of Acknowledgement*. Lafayette, IN: Purdue University Press.

Kierkegaard, S. (1980). *The Sickness unto Death*. Princeton, NJ: Princeton University Press.

Kierkegaard, S. (1986). *Fear and Trembling*. New York: Penguin Books.

Marcel, G. (1950). *The Mystery of Being*. London: Harvill Press.

May, R. (1950). *The Meaning of Anxiety*. New York: Pocket Books.

McGlashan, A. (1988). *The Savage and Beautiful Country*. Einsiedeln, Switzerland: Daimon Verlag.

Pelias, R. (2011). *Leaning: A Poetics of Personal Relations*. New York: Routledge.

Percy, W. (1960). *The Moviegoer*. New York: Avon Books.

Poulos, C.N. (2006). 'The Ties That Bind us, the Shadows That Separate Us: Life and Death, Shadow and (dream)Story'. *Qualitative Inquiry*. 12(1): pp. 96–117. https://doi.org/10.1177/1077800405278780

Poulos, C.N. (2012). 'Stumbling into Relating: Writing a Relationship with My Father'. In Wyatt, J. and Adams, T. (eds.) (Special issue on father-son relationships). *Qualitative Inquiry*.18(2): pp. 197–202. https://doi.org/10.1177/1077800411429099

Poulos, C.N. (2014a). 'My Father's Ghost: A Story of Encounter and Transcendence'. *Qualitative Inquiry*. 20(8): pp. 1005–1014. https://doi.org/10.1177/1077800414530317

Poulos, C.N. (2014b). 'Writing a Bridge to Possibility'. *International Review of Qualitative Research*. 7(3): pp. 342–358. https://doi.org/10.1525/irqr.2014.7.3.342

Sartre, J-P. (1993). *Being and Nothingness*. New York: Washington Square Press.

Sartre, J.P. (2007). *Existentialism is a Humanism*. New Haven, CT: Yale University Press.

Schrag, C. (1986). *Communicative Praxis and the Space of Subjectivity*. Lafayette, IN: Purdue University Press.

Shakespeare, W. (1992). *Hamlet*. New York: Simon & Schuster.

Tillich, P. (1952). *The Courage to Be*. New Haven, CT: Yale University Press.

Tillich, P. (1957). *Dynamics of Faith*. New York: Harper & Row.

Tolstoy, L. (1960). *The Death of Ivan Ilych*. New York: New American Library.

10

THE PERSONAL EVOLUTION OF A CRITICAL BLACKGIRL FEMINIST IDENTITY

A Philosophical Autoethnographic Journey

Menah Pratt

Introduction

A core philosophical inquiry is about identity: "Who am I?" "How do I define myself?" (Green, 2017). What does it mean to "know thyself" in the words ascribed on the Temple of Apollo in Greece? (Green, 2017). If one does in fact understand who one is, what responsibilities might be associated with that knowledge? Black women philosophers have provided a unique perspective to this question of self-identity. Dotson (2011), in her aptly titled article "Black feminist me: answering the question 'who do i think i am'," writes: "My name is Kristie Dotson. *One way* to describe me is to say that I am a black American feminist, professional philosopher." (p. 109). Her self-assertion is an attempt to begin to answer the question: "Who do I take myself for?" (p. 109). Her answer reflects "the story of someone, located somewhere, with certain political commitments and a certain type of commitment within of the philosophy of Africanity" (p. 110). Her self-definition is complex, incorporating race, gender, political, and philosophical identities.

Likewise, V. Denise James (2014) explores a similar question in her article "Musing: A Black feminist philosopher: Is that possible?" She examines whether it is possible to be a Black feminist philosopher and the implications of that identity on her scholarship. In answering that question, James affirmatively states:

> I am a black feminist philosopher. I want to work on projects that will contribute to understanding the lived experiences of black women and

DOI: 10.4324/9781003274728-10

girls. I believe that philosophy done from a black feminist standpoint can help to define, clarify, assess, and suggest changes in our social world that would greatly improve the lives of all people. I believe that my standpoint is both a political and philosophical commitment. I am happy to admit that commitment to this standpoint is a rejection of the supposed neutrality and universalist claims often made by other philosophers.

(p. 189)

Like Dotson, her self-definition incorporates race, gender, political, and philosophical identities. In acknowledging and affirming her identity as a Black feminist philosopher, James (2014) shares the ambivalence she has worked to overcome:

It is also a self-designation that has at times drawn blank stares, looks of confusion, outright derision, and at least once, disbelief in the tenability of such a pursuit from the person to whom I offered it as a description of my work. The astute senior philosopher looked me over and asked, "A black feminist philosopher? Is that possible?" I must admit there are times that I have my doubts.

(p. 191)

In attempting to justify her self-designation, she acknowledged that she struggled to legitimatize her place within the dominant White male cannon by selecting the pragmatist John Dewey in response to the question, "Who is your guy?" (James, 2014, p. 192). Uncomfortable with her alignment with a White male philosopher as a Black feminist philosopher, she wonders:

if my greatest successes are found in . . . how dexterously I layer some black feminism on top of the more important and more properly philosophical thinking of mostly dead, white, US men, am I doing something worth labeling black feminist philosophy at all? Is it possible to be an academic, professional philosopher and privilege black feminism? I was left to ask, does black feminist philosophy exist? Is it possible?

(p. 193)

While affirming her identity, she also continues to question if she is in fact who she has claimed to be. She wonders if she is doing Black feminist philosophy as a Black feminist philosopher or if she is merely a Black woman doing philosophy in the dominant White male hegemonic traditions of philosophy.

Kathryn Gines, another Black woman philosopher, also explores this issue of identity. In privileging White men in philosophical discourse, she asks: "Why wouldn't I (or shouldn't I) because of (or in spite of) my embodied existence – that is, my embodiment as a Black woman – be interested in philosophical reasoning and fields of inquiry?" (Gines, 2011, p. 433) She insists on being a role model and inserting herself and other women and people of color into a "space that has been constructed as explicitly white and male," to challenge what qualifies as philosophy and who qualifies as a philosopher (p. 434).

Anita Allen, a Black female philosophy professor at the University of Pennsylvania, notes that African-American philosophers have been addressing a range of important issues. These issues are influenced, in part, by the political, social, and cultural realities of their identity as African-Americans:

> African-American philosophers have been critiquing law and government; analyzing power, and institutions and practices of oppression, subordination, slavery, class, caste, colonialism, racism, sexism and homophobia; articulating the bases of African-American identities and the grounds of responsibility, community, solidarity and collective action; expressing African-American existential, spiritual, psychological and moral joys and discontents; celebrating and interpreting African-American art and culture; and assessing the discipline, canon and history of Western philosophies, by reference to gaps, logical and moral inconsistencies, methodological limitations, epistemologies and exclusions.
>
> *(Yancy, 2018)*

Dotson, James, Gines, and Allen, as Black women philosophers, are exploring fundamental questions of identity. Who are we? How do we define ourselves? What is the evidence and justification for our identity? What are the responsibilities and obligations associated with our identity? Answering these questions of identity and responsibility as Black women philosophers is compounded by the visual representation of the most commonly recognized image of a philosopher, Rodin's *The Thinker*:

> The *Thinker* is a man sitting alone, head in hand, with furrowed brow, suggesting he is deep in thought. This image can be found on the covers of books, conference programs, and workshop flyers about critical thinking. In tracing the roots of current critical thinking theories back to ancient Greece, we found that it is no accident that critical thinking is commonly associated with the *Thinker*.
>
> *(Thayer-Bacon, 2000, p. 144)*

As a result, Black women philosophers are constantly pushing against the assumption that only White men can engage in philosophical discourse:

"I am constantly aware of and tirelessly (or tiredly?) resisting controlling images and defining (and redefining) myself with and against stifling, inter-secting, racialized-gendered-classed expectations" (Gines, 2015, p. 2342). This work of contesting and defining one's identity is a core element of Black feminist thought: "[M]uch of the best of Black feminist thought reflects this effort to find a collective, self-defined voice" (Collins, 2000, p. 110). This self-defined voice is a voice that is often a relational identity influenced and informed by family, community, and diasporic realities. It is an individual and collective voice impacted by the intertwined identities of generations, gender, sexuality, race, religion, and class (Collins, 2000).

How do Black women scholars, particularly, find and articulate this voice and identity? What are the experiences that shape the development of this self-defined voice? How do we share the stories of someone, located somewhere, with political and professional commitments influenced by race, gender, and academic background and training? Blackgirl autoeth-nography and Black feminist autoethnography provide an answer to this question. Black feminist autoethnography can be understood "as a theo-retical and methodological means for Black female academics to critically narrate the pride and pain of Black womanhood" (Griffin, 2012, p. 138). It blends autoethnography and Black feminism to facilitate analysis and interrogation of the experiences of Black women in the academy. It enables a looking inward at oneself and identity, as well as looking outward to the larger community (Griffin, 2012). Similarly "blackgirl auto/ethnography" facilitates "praxis for black and brown women to do the home/work of self-construction" (Boylorn, 2016, p. 46). Blackgirl auto/ethnography acknowl-edges the embodied nature of Blackness and femaleness. Boylorn (2016) notes:

> I write blackgirl (one word) auto/ethnography because it speaks to the twoness and oneness of my raced and gender identity that is ever present in my work, alongside my class background. I am never only black or only girl/woman, but always both/and at the same time, and that colors and situates my lived experience . . . I see blackgirl and black (space) girl as distinct and not the same, so I merge the words to make them touch on paper the way they touch in my everyday existence.
>
> *(p. 49)*

Blackgirl autoethnography is about showing, telling, and providing exam-ples of lived experiences and then explaining why those experiences are important to self-definition: "Blackgirl autoethnography includes an analy-sis and cultural critique of racism, sexism, classism, and the matrixes of those oppressions in the lives of women of color" (Boylorn, 2016, p. 56). It provides "an alternative epistemological standpoint, another way of knowing how I know what I know as a black woman" (p. 56). The documentation of this knowing most often requires "home/work." It is about the work of finding, defining, and claiming home as Black women and girls.

My journey of self-definition has been evolutionary, involving multiple stages. It began with the awareness of a BlackGirl identity. I chose to capitalize both Black and Girl to illustrate the equal salience of both identities. Developing a deeper self-awareness led to the development of a Black feminist consciousness. Over time, the Black feminist consciousness evolved into a critical Black feminist identity and then to a critical Black-Girl feminist scholar-activist identity. Using "data" from personal journals and autobiographical reflections, this chapter documents the evolution of a critical BlackGirl feminist scholar-activist identity through a Black feminist and Blackgirl autoethnographic lens.

A BlackGirl Identity

I watched *Roots* when I was 9 years old. It aired from January 23 to January 30, 1977. The movie made a lasting impression on a very vulnerable, innocent, and impressionable mind. For months, I would have recurring memories from the documentary, particularly the brutal scenes of violence and whippings. Why, I wondered, are the White people being so mean? Is it just because the people are Black?

I learned very early that skin color and Blackness in America is a complicated identity. I also knew that my Blackness meant that my life was going to be challenging. My parents told me that I was going to have to work twice as hard to achieve my goals. Their lives were living proof. My father, an immigrant from Sierra Leone, West Africa, had a PhD in Nuclear Physics. He received it in the 1960s from Carnegie Mellon. My mother had a PhD in Social Work. She received her degree in the 1960s from University of Pittsburgh. My mother became a full professor, in spite of enduring unimaginable instances of racism and sexism. My father's journey in the academy was not successful. As a consequence of blatant discrimination based on his national origin and race, his faculty contract was terminated after three years. My father had to reimagine his future and that of his family. He decided to raise his family to be independent of the White racist system that had stolen his career. My brother and I were introduced to classical piano, classical violin, and tennis. My brother chose the classical music route, and I was led into tennis, with my father as my coach.

I was raised in an almost all-White community and was the only Black student in my high school graduation class of almost 400. I graduated from high school at 16 and played professional tennis for two years, experiencing the stark reality of often being the only Black tennis player with all White girls. I remember frequently experiencing racism on the tennis circuit. These two years were very formidable in my identity development. I had written in journals since I was eight years old as a way to understand and process my life. My reflections were often on day to day realities. At the age of 17, I wrote in my journal: "I'm at the stage of going mentally and emotionally from a girl to a woman and I guess that's not an easy time for me. I'm a Black woman in a male-oriented, White society" (Pratt, 1984, personal correspondence). This self-definition as a "Black woman in a male-oriented, White society," reflects my first articulation of my BlackGirl identity.

I would continue to explore this identity when I enrolled at the University of Iowa. In my freshman year, I took a Black poetry class. Three poems from my freshman poetry journal reflect a growing awareness and articulation of a BlackGirl consciousness. One poem focuses specifically on race:

Untitled (December 8, 1985)

Ominous clouds of Black and White
Circulating
Surrounding
Blending
Merging
Combining
Torrential outputs of filth
Full of their filth
Their perceptions of
My Whiteness
My Blackness
The non-dialect is White
The lack of Black friends is White
The lips too thick
The hair Black textured
The skin African tar black
Being checked out
My credits
My debits
The balance . . .
The bottom line . . .
Too White-oriented
Too Black-featured
Sometimes
Oreo cookies

Don't do good
With
Fudge or Cool Whip

In this poem, I specifically examine the social construction of race and what it means to be seen as both Black and White. I reference my speech and lack of Black friends as being identified as White; and my lips, hair, and skin as Black. In the stereotypical phrase "Oreo cookies," I lament being seen as "too White-oriented" and "too Black-featured." Being "checked out" is part of the way my identity is being constructed by others. The implications of this racial identity are reflected in another poem a few months later.

Untitled (February 1986)

When you're Black
and things don't work out
You wonder, sometimes
"Is it me, my skin, or them?"
One can't ask
'cuz they'll deny the two
And point it all to you.
You know you're getting
The rotten, bottom end
But think you can't speak 'cuz
They'll say "You're paranoid . . .
Causing trouble when none exists."
They think you're too stupid and dumb
To see the subtleness
They lack the courage to boldly display
So,
It's either suffer in silence
Growing bitter
Always wondering
Is it me, my skin, or them?
Or
It's speaking out
Growing stronger
Knowing it's not you
But your skin and them.

This poem explores the impact of my experiences with the "rotten, bottom end" of racism and Blackness. Though written in second person,

I specifically acknowledge being Black with the words "When you're Black." I acknowledge the challenge of skin color and not knowing whether it is "me, my skin, or them." I end the poem with two options: being silent and growing bitter or speaking out, growing stronger, knowing that it is not me, but my skin and them. As another poem in my journal reflects, I would not suffer in silence. I would continue to write about my feelings about race. Not only would I write about race, I was also beginning to explore my relationship with gender.

Untitled (Undated)

I am black – coal black, mind you.
It bothers me.
Should the distinction be made?
I am a woman.
It doesn't bother me.
The distinction must be made.
I am defined by my color.
I hate it.
I also hate the words
Black
Negro
Nigger
White
Whiteness
Purity
Cleanliness
I hate all of them.
I am bitter.
Women
Weak
I hate them.
Men
Black
White
Egos
Insensitivity
I hate them.
America
Forgotten dreams
Lost chances
Ignorance

White
I hate it.
Me
A woman
African descent
In
America
I hate it.

This poem specifically references my race and gender: "I am black"; "I am a woman." I explore words and labels associated with the social construction of race and Whiteness: purity and cleanliness. I acknowledge that I am defined by my color. I also explore gender and the attachment of certain adjectives to the construction of gender with women as weak and men with egos and insensitive. Finally, I examine the construction of America's identity as a place with forgotten dreams, lost chances, ignorance, and Whiteness. I end the poem with a statement of identity: "Me A woman African descent In America I hate it." I was developing and articulating a BlackGirl identity, and also understanding the reality of that identity in America.

These poems reflect an emerging BlackGirl identity and accompanying anger that would continue to evolve over my five years at Iowa. This identity would be shaped by experiences within the classroom, as well as outside the classroom. Outside the classroom, I was dating White and Black men; working in a underrepresented student support office; tutoring minority and low-income high school students; working in an after-school program for Black 6th grade girls; exploring Islam at the all-Black Nation of Islam meetings; and playing piano every Sunday at the all-White Unitarian Universalist meetings.

In the classroom, I majored in literary studies and minored in philosophy and African-American studies. In literary classes, I mainly read the classic cannon: America, British, Russian writers, predominantly male and White. I fell in love with William Faulkner, as one of the few authors who wrote about race. I did an honors thesis examining his portrayal of Black characters in five novels, and also wrote a master's thesis examining race and Southern culture. In philosophy classes, I also read the classics: America, European, and Russian philosophers, exclusively male and White. It was in African-American studies, however, that I was able to more fully explore my BlackGirl identity. Most classes focused exclusively on race. I learned about the Middle Passage; the enslavement of Africans in America; the Civil War; the Radical Reconstruction; the Freedmen's Bureau; Jim Crow and race codes; and the Civil Rights movement. Although most of the texts were by Black men, there was one Black literature class that focused on

Black women. In that class, I was introduced to bell hooks, Alice Walker, Toni Morrison, Nikki Giovanni, and Gloria Naylor, among others. It was in these classes that I began to learn about what it meant to be a BlackGirl in America.

As I developed a deeper understanding of what it meant to be a Black-Girl, I began to more deeply feel the rage, anger, and hate that I wrote about in the undated and untitled poem. My experiences at Iowa not only helped defined my BlackGirl identity; Iowa also gave me anger – a wild, undirected passion, a righteous indignation at the world; at life; at the unfairness of it all. Like Griffin (2012) who proclaimed, "I AM an Angry Black Woman," I, too, was an angry BlackGirl. As Griffin shares:

> Countless times in my life, I have been asked from someone using an exasperated tone, "Rachel, why are you so angry?" as if the expression of my anger should come with a warning sign, an apology, and a cleanup crew. On most occasions my response is to pose questions back by saying, "Look into the world. How can I not be angry? How can you not be angry?" On a day when sass spills off the tip of my tongue, I might add, "How can the whole damn world NOT be angry?"
>
> *(pp. 145–146)*

The key question for me was what should I do with the anger? How could I channel and direct the anger for good and for justice? Could I use the anger to make the world better for BlackGirls? That desire to make the world better was the advent of developing a Black feminist consciousness. I did not, however, have the tools and training necessary to become an activist or advocate. I decided then to pursue a joint law degree and doctorate degree in sociology. I would continue my "home/work" at Vanderbilt University in Nashville, Tennessee.

A Black Feminist Consciousness

I moved to Nashville in 1990 and began to experience the impact of race and the legacy of enslavement and segregation in a southern city. I was living in walking distance to Vanderbilt in mid-town Nashville, a largely White community. Vanderbilt was predominantly White and wealthy, and the wealth of students was apparent in the presence of luxury cars in the parking lot. The predominantly White student body created a very discernible contrast to a largely Black service community of gardeners, housekeepers, and janitors. I remember thinking to myself that Vanderbilt felt like a plantation. This reality of race would play a critical role in my development of a Black feminist consciousness.

Similar to Iowa, my experiences include classroom and out of classroom experiences. In the classroom, the joint degree program was structured to combine law and sociology classes. The first year was all traditional law classes: contracts, torts, property, constitutional law, and criminal law. Most of these classes did not discuss race or gender. The second year of the program was largely sociology classes. Not having taken any sociology classes at Iowa, I was learning a new discipline and a new canon. The sociology classes were essentially the traditional sociology canon of Durkheim, Marx, Weber, and other White men. Like my undergraduate classes in philosophy and literature, the canon again was mainly White and mainly male. Most courses and curriculum were largely devoid of any extensive discussion of race or gender. The third and fourth year of the joint programs were combined law and sociology classes, with a few more classes exploring issues of race, gender, and civil rights.

As a result of an academic experience that was largely race-neutral or in which race was invisible, it was mostly experiences outside of the classroom that provided a space for my evolving self-identity as BlackGirl. In my second semester of law school, I had the opportunity to teach English at the men's maximum-security prison through American Baptist College. I would see the disproportionate representation of Black men in the prison. My first summer in Nashville, I worked downtown in two White law firms for my internships, noticing so many Black people waiting for public transportation. After my first year in Nashville, I moved into the Black community, buying property on Jefferson Street, a prominent street for Black businesses. I would operate a frame shop and art gallery and participate in conversations about Black business success. In addition to teaching at the men's maximum- and minimum-security prison through American Baptist College, I would also start teaching at Fisk University. At Fisk, I would teach English classes that included the integration of grammar, writing, and literature about the Black liberation struggle. My employment experiences continued to influence my understanding about the impact of my BlackGirl identity. These experiences were largely focused on race and issues involving Blackness. It was not until I started working on my dissertation that I was able to more fully explore and develop a Black feminist consciousness.

As Gines et al. (2018) note:

Philosophy, as a profession and academic discipline, has constructed a Western philosophical canon that is overwhelmingly white and male and that routinely excludes the scholarly contributions of women and people of color . . . It is necessary for the field of philosophy not only to take Black feminism seriously as an area of study, but also to reevaluate central claims by canonical figures in light of Black feminist and intersectional contributions . . . Feminist philosophy has often approached issues through a White female lens and critical race philosophy has often focused on a Black male lens: "In white women's feminism and Black men's philosophies of race, Black women's lives are posed as derivative of those others, male or white."

(pp. 145–150)

This critique of philosophy can also be applied to sociology. The discipline of sociology was steeped in the "traditional" canon, and if not for having a Black woman dissertation adviser, I would not have been introduced to Black feminism. I would not have known that there was a framework that I could use to analyze issues impacting Black women and girls, not from a Black male standpoint, or a White female standpoint, but from a Black feminist lens, recognizing the complexity of an identity intertwined and impacted by race, class, gender, and Black nationalism.

My dissertation adviser, a Black woman, introduced me to Patricia Hill Collins (2000) and her book, *Black Feminist Thought*. Her book changed my life. As Gines (2015) notes:

Hill Collins's Black Feminist Thought is one of my transformative, eye-opening, earth-shattering, life-changing books. Having read a plethora of white feminist thought without recognizing myself and my lived experience (or the lived experiences of my mother, grandmother, great-grandmother, and countless godmothers, aunties and big sister-mentors), I celebrate and appreciate the ways that Black Feminist Thought speaks to us. I understand that Collins did not know me at the time that she wrote it, but Black Feminist Thought has always felt like a book written especially for me, as if she said: Kathryn . . . I acknowledge you. I believe in you. I affirm you. I celebrate you. You are a part of a legacy of Black women laborers, activists, intellectuals, writers, and teachers. You are drawing from a wellspring of knowledge, wisdom, and understanding. You will not face any challenges that have not already been faced and overcome. You can do this!

(p. 2341)

I, too, felt like *Black Feminist Thought* was written to and for me. *Black Feminist Thought* validated my BlackGirl identity. It gave me permission to see myself not only through a race and gender lens, but also provided a framework for understanding my experiences as a consequence of both race and gender. It facilitated the development of a Black feminist consciousness. I was able to attach an ideology and consciousness to my identity as both Black and female from an intersectional lens. It also meant that

I could have a unique and valid perspective, standpoint, and philosophy about the world and my role in it as a BlackGirl.

The feminist philosopher Botts (2017) notes that intersectionality is closely connected to standpoint epistemology:

> standpoint epistemology begins with the idea that all social knowledge claims are not only gendered but also drawn from, bear the marks of, and perpetuate structures of power and privilege that are sustained as much by racial, class, religious, ethnic, age, and physical ability differentials as they are by a sex/gender system that could be discretely and univocally characterized.
>
> *(p. 347)*

Feminist philosophy through an intersectional lens challenges the traditional mainstream philosophical notions of universality and objectivity often informed by "Eurocentric, androcentric, homophobic biases" (Botts, 2017, p. 353), and encourages the acceptance of "knowledge production of those historically excluded from the philosophical canon" (Botts, 2017, p. 350).

As such, my dissertation advocated for "an Afrocentric feminist epistemology" that would challenge the "Eurocentric masculinist knowledge validation process" (Pratt-Clarke, 1997, pp. 16–17). As part of the limitations of the study section, I acknowledge my status and experience as a Black woman "inevitably influenced" the analysis, though I emphasize that my analysis was grounded in sound theoretical and methodological principles (p. 17). Because BlackGirls were the key subject of the dissertation, the research strategy was influenced by a Black feminist standpoint epistemology, grounded in intersectionality. I explored the BlackGirl identity of my research subjects through a Black feminist lens.

My dissertation was called "Where are the Black Girls?: The Marginalization of Black Girls in the Single-Sex School Debate in Detroit" (Pratt-Clarke, 1997). The work examined the BlackGirl experience as part of the single-sex school debate in Detroit in 1992. It documented the impact of White racism, White feminism, Black male sexism, and Black nationalism on BlackGirls. It explored issues of race, class, gender, and nationalism in the Detroit African-American community through a Black feminist lens.

Several key findings emerged. One finding was the prevalence of race loyalty in the Black community. It was loyalty so strong that the rallying cry at public marches in support of three all-Black-male K-6 academies was "Keep your girls at home." This reflected the literal and symbolic perspective about the role and place of African-American girls and women in that community. Another key finding was the powerlessness of "White" feminism to effectively address the issues of BlackGirls through the National Organization of Women Legal Defense Fund (NOWLDF) representation. Though there was a temporary injunction issue, the eventual settlement resulted in 136 seats out of 560 seats being allocated for girls, with only 36 girls attending. A third key finding was the silence and absence of Black feminist activism on behalf of BlackGirls. There was no strong or visible presence of Black feminist activism. As a result, BlackGirls were told to "stay at home" – hidden, invisible, marginalized, uneducated, and silenced.

My academic journey at Vanderbilt had introduced me to a Black feminist consciousness to complement my BlackGirl identity. I had developed tools and language to not only articulate my own identity, but to also advocate for BlackGirls through my scholarship. The next step for me was to explore another related component of identity. What did it really mean to have a Black Feminist consciousness? Was I a Black feminist? Was it enough to just write a dissertation about BlackGirls? As a Black feminist, did I have certain obligations to Black people, and to Black women and BlackGirls in particular? And if so, what were they?

This is the question that Black woman philosopher Barbara Hall (2000) explores: "As an African American, do I have certain obligations to all other African Americans *per se*?" She asks, "Do I have a special duty to try to support and uplift my race or group? . . . What does it even mean, to uplift . . . the race?" (p. 168). She explores the question: what are "an individual member's obligations or moral responsibilities to her particular subgroup (racial, ethnic, gender, etc.)"? (p. 169). Once one has developed an awareness of injustice, what is the responsibility related to that awareness? Parekh (2017), who explores the intersecting concepts of feminism, structural injustice, and responsibility, suggests that feminist philosophy facilitates an interrogation of how to understand structural injustice and the resulting responsibility: "Political responsibility is a duty for individuals to take public stands about actions and events that affect broad masses of people, and to try to organize collective action to prevent massive harm or foster institutional change for the better" (p. 625).

The question for me was as a BlackGirl with a Black feminist consciousness, *did I have a particular political responsibility that I needed to fulfill? If so, what was it? What should I do?* The identity of being Black and female in America doesn't by default require activism, but it can. Certainly for Kristie Dotson's mother, the mere identity as a Black woman is a call to activism. As such, her mother could not reconcile the identity of a philosopher with an identity as a Black woman, as Dotson shares:

> However, for my mother who believes that the simple fact of living in the United States as a black woman is already in itself a call to activism, an

activity that does not tend towards a precise action [it] is, to put it frankly, a waste of time. And while wasting time is inherently human, devoting most of one's existence to an activity that leads nowhere is downright laziness. But my choice to turn to philosophy had another consequence, this one much more serious. My decision seemed to imply that my mother had not raised a black woman, steeped in black culture and life, but rather a "Western" philosopher. I could be either a black feminist and activist or a professional philosopher – but clearly not both. The fact that she couldn't reconcile these two "ways of being" bothered me. Her words reflected a rigid dichotomy between activism and philosophy. The *mere* theorizing of life, what philosophy amounted to in her eyes, was incompatible with the status of a black woman deeply concerned by her community.

(Dotson, 2011, pp. 110–111)

Feeling a similar tension, I wanted to understand my obligations to the community as a BlackGirl with a Black feminist consciousness. Was I doing enough to fulfill my obligation if I only wrote about Black feminism? As a sociologist and a lawyer, was it enough to merely be a scholar, without a critical lens and approach?

Although I did not explicitly mention critical race feminism, critical race theory, or intersectionality in my dissertation, I was beginning to think about those issues. As Sheth (2017) notes, Crenshaw describes Critical Race Theorists as having two common interests:

(1) An interest in the way white supremacy, as a political framework, enabled the maintenance of "the subordination of people of color . . . in America"; and (2) The "desire not merely to understand the vexed bond between law and racial power but to *change* it."

(Sheth, 2017, pp. 358–359)

To change it! What could or should I do to change it? I needed to develop a "critical" lens to my Black feminist framework. I would need to leave Nashville to find it and would need to do more "home/work."

A Critical Black Feminist Scholar-Activist

Ten years after my dissertation in 2006, I moved back "home" to Illinois, living 45 minutes away from my mother. I joined the Office for Equal Opportunity and Access at the University of Illinois in Urbana-Champaign as a civil rights administrator. My responsibility was to ensure compliance with the Affirmative Action Plan and Equal Employment Opportunity laws.

I would investigate allegations of discrimination based on identity and support accommodations for employees with disabilities. I also started teaching in the law school and in the African American Studies department. I started teaching Black Feminism, Critical Race Theory, and Critical Race Feminism.

In 2007, I wrote:

> The spring of 2007 represented a turning point for me . . . . I began again to contemplate my mission and meaning in life. The questions began again in my mind: Who was I? What did I want to do with my life? What did I have an obligation and responsibility to do as a Black woman?
>
> *(Pratt-Clarke, 2010, p. 5)*

Several defining national events impacting Black women were in the media: sexist and racist comments about the Rutgers' women's basketball team; Anucha Browne Sanders' lawsuit against New York Knicks; Dog the Bounty Hunter's use of the "n-word"; Clarence Thomas's book about Anita Hill; Patricia Hill Collins' continuing work; and the work of Johnetta Cole and Beverly Guy-Sheftall on Black women. These events began to influence my own sense of responsibility and obligation:

> It seemed all of sudden that the energy in the universe was calling me to tell the story of Black girls in Detroit . . . . It was as if the Black women were telling me that they still had a story to tell; that their story could still make a difference in the world; and that I needed to use the aloneness, loneliness, and quietness of Champaign-Urbana to begin to write and revise my dissertation to tell their story.
>
> *(Pratt-Clarke, 2010, p. 6)*

In revising my dissertation to a book, the introduction to the book begins with "A Black Girl's Story." In part, it includes the reason for writing the book:

> I am writing because I what I wanted to read was not written. I wanted to read about how to simultaneously work in different academic disciplines and blend strengths from each discipline to produce a revolutionary and transformative approach to understand society. I wanted to read about the intersection of academic disciplines and their role in helping to explain the relationship among the interwoven identities of race, class, and gender, and the interlocking social institutions of the education system, the legal system, and the media. I wanted to read about how to transform institutions that perpetuated oppression and injustice.
>
> *(Pratt-Clarke, 2010, p. 1)*

I continue:

> There is another reason that I am writing. I am writing this book because I am a Black woman and I have five degrees: A bachelor's degree, two master's degrees, a law degree, and a doctorate. I have quietly carried these degrees around trying to find the appropriate use for the responsibility they entail. For almost fifteen years I have not been able to fully actualize the potential associated with these degrees. Until now, they were unfulfilled potential. But now, I am writing because I must honor the sacrifices of my family, of other African-Americans, and especially of Black women.
>
> *(Pratt-Clarke, 2010, p. 1)*

I continue:

> I am writing because of my responsibility as an educator to participate in the "community" and to contribute to the collective understanding about issues of education, race, class, and gender . . . . I see myself as part of a long line of revolutionary Black feminist scholar-activists.
>
> *(Pratt-Clarke, 2010, pp. 7–8)*

I had found a new identity: a revolutionary Black feminist scholar-activist. In this role, I affirm that I am committed to not only being a Black woman scholar and sharing theoretical approaches, but also engaging in praxis. For me, the book represented that effort to combine theory and praxis. In the work, I share my development of a transdisciplinary method that helps explain how oppression is reproduced and perpetuated to begin a process to explore "the possibility for radical transformation of systems and structures that traditionally reproduce and perpetuate domination and oppression" (Pratt-Clarke, 2010, p. 9). Building upon the dissertation, which presented qualitative findings and analysis of the experience of Black girls in the single-sex school debate in Detroit, I offer the Transdisciplinary Applied Social Justice model as a tool for understanding complex social problems and exploring potential intervention strategies.

Critical Race, Feminism, and Education: A Social Justice Model (Pratt-Clarke, 2010) reflected my attempt to understand systems of oppression and to propose a tool for social justice change. The Transdisciplinary Applied Social Justice (TASJ) model (Pratt-Clarke, 2010) is a tool of empowerment that uses theory, methodology, and praxis with the goal of transforming society. The model (Pratt-Clarke, 2010) is designed to help increase the likelihood of successfully addressing and responding to systematic and institutional oppression. The model encourages an interrogation of the elements that perpetuate oppression: power, philosophy, people, processes, practices, policies, perceptions, and privilege. It incorporates concepts from social movement theory, Black feminist thought, and Critical Race Feminism. It argues that responding to issues of social justice and the traditional and historical marginalization of populations based on their intersecting identities requires a strategic approach influenced by multiple disciplines (Pratt-Clarke, 2010).

The TASJ model draws from Collins' (2000) concept of power domains. The model incorporates four interrelated domains where power is organized: a hegemonic/cultural domain where ideologies such as White supremacy, patriarchy, heterosexism, and religion are constructed, shared, legitimized and maintained; a structural domain where social institutions of a society, such as banks, hospitals, schools, the military, and churches exist as almost impenetrable social structures; a disciplinary domain where modern bureaucracies and social structures are maintained through policies, practices, procedures, rules, and laws; and an interpersonal domain where relationships between individuals influence outcomes on an everyday level of social interaction. The domains operate through individuals who enforce and execute the policies, practices and procedures as influenced by the biases and prejudices that they bring from the hegemonic domain. The interpersonal domain, as the location for day-to-day interactions and encounters between individuals, is the space in which racism, sexism, and other biases including microaggressions and macroaggressions are carried out. More importantly, though, it is also a space in which acts of resistance, self-empowerment, and activism exist. The domains reflect both challenges and opportunities. They are the sources of oppression, but also opportunities for activism.

To create sustainable change within any organization, one must be knowledgeable and aware of the domains, understand their operations, and then seek to reimagine and repurpose them from sites of domination and power to sites of resistance and social justice. These domains of power (ideologies of oppression; structures of oppressions; rules of oppression; and relationships of oppression) almost operate invisibly and are stitched into the fabric of American society, into our minds as culture and the way things are and – we are made to believe – should be. Changing culture can only happen by an interrogation and understanding of power, and a strategy and a tool to address, mitigate, and shift power. This is in fact the work of social justice and of creating sustainable institutional transformation.

Understanding the model enables us to have tools to challenge institutional structures, ideologies, and individuals who seek to inhibit the advancement of equity. The model enables the careful consideration of a counter strategy, a counter movement, and a counter narrative to combat the power of the domains, because social justice work is about disrupting the status quo and dismantling existing systems and structures. This is consistent with James (2017, p. 139), who notes that:

Black feminists are simultaneously envisioning incremental changes and radical transformations not only within Black communities but throughout the broader society as well. Ultimately, the humanistic visionary pragmatism of theorizing by Black feminists seeks the establishment of just societies where human rights are implemented with respect and dignity.

For me, the "homework" of finding home has always involved classroom and out of classroom work. I was able to align my scholar-activist identity at Illinois where I became a tenured professor in the College of Education, and Associate Chancellor and Associate Provost. My identities were inseparable. I was in fact being a Black feminist scholar-activist. I was not only working every day to dismantle oppression, I was also offering through my scholarship strategies to dismantle oppression. I had connected theory with praxis: "Those who are dedicated to interlinking theory with praxis face another hurdle, waiting to be acknowledged as both an academic and an activist" (Gines et al., 2018, p. 148). I would not wait to be acknowledged. I would acknowledge myself.

A Critical BlackGirl Feminist Scholar-Activist

I am a critical BlackGirl feminist scholar-activist. As part of that identity, I work at Virginia Tech as the Vice President for Strategic Affairs and Diversity and Professor of Education. I also write blog posts on issues of identity and humanity, focusing on empowering the powerless on my website at menahprattclarke.com. It is my commitment to addressing and ensuring visibility to mitigate the "politics of extinction" (Hawkesworth, 2010, p. 694). As Hawkesworth notes:

Within academia, feminist theory and critical race theory have posed dramatic challenges to traditional accounts of the world, taking issue with dominant disciplinary approaches to knowledge production and repudiating universal claims prized by many political theorists. They have contested androcentric, Eurocentric, and colonial "ways to truth" that universalize the experiences of a fraction of the human population. They have challenged the power dynamics structuring exclusionary academic practices that have enabled unwarranted generalizations to remain unchallenged for centuries or indeed millennia. They have sought to identify and develop alternative research practices that further feminist and antiracist goals of social transformation. Challenges of this magnitude call for direct engagement, not for dismissal, neglect, or erasure.

(p. 689)

As a critical BlackGirl feminist scholar-activist, I will not be neglected, erased, or dismissed. I will write. I will speak up. I will educate. I will act. I will empower. If Black feminist scholar-activists are not extinct, we can continue to proclaim who we are. My name is Menah Pratt, and one way to describe me is a critical BlackGirl feminist scholar-activist.

References

Botts, T.F. (2017). 'The Genealogy and Viability of the Concept of Intersectionality'. In Garry, A. (ed.) *The Routledge Companion to Feminist Philosophy (1 [edition], Ser. Routledge philosophy companions)*. pp. 343–357. London and New York: Routledge.

Boylorn, R.M. (2016). 'On Being at Home with Myself: Blackgirl Autoethnography as Research Praxis'. *International Review of Qualitative Research*. 9(1): pp. 44–58. www.jstor.org/stable/26372178

Collins, P.H. (2000 [1990]). *Black Feminist Thought: Knowledge, Consciousness, and the Politics of Empowerment*. 2nd Edition. New York: Routledge.

Dotson, K. (2011). 'Black Feminist Me: Answering the Question "Who do i Think i am."' *Diogène*. 235–236(3): pp. 109–109. https://doi.org/10.3917/dio.235.0109

Gines, K.T. (2011). 'Being a Black Woman Philosopher: Reflections on Founding the Collegium of Black Women Philosophers'. *Hypatia*. 26(2): pp. 429–437. https://doi.org/10.1111/j.1527-2001.2011.01172.x

Gines, K.T. (2015). 'Ruminations on Twenty-Five Years of Patricia Hill Collins's Black Feminist Thought: Knowledge, Consciousness and the Politics of Empowerment'. *Ethnic and Racial Studies'*. 38(13): pp. 2341–2348. https://doi.org/10.1 080/01419870.2015.1058505

Gines, K.T., Ranjbar, A.M., O'Bryn, E., Ewara, E., Paris, W. (2018). 'Teaching and Learning Philosophical "Special" Topics: Black Feminism and Intersectionality'. In Perlow, O.N., Wheeler, D.I., Bethea, S.L. and Scott, B.B.M. (eds.) *Black Women's Liberatory Pedagogies: Resistance, Transformation, and Healing within and Beyond the Academy*. pp. 143–158. Cham: Palgrave Macmillan.

Green, M.S. (2017). *Know Thyself: The Value and Limits of Self-Knowledge*. London and New York: Routledge.

Griffin, R. (2012). 'I AM an Angry Black Woman: Black Feminist Autoethnography, Voice, and Resistance'. *Women's Studies in Communication*. 35(2): pp. 138–157. https://doi-org.ezproxy.lib.vt.edu/10.1080/07491409.2012.724524

Hall, B. (2000). 'The Libertarian Role Model and the Burden of Uplifting the Race'. In Zach, N. (ed.) *Women of Color and Philosophy: A Critical Reader*. pp. 168–181. Malden, MA: Blackwell.

Hawkesworth, M. (2010). 'From Constitutive Outside to the Politics of Extinction: Critical Race Theory, Feminist Theory, and Political Theory'. *Political Research Quarterly*. 63(3): pp. 686–696. https://doi.org/10.1177/1065912910367496

James, V.D. (2014). 'Musing: A Black Feminist Philosopher: Is That Possible?' *Hypatia*. 29(1): pp. 189–195. www.jstor.org/stable/24541961

James, V.D. (2017). 'Feminist Pragmatism'. In Garry, A. (ed.) *The Routledge Companion to Feminist Philosophy (1 [edition], Ser. Routledge Philosophy Companions)*. pp. 132–142. London and New York: Routledge.

Parekh, S. (2017). 'Feminism, Structural Injustice, and Responsibility'. In Garry, A. (ed.) *The Routledge Companion to Feminist Philosophy (1 [edition], Ser. Routledge Philosophy Companions)*. pp. 620–630. London and New York: Routledge.

Pratt, M. (1984). Personal Correspondence to Self.

Pratt-Clarke, M. (2010). *Critical Race, Feminism, and Education: A Social Justice Model*. London: Palgrave Macmillan.

Pratt-Clarke, M. (1997). 'Where Are the Black Girls? The Marginalization of Black Girls in the Single-Sex School Debate in Detroit'. (Doctoral dissertation) Vanderbilt University.

Sheth, F.A. (2017). 'Critical Race Theory, Intersectionality, and Feminist Philosophy'. In Garry, A., Khader, S.J. and Stone, A. (eds.) *The Routledge Companion to Feminist Philosophy*. New York: Routledge.

Thayer-Bacon, B.J. (2000). *Transforming Critical Thinking: Thinking Constructively*. Columbia: University Teachers College Press.

Yancy, G. (2018). 'The Pain and Promise of Black Women in Philosophy'. 18 June. www.nytimes.com/2018/06/18/opinion/black-women-in-philosophy.html

11

TALKING WITH OTHERS

Autoethnography, Existential Phenomenology, and Dialogic Being

Shelley Rawlins

Twilight of Hammers

One of the best things I have done in my life so far is to read everything Friedrich Nietzsche published during his lifetime. From June 2014 through February 2016, I studied Nietzsche's style, irony, humor, and his inspired use of clever and damning comparative examinations of historical and ongoing cultural practices. He announced in *Twilight of the Idols* (1889) that to "philosophize with a hammer" is to call into question all the puzzle pieces of life that seemingly fall into place – making our worlds intelligible, familiar, and meaningful (and even apparently "natural"). I wrapped myself in the welcoming warmth of his nihilism, which many people seem to misconstrue by reducing it to its barest interpretive bones, translating the word from German to English as "nothingness."

Nietzsche was playful with his audience, making us work for understanding. *The Will to Power* (1901) contains his most "comprehensive" definition of nihilism as the process by which the *"highest values devalue themselves"* (II). In his view, cultural entities possessing the most power and influence set about "transvaluating" other lower entities to reify their control, thus devaluing their own moral stature. Nietzsche's famous exemplar is the nihilism of Christianity through its psychosocial imposition of contrived human-made moral dictates. He mused:

> Supposing that nothing else is 'given' as real but our world of desires and passions, that we cannot sink or rise to any other 'reality' but just

DOI: 10.4324/9781003274728-11

that of our impulses – for thinking is only a relation of these impulses to one another.

(1886, II: p. 36)

His keen observations opened previously unknown existential doors for me. Today I see him all the time in the world when powers collide with resistance, when people ask, "Why does it have to be *this* way?" and from the tattoo of his face on my left thigh, gazing up at me or outward from my body, depending on how I'm positioned.

Introduction

For ages, philosophy has both weathered and inspired implications of its tradition of generating alternative perspectives, reifying norms, and challenging conventional ideals. Brave thinkers have put their words, bodies, and sometimes even their lives and those of their loved ones on the line for the sake of speaking their truths. Deliberations about origins, values, and traditions populate the pages of philosophical works as thinkers explore their motivated life experiences, at times through abstract meditations about presumably universal practices. I adore philosophy, but I admit that I am drawn to the traditions that equip me to locate myself and my lifeworld within a framework that enables a recognition of other persons' living possibilities and understandings. I want to be able to *use* philosophy. Like a hammer.

Likewise, autoethnography provides an intriguing lens for reflecting on personal experiences and considering broader cultural contexts and interconnections. These explorations feature a variety of styles, approaches, and topics. Through writing stories in a deliberate compositional style, an author establishes a relationship among their self, cultural issues, and an intended audience. While I value autoethnography's rich potential for gleaning self-reflexive insights, I maintain this approach can be supplemented with an externalized focus on others' accounts of experience. After all, we each exist in contingent social and cultural contexts as we co-create shared meanings and develop personal understandings that will inevitably change over time. In a previous article, "Stranger and Stranger: Living Stories on Others' Doorsteps" (2017), I demonstrate a complementary collaboration between autoethnography's self-focus and existential phenomenology's vivid and outwardly other/wise-attentive descriptive praxis. I appreciate the productive tensions between these complementary approaches that describe and disclose lived experience:

> Autoethnography tends to privilege Self-reflexivity as the starting point of analysis, while phenomenology destabilizes or refuses that privilege by insisting on intersubjective being and social embodiment. The concept of "Self" is produced in tandem with the emergence of the concept of "Other." As such, we are not preeminently a Self; rather, we construct a fluid sense of Self, albeit partial, through our experiences facing Others.
>
> (Rawlins, 2017, p. 102)

Reflecting on experiences with known and unknown others from this joint perspective can enable rich descriptions about the conditional relationality of the living contexts we create with others. Here, I delve a bit deeper methodologically and philosophically as I introduce various existential probes (or "hammers") inspired by the works of Edmund Husserl, Martin Heidegger, and Jean-Paul Sartre. In applying these existential frames to consider my story about a recent experience participating in collective protest, I will demonstrate the productive potential of incorporating others' accounts alongside our own in autoethnographic work.

In this chapter, I describe my engagement with existential phenomenology and selected concepts that can inform autoethnography. I emphasize here the importance of investigating others' accounts alongside our own, as well as how to incorporate some of these insights within our autoethnographic accounts. I contend that no one tells a story alone. As Mikhail Bakhtin (1981) observes, each of our distinctive narrative styles paints a picture for others that contains (and at times imposes) our distinguishing "taste." Owning and reflecting upon such intersubjective choices of representation, constraint, and possibility ought to inform robust autoethnography. In talking with others about what it means to exist in a world fraught with uncertainty, we necessarily perform a dialogic reflexivity, and we are better for it. Collective experiences such as rallies or protests present living dynamics that always involve strangers, stories, and ethics. Consequently, protest exemplifies embodied existential stakes and shared vulnerabilities that both beckon and challenge sophisticated autoethnographic exploration by individual authors.

Accordingly, this work is guided by the overarching question: *How might existential phenomenology productively supplement autoethnography in exploring the shared cultural meanings of collective public experiences?* I approach this inquiry in three parts, guided by the following questions: (1) How might I story the progression of existential phenomenology across Husserl, Heidegger, and Sartre? (2) How might guiding existential themes and modality probes (termed "hammers" in this work) productively inform autoethnographic explorations of collective experience? That is, how can they help in connecting personal and collective experience across private and public contexts? (3) What does this look like in application? I begin by sharing a story about a recent protest experience of mine. Next, I provide a brief survey of the development of phenomenology and existential phenomenology across Husserl's, Heidegger's, and Sartre's distinct approaches. It could be argued that each thinker employed autoethnography before it was so aptly named in their philosophical pursuits to account for lifeworld complexities of context, contingency, and relational being. While these three men may diverge in how best to discuss philosophy about situated human existence, they still identify characteristic relationships and conceptual terms that define distinct yet overlapping philosophical trajectories concerning life, reality, and being. Along the way, I analyze my protest story from each thinker's perspective. In doing so, I locate existential hammers from these thinkers and demonstrate their conceptual utility for conducting qualitative research about individuals' experiences of communal activities. Then I (re)consider my story about what it means to (dis)engage in collective protest with others.

My Protest Story: "I Think I Need to Go . . ."

It is a blustery day, unusually cold for late March, as we gather in downtown Carbondale, IL, to celebrate the Transgender Day of Visibility (TDoV). Rachel Crandall established this annual holiday on March 31, 2009, to focus "on all the good things in the trans community, instead of just remembering those who were lost" (Carreras, 2009). It's always important to me to support the transgender community, but especially on this day because my friend Marisol[1] is speaking at the event. Swirling winds sweep raindrops through the open sides of the old wooden pavilion. This town square pavilion dates to 1854, when Carbondale's founder Daniel Harmon Brush erected it in anticipation of the upcoming railroad expansion. On July 4, 1854, the pavilion hosted its first public celebration with locals cheering as the first train pulled into town (Explorecarbondale.com). Today we are here to celebrate the lives and cultural contributions of our trans siblings.[2]

I attend the rally with my friend, Les. We are both allies of the community and are cisgender, straight White people – he is a man (named Leslie), and I am a woman. We watch the three presenters with open eyes, open ears, and active hearts. Recently, Les's child informed him that he is transgender (unfortunately, he has a scheduling conflict and cannot join us). The first speaker, a trans woman, speaks passionately about the importance of trans people being seen and heard, and to safeguard the potential for trans kids to lead authentic lives. She shares that as a youth, "transgender" was not an identity she could claim because she had never met nor heard of a transgender person before. The second speaker, my friend, a beautiful trans woman, speaks about the importance of challenging transphobia anytime we see it in the world, but also to remember to embrace the hope and positivity exemplified by the vibrant close-knit LGBTQIA+ community and supportive allies. The third speaker is a trans activist and community organizer who traveled five hours from Chicago for the occasion. He speaks about how inspiring it is to see so much support "in a small rural town" (like ours) that reminds him of where he was raised. He mentions that being trans in smaller "country towns" can make life almost unlivable for young people trying to assume their authentic identities and selves. After the speeches we socialize a bit, congratulate the speakers, and play some trans pop culture trivia games. There are tables with markers and posters for people to make signs for the upcoming rally. We hear that the march will start in 30 minutes, so we decide to scramble through the rain to a nearby bar to use the restroom and have a quick cocktail.

Inside the bar I encounter a couple acquaintances that I haven't seen in over three years, back in "pre-covid" times. During small talk, Matt eyes the blue, white, and pink trans pride pin on my coat, and says,

"Oh! I had no idea. Wow."

I opt to ignore whatever this "epiphany" in his mind concerns, and reply,

"Yeah! There's a rally today – it's the Transgender Day of Visibility. The march starts soon at 7:00 – you should come!"

Matt appears to stall, looking around the bar somewhat quizzically before saying,

"Nah, I don't think so. I'm about to go get some food, but I'll be back here if you want to stop in afterwards."

Les and I finish our drinks and exit the bar just in time to join in at the back of the march. We trail behind a couple carrying a huge blue, white, and pink trans flag as rain begins again. As we advance, we can view the assembled collective stretching for a block down the sloping city sidewalk. I estimate that around 40 people are participating as some individuals lead us in chants with bullhorns:

"We are trans and we are people!"
"Save our Black sisters!"

"I am not your fetish! I am not your boogeyman!"
"Trans rights are human rights!"
"Trans lives matter! Trans lives matter!"

Then, a shift:

"Trans lives matter; Blue lives don't!"

Les and I instantly exchange puzzled looks of discomfort and I say, almost without thinking:

"I think I need to go; I can't do this."
"Same here, let's roll."

We head back immediately.

***

Notes on Autoethnography

I am confident that autoethnography has been thoroughly defined for the reader of this volume – as a self-centric examination of cultural experiences. Consequently, I understand autoethnography as a lens for self-reflection that must include "an explicit turn outward" that connects one's narrative with larger cultural happenings (Gingrich-Philbrook, 2015, p. 209). The effort to achieve an existential balance among the universal/particular facets of lived experience perhaps most differentiates "good" autoethnographies from less impressive attempts. The self is central to the autoethnographic project but in many cases, examining self-stylized and unchecked egos sheds much of its rigor, realism, and intriguing appeal to others when such "easy access" dwindles in a silo all by itself (Gingrich-Philbrook, 2005, p. 298). Autoethnography thus grapples with the project of achieving a correspondence between the particularities of personal accounts and more universal cultural themes. Communication studies house much autoethnographic work, and this makes sense as the field searches for relational and cultural contingencies with hopes of identifying and overcoming barriers obstructing equity and justice. Perhaps the greatest obstacle autoethnographies face is the common critique that such work is overly solipsistic or exhibits "navel-gazing" (Chang, 2008). Autoethnographic inquiry should not begin and end with a self's world with little perceivable effort to connect with others' worlds. Informed by these ideas and concerns, I next discuss and demonstrate how I envision existential phenomenology as a fitting complement to these perceived autoethnographic limitations.

Phenomenology and Existential Phenomenology

In this section, I consider Edmund Husserl's foundational understandings of what phenomenology is and does, as well as conceptual contributions made by his existential successors, Martin Heidegger and Jean-Paul Sartre. Phenomenology spans multiple interdisciplinary realms with distinct methodological protocols and assumptions. In general, phenomenology is a philosophy and method that focuses on consciousness, perception, and lived experience (Husserl, 1913, pp. 24–25). By attempting vivid and unbiased descriptions, a researcher seeks to uncover the structural essence(s) constituting "an object of perception," or the experience of perceiving the meaning of said object-thing (Sartre, 1943, pp. 14, 106). Existentialism is a dynamic philosophy concerning the general yet concrete business of existence and existing. This chapter advances my own adapted methodological protocol for performing qualitative existential phenomenology in cooperation with autoethnography – that is, for providing, eliciting, and interpreting my own and my co-researchers' accounts of experiencing collective protest.

Edmund Husserl's Phenomenology: Intentionality and Description, Reduction, and Interpretation

Phenomenology has a rich history as both a philosophy and method that addresses people's subjective experience of their situated existence, or lifeworld. This philosophical orientation believes one's consciousness of lived experience reveals underlying structures of meaning that give shape and intelligibility to any experience as such. Innovator Edmund Husserl's foundational phenomenological structure of experience is *intentionality* – or "the property of being a 'consciousness of something'" (1913, p. 120). In *Ideas* (1913), Husserl critiques prevailing positivist empirical practices for frequently dictating rather than investigating social phenomena. He focuses his phenomenology approach on countering positivist assumptions about human universality and scrutinizing the grounds of such objectively-derived determinations – how do objects and others become known and thus familiar to a person? For instance, how do I know what I am looking at? Husserl reasons, "An experience has no perspectives," and thus meaning arises through human consciousness *of* and intentional encounters with other(s)-world-things (p. 135). Meaning develops relationally, through our interactions and contact with the other people and things in our lifeworld. Husserl states that his mission is to return the focus of research agendas "to the things themselves!" (p. 135) Husserl seeks to challenge and transcend some of the recurring limitations of objective certainty by encouraging researchers to investigate lived experience and (re)consider the source of meaning-making as well as how individuals perceive the same things in different ways.

Methodologically, phenomenology cycles through three interconnected steps: description, reduction, and interpretation. Husserl's phenomenological method begins with the selection of a phenomenon or object for analysis. Following this selection, one then induces *epoché* – considered to be the first "reduction" – as preconceived impressions of the world-thing are transcended, opening the possibility of examining the structures of one's own consciousness of the phenomenon/object. These eidetic (vividly detailed) descriptions of a phenomenon of study – without any "rationalized" associations – form the first step of Husserl's three-step method. Following the description is a *reflection* on *how* an object is meant or intended – or the experience of the meaning or content (also termed the "reduction"). During the description and reduction stages, researcher beliefs remain suspended, as all potential interpretations are *horizontalized* – or taken as equivalent prospective meanings with no preordering hierarchy (Husserl, 1913, p. 210). This substitutional exercise is informed by the practice of *free imaginative variation*, which posits possible variations in constitution and meaning to establish which structures are essential to an entity's foundation, and which are not (Husserl, p. 57).

After codifying necessary and invariant "ingredients" of a particular phenomenon, "the realm of transcendental consciousness" is revealed as the domain of "absolute Being" (Husserl, p. 210). From here, a researcher engages the third step of interpretation, in which they explore and compare the variant meanings constituting the lived experience of the phenomena under examination. By recursively cycling back through the detailed descriptions and core characteristics identified during the reduction, Husserl insists that researchers take care to ensure their interpretations of phenomena remain true to the lived experience of the phenomenon. Husserl's phenomenological method became known as descriptivist, eidetic, or transcendental phenomenology because the most important aspiration is a bracketed and richly detailed description, which he believes provides access to the intentionality of the structural logic making "this experience" none other than *this experience*.

Following Nietzsche's wisdom about the purposeful use of philosophical "hammers" to deconstruct and examine features of lived experience and social practices, I identify some of the philosophical hammers wielded by each thinker. These hammers represent the distinctive ways these theorists *do* philosophy.

Husserl's hammers: *intentionality* (our visual orientation toward an object of consciousness); *epoché* (an active process of bracketing preconceived notions about a thing/experience); *description* (unbiased and bracketed), *reduction* (locating in/variant features that make up a thing/object of perception, including people), and *interpretation* (considering how things appear to us, as well as how they might appear otherwise to others).

The Transgender Day of Visibility: Husserlian Explication

Husserl focuses his method on rendering a vivid but bracketed description of a visible phenomenon to reveal the structural features in our consciousness that direct our understandings.

Description: The rally I attended for the TDoV presents a dynamic experience. I was invited by my friend to celebrate the day and joined other people in an old pavilion. This occasion featured presenters – two women and a man – who spoke about their experiences being trans. After the speeches, I needed to use a nearby restroom. We returned 30 minutes later to join the celebratory march. During the march, chants ensued, flags waved, and I left.

Reduction: This rally of visibility changed forms as we pivoted from uplifting speeches to apparent protest. In a few minutes of marching, participants' chants shifted from supportive to critical. This rally became a protest.

Interpretation: We are continuously orienting ourselves toward appearances through our perception, and we are always partly engaged in its revelation. My consciousness of this event transformed in-step with the other participants as I realized the intentionality of a celebratory march became a protest. I was not intending to protest that day. I was caught off-guard by the rhetorical deployment of "Blue lives don't [matter]," but perhaps I missed something in my orientation. There may well be a different intentionality toward this claim that speaks to others in a manner that it does not to me.

Husserl encourages us to resist taking the appearance of things at face value and instead to scrutinize the variant appearances of things to thematize how a thing displays (its) face value/s. However, this correspondence between the experience of orienting to an appearance and the experience of being experienced as an appearance has not yet acknowledged its affective presence. What role do the embodied others surrounding me play in this event? Husserl's pupil, Martin Heidegger, considers some temporal implications arising from a being's relational lifeworld in pondering how things show themselves to us, as one being situated among many others as time persists and affects our apprehension.

Martin Heidegger's Existential Phenomenology: Being, Time, and Hermeneutics

In an explicit retort to Husserl ("To the things themselves!"), Heidegger (1926) pronounces: "To letting the things show themselves!" By this statement, Heidegger asserts that all our activities are always already "in the world" and thus the entirety of our existence revolves around our "being-in-the-world" *and* our "being-with-others" (p. 33). In his view, consciousness is not the foundational universalizing structure of being. Rather, Heidegger uses Husserl's phenomenological method to examine ontology itself. Ontology refers to the philosophical consideration of what exists, is real, and thus contributes to our sense of reality. Whereas Husserl focuses on how meanings emerge in consciousness and perception to an engaged researcher, Heidegger projects his phenomenological inquiry toward the inescapable existential project of existence itself (*Dasein*) – including that of the researcher (p. 26). Departing from Husserl's definition of *Dasein* as "the apprehension of concrete existence" (1913, p. 58), Heidegger interrogates the very notion of Being as an active doing and questioning of and about existence (1926, p. 61). This inward turn leads to a second phenomenological arena – that of interpretivist, hermeneutic, or existential phenomenology.

Heidegger refutes several of Husserl's ontological stances, especially the idea that we can identify and/or bracket and subsequently "transcend" personal biases to access our subjectivity in isolation. Heidegger takes to task ontology itself – what is being? – in his hermeneutic or existential phenomenology. He points out that Husserl's prospect of identifying pure essences through phenomenological reductions is unachievable since descriptions and free imaginative variation are always already part of an interpretive process subjectively situated in social, cultural, and historical contexts. He terms this understanding "historiological" (p. 62). Heidegger refers to the process that informs and directs one's interpretative scheme as hermeneutics. Hermeneutics is "the methodology of those humane sciences which are historiological in character" (Heidegger, p. 62). As such, Being-in-the-world is the fundamental structure of *Dasein* (*this* existence, *here*) (p. 65), and any "structures" arising outside from *Dasein* are "hazy [and] indefinite," or else catch-all "pregnant structures that may be structurally indistinguishable from certain ontological characteristics of an *authentic* Being of Dasein" (Heidegger, 1926, p. 70). Heidegger focuses his phenomenological approach on the essential relations that characterize an entity (being) and its mode/s of Being (how it exists and what possibilizes or actualizes this existence as it changes across time) (p. 37).

Heidegger's existentialism redirects the focus of transcendental phenomenology from eidetic descriptions considered to capture intentional structures of conscious experience (perception), toward an emphasis on the importance of our situated existence *in* and *across* existential *time-space/s* that shape and enact our becoming. Heidegger says: "the Being of Dasein can be indicated provisionally. Its existential meaning is *care*" (p. 65). Heidegger's phenomenological exploration tends toward existential questions about a Being's fleeting temporality because time rushes through whatever this existence may be. Life is unsteady, unlike structurally stabilized appearances, and Heidegger contends there is no phenomenological transcendence or possibility of escaping or fully knowing what one is. Instead, there are only "possibilities" of Dasein's protracting "explication of time as the transcendental horizon for the question of Being" (Heidegger, 1926, p. 63). I am a being-in-the-world-with-others in specific time-spaces and contexts; what am I doing here?

Heidegger's hammers: *Being/being* (a reflexive awareness of existence, the self); *time* (the constant tracker of our unfolding lifeworld-with-others); *being-in-the-world-with-others* (this pluralistic ontology is the foundation for realizing authenticity in lived experience); *hermeneutics* (ontological foundations of lived experience – a recursive backchecking approach that strives to account for our interpretive moves across experiences, reflection, and analytic outcomes).

The Transgender Day of Visibility: Heideggerian Explication

Heidegger's approach to existential phenomenology involves dual meditations about personal existence (B/being) as it entwines with our lifeworld relationships (with-others). These existential vectors influence our experiences of our situated selves, across time, in our discrete life-worlds.

Account (Description): It is important to me to be here today. I am pleased to see a good turnout despite the rain. I watch the speeches in empathetic admiration as I connect with the worthy plight of wanting to live authentically as oneself. It is a rewarding experience to learn about others' life journeys, but as the sentiment shifts during the march ("Trans lives matter; Blue lives don't [matter]"), I want to break my association with the group.

Being/Dasein (Reduction): My site of reflection is my *Dasein* – this existence here and now. I associate myself with the positive vibes and inspiring atmosphere of the day. I go to use the restroom and grab a drink, all of which feels fine. But then, I feel self-conscious about my Being, in concert with others walking down Main Street and chanting for the unimportance of "Blue" lives alongside the importance of trans lives. In the space of an hour, I feel different about participating in this event; I experience two distinct modalities. First, I am comfortably supportive and inspired by the speeches in the pavilion (a mode of participating in this event). Second, I am put off during the march when things take a more critical direction than I had intended to participate in.

Explication (Interpretation): In this rally/protest/visibility time-space, I experienced Being-in-the-world-with-others – in one positive encouraging way, and then in another, more concerning manner. In retrospect, I felt troubled by my escape: Was I wrong to leave? I care and support the tenuous cultural walks trans people and other marginalized members of society endure, and it is important to me to affirm these various communities. Yet I knew I had to leave, and it seemed that my friend felt the same way. Hermeneutics calls for us to cycle repeatedly back and forth from the particular to the universal. I wondered if Les and I were alone in our discomfort. I felt guilty for leaving and hoped nobody saw me duck out. Was I true to my authentic Being/self? Did my decision to leave only affect me? How can I know, and would I do the same thing again if there is a next time? What did I gain from this experience that I now carry with me?

As Heidegger observes, existence is not available as an ontological fact; it is constantly up for debate even as it evades its own examination. The mystery of existence is never solved, although it is lived across various modalities of experience as we traverse endless contexts with others across time. Consequently, how might this experience at the TDoV change my future orientations toward protesting with others? What are my political and ethical obligations to others?

Jean-Paul Sartre's Existential Phenomenology: Thrownness, Embodiment, and Contingent Freedom

While incorporating aspects from Husserl and Heidegger, French existentialist Jean-Paul Sartre considers relational ethics in his existential phenomenology concerning intersubjectivity, freedom, and choice. Sartre (1943) characterizes human existence, or being, as a consciousness lacking fulfillment that materializes across its own unfolding engagement with the world as subjects endure the interminable task of constantly making choices in order to live (pp. 23–26). Sartre agrees with Husserl that all consciousness is a consciousness *of* something, similarly noting that "consciousness has no content" of its own (p. 11). Therefore, "all consciousness is a positional consciousness *of* the world" as consciousness "transcends itself to reach an object, and it exhausts itself in this same positing" (p. 11). Sartre admired Heidegger's work *Being and Time* (1926), but took issue with the idea that *Dasein* is a being whose Being is in question, for there is no "mode of being which manifests being and veils it at the same time" (Sartre, 1943, p. 25). For Sartre, Heidegger all but forgets the importance of consciousness in existential thought. Sartre famously states that "existence precedes essence," reflecting the idea "that man[3] first exists: he materializes in the world, encounters himself, and only afterward defines himself" (1947, p. 21). When a person discovers pathways to personal freedom, Sartre insists it then becomes their ethical obligation to guide others in their own liberating pursuits of better life possibilities. For Sartre, existentialism "is a doctrine that makes human life possible and also affirms that every truth and every action

> I exist in my body: this is the first dimension of being. My body is utilized and known by the Other: this is its second dimension. But in so far as *I am for others*, the Other is revealed to me as the subject for whom I am an object. Even there the question, as we have seen, is of my fundamental relation with the Other. I exist therefore for myself as known by the Other – in particular in my very facticity. I exist for myself as a body known by the Other. This is the third ontological dimension of my body . . ..
>
> Thus, my body is not given merely as that which is purely and simply lived; rather this "lived experience" becomes – in and through the contingent, absolute fact of the Other's existence – extended outside in a dimension of flight which escapes me. My body's depth of being is for me this perpetual "outside" of my most intimate "inside."
>
> (Sartre, 1943, pp. 460–461)

imply an environment and a human subjectivity" (1947, p. 18). No one lives life entirely alone.

Sartre explicates his ontology of people's inherent and inseparable (self-other) relationality in a brilliant distinction among three ontological modes of embodied being:

Sartre explains that we do not exist through "our" intentional consciousness of reality that populates the outside from within *our* interiority (as Husserl believed). Rather, Sartre considers the realization that when "we" (or the embodied "I") face another person, we are transcended as a mere object-for-the-other because the two-way reversibility of this epiphany reflects our very existence back to us. Sartre says:

> I exist in my contingency. . . . My body is there not only as the point of view which I am but again as a point of view on which are actually

brought to bear points of view which I could never take; my body escapes me on all sides.

(1943, p. 461)

Sartre's intersubjectivity posits that our futile efforts to flee our own body to be with the Other (in-itself) affirm our existence as a being for-itself. But the Other is a similarly mimetic being (for-itself), mirroring the interrelational and existentially reversible nature of corporeal forms (we are similarly perceived as an Other in-itself). For Sartre, people experience a weighty *choice* of how we shall exist with Others. Anguish symbolizes the irreducible interrelationship of a dependent existence, one that often obscures one's constituting partner from the event because we cannot see ourselves; we only see the Other. But we share a co-presence as the Other seems to be returning *my* gaze, which in turn bears my being as a concretely relational embodied Being. I exist. Concern for the Other concerns me.

Sartre's hammers: *thrownness* (the state of being "flung" into existence without any control over the material conditions and/or social prejudices in which we find ourselves, live, and survive); *intersubjectivity/self-other* (we become known to ourselves through our interactions with others – we experience ourselves through shared interanimating experiences of "you," "me," and "us"); *embodiment* (our body is central to our world-dealings – it both enables and delimits our life possibilities "even as it evades our own examination"); *choice/contingency/freedom* (social responsibility; everyone is confronted with the existential "choice" to live or not, opting for life subsequently involves an endless barrage of choices that both open up and foreclose other options – for ourself and others; freedom is the ideal lifeworld that *ought to be* populated by all living beings).

The Transgender Day of Visibility: Sartrean Explication

Sartre's existential phenomenology assumes a more political and relational approach than his predecessors. Imprisoned and later released during WWII (Desan, 2022), he experienced radically absent control over his own freedom, which likely influenced his concentration on the concepts of choice, freedom, intersubjectivity, and collective contingency/consequences in his approach to existential phenomenology.

Account (~~Reduction~~): There is more happening today than my mere presence, as several other people are here. Initially, I do not know many of these folks personally, but I recognize this event supports trans-inclusivity, an acknowledgment of the high rate of violence against trans people, but mainly an intentional celebration of trans lives and cultural contributions. I wonder to myself if I should have worn something more festive, but I also don't want to look like an imposter. What should I look like and do to affirm trans lives and visibility? How visible should I be on this day?

Authenticity/Explication: Today is not about me; it is about showing my support for trans lives – those lost, those present, and a future that embraces all trans lives. My eager support makes me a bit self-conscious as I strive to put my personal freedom in the service of affirming my local community members. I feel good during the positive celebratory moments, grieve in remembering lives lost, and subsequently am trapped between contrasting modalities of marching. I want to stand, march, and live in solidarity with this cause. My future remains open-to-the-world and I will continue to make choices about my involvement and investment in others, my responsibility to freedom. How can I learn to live with and reconcile my splintered discomfort? I return to this question later.

Existential Hammers: Tools for Accomplishing Qualitative Analytical Autoethnography

Existential phenomenology follows a hermeneutic interpretive cycling that dialectically ripples between conceptualizing existence as the "lone" self-project of distinct individuals, and existence as an interactive, collective, historical, social, and cultural continuity, anchored by and within exclusively embodied time-spaces. Thus far, I have identified several "hammers" inspired by Husserl, Heidegger, and Sartre. These conceptual tools follow Nietzsche's nihilistic approach to challenging and deconstructing norms and serve as critical probes for backchecking autoethnographic accounts as being fully formed and aptly known, without including others' input. Husserl's hammers challenge the world of appearances as readily known through a researcher's perspective by including the importance of "bracketing" (*epoché*) preconceived opinions and perceptions about a thing/object/person of perception during eidetic description (vivid and detailed). Disclosing the intentionality of the lived experience of an object of perception aspires to reveal *one's structural consciousness and perception of a world-thing* (how do I know what I am looking at?). Likewise, my perceptual intentionality motivated me to exit the protest. Others' intentionalities stayed on course with co-participants and weathered the march. There are multivariant perspectives situated in concretely lived realities that inform our elections to stay or leave.

Heidegger's hammers chip away at assumptions of the visible world by turning the phenomenological project inward toward the very notion of being a Being in existence with others who have their own unique perspectives. His existential outlook about concrete existence *binds self- and other-consciousness as irrevocably historicized, cultural, and interconnected.* Being-in-the-world-with-others unfolds in distinct time-spaces that we cannot elect to avoid. We are already here, and to exist we must *care* about our common existence. Sartre's hammers locate an unequal yet shared humanity possessing an intrinsic potential to participate in a collective response to ever present oppressions and multifarious evils in/of the world. Sartre thus advocates for an increased awareness and initiation of a *humanistic collective consciousness of social responsibility.* Taken together, these insights thematize windows into the intersubjective constitution of personhood. Participating in daily life immerses us within institutions, historical conventions, backyards, public parks, subway seats, and unexpected protests, for we are always alongside others. The solo existential project does not and cannot exist alone. Next, I (re) engage with this experience and reflect on conversations I had with two friends following the event. These exchanges helped me reconcile some of the anxieties I felt after leaving the rally. Afterward, I incorporate some selected existential "hammers" I have identified and draw this chapter to a close.

Talking with Others

Following my experience at the TDoV, I reach out to my friends Marisol and Bea. I take detailed notes as we speak, and both of my friends review and authenticate my depictions of our conversations in the following accounts. I argue that this effort to seek feedback from others strengthens autoethnographic rigor.

Talking with Marisol

Two days later, I am still wracked with guilt about leaving the rally. I decide to text Marisol to see if we can please chat for a few minutes. She quickly replies,

"Absolutely! Call whenever!"

I do, and we talk about the TDoV, how fantastic her speech was, and then I confess:

"So, I'm not exactly sure how to say this . . . I'm just gonna go for it."
"For sure! You can tell me anything, girl!"

I apprehensively tell Marisol that Les and I didn't complete the march and explain how the inspiring chants ("Trans lives matter!") shifted to "Blue lives don't [matter]." I ask if she was at the march and heard this happen. Marisol surprises me with her response:

> "Oh shit, that sucks! I was afraid things might turn out that way. I was on the planning committee, and I never wanted to have a march at all! I was stoked to give a speech, but I wanted the day to be positive. The core of the Trans Day of Visibility is a positive one. For me, personally, protest says something is wrong and nothing horrible had happened recently. I mean, of course there are terrible acts of transphobic violence and discrimination that happen every day, but I only march when I feel *endangered* because it holds so much symbolic weight. We need cis allies! Also, I'm sure you noticed that I wasn't wearing Pride gear or trans colors because I didn't want to get clocked![4] But mainly, you attract more bees with honey, and we're a marginalized group. We've been fighting to exist in society forever and we don't help things by villainizing other groups. I think it's fine that you left – if that's what you felt – always follow your heart. I'm so sorry that things turned out like that."
>
> "Oh, don't be sorry! It's not your fault and it was still an awesome day!"
>
> "We should get together soon and chat more about this over some wine."
>
> "That is a great idea! Thank you so much for talking with me about this. I was worried that you might be disappointed."
>
> "Oh my god, no! I actually love the opportunity to share my thoughts on protest and being trans – I don't really have anybody to talk about this with! I have actually never spoken about this with anyone! Sometimes I worry that I might come off as pretentious or anti-trans. Thank you for asking and hearing me out!"

***

Talking with Bea

I am the type of person who seeks advice from others. It's not that I don't trust myself and my perceptions; it's just that I have been "wrong" about situations so many times in my life and I appreciate talking things over with my friends. This helps give me some footing in a complicated world. Bea is my best friend and works as a mental health social worker and advocates for her clients with debilitating lifelong mental health challenges to live on their own (and not become institutionalized). We're both night owls and often talk late into the evening. I tell her about my experience at the TDoV, fill her in on my conversation with Marisol, and ask for her thoughts. After listening intently, Bea breathes deeply:

> "Well, dude, this is a tough one, you know? On the one hand, you have to live and be your authentic self and you have the right to leave anywhere if you don't feel comfortable. That's very understanding of Marisol to support you on that position. And that is Marisol's call to be where she feels comfortable. On the other hand, in terms of you being at the march and leaving, it's important to remember that you don't have the shared experience of being transgender. Imagine getting arrested by a police officer, going to jail, and getting misgendered. In many cases, now you're in a men's jail and you're a woman. I can recognize the fear and pain involved in these scenarios that happen all the time. Think about *you* being arrested for something and going to jail – not that this would happen, but it *could*. Now, think about being arrested as a Black trans woman and wondering what is going to happen to you – *where* are you headed? These are the things that we must keep in mind as allies."

Collective Participation, Autoethnography, and Existential Phenomenology: Presence, Exit, and Afterwords with Others

I have worked to illustrate the productive complementary relationship between autoethnographic and phenomenological approaches to understanding and participating in collective action. I am both a participant and a researcher. Throughout, I have considered phenomenological dimensions of my experience at the Trans Day of Visibility. Drawing from Husserl, Heidegger, and Sartre, my story assumed different perspectives, depending on the phenomenological and existential features soliciting my perception, reflection, and conscious awareness of myself alongside others. Analyzing my experience from Husserl's approach helped me consider "what things and others appeared to be," *to me*, in daylight as a celebratory rally transformed into a protest. I had not intended to participate in protest on this special day. From a Heideggerian existential perspective, my account turned inward, contemplating my experiences of myself being with others, feeling heartened, and then feeling uncomfortable. Sartre's existentialism reframed my perspective as not merely "my view of the world," nor "my experience of myself-in-the-world-with-others," to a focus on "my responsibility to (the) Other/s" and the role I *ought* to play in supporting transgender visibility and freedom. Perhaps the best thing I could have done that day was to stay and dwell in a liminal state of culturally privileged discomfort.

I have considered my experience of the TDoV as an autoethnographic story, which I then reflexively explored using three distinct phenomenological "hammers." To better understand my personal experience, I also sought counsel in conversations with my friends Marisol and Bea, from which I offer two final takeaways.

Dialogic Hermeneutics: Self-Reflexivity-With-Others

Autoethnography hinges on the notion of self-reflexivity, yet this living effort is too often preoccupied with the confines of the self. This exercise can be enhanced by pursuing inclusive dialogue with others and inviting their world-understandings of our collectively performed cultural experiences. By meditating on the relational complexities informing my lived experience, I gain insight about my experience of others, and their experience of me. I value dialogue with my supportive friends and their distinct perspectives. In talking with Marisol, we both assumed a risk in going outside of ourselves – we live different lives. I could have offended her, but Marisol expressed that she too felt disengaged from the march. It surprised me to learn how similar our feelings were. Intriguingly, we both sought control over the visibility of our bodies with others. Although I don't have to worry about getting "clocked" and outed as a member of the trans community, I have realized that we each walk a tightrope in life, in shared and divergent modes. Speaking with Marisol disclosed aspects of the experience that were not readily apparent to me. Hearing her, I don't take the ease of my cis visibility nor Marisol's self-protecting visual vulnerabilities for granted. I will continue to be an ally and work on becoming a more visible advocate.

Standpoint and Representation: Identity and Collective Experience

Representing and narrating our experiences of others lies at the heart of autoethnography. But how we go about achieving these depictions calls for multiple perspectives. I made an appearance at the rally and joined a collective protest but grew concerned about being seen by others as anti-police. This feeling of abandoning my trans siblings haunted me and colored my reflections made after the fact. Hannah Arendt (1993) discusses this "process of representation" as necessitating multiple viewpoints and an ability to *imagine* the positional perspectives of others who are present on the scene, as well as those who are absent (for good reason) (p. 241). In other words, what "I" see is not all that there is to see or know in any given situation. Admittedly, I did feel better after Marisol told me she didn't attend the march either. But in talking with Bea, I reconsidered my experience at the TDoV. Bea reminded me that I don't share Marisol's experience as a trans woman. I have never felt *endangered* in my life, and I cannot imagine what that fear might feel like – how it would change me, alter my practices, my routine, my outlook, *me*. Exploring such relational cultural space can be autoethnography's wheelhouse. Uncovering insights about others' lives are perspectives that I cannot assume because I do not live those realities; I'm trapped inside me. I am advocating for enriched autoethnographic practices that self-consciously broaden the scope of "personal" experience as a landing point, in favor of greater existential meditation and dialogic reflection with others. I do not hold "truth" in my ability to word an experience because reality is beyond my or any linguistic grasp. Self-focused representations can unduly constrain our accounts and exclude others' voices. Sometimes those of us who don't live "the experience" can offer relevant insights to those who do. This meaningful interchange of uncovering and affirming other viewpoints ought to be an important activity of autoethnography when it consciously seeks out and discloses the relational-existential-world-with-others.

Notes

1 I have changed people's names to protect their identities (other than my own and my friend, Les, who gave me permission to share his name). My friends chose their own pseudonyms.
2 Marisol explained to me that it is appropriate to shorten "transgender" to "trans" in academic writing. She also shared that it is important to honor the fact that a spectrum of identifications exist in the community beyond "brothers and sisters" to include non-binary trans persons; thus, siblings is used to honor this understanding.
3 Sartre's androcentric style of writing that was common during his time is preserved for readability. (Personhood and humanity are universalized as "man" or "men.") While I maintain this strategy throughout the present work, it is important always to use inclusive and gender-neutral language.
4 In the transgender community, being "clocked" indicates "that someone transgender has been recognized as trans, usually when that person is trying to blend in with cisgender people, and not intending to be seen as anything other than the gender they present" (Ennis, 2016).

References

Arendt, H. (1993). *Between Past and Future: Eight Exercises in Political Thought*. New York: Penguin Books.
Bakhtin, M.M. (1981). *The Dialogic Imagination: Four Essays*. Translated by Emerson, C. and Holquist, M. Austin: University of Texas Press.
Carreras, J. (2009). 'Transgender Day of Visibility Plans Erupt Locally, Nationwide'. *Web Archive*. https://web.archive.org/web/20130327152446/www.pridesource.com/article.html?article=34351 (Accessed: 16 April 2022).
Chang, H. (2008). *Autoethnography as Method*. Walnut Creek, CA: Left Coast Press.
Desan, W. (2022). 'Jean-Paul Sartre: French Philosopher and Author'. *Britannica*. www.britannica.com/biography/Jean-Paul-Sartre (Accessed: 8 April 2022).

Ennis, D. (2016). '10 Words Transgender People Want You to Know (But Not Say)'. *The Advocate*. www.advocate.com/transgender/2016/1/19/10-words-transgender-people-want-you-know-not-say (Accessed: 16 April 2022).

Explorecarbondale.com. Landmarks. Town Square Pavilion. www.explorecarbondale.com/371/Landmarks (Accessed: 1 April 2022).

Gingrich-Philbrook, C. (2005). 'Autoethnography's Family Values: Easy Access to Compulsory Experiences'. *Text and Performance Quarterly*. 25(4): pp. 297–314. https://doi.org/10.1080/10462930500362445

Gingrich-Philbrook, C. (2015). 'On Dorion Street'. In Chawla, D. and Jones, S.H. (eds.) *Stories of Home: Place, Identity, Exile*. pp. 199–214. Washington, DC: Lexington Books.

Heidegger, M. (1926). *Being and Time*. Translated by Macquirrie, J. and Robinson, E. New York: Harper Perennial Modern Thought, 2008.

Husserl, E. (1913). *Ideas*. Translated by Boyce Gibson, W.R. New York: Palgrave Macmillan, 1982.

Nietzsche, F.W. (1889). *Twilight of the Idols*. Translated by Ludovici, A.M. In *A Nietzsche Compendium*. pp. 297–378. New York: Barnes & Noble, 2008.

Nietzsche, F.W. (1901). *Will to Power*. Translated by Kaufmann, W. and Hollingdale, R.J. New York: Vintage, 1969.

Nietzsche, F.W. and Taffel, D. (1886). *Beyond Good and Evil*. Translated by Zimmern, H. In *A Nietzsche Compendium*. pp. 1–173. New York: Barnes & Noble, 2008.

Rawlins, L.S. (2017). 'Stranger and Stranger: Living Stories on Others' Doorsteps'. *Departures in Critical Qualitative Research*. 6(4): pp. 87–110. https://doi.org/10.1525/dcqr.2017.6.4.87

Sartre, J.-P. (1943). *Being and Nothingness*. Translated by Barnes, H.E. New York City: Washington Square Press, 1992.

Sartre, J.-P. (1947). *Existentialism is a Humanism*. Translated by Macomber, C. New Haven: Yale University Press, 2007.

12

OUR BODIES KNOW ABLEISM

An Existential Phenomenological Approach to Storytelling through Disabled Bodies

Julie-Ann Scott-Pollock

Bodies Know: A Summary of What is to Come

He stops
Trembles
Stiffens
Irregular breaths
Flushed
Hands in the air
He grips a table
Or chair if there is one
Or
He falls
It's all over in 5 or 20 seconds
It.
Feels.
So.
Much.
Longer.
Taunt limbs
Gritted jaw
Grabbing Invisibility
The energy is mysterious
Waves vibrating through his frontal lobe
Through tissues that generate our emotional response
Both when awake and asleep

DOI: 10.4324/9781003274728-12

They envelop his fear center
And then
He gets up
He lives
He remembers it happened
He knows it will happen again
And moves on
He resumes
Eating
Swimming
His Spanish homework
Defending a soccer goal
For him
It's over
Until the Next one
Which could be months away if the meds are working
Or Hours
Or Minutes if they're not
It's his reality
He knows his body
He accepts
Is at ease
Will explain
With patience beyond his ten years
But people around him are frightened
They ask me why the seizures aren't gone
Why he is this way
Why I
His mother
Allow this to happen in front of them
Why I haven't found a way to suppress this energy
Or to keep him home
Away from them
until they stop
It could be months before the correct cocktail of meds suppresses them
again
Their Request is Unreasonable
Wrong
Rooted in fear
Their Hatred of difference they see as Deficient
And my body knows their judgment
Their Ableist marginalization

Their belief that bodies that make them uncomfortable should be
controlled
Hidden
Apologetic for Our presence
And my tight limping muscles clench in defense
The memory of when my body was young
Perched on turned in toes
Back hunched
Unsure
Rejected
Expected to not Expect anything
To accept exclusion
Alienation
I Longed for advocates absent from my story
And my body is present
Snipped Broken and Mended
With a straight back and feet after decades of surgery
Passing
As ALMOST (but not quite) Normal
Ready
Angry
Rigid with Defensive Resistance
Poised for the role in my son's story that mine was lacking
And A well-crafted challenge
Delivered with force and finality
My body's response make those who don't embody marginalization
pause
Confused
Even if they know the laws
the protocols
the medicine
Stigma Does Not Live in their bodies
My body knows
So does my son's
And I believe they will learn
They may never know like we know
But they can access
Understand
Change
Support
So we Keep Going
Our bodies know their Rejection

But we also know Hope
We Believe that which we pursue but have not experienced
For this reason I tell our story

Advocacy, Parenting, and Embodied Responses

This essay is an existential phenomenological critical autoethnographic response to my cerebral palsied body's lived experience of parenting my son, Tony, who is 10 and lives with seizures. I tell our story. He reads drafts, responds, and clarifies. Together we map how resistance emerges from our bodies' knowledge of stigma, judgment, and marginalization that others interpret as too emotional, too angry, too unforgiving, too much. Through telling our story, we hope to compel people to value the deep, fleshed knowledge of ableism that those of us marked as disabled and/or chronically ill react to as our bodies move through cultural spaces. Tony and I know, just as we cannot fully access each other's physical experience, the experience of ableism may not ever be truly accessible to those marked as 'normal' in culture, but we hope that empathetic listening can open up space for a kind of knowing that manifests in allyship and productive advocacy. We are committed to engaging in this methodology in hopes of creating shared knowledge that values the lived knowledge of disabled bodies.[1]

Tony and I live Rosemarie Garland Thomson's 1997 observation that culture defines our medically diagnosed and categorized bodies as the opposite of 'normal.' We are among the 'marked bodies' that define what normal is not so that others can exist unquestioned, moving through the world as the representation of what a good, easy, respectable, normal body should be. We desire the greater culture's acceptance of our lived, cripped[2] way of producing meaning, and out of this desire we turn to an existential phenomenological approach to critical autoethnography that emphasizes the power of a body analyzing how it is experienced and interpreted in daily life. I will explain this method in greater detail, but first, a story.

He Doesn't Have Grand Mal Seizures

I'm sitting outside of one of the three gates in our small coastal airport. I'm 22 weeks pregnant with my fifth baby. I'm sore, and anxious to be flying during a pandemic, but my national organization's annual conference is in Seattle. I'm on the executive committee for three interest groups, a program planner, and an elected voting member of legislative assembly. I need to go. My doctors deemed it an overall 'low-risk' trip. His exact words: "The best thing you could do for the health of your baby right now is not only go to Seattle, but not come back. They're being much more cautious than we are." Seattle is handling COVID far better than cities in the southern US, so I'm ready for the cross-country flight.

I'm anxious to ensure that I get my opportunity as a disabled flier to board first since being slower than others with compromised balance makes me anxious when there is a line behind me. As I see the red digital sign over the doorway shift to "Now Boarding," my phone rings. It's my sons' magnet school, so I answer.

"Hello. This Is Julie-Ann Scott-Pollock."

"Oh. Hi. Yes. This is Nurse Emily from The International School at Gregory."

"Hi. Is everything okay?"

"Well, everything is okay now. Tony had a seizure today in the cafeteria and it was a grand mal which doesn't match his paperwork."

"Tony doesn't have grand mal seizures. It was a myoclonic seizure with awareness."

"He fell down and he closed his eyes and was shaking all over for about five seconds."

"Right, he loses his balance sometimes during his seizures and his body stiffens. He has some minor involuntary movement during an episode. Did he get up after?"

"Yes, immediately after, but he fell to the ground."

"Okay, well, sometimes he loses his balance when his body stiffens, and he will close his eyes and tense up, but he didn't have a grand mal. He doesn't get grand mal seizures, and grand mal seizures don't have awareness and immediate recovery."

"Well, I described it to my county supervisor and she said it was a grand mal."

"His neurologist team who performed brain surgery and have worked with him since he was two years old are confident that he does not have grand mal seizures. His seizures are located only in the frontal lobe, not his entire brain."

"Well, it is my opinion and my supervisor's opinion that he had a grand mal."

"Was he aware of the fact that he had just had a seizure and how long it took?"

"I don't think so. His eyes were closed."

"You can still sense the world around you when your eyes are closed. You cannot during a grand mal seizure. Did you ask him and see if he could remember what happened?" I breathe heavily with exasperation into her ear and I don't feel bad about it. I will not expend the emotional energy to conceal my frustration. I'm irritated that she is attempting to re-diagnose my son and I want her to feel that agitation. Diagnosis is not the role of the school nurse in my son's life. My family has spent hundreds of hours with neurology specialty teams tasked with diagnosis and treatment. Her role is to follow their directions that are in his paperwork.

"I didn't think asking him anything was necessary. It's not in his health plan from last year." I sense defiance and defensiveness in her voice. Her words are higher and tighter than when she first called.

If my husband, Evan, were also on the call, he would say after we hung up that I'm 'unnecessarily escalating the situation.' My chest tightens. It feels necessary to me. I continue:

"It's only necessary to ask him if you're trying to undermine his neurologist's diagnosis. Listen, I need to get on a plane. Please refrain from diagnosing my son on your own. If you'd like updated paperwork from his neurologist, he has an appointment on Friday. We're going to try to alter meds and turn up his Vagal Nerve Stimulator to see if we can get these seizures under control again. This growth spurt has been hard. We will have paperwork for you on Monday."

I hang up and board the plane with other disabled passengers. Once I'm settled in my seat, I call Evan.

"Hey, there's a new nurse at Tony's school and she sounds younger and potentially not as bright as the one last year. She's trying to diagnose Tony with grand mal seizures."

"Ah, last year's nurse was competent. Why does the county have to keep changing them around each year?"

"Ugh, I know. We're always starting from scratch and this one is as tiresome as the one in his kindergarten year. Instead of just of calling an ambulance every time he has a seizure, she's trying to be his neurologist."

"Well, at least we won't be paying the deductible for an ambulance with this one. I just got them off the bus. Tony fell today in the cafeteria but he says it was like all of his other seizures. He just lost his balance since there was nothing to sit down on. He was so proud that he managed to get his tray to the table before he fell. I told him to just sit on the floor next time."

"We always tell him that. He never does. Listen, just make sure you get an updated diagnosis from the neurologist for him. This nurse doesn't even seem to know that you're not supposed to say 'grand mal' anymore, that the correct phrase is 'tonic-clonic.'"

"Did you correct her?"

"No, I didn't. I was trying to keep her focused on the fact that no matter what they are called, they are not part of our son's diagnosis or his lived experience."

"Yeah, I see why you'd want to keep the conversation on track, but you may have missed a teachable moment. I'll call you while we are at the neurologist on Friday, okay? I love you. Be safe."

"I love you, too. Thanks. I will."

I lean back in my seat and try to get comfortable with my growing belly and tight muscles. The nurse did not respond to me like a student to teach. She is a tiresome obstacle to overcome. I'm about to turn my cellphone to airplane mode when a message dings. It's from Ella, another professor at my university. Her daughter Jade and our son Tony have been in the same class since preschool. I read her message:

> Hi, Jade just said she heard the nurse tell their teacher in the lunchroom that Tony has grand mal seizures now. I'm so sorry. That has to be such hard news. I know how happy you'd been about the decrease in seizure activity since his surgery. Do you need anything? How can we help? We're here for Tony and for you.

My jaw tightens. My toes curl in a spasm. I quickly type:

> Hi. Tony still has seizure activity. It's normal growth spurt stuff. We need to turn up the Vagal Nerve Stimulator and maybe swap out one of his meds for a new one, but his seizures are the same. The nurse doesn't know what she's talking about. He just fell during one, like he did at your house during Jade's birthday party. Thanks so much though. We're okay. Just make sure Jade knows that Tony doesn't have grand mal seizures. They're the same as before.

Ella responds with a heart emoji.

I click my phone to airplane mode, knowing that the 504 plan meeting for Tony's seizures is going to be tense. Every interaction I have as an advocate for my son is tense. My body knows tension. I have spastic cerebral palsy. My body is defined by the unusual presence of tension. It is my daily experience, my diagnosis, and my identity. Before I continue my story of a disabled advocate for my son as a disabled parent, you need the prologues to this story. You need Tony's body's story, my body's story, and the lens I approach with to understand how Tony and I move through cultural space as mother and son. I will start with Tony's story.

Our Big Strong, Seizing Boy

Tony is strong and muscular with bright green eyes, thick, sandy brown hair, and skin that naturally soaks up the summer son on the North Carolina beach where we live so that he has a tan for seven months out of the year. He's always been strong. He was born three weeks early so he did not have time to put on the amount of usual weight in the womb before birth. The doctor marveled at how his calve and triceps muscles rippled as he arched his back right after birth and lifted his head.

She commented moments after delivering him, "This is the strongest newborn I've ever seen."

His calves and arms are thick. At 10 years old, his shoulders are as wide as his six-foot- tall former football player father's shoulders. They share size medium men's t-shirts. He is 5 foot 3 and 130 pounds. Other fathers marvel at his size. Grown men have commented on how muscular his legs are on the soccer field since he was three years old. They look at my husband enviously for having such a large, strong son (Scott, 2020). One father at the soccer field asked incredulously when he was three, "Does Tony lift weights?" as his broad shoulders and chest stretched the largest preschooler jersey available to its limits. We both just smiled. "He's just a big, strong boy."

That soccer season Tony's medication was working well. He was only on one daily dose when he was three. And his seizures had disappeared for almost eight months. In that moment of time, they seemed like a past experience that he had come through. He just needed a syringe of medicine with his gummy vitamin each morning and before he brushed his teeth each night. We did not understand what it meant to be a growing child with seizures in the frontal lobe back then. We did not realize how present seizures would be for Tony. We learned. Tony's identity is entangled in seizures, diagnoses, medications, surgeries, and educational plans for a boy that culture initially reads as so healthy. We know that now. So does he.

The Diagnosis

Just a few months after Tony's second birthday, he started to stop suddenly, grit his teeth, and raise his hands in the air. His face would flush, and he'd hold his breath for a few seconds as he trembled. The first time, we were startled but thought maybe he was about to trip and was just catching his balance. Looking back, we knew it was something more serious, but he was so healthy, big, strong, and smart. He had great diction, an impressive vocabulary, balance, and the ability to already carry a tune when he sang even though he was just a toddler. We assumed nothing could possibly be *really* wrong.

I'm embarrassed as I reveal my initial response to his seizures. I'm reminded how pervasive ableism is. I'm an identity scholar with a specialization in disability. I know that all these qualities do not mean that one cannot also be disabled. I know this intimately through my own body. Still, I desperately wanted to believe that it was a temporary experience that would not define his life in so many ways like having cerebral palsy has defined mine. I know disability stigma and ableism so deeply that I did not want a child I loved so much that it ached to ever have to share this embodied knowledge.

Over the course of a week, that one seizure turned into 20 5–10 second seizures each day. We did not know that they were seizures at that time. I don't think we named them. We did not know what to call them and hoped that they were not significant enough to call anything. We called the pediatrician and described what was happening throughout the day and night. By the time we had the appointment Tony was having up to 30 a day. We were terrified. Our toddler's round face began to look drawn. Our happy little boy cried more easily. He was frustrated and more prone to tantrums. He was exhausted from being woken up so often by his seizing brain. His preschool did not want him to return to class until we knew exactly what was happening and how to fix it. His pediatrician, a kind father of five with a solid balance of home remedies and medications in his prescriptions, told us not panic and assured us that we would figure it out. Tony, with dark circles from having his sleep repeatedly interrupted by his stiffening body for over two weeks, was healthy based on his doctor's check-up and he was sure no damage was happening to him, but he needed to see a pediatric neurologist. He told us to give Tony melatonin to help him sleep through what he thought were short seizures until we could have a meeting with the child neurologist who came down from the medical school in Chapel Hill once a week. The melatonin did not help. We waited for the appointment at the end of the week.

Dr. Tennison was the head child neurologist at Chapel Hill University Hospital. He drove the two hours to our city's neurology clinic once a week. He was already in his seventies when we went him, tall, lanky, with gray hair, a strong jaw, patient eyes, and a powerful voice. He commanded attention and radiated comfort simultaneously. I liked and trusted him. He watched Tony seize during our appointment and immediately diagnosed him with simple partial frontal lobe seizures that within the next few years would be renamed myoclonic seizures with awareness. The diagnosis did not change, just the terminology. Dr. Tennison prescribed a standard, well-known prescription to treat them that had minimal side effects, oxcarbazepine. It is still Tony's base medication today, though they went on to add two others and a Vagal Nerve Stimulator in an effort to continue to suppress his seizures as he grew. Dr Tennison ordered magnetic resonance imaging (MRI) and an overnight electroencephalogram (EEG). The MRI was normal, and the EEG had a difference of brain activity that ordinarily is read as being asleep versus waking up. It is only because our toddler was being video recorded that we knew those changes in brain activity were seizures. In fact, had this happened as a teen or adult, they said they would take time to rule out simple anxiety or attention-seeking behaviors before prescribing medicine. They assumed a child so young, with such tired eyes, would not be faking the condition. We still feel relieved that doubt of the authenticity of what they were observing was not another obstacle to his care. A two-year-old does not evoke questions of willful deceit or emotional manipulation like an older child or adult may. The observations were readily accepted as involuntary and in need of treatment. We had a boy with a healthy brain without a reason for seizure activity in the frontal lobe. Dr. Tennison was both relieved and apologetic:

> "The good news is that your son is healthy. His brain looks great. He's meeting all of his milestones ahead of schedule. The bad news is that given where the seizures are located and what the EEG showed us, we probably won't ever really know why he has seizures or if there is a specific part of the frontal lobe that could be removed to eliminate them. If they were in the motor cortex that would be a strong possibility. You see, the frontal lobe is where we process all of our emotions. It's active even when we're sleeping unless there is sedation, and if we sedated him to the point to quiet all that activity, it would also quiet the seizures, so we wouldn't see them. That said, oxcarbazepine has been around a long time. It's an established med with minimal side effects, and it's already working. When we up the dose a bit, his seizures should be completely suppressed. If they stay that way as he grows, we can slowly wean him off the medication and see what happens. So, for now, we have a treatment."

Evan and I left that doctor's office with a very happy two-year-old. And for about a year, a syringe of liquid once a day kept his seizures suppressed. As he grew, the needed medication went up to two syringes, then three. At four years old, Dr. Tennison added a second medication, then a third, that he called "toppers," to suppress the seizures that his base med was missing. These two topper meds evolve every few years as we navigate new side effects and unsuppressed seizures. He explained that there are "families" of seizure medications that work the same way but have varying side effects. So, if one is working to suppress seizures but causing other physical or emotional symptoms, we can switch to a different medication in the same family. However, if the medication is not suppressing seizure activities, a different member of the same family of medications will not either. Nine years later we are on the last 'family' of medications. I'll explain more about that later.

Dr. Tennison retired a few years ago, and our own city hospital grew to include a new child neurology unit, with the head doctor being a former student of Dr. Tennison's. Dr. Taravath suggested that since three medications were not suppressing Tony's seizures effectively that he should undergo surgery to install a vagal nerve stimulator (VNS) that would send electricity to his vagal nerve that connected to his brain in hopes of interrupting seizure activity. Tony underwent the operation when he was nine and it was deemed a success.

The doctor who installed the VNS noted: "It's so nice to work on someone so high functioning. He is so smart and so big and so strong. This kid has a real chance of this being life-changing." I smiled and nodded. I understood what he meant. I saw the majority of children with unsuppressed seizures that needed a VNS had compounded health problems and seizures that deprived their brains of oxygen. Their disabilities hindered their movement, ability to communicate, and their cognitive processing. Tony has seizures, but he is a big, strong, smart boy. In the hierarchy of ableism, which values independent, strong, mobile bodies with what is deemed normative cognitive processing, he has more opportunities. Still, I worry. I wonder what it will mean to have unsuppressed seizures as an adolescent and adult. I wonder how it will impact his career options, his relationships, and his independence if the end of growing does not result in the end of his breakthrough seizures. For now, we watch, and we hope.

My Tense Cerebral Palsied Embodiment

My fear of Tony experiencing disability stigma stems from my embodied experience. I have spastic cerebral palsy. Like Tony's, my brain sends involuntary signals to my body, but the manifestation is markedly different. My brain sends constant, involuntary impulses to my muscles to tense over and over again throughout the day. My muscles grow tight and sore and require constant stretching and movement to stay mobile. As a child, I was perched on turned-in toes, with my back hunched to accommodate my irregular gait. Both grown-ups and children stared at me. Strangers offered condolences to my mother in the grocery store, speaking to her about my obviously unfortunate existence as though I could not hear them. I could hear them. At first, they confused me as a little girl who adored life despite my chronic pain and atypical gait. Confusion evolved to shame and embarrassment, then anger as I grew older and realized the violence of ableism that obstructed my opportunities for social inclusion.

From age four to 24, I underwent a series of operations that transformed my body. They sliced into me to snip, stretch, and stitch tendons. They broke my feet and repositioned them, and sawed my femurs in half, rotated them 30 degrees, and nailed them back together again. I still have a noticeable limp, but my back is straight, my heels touch the ground, and my feet face forward. At times, I even pass as 'normal' with a temporary injury rather than permanently 'deficient.' Right now, people assume my limp is due to carrying my growing pregnant belly. I'm my most immobile in my last months of pregnancy, yet it is when people assume I'm the most 'normal' as a fertile woman about to give birth who is limping due to the extra weight that I'm carrying that will become a new life. Pregnancy is considered a sign of health and relative youth despite how it impairs the body. When leaving my barre studio, people assume that my stiff, unbending knees are just from working out too hard. I'm told to "take it easy." I smile, knowing that if I take more than a day off between barre classes, my knees and feet will be so much stiffer.

An Almost Passing Disabled Body with Intersectional Privilege

I benefit from multifaceted intersectional cultural privilege as a white, cisgender, heteronormative, married, upper-middle class, educated, ambulatory woman just as Tony benefits from being a big, strong, upper-middle class, white, cisgender, heteronormative boy who does well in school. I'm well-known and celebrated in our community as a performance artist and social justice intellectual. I give invited talks and radio interviews on a regular basis and my one-woman shows, research, and directed ensembles have received awards from the local to international levels. Still, disability stigma is etched into my muscles, bones, nerves, and flesh. I know it deeply and intimately. My body remembers and responds with an emotional tightness, a stiffening in my chest that mirrors my involuntary muscular spasms, that is made tangible through active resistance and advocacy.

At this moment in time, this advocacy is rarely for myself. Overall, I move through my daily life without being denied the medical care and flexible schedule I need to thrive. I have good health insurance and as a tenured, full professor, I'm granted the authority to design a work week that enables my maximum mobility. My friends are accepting, and strangers – while curious and at times invasive in their questions – are never hostile. No one denies me access to cultural and physical spaces like they did when I was a child. I no longer desire to play organized sports or participate in mainstream theatre. I don't worry about unkind people not wanting to invite me to parties since my friendships have evolved away from those that I may have wanted to be friends with for social power as a child and young adult. I can gain social power through my work and extensive networks through my husband and children. I have a PhD and a publication record that means no one questions my intelligence like they did when I was a child. Still, stigma and rejection are deep within my body. I know disabled marginalization.

An Existential Phenomenological Approach to Critical Autoethnographic Inquiry

I tell you these stories to explain how my methodology stems from autoethnography's call for the "turning of the ethnographic gaze inward on the self (auto), while maintaining the outward gaze of ethnography, looking at the larger context wherein self-experiences occur" (Denzin, 1997, p. 227). Critical autoethnography maps how cultural power relations become tangible through storytelling, recognizing how privilege, power, and difference are influencing our experience and response in the world (Alexander, 2006; Denzin, 2014; Diversi and Moriera, 2009; Pelias, 2015; Scott, 2018; Shoemaker, 2011; Spry, 2016; Toyosaki and Pensoneau-Conway, 2013). Critical autoethnography allows a reflexive analysis of self, mapping how meanings and understandings surrounding identity are surfacing and struggled over through one's lived, embodied experience. Critical autoethnographic stories not only uncover marginalization, stigma, and prejudice in our personal stories, but also look toward means to resist it. My resistance stems from my embodied response to others' responses to my body in the world.

I'm drawn to existential phenomenology, a philosophical lens that grounds knowledge in the fleshed, lived experience to understand the stories I live and choose to tell. Throughout my life I have navigated the able-bodied, normative cultural gaze. Rosemary Garland Thomson (2009) reminds us that the disabled body evokes not only the stares of the dominant culture, but also the demand for one's story. People want to know 'What happened?' And more importantly, "If whatever ever happened to me it could happen to them, or anyone that they care about" (Scott, 2022). Everyone, from students in my classes to strangers at the grocery store, wants the story of my body. Perhaps that is why I'm drawn to the visceral experience that brings about storytelling (Scott, 2018). The stories we choose to tell happen due to our fleshed reactions to the world around us, to the deep sensations of our body. Our bodies 'know' when a moment matters. I think to the tightness in my lungs as I conversed with the nurse and how only when speaking to Evan did I realize how much I needed air. I remember how my toes curled as I read Ella's message, and how hard I pressed the keys of my phone to respond.

Existential phenomenology focuses on the flesh, blood, bone, and organs as our access to what is real, true, powerful, and meaningful. Our bodies are the "foundations of consciousness" that engage with and are "transformed by the world" (Sobchack, 2004 p. 2). An existential phenomenological perspective emphasizes the body's role in the creation of personal and cultural identity; all of which are contingent upon our human tissues that allow us to experience our world – to feel, see, hear, smell, and touch, and to *be* felt, seen, heard, smelled, and touched (Merleau-Ponty, 1964a). The founder of existential phenomenology Merleau-Ponty (1964b, p. 290) explains:

> "The enigma is that my body simultaneously sees and is seen. That which looks at all things can also look at itself and recognize, in what it sees, the 'other side' of its power of looking. It sees itself seeing; it touches itself touching; it is visible and sensitive for itself.

As I tell my stories, my focus is on my body as the main character in relationship with other bodies. My body is also the creator of the story. I'm aware how the tissues of my brain hold the experience, allowing my fingers to type it to you as my eyes read, reexperience, struggle, and negotiate with you, an audience that consists of some that I may know and some that I inevitably do not. Existential phenomenology embraces knowing that comes from living in a body that interprets the world, is interpreted by the world, and interprets the world's ongoing interpretations in a never-ending re-understanding of self and others.

I'm drawn to an existential phenomenological approach to critical autoethnography because my embodiment is so highlighted in my ongoing interactions. Existing as the antithesis of a 'normal' body means that culture continues to draw my attention back to my body and others' responses to it. This focus on my body is intensified by needing to manage my body's chronic pain and the tightness that can lead to lack of mobility without a rigid exercise schedule. Since my senses are already heightened to how others perceive my involuntarily spasming limbs, my son's involuntary seizures and culture's responses to him resurface the embodied memories of marginalization when I was denied mainstream schooling, theatrical roles, and social inclusion based on how my body made others uncomfortable.

My body knows social marginalization and ableism in intimate ways that my able-bodied, athletic husband's body does not. Both medical and educational professionals would rather converse with him, who does not read their ableist viewpoints as marginalizing, but simply uninformed. He

expresses that through education, ableism will disappear since he personally has transformed his thinking through learning from my son and me.
In contrast, my lived experience knows intimately how medical and educational knowledge of disability is rooted in ableism that is comfortable
diagnosing our marked bodies as disruptive and in need of managing with
the minimal number of resources possible that extend the greatest profit
to these institutions. The power that comes from knowledge surrounding
disabled bodies is not guaranteed to lead to acceptance and inclusion. In
fact, in my lived experience, it usually does not. The positioning of our two
bodies, with different understandings of how knowledge moves through
and alters culture is accessed through an existential phenomenological lens
to our family's stories.

The Normative Body's Befuddled Response to My Tense
Response to Marginalization

My phone rings during a panel at the conference. It's Evan. He is attending
a performance with one of my traveling troupes this week since I can't be
there. I glance at the time and realize that the performance should have
ended about 20 minutes ago. I step out of a panel to take the call. I find
a chair that seems moderately private since it is against the wall in a narrow walkway that does not invite people to pause in without obstructing
others' paths. Right now, with panels going on mid-day, the convention
halls are noticeably empty. Unlike most of our national conventions, this
one is not crowded. There is somewhere between one-third and one-half
the normal attendance due to the pandemic. The space feels large for the
number of people who are in attendance and offers pockets of privacy and
solitude in the hallways. I'm thankful a candid conversation is possible.

"Hi. How did the performance go? Thanks so much for being there with
them. Ordinarily I'd just have them attend alone, but with the pandemic
and so many changes to the schedule once we get there, I think having
a professor there was comforting."

"It went fine. You have a good group."

"Yeah, they're kind people. I like them. They're doing so well during
a pandemic."

"It is nice to take a break from large lecture physics to organize your
troupe. They are very different than physics students. Listen, I called
because the school nurse asked me three times during the performance
to stop by her office, so I did. She had Tony's revised paperwork to give
me. It says he has grand mal seizures. I asked if she had talked to you
about his diagnosis and she said, 'Yes, but she saw what she saw and

this is her supervisor's and her opinion so that's what needs to be on the form.'"

"So what did you say?" I notice my voice is rising a bit as I respond without pausing a moment to take in any air. I consciously take a deep breath. The nurse's behavior is not Evan's fault and I'm talking to him, not the nurse.

"I said that we may have some adjustments once we talk to his doctor tomorrow."

"You didn't say, 'He doesn't have grand mal seizures and this is inaccurate, so get it out of his file.'"

"She's so young, Julie. She's trying to do a good job. She had on foundation that was two shades darker and about an inch thicker than it needed to be with such bright make-up. She reminded me of a teenager pretending to be a grown-up. She's taking everything she's hearing from her supervisor as gospel. She doesn't know us. She'll get it. She's eager. This can be a growing experience for her. We don't want her to shut down."

"She needs to be corrected, Evan. This is completely unacceptable. She is disregarding what I'm saying as his mother based on his neurologist's diagnosis. She's calling Tony's seizures 'grand mal' to his teachers and other kids are hearing that and repeating it to their parents. It has to stop."

"It will. We'll get the paperwork and make sure she understands not to try to diagnose him herself at the 504 meeting."

"You should have shut down this whole diagnosing our son with her supervisor who wasn't even present during the seizure when you talked to her. Listen, I need to get back into a session. I'll call you tonight."

"Don't let this upset you. She's harmless. We'll teach her."

"Okay, bye."

I hang up the phone. My legs tighten in a spasm. The tendons in my neck are taunt as I clench my teeth in frustration. My body responds to the school nurse's dismissal of my son's official diagnosis. How often people have misdiagnosed my disability surfaces through this conversation. My body knows the marginalization that comes from misdiagnosis. People would repeatedly mistake my brain injury for a progressive illness. Assumptions that I had muscular dystrophy, not cerebral palsy or an accompanying intellectual disability (which is common with cerebral palsy since cerebral palsy results from a lack of oxygen to the brain), meant simultaneously more pity and fewer opportunities. The danger of misdiagnosis is not part of my husband's story. The nurse is naïve but not dangerous.

I understand why my husband, who is white, tall, smart, athletic, from an educated, financially stable background, reacts differently than I do to people's assumptions surrounding Tony's seizures. As an educator and father, he has patience with Tony's school nurse. He relates to her as a person to teach and mentor into her role as a supporter of our son. His mother was a school nurse and his father was a high school science teacher before they both retired from the public school system seven years ago. Talks of how unreasonable and uninformed parents of K-12 students are reverberated through his family conversations. I'm also an educator, but a first-generation college student. My family's blue-collar background placed us at odds with teachers and administrators who sought to remove me from the mainstream classroom. Valuing, protecting, and supporting healthcare workers and educators as imperfect but competent well-meaning professionals is as etched into his human tissues as deeply as resisting potential marginalization and lost opportunity from their judgments are etched into mine. For this reason, staff at our son's school tend to prefer to talk to Evan about Tony's seizures, but we are both always at the meetings.

The Annual 504 Meeting

Evan's and my emails ding simultaneously. It's the notification that the Zoom link for Tony's annual 504 meeting has come to our inboxes. He sits at the table by the window and I move to the rocking chair in the living room to tune in. Boxes emerge with familiar faces. First the principal of the school, with her broad shoulders and perfectly coiffed blond bob, the petite vice principal, a nondescript administrator from the county who has to be present for the meeting to take place, the round-faced school nurse, Tony's Costa Rican Spanish teacher, Senora Rudi with her dark hair swept up in a pretty scarf, and his surfer/English teacher, Mr. Boone, who recently arrived from California in search of a more affordable beach town than Santa Cruz.

Overall, the meeting is uneventful. Tony is having five or more breakthrough seizures a day, but his grades are high. Other than extended time to complete assignments because seizures slow him down, both his Spanish and English classes are progressing well.

Ms. Rudi politely offers after the discussion about his grades, "We have seen that Tony is crying easier than he ever has lately. He's fighting with the other boys on the playground during gaga ball."

Mr. Boone readily agrees:

I mean he's such a big, strong, smart kid, and he's letting kids half his size that are really just trying to join forces so they have a prayer of winning reduce him to tears. He lets them get to him. It seems atypical for such a big, smart, thoughtful kid."

I wait a moment for Evan to respond. I probably should have waited longer, but I feel my body tense with the critique.

"We've been working with Tony on strategies to help with this, but it's a lot for him. He hasn't had uninterrupted sleep for six months since he started having breakthrough seizures. He's exhausted. Those kids just get under his skin. He doesn't have a lot of coping mechanisms right now. He has all he can do to concentrate and get through the day. He is competitive by nature, and he is really at his limits. Feeling ganged up on is a lot for him right now. Is his response breaking school rules?"

"Well, no. It's just, well, surprising."

"Well, a fifth grader having five seizures a day is not typical. We will keep working with him. He may be a big, strong, smart boy, but he's still a child. And while an emotional large boy may be more surprising and uncomfortable than a smaller child or a girl, he's a kid and emotions are natural."

"Of course, and we are ready to support him," the vice principal answers quickly.

"Actually, one thing you could do to support him is to please stop referring to his seizures incorrectly. Tony does not have grand mal seizures, or tonic-clonic, as they are now called. This was said out loud by the nurse to his teachers in the cafeteria and his friends overheard. It was stressful for Tony to have to come to school the next day and explain to multiple children that the nurse was wrong. Unfortunately, tonic-clonic seizures have a stigma in society due to the severity of the episodes. Please do not take it upon yourselves to diagnose our son. He has a team of health professionals to do that. His paperwork says myoclonic seizures with awareness, and that is how you should be referring to them."

No one responds as I finish. A message from Evan pops up on my MacBook: "You're rocking really hard. It's going to make people seasick."

I grip the hardwood floor with my bare toes to stop my rocking chair as the principal responds.

"Um, yes. We were sent a screenshot of your conversation on Facebook. We want to assure you that we were not intentionally violating HIPAA in anyway."

"I'm not concerned about you violating HIPAA. Tony's seizures are public. Everyone sees them. They are not a secret. He, and we, are not ashamed of them. We just don't want you to diagnose them since his neurologist isn't on your staff."

"Of course not."

"I didn't mean to, um. . ."

"Of course you didn't. And we won't do that, will we?" The principal cuts the nurse off. She flushes. The teachers look down uncomfortably.

"I also want to emphasize that my post on Facebook was asking my network how to approach the fact that Tony's seizures are being misdiagnosed by the school nurse and her supervisor even after multiple corrections. It was a private post. I'm not upset that someone sent it to you. I had every intention of sharing my concern today, but that was not a public conversation and I'm free to discuss my experiences on my social media."

"I understand. It won't happen again." The principal blinks several times and forces a smile.

"Thanks for that assurance."

I receive another message from Evan:

"That was harsh, but you get things done. Tony is lucky to have you."

I smile. I realize that at some level, Evan does understand ableism and its dangers, and appreciates my response. Tony and I are part of his story.

In Conclusion: Embodied Knowledge, Hope, and Cultural Transformation

This story is unfinished. Ableism and disability stigma did not end at that Zoom call. We are still negotiating medications for Tony and fear we are running out of options. His teachers are still frustrated with his increasingly emotional responses to daily challenges within and beyond the classroom. I continually struggle with the relief that Tony and my embodiments allow us to move among those marked as 'normal' bodies with relative ease and grief that ableism hinders the daily lived experiences of so many. Dismantling ableism is large and overwhelming, and I get caught up in our ongoing lived struggle. I hope that our embodied knowledge of disabled identity and ableism can become accessible through our stories. Perhaps our stories can become part of the stories of our readers and resurface across consciousnesses as limping or seizing bodies make others uncomfortable. With this knowledge, there is hope that others will resist the desire to expect someone to resolve the perceived disruption or offer an explanation to restore ableist comfort. An existential phenomenological approach to critical autoethnography maps how the living through a body provides knowledge of the world and offers the potential for that knowledge to be accessed, shared, and etched into the stories of readers. Storytelling allows the exchange of knowledge across bodies, and while that knowledge can never be known at the deep level of the body that lived it, it can compel us to revise shared cultural narratives and dismantle marginalization. With this hope, we share our body's knowledge through storytelling.

Notes

1 I reject the person-first language that is prevalent in US discourse surrounding disabled identity. I believe that it is most inclusive to refer to my disability as an identity marker. I'm not a woman with whiteness, I'm a white woman. For this reason, I also refer to myself as disabled. To relegate my disabled identity to person-first language signals a discomfort and further marginalizes my body.
2 To 'crip' culture, meaning, and identity is to infuse with an affirmative, embodied disability consciousness, understanding, and commitment to equity.

References

Alexander, B. (2006). *Performing Black Masculinity*. Walnut Creek, CA: Altamira Press.

Denzin, N. (1997). *Interpreting Ethnography: Ethnographic Practices for the 21st Century*. Thousand Oaks, CA: Sage.

Denzin, N. (2014). *Interpretive Autoethnography*. 2nd Edition. Los Angeles, CA: Sage.

Diversi, M. and Moriera, C. (2009). *Betweener Talk: Decolonizing Knowledge Production, Pedagogy, & Praxis*. Walnut Creek, CA: Left Coast Press.

Garland Thomson, R. (1997). *Extraordinary Bodies: Figuring Physical Disability in American Culture and Literature*. New York, NY: Columbia University Press.

Garland Thomson, R. (2009). *Staring: How We Look*. Oxford: Oxford University Press.

Merleau-Ponty, M. (1964a). 'Eye and Mind'. In Edie, J. (ed.) *The Primacy of Perception*. Malden, MA: Northeastern University Press.

Merleau-Ponty, M. (1964b). *Phenomenology of Perception*. New York, NY: Routledge.

Pelias, R. (2015). 'A Story Located in "Shoulds": Toward a Productive Future for Qualitative Inquiry'. *Qualitative Inquiry*. 21(7): pp. 609–611. https://doi.org/10.1177/1077800414555073

Scott, J. (2018). *Embodied Performance as Applied Research, Art and Pedagogy*. London, UK: Palgrave Macmillan.

Scott, J, (2020). 'Disrupting Compulsory Performances. Snapshots and Stories of Masculinity, Disability and Parenthood in Cultural Currents on Daily Life'. In Johnson, A. and LeMaster, B. (eds.) *Gender Futurity/Intersectional Autoethnography: Embodied Theorizing from the Margins*. pp. 24–37. New York, NY: Routledge.

Scott, J. (2022). 'Gazed at: Stories of a Mortal Body'. *Liminalities: A Journal of Performance Studies*. 18(2): pp. 1–17. http://liminalities.net/18-2/gazedat.pdf

Shoemaker, D. (2011). 'Mamafesto! (Why Superheroes Wear Capes)'. *Text and Performance Quarterly*. 31(2): pp. 190–202. http://dx.doi.org/10.1080/10462937.2010.551138

Sobchack, V. (2004). *Carnal Thoughts: Embodiment and Moving Image Culture*. Los Angeles: University of California Press.

Spry, T. (2016). *Autoethnography and the Other: Unsettling Power through Utopian Performatives*. New York, NY: Routledge.

Toyosaki, S. and Pensoneau-Conway, S. (2013). 'Autoethnography as a Praxis for Social Justice: Three Ontological Contexts'. In Holman Jones, S., Adams, T.E. and Ellis, E. (eds.) *The Handbook of Autoethnography*. pp. 557–575. Walnut Creek, CA: Left Coast Press.

13

ASSIMILATION AND DIFFERENCE

A Māori Story

Georgina Tuari Stewart

Introduction

This chapter continues an ongoing exploration of what it means to be Māori today, as an example of living cultural difference, even after several generations of my people having spent their entire lifetimes under British settler derived conditions. The 19th-century British colonisation of Māori was based on policies of assimilation of Māori to British-imposed conditions. The two names for one country are used strategically in this chapter, to recognise that "New Zealand was created in Aotearoa by the British" (Willmott, 1989, p. 2). In the emerging modern nation-state of New Zealand, Māori were expected to abandon their traditional lifeways and conform to European/White norms. Claims of cultural difference such as those in this chapter are made by Māori people who are, to all outward appearances, fully assimilated to the dominant Western culture of New Zealand today. But the assumption of 'full' assimilation overlooks symbolic culture, seeing 'culture' only in tangible forms such as clothing, food, technology, and so on. So in this chapter, I want to bring an analytical microscope to the concepts of cultural assimilation and cultural difference, as applied to a person (such as myself) who identifies as Māori today, in the brave bicultural new world of Aotearoa New Zealand.

The key argument of this chapter, which I will pursue through both original narratives and close readings of credible sources, is that Māori identity as cultural difference still exists today, but over time has increasingly moved towards symbolic levels of ethnic culture, and incorporates a strong element of 'struggle' (Webster, 1998), such that political subjugation is part

DOI: 10.4324/9781003274728-13

and parcel of Māori identity, almost independent of personal financial circumstances. One effect of this link is that even being in a privileged position, such as a senior university academic, does not protect a Māori person from racism in the workplace. As such, this chapter is written as Māori testimony. It is not trying to be a resource for White educators, but if found useful for such a purpose, well and good.

Colonisation of Māori is generally glossed in national discourse as having 'saved' Māori from extinction, and/or vastly improving Māori lives. The ill effects on Māori of being alienated from their traditional lands is being recognised through the Waitangi Tribunal, and the state also recognises its responsibility to help protect the endangered Māori language from extinction, but less obvious are the losses that Māori have suffered as a result of becoming alienated, to a greater or lesser extent, from traditional Māori knowledge and ways of thinking (Jackson, 1992). Colonisation by assimilation aims for Māori becoming the same as non-Māori, thereby deleting distinct Māori identity. After WWII, the state's official policy softened to 'incorporation' and 'integration' but these modified, rather than transformed, the overwhelming direction of assimilation (Hunn, 1961).

Assimilation is so strongly embedded in Māori experience that it is seldom even mentioned, being either assumed or ignored. Using my own experiences and observations as one source of data, I approach the question of Māori assimilation and difference using a combination of two major theoretical traditions: Kaupapa Māori – the word 'kaupapa' has many levels of meaning, from 'base' to 'topic' to 'philosophy,' as explained in the next paragraph (Smith, 2003, 2011), and philosophy of education, as interpreted in the local academy (Marshall, 1987; Roberts, 2015). These two traditions underpin my research framework and an approach to collecting and analysing data that opens space for 'autoethnography' as explained in the paragraph after the next one, and 'writing as a method' (Richardson and St. Pierre, 2018) which I extend to Māori/Indigenous research (Stewart, 2021b). I collect and analyse various sources, data and insights to produce 'layered texts' (Rath, 2012) in an approach I call 'Kaupapa Māori Autoethnography' (Stewart, 2023).

Kaupapa Māori theory originated as a set of principles associated with an Indigenous community-driven form of education in Aotearoa (the Māori part of New Zealand), which was seeded in the early 1980s and has since grown into a widespread social and intellectual movement (Hoskins and Jones, 2017). In thought and action, Kaupapa Māori is based on the principles of being:

- related to 'being Māori';
- connected to Māori philosophy and principles;

- committed to the legitimacy of Māori language and culture; and
- concerned with 'the struggle for autonomy over our own cultural well being'

(G. H. Smith, cited in Smith, 1999, p. 185)

Kaupapa Māori research methodology can be placed like a lens or filter across a method like autoethnography, because although it guides research paradigm and ethics, Kaupapa Māori does not specify any particular data collection methods that must (or must not) be used in research. Autoethnographic methods have great potential to be more widely used in Kaupapa Māori research, especially by those researchers who are immersed and/or expert in their topics.

About te reo Māori in this chapter: Te reo Māori is an important plank of Māori identity; so is an essential feature of Kaupapa Māori research, as spelled out in the principles discussed prior. In this chapter, Māori words are in plain font, in line with the status of te reo Māori as an official language of Aotearoa New Zealand (New Zealand Government, 1987), and supported by the principle of sociolinguistics to the effect that normalising indigenous languages is a legitimate practice (May, 2012). Māori words (excluding names) are translated in brackets on first appearance; Māori words used more than once in the text are also listed in a glossary immediately following the main text.

Autoethnography and other recent post-qualitative methodologies (Adams and Herrmann, 2020; St. Pierre, 2018) emerged as a result of the 'crisis of representation' in research and theory, which destabilised the authority of the text and the autonomy of the author. In qualitative research, these changes greatly increased the importance of positionality – that is, the relationship between the researcher and the research. Autoethnography is a leading research methodology that aspires to complete the mission of qualitative research by stepping fully out of the shadows cast by science over educational research, in particular questions about truth and the reliability of findings.

To record and study one's own life under the banner of autoethnography inevitably involves a significant element of narrative writing, in the form of biographies and vignettes based on one's experiences, thereby bringing narrative genres more centrally into research and scholarship in education. This chapter includes the most extensive account of my personal history of any of my academic writings to date. In the next section, I capitalise on my side role in my personal life as a whānau (extended family) researcher and holder of information about family history. This other role allows me to give a more detailed account than in previous writing of the basis upon which a typical Māori person (such as myself) understands their ethnic identity today. In writing about my life, I am reminded that all writing, including scholarly writing, is a 'curation' – a few points or snippets, carefully selected from the whole 'buzzing' stream of one's experience of reality.

As a Māori person undertaking educational research, for whom Kaupapa Māori is 'home ground,' I also find value in 'philosophy of education' and 'autoethnography' based on my personal experience as one of just a handful of Māori-speaking qualified teachers of senior school science. My research builds on my history of involvement since 1993 with teaching, developing and researching Pūtaiao, the Māori science curriculum (Ministry of Education, 2020; Stewart, 2020), eventually completing a doctorate on this topic, reading curriculum theory and philosophy of science, and inventing the original concept of 'Kaupapa Māori Science' as a local critique of science (Stewart, 2007).

The central curriculum question for Pūtaiao concerns the relationship between science and Māori knowledge – an extremely complex, deeply philosophical question, which demands consideration of the impact of science on all aspects of contemporary education practice and theory yet is consistently, problematically reduced to a binary question: 'Is Māori knowledge a form of science, or not?' (Stewart, 2019). The problem is that this question has no correct 'hard' or scientific answer, due to the slippage in meaning of its constituent terms. The only truthful answer is 'it depends' on how we are defining both science and Māori knowledge. To investigate this relationship requires sound arguments supported by reliable evidence, as demonstrated in the breach by the history of published debate, in which many authors (both scientists and Māori writers) fail adequately to represent either one or both forms of knowledge.

In this chapter, I am grappling with a linked set of complex concepts: binaries, representation, authenticity, relativism. To study the question of Māori cultural assimilation opens up to all these concepts. First of all, it raises the questions discussed prior: 'What is a Māori?" and 'Do Māori still exist today?' Next come the questions: 'Can anyone become a Māori?' 'Who counts as 'real' Māori?' and 'Who owns the definition of 'Māori'?' (Stewart-Harawira, 1993). Underpinning all of these questions is the 'hoary chestnut' of relativism vs. universalism, and whether philosophical universalism is actually a disguise for majoritarianism, including the White patriarchy. I will pick up these questions again in the penultimate section.

I am interested in probing such philosophical questions using auto-writing in the form of original stories and vignettes of experience, cognisant of the description of stories by Thomas King (2003) as both 'wondrous' and 'dangerous.' Story can bring the reader up close and personal to confront a complex topic, embedded in complex socioeconomic systems and assumptions, and thus acts as a powerful teaching tool. Story as a genre transgresses the usual standards to which academic research is held, yet is acknowledged as a universal and ancient form of teaching and learning (Herman, 2003). To write about one's own experiences is inevitably done in the form of stories. In Māori research, the identity of the researcher is always of interest, so the following section introduces me and the background I bring to this work.

Antecedents to My Personal Identity as Māori

I grew up in a bicultural Māori-Pākehā (New Zealand European) family in 1960–1970s Auckland and received an excellent education in the state schools in Aotearoa New Zealand. My parents had bought the 'worst house in the street' as our family home in order to be just inside the Grammar Zone, the area of Auckland where children could by right attend the city's oldest and most prestigious secondary (high) schools. An annual school census is one of my childhood memories of being marked as Māori. At school assembly, it would be announced that all Māori students had to stay behind after assembly. This annual ritual was lonely, since I was invariably the only student from my class to stay behind to be counted. I felt like I had to mentally 'grit my teeth' and stand up for my right to self-identify as Māori, despite (or because of) being in the top class in my year. It was a point in the school year where my ethnic difference from my classmates came into focus. This ethnic census is one way the national education system 'performs' Māori ethnicity. That experience (among others) triggered an inchoate inner sense of the questions I am still investigating today, including in this chapter.

One important childhood memory is a family discussion about 'how much Māori' we were. My father counted himself three-quarters Māori, so from him we were 3/8. Adding on the 1/32 from my mother, we decided we were 'three-and-a-bit eighths' or 'just under half.' It was a potent fractions lesson: right away I resolved to myself that I would 'marry a Māori' so my children would not again have their 'blood' halved. Decades later, my two siblings and I all have children with full Māori partners; a surprising claim given the strength of the notion that no 'full' Māori remain alive, yet entirely reasonable if Māori identity is understood as an ethnicity, rather than through the racist pseudo-concept of 'race.'

The dominant notion of Māori identity as based on a 'fraction' of a person's 'blood' is racist because it falls prey to the pseudo-concept of 'race' as a scientific or real category, determined by a biological essence to do with something physical such as the 'blood' or 'genes' of an individual. The notion of Māori identity as ethnicity, on the other hand, is more about the self-identity with which we grow up. I think that if a person's four grandparents understand themselves as Māori, one is full Māori in an ethnic sense. This is not a full and final definition of what it means to be Māori, but it suggestively illuminates the nature of ethnicity as a self-understanding of belonging to a particular cultural group within the society/country/nation of one's upbringing.

In early New Zealand (here purposely using the name of the colony), the children of Māori mothers and British/White fathers often grew up in Māori whānau (extended families) and were culturally and ethnically Māori. My paternal great-grandfather Paraika Tuari (transliteration of Frank Stewart) was one such. His father, John Timothy Mangles Stewart (1826–1891) was a shipman of Scottish ancestry from across the Tasman Sea in Australia, who plied a trade in Northland kauri timber for the booming housing markets of Sydney, Melbourne, and the other Eastern seaboard Australian cities, in the same vessel in which his father, Thomas Stewart (Senior), had left Bristol, England, in 1839 with his wife, children, and in-laws, bringing them to colonial Australia. John's oldest brother, Thomas Stewart (Junior) stayed and lived out his life in New Zealand, a well-known early European settler at Ngunguru, on the coast east of Whangarei, where kauri logs cut in the local forests were brought by river to the coast.

After his father John Stewart had left Northland for the last time, Paraika was born in 1859 and grew up with his mother, Mere, amidst the iwi (people, kingroup) of her second husband, ranking local ancestor Waata Te Maru, at Whananaki, a stunningly beautiful coastal village, further north up the same coast from Ngunguru. Paraika took after his Stewart side, with fair skin and greenish eyes, but was an accomplished native speaker of te reo Māori and a person of mana (prestige) in both Māori and Pākehā circles of the Whangarei district of the late 1800s and early 1900s. He was well-known amongst the coastal whānau, still living on their ancestral lands (now 'millionaire row' beach homes owned by wealthy Pākehā) for travelling the rohe (district) by walking up and down the coast, his white sand-shoes hanging around his neck, stopping in at each beach to visit the kāinga (Māori homesteads) between Taiharuru to the south and Whangaruru to the north. Paraika really did not show his age; in his 90s he was still taken as being in his 60s. Paraika died in the early morning of the 4th of October, 1954, at Pātaua (one of those kāinga), at the back steps of an old house that still stands there today. At the time it was the home of his cousin, Ngaronoa Mahanga. In his memory, the Mahanga whānau buried Paraika's pipe, set in concrete, by those steps.

Paraika and Ema, a woman from Wainui, had a son, my grandfather, whose name was Nuku Stewart (1899–1960). In the late 1910s, Nuku was betrothed by the elders in the indigenous Māori custom of 'tomo' to a highly-ranked Māori woman from Matauri, by the name of Tangiaranui Te

Karaka (1900–1981). Nuku and Tangi went on to have 15 children born between 1919 and 1941, of whom one was my father, Wiremu (Wina) Stewart (1927–2007).

My father was a native speaker of te reo Māori: it was the first language he learned as a small child in his home. He spent the first few years of his life living with grandparent figures in a Māori whare (the word here meaning a handmade shack) with a dirt floor. By the time of my childhood, my father was working in Auckland as an owner-operator with Co-op Taxis. I remember as a child watching his mouth moving silently as he read the newspaper. He told me about learning English on turning five and going to school, and how he was 'given the supplejack' (hit with pieces of a vine cut from the local bush) by the teachers when they heard him speak a word or two to his siblings in Māori, which school rules considered 'swearing.' He told me about moving as a young man from his home in Northland to live in Auckland, and the culture shock of that move. For many years he translated English into his own reo (language) in his head as he conversed with others. He recalled being married to my mother, his second wife (his first wife was also a native Māori speaker, from Rotorua) before he could converse in English without that mental translation process.

With my family background of both my mother and her mother being teachers and avid readers, as well as poets, from an early age I enjoyed generous access to books, and reading was my first and abiding favourite activity or 'passion,' as we would say tsoday. So, teaching was 'in my blood,' but it was not my first career choice – that became to help save the Takahē (a flightless native bird) from extinction after reading *Two in the Bush* by Gerald Durrell. When I left secondary school in 1978, that impulse saw me enrol in a Bachelor of Science degree at Auckland University, resulting in a first class MSc in organic chemistry in 1981. Following that, I worked first as a research technician in the Cancer Research Laboratory in the Auckland Medical School, and later in sales and customer support of chemical analysis equipment.

At the end of 1988, I left my job and went north to live at Matauri in an effort to reconnect with 'my Māori side' from which I felt I had moved too far away for comfort. From there, I went further north to live with Mangu Awarau at Waimanoni, near Kaitaia, where I first heard about Kura Kaupapa Māori (Kaupapa Māori schools) and extended my limited earlier knowledge of te reo me ngā tikanga (Māori language and customs). In 1991, I returned to Auckland and completed secondary (high school) teacher training at Auckland College of Education. After a year teaching Te Reo Māori at Onehunga High School, in 1993 I was appointed as an inaugural teacher at one of the first Māori-medium secondary schools, Te Wharekura o Hoani Waititi Marae, in Oratia, West Auckland, until wanting to live in Te Taitokerau

(Northland) drew me to take up the Head of Māori position at Tikipunga High School in Whangarei in 1996.

My teaching and ongoing involvement with various national curriculum projects in Māori-medium education spurred me on to enrol part-time in doctoral studies in 2001 for a chance to investigate the Māori science curriculum. After graduating in 2007, I held short-term research positions before being appointed in 2010 as a Lecturer in Education, University of Auckland, based at the Tai Tokerau campus in Whangarei. In mid-2016, I moved to AUT in Auckland, where I am now Professor in Māori Philosophy of Education, in Te Ara Poutama, the Māori faculty.

I have developed a delineation of Māori philosophy that pays attention to the symbolic level of culture in colonising histories (Stewart, 2021a). Māori Philosophy as I understand it considers how identifying as Māori and working with Māori knowledge influence one's everyday thinking about social matters of all kinds. I use the Kaupapa Māori principles discussed prior to guide a process of critically reading through and past the chauvinism of Eurocentrism and patriarchy found in most published work on Māori. I think of this approach as rehabilitating and repurposing older (Eurocentric) scholarship about Māori philosophy for indigenous scholars and their work, under the umbrella of the Kaupapa Māori intellectual project.

My research explores Kaupapa Māori approaches to blending narrative and analytical genres and registers, within an overall concept of writing as a Māori/Indigenous method of inquiry (Richardson and St. Pierre, 2018; Stewart, 2021b). The following two previously unpublished autoethnographic vignettes are attempts to use the power of 'story' to illustrate contemporary Māori difference, as I know it.

Story 1: Te Hīkoi Ngāhere – the Bush Walk

May, 1993: I had been appointed as the inaugural teacher of Pūtaiao (Science) at one of the first Māori-medium secondary schools to be recognised by the state schooling system – Te Wharekura o Hoani Waititi Marae, situated at Parrs Park in Oratia, Waitakere City, West Auckland. It so happened that an elder from Tūhoe (kingroup name) was living nearby; I was put in contact, had an initial visit, and arranged a bush walk with the students (a small group of about 15). In retrospect, it is unfortunate that I did not arrange to record this trip on video, or even photographs and audio files. All I have at this distance of time are my memories.

At the time, I felt under pressure to come up with an answer to the question 'What is Māori science?' I remember feeling a sense of longing for the elder who was leading us to finally delineate for me what Māori science actually is. On the day, we met up at the Arataki visitor centre in the

Waitakere ranges and went for a walk in the ngāhere (forest/bush) along the well-constructed pathways. As we walked into the bush, the elder spoke about his connections to the various plants we encountered. He told us stories about going into the ngāhere as a young child with his grandmother to collect plants for rongoā (herbal medicines), and so forth. I was experiencing an intense inner cognitive dissonance between my teaching subject of 'Science' and the stories the elder was telling, but I kept silent and tried not to show how I was feeling. That query took years of reading and thinking before I knew the answer: 'Māori science' is more of a political than an epistemic concept; a provocation, rather than a useful element for a model of Māori or indigenous thought (Stewart, 2022).

In retrospect, that field trip to the ngāhere was a classic example of the gap between Māori knowledge (by which I mean the same as Mātauranga Māori) and 'Science' as per the secondary school curriculum. That experience (and others) made me realise the problem of trying to equate Māori knowledge with science. The elder spoke about his Māori knowledge of the native plant species by telling 'holistic' stories of his life, not filtered through the sieve of science criteria. Someone like this elder who is Māori by upbringing does not necessarily have a perspective from which they can theorise their identity in terms that make sense in a 'science' framework. Māori knowledge as demonstrated by the elder is non-abstracted, non-theorised knowledge, part and parcel of a holistic sense of reality as a simple rendition of 'ontology' – as well as epistemology as theory of knowledge and ethics as a framework to guide right action in the world.

The elder was from Ngāi Tūhoe (kingroup name), the children of the vast Urewera forest in the mountainous heart of the North Island of Aotearoa New Zealand. He demonstrated that Māori knowledge is still within living memory, in contradiction to the assimilationist propaganda of the dominant national discourses. According to dominant ideologies, all things Māori are inferior to all things Pākehā, and 'real' Māori died off from 'natural causes' many generations ago. All this experience of struggle and resistance at symbolic and intellectual levels is captured in my notion of Māori philosophy, described prior. While Māori have been subject to more subtle forms of colonisation, compared with Indigenous peoples in Australia, South Africa, etc, the underlying thinking beneath all forms of colonising ideology has been the same.

Story 2: Te whakanui i te kotahi rautau o te wharenui – Celebrating the Centenary of the Meeting House

December, 2021: It is the end of a long hard year in my role as a senior Māori academic at one of the local universities. Like every other university in the international Anglophone academy, we have been badly impacted by the pandemic and response; international students and research, on which we rely, have been the most affected.

A date has been in my diary since last summer for the centenary celebrations of the wharenui (meeting house) at our marae (Māori community centre) in Wainui, Whangaroa, Te Taitokerau Northland. By the time the date arrives, the pandemic response has meant working off-campus for about four months. A recent change in the national public health settings means there are no travel restrictions within the region, but strict legal limits on the numbers of people at events. I set off alone after lunch on the Friday, and a few hours later arrive at the village at the top of the hill leading down to the beach, where my sister lives in the house left to us by our father. It is great to catch up after so long apart, and we raise a few glasses of gorgeous Marlborough sav blanc.

The pandemic restrictions have resulted in the centenary celebrations adopting an unusual programme for the day, consisting of several sequential pōwhiri or welcome ceremonies for the peoples (hapū or marae) of the surrounding areas, focusing on those 'under the mountain' of Whakarārā – our local maunga (mountain – indigenous Māori identities are associated with local landmarks such as peaks and rivers), so uninspiring up close, yet visible at a distance in all directions from sea or land. The first ceremony is timed for pre-dawn for locals and experts; we decide to attend that one. The alarm goes off at 3.15 am and I briefly consider saying I can't go as I feel terrible, but I soldier on and have a quick shower, make a cup of tea, and wake my sister. We get ready and go an hour later into the 'dark before the dawn' time. We travel separately since we must head off in different directions from there. I follow her a few kilometres down the coastal road, then turn inland towards one of our family's two main ancestral marae. These are places I have visited and known intimately for as long as I can remember.

Our marae are just like those dotted around all over the north; none of them have any carvings, apart from the tourist-oriented ones at Waitangi, and the war memorial-funded Ōtiria marae in Moerewa. Many of the existing buildings on the smaller marae around the north were made by hand by the local people, including our uncles, in the period between WWI and WWII, when the wood cut down by hand was converted to building timber at small local mills. Our Wainui marae is for the kingroup (hapū) who know ourselves as Ngātiruamahue – the descendants of the ancestress Muimui, a survivor from the hapū (kingroup, often glossed as 'sub-tribe') of Ngare Raumati, who were wiped out by intertribal warfare in the early 1800s, before the signing of Te Tiriti o Waitangi (Māori name for the Treaty of Waitangi, 1840). This small handmade building that we call the wharenui (meeting house – lit. 'large house') was opened in December 1921, almost exactly one hundred years ago to the day on which we are heading there now.

Mainly through social media, I have been following the progress over the previous months as the locals (i.e. my whānau) have defied pandemic restrictions and winter weather to complete extensive renovations: replacing and enlarging the concrete footpaths around the buildings; repairing all damages and replacing some of the wooden surfaces and windows; new carpets, blinds, and of course fresh paint inside and out. In the last few weeks on social media, I had seen talk of carvings and warnings (especially to women) to stay clear. As with all the small community marae I know of in Te Taitokerau Northland, our wharenui has stood, simple and uncarved, bereft of any Māori iconography, since all carvings and other decorative elements such as tukutuku (patterned woven wall panels) were ordered to be destroyed by early European missionaries (mainly Anglican and Catholic) who infiltrated the peoples of Northland very early on, before encountering other iwi in other parts of Aotearoa. Our wharenui building is so small and homely I was finding it difficult to imagine what it could possibly look like as a whare carved in the traditional Māori style. For some reason, I got the idea that a pou (carved pole) may have been erected near the building, rather than carvings affixed to the building itself.

We park up and walk through the dark towards where indistinct voices and shadows of people are gathering in knots, slowly forming and moving towards the position at the end of the path leading up from the carpark to the wharenui. We stand about with our old friend, the (Māori) Bishop, and others. Many cars are already parked, and we can vaguely make out a group of people seated to one side of the main building. Behind and to one side is some light and activity from the kitchen, and from around the back the hāngi (earth oven) fire sends up sparks like fireworks into the crisp dark air. A car pulls into the spot next to us and another old friend, now an elder expert in the Māori world, gets out.

In the glimmering of the pre-dawn over the hills surrounding this peaceful inland valley, the wānanga (focused discussion) emerges; a kaupapa (process) is outlined, an opening karakia (prayer) is offered, and our group turns to move purposefully towards the whare. In the next minute or so I have one of those strange experiences one can only attribute to the spiritual-metaphysical aspects of being human. All I am doing is walking slowly, next to my sister, up this little path I have walked so many times before. My eyes are transfixed by the indistinct sight ahead of us in the gloaming of a tekoteko (carved figure) standing above the apex of the roof, atop vague visual hints of a carved house front. My ears and mind are full of the formal language of the karanga (calling) issuing towards us from the women standing in front of the building, and the tauparapara (incantations) of the elders moving alongside us, delivering their oratory power as they walk, slowly and ceremoniously, towards the renewed building, brandishing their toko-toko (walking sticks) as they go. Suddenly I feel a deep, strong, peaceful sense of being pulled towards the building by some invisible but inexorable force; my feet are shuffling forward without any conscious will on my part.

We arrive as a group at the new wider concreted area in front of the building, and move to the right to walk in a circle around the outside of the whare, an activity in which many others join, touching the walls as we go. The incantations continue without pause or break. Returning to the front of the building, where the carvings are now subtly lit by well-placed lights, my sister and I retreat to the plastic chairs set out for us to the side, drinking in the sights and sounds as the core group of tohunga (experts) head inside to complete their process.

As a competent listener of te reo, it is a real treat on this day of celebration of a hundred years of our wharenui and marae to sit and listen to the mihimihi (oratory), the kauhau (explanations), the stories, the giving and receiving of gifts, the memories, the songs. These utterances are the taonga (treasures) of Māori language, thought, and philosophy that keep alive the Māori world, and should never be expected to be assimilated.

The next section considers two policies, assimilation and apartheid, imposed by European powers on indigenous populations, using apartheid as practised in South Africa as a dis-analogy for assimilation as practised in New Zealand.

Assimilation and Apartheid: Two Sides of One Colonial Coin?

The two ex-colonies, New Zealand and South Africa, share much history in common, but also display vast differences in the dominant attitudes of contemporary 'White' culture towards the Indigenous peoples of their respective homelands. Between 1948–1994, South Africa followed an official policy of **Apartheid**, where people were kept apart on the basis of their skin colour, with interracial love and marriage subject to heavy legal and social sanctions. Generations of such racist social ontology, which completely reifies the binary between White and non-White skin colour, cannot be overcome simply by making a decision not to be racist. In practice, the most common result of such a decision means teachers taking a 'culture-blind' position, ignoring ethnicity and the effects of racism altogether.

By contrast, in New Zealand history, the European colonisers followed a policy of **Assimilation**, whereby Māori were expected to assimilate to the culture and values imposed by the British settler government. Assimilation in principle anticipates a time when 'Māori' no longer exists as a separate identity. Histories of happy Māori-Pākehā marriages seemed to confirm the success of assimilation. 'Apartheid' and 'assimilation' may seem like two opposite policy approaches to governing bi-ethnic societies, but they both aim to replace pre-existing indigenous cultures by hegemonic White systems, and both are justified by appeal to the same basic racist ideas, in which Europeans or Whites have a natural right to dominate and rule over their indigenous and non-White fellow citizens.

The topic of apartheid came to a head in New Zealand with the 1981 Springbok rugby tour, against which an extensive campaign of protest was organised to support the anti-Apartheid movement in South Africa. This movement, seeded in the Black universities, was gaining momentum at home and support internationally, strengthened by reports of the violent crackdowns by the government against the protestors. In 1981, the Springboks were still being selected on apartheid grounds; national representation was denied to non-White rugby players. Similarly, in previous decades, apartheid policies had prevented Māori All Blacks from touring South Africa, or led to them being dubbed 'honorary Whites' (Keane, 2012). The legendary historical rugby rivalry between the All Blacks and the Springboks, combined with the history of protest in New Zealand against using apartheid policies against Māori All Blacks, meant the 1981 tour was bound to catalyse strong emotional national debate.

As a 20-year-old university student at the time, I borrowed a motorcycle helmet and joined many others to march and shout slogans of protest in the streets near Eden Park, the hallowed ground of New Zealand rugby, where the final test of that tour was played under dramatic conditions. I remember marching up and down for a while before turning a corner and being confronted with lines of police advancing with batons, at which point my platoon of the protest turned and ran away.

That rugby tour was a touchstone of inter-ethnic relations in Aotearoa New Zealand: the point in time when many White New Zealanders 'became Pākehā' in realising how the same racist policies to which they were objecting in South Africa also applied to Māori at home. The phrase 'becoming Pākehā' here refers to accepting a White identity founded upon relationship with Māori (King, 1985).

Today the concept of Māori identity remains as contested as ever, as expressed in the poignant question I am often asked: 'What is a Māori, really?' While I am certain of the answer, it is not a formula. It is a question that defies succinct definition, but rather invites an holistic or experiential response, which narrative and autoethnographic writing seek to evoke. As an ethnic identity, Māori a relational category, meaning one that only comes into being as a result of contact between different cultural groups.

In recent generations, Māori cultural difference has moved away from the material and towards the symbolic levels of culture. This means that

Māori symbolic culture in all its forms – language, thinking, values, philosophies, narrative genres and repositories, and others such as facial tattoo and the arts in general, are more important than ever before, to keep alive a sense of what it means to be Māori. The purpose of the two stories in the previous section is to provide detailed accounts of Māori difference in terms that will be recognised by Māori (and other Indigenous) readers, and may also have educational value for Pākehā/White readers.

Compared with telling stories, bald synoptic assertions can be confronting, as I have found in my own attempts to teach about Māori-Pākehā relationships, which sometimes invoke negative reactions when a Pākehā/White listener 'takes it personally' in response to my efforts to describe the reality of Māori life. Based on the North Shore in Auckland, I am in a community and teaching sector in which (mostly White) South African immigrants are strongly represented, after 25+ years of active recruitment by the New Zealand government of teachers from South Africa, large numbers of whom have taken the opportunity to leave behind the unsettled conditions in their home country.

But there is a conceptual gap in social ontology for teachers bred from the heavily racialised thinking of South Africa, who migrate to live and teach in Aotearoa New Zealand. This gap was expressed to me by a university manager using the phrase 'real racism' to refer to South Africa – a wording that carries the implied assertion that anti-Māori racism in New Zealand either does not exist or is 'not real racism.' This thinking is problematic because it denies the effects of history and philosophy on current ethnic gaps. National memory is pushed below the surface of mainstream social discourse, invisible to the outsider, including most White South African educators.

My experience suggests this gap supports how Māori are being re-colonised within the local academic and university system. This gap in understanding returns to a deficit model of Māori equity and reduces cultural responsiveness – the state's policy solution for Māori underachievement in schools – to a checklist and some classroom tips and tricks (Krzyzosiak and Stewart, 2019). A critical view of 'cultural responsiveness' sees through it as an attempt to ameliorate the effects of racism, without acknowledging its existence. Cultural responsiveness on principle cannot effect equity, which would require eliminating the ethnic wealth gap (which is instead accelerating). The covert purpose of cultural responsiveness as a response to ethnic educational inequity is to assuage the guilt of White educators, rather than to help those populations, including Māori, which have been harmed by racism in schooling and society.

Policies of apartheid and assimilation may appear at first sight to be opposites, but closer inspection shows that both arise from the same central

244 Georgina Tuari Stewart

notion of European/White superiority and Indigenous/non-White inferiority, adapted and elaborated into specific local conditions within each social context. While South Africa and New Zealand may represent the clearest examples of the workings of apartheid and assimilation, respectively, aspects of both approaches can be seen in other ex-British Empire countries, including Australia, Canada, and the US.

The next section drills down into contemporary effects of Māori assimilationist policies in education.

Making a Difference: Contemporary Māori Identity

There is widespread racial complacency within the dominant Pākehā/White culture of New Zealand, bolstered by a longstanding reputation for the 'best race relations in the world' (Human Rights Commission, 2017), and maintained by ideological beliefs about national identity, such as that Māori willingly ceded sovereignty by signing the Treaty of Waitangi, despite evidence to the contrary (Māori Law Review, 2014). The subtle and embedded nature of racism in Aotearoa New Zealand renders it invisible, except to its victims in the moment, which allows it to continue unchecked.

Equity and diversity are key education policy drivers in Aotearoa New Zealand that build on the underlying assumption of Māori assimilation and the notion of a 'level playing field' – but without explaining why the playing field is skewed to start with. In the absence of critical analysis, the effect of equity policy in education is to induce positivistic responses, such as the intense competition between universities for a very small number of Māori and Pacific doctoral scholars who are not already in academic jobs (McAllister et al., 2019). Simultaneously, there are ongoing losses of Māori and Pacific academics from the universities as they burn out and leave, seeking greener pastures.

The implicit nature of the dominant assumption of complete Māori assimilation and sameness has the effect of rendering Māori cultural difference invisible. The right to self-identify ethnicity is a basic democratic right in Aotearoa New Zealand, yet Pākehā often seem to find it difficult to understand the Māori desire to retain their own culture and ethnic identity – so engrained are the old ideas about European superiority. One of the hardest concepts for non-Māori people at all levels of education to understand is that Māori people have their own interests that lie beyond the equity obsession with 'closing the gaps' – most Māori academics are not interested in being career cultural advisors for their non-Māori colleagues.

To reject the racist concept of Māori identity as based on 'blood quantum' (Smith, 1999, p. 72) allows claims about 'being Māori' to return to a more genuine indigenous criterion of ancestry, or whakapapa (genealogy). A minimal claim to Māori identity is being able to trace one's whakapapa back to one or more Māori ancestors, the tangata whenua (indigenous peoples) of Aotearoa.

Today, Māori-Pākehā misunderstandings and clashes of perspective on social issues are significant markers of cultural difference.

At more general levels, binary concepts as such have gained a bad reputation among social scientists from being associated with hierarchical thinking, which invariably favours the wealthy societal elite. As a Māori researcher concerned to answer the question of whether or not Māori cultural difference still exists, I am centrally concerned with binaries, real and reified, and the difference between them. The topic of Māori cultural difference, as I have argued, invokes a mixture of both. My conclusion is that one or two 'real' or scientific binaries exist, which are refracted through multiple lenses to produce a spectrum of reified binaries in relation to Māori identity, including that of 'Māori science.' The mainstream reaction is to conclude that binary thinking is in itself 'wrong' or inadequate. Conversely, a Māori analyst (such as myself) might wish to play with and invert the binary, rather than pretending it never existed.

It remains evident to me that a binary concept is a powerful basic tool for language and thinking, since it follows the logic of identity: same + different. We learn language by refining binary concepts – a word refers to *this* and not *that*. The human brain, it seems, is geared to using binaries in learning, knowing, and teaching. There is a 'real' i.e. scientific language binary at the core of the national identity of Aotearoa New Zealand, since all natural languages, including te reo Māori, are considered equally valuable in cognitive terms by contemporary sociolinguistic theory (May, 2012).

Conclusion

Using a Māori philosophy framework, I have sampled from my own life and history as supplementary sources in order to provide a detailed account of Māori cultural difference and its significance for today's generations of Māori people. The dominant view of New Zealand remains that of an Antipodean replica of 'mother country' Britain, but my counterview, through a critical, Māori-centric lens, is cognisant of the ongoing shadow existence of 'Aotearoa' – the marginalised Māori part of the contemporary nation-state. My arguments lead me to conclude that 'Māori identity' and 'Pākehā identity' form a real binary, because a person can either claim whakapapa as Māori or not. Māori identity thus constitutes a second social scientific category, in addition to the linguistic binary of te reo Māori and English. The refraction of language and identity throw up a series of reified binaries across the entire social field in its many domains – media, schooling, science, public works, recreation, museums, tourism, and so forth. There are many lifetimes of work remaining to be done to fully explore the richness of the intercultural encounter of being Māori.

Glossary

As used in this chapter

Aotearoa	Māori name for New Zealand
Hapū	Smaller kingroup made up of several whānau
Iwi	Larger kingroup made up of several hapū
Kāinga	Home, homestead
Kaupapa	Base, cause, philosophy – a word with many meanings
Kaupapa Māori	A Māori social/intellectual movement originating in education
Māori	Self-identity of indigenous peoples of Aotearoa
Marae	Māori community centre
Mātauranga Māori	Māori knowledge
Pākehā	European New Zealander, esp. descendants of British settlers
Te reo (Māori)	The (Māori) language
Whakapapa	Genealogy
Whānau	Family, extended family, or local/school community
Whare	House, building
Wharenui	Meeting house, lit. 'big house'

References

Adams, T.E. and Herrmann, A.F. (2020). 'Expanding Our Autoethnographic Future. *Journal of Autoethnography*. 1(1): pp. 1–8. https://doi.org/10.1525/joae.2020.1.1.1

Herman, D. (ed.). (2003). *Narrative Theory and the Cognitive Sciences*. Malvern, PA: CSLI Publications.

Hoskins, T.E. and Jones, E. (eds.). (2017). *Critical Conversations in Kaupapa Māori*. Wellington: Huia Publishers.

Human Rights Commission. (2017). *Race Relations Commissioners and Conciliators Mark Significant Anniversary*. Wellington: Human Rights Commission (hrc.co.nz)

Hunn, J.K. (1961). *Report on Department of Maori Affairs: With Statistical Supplement*. Wellington, New Zealand. Report on Department of Maori Affairs . . . | Items | National Library of New Zealand | National Library of New Zealand (natlib.govt.nz)

Jackson, M. (1992). 'The Treaty and the Word: The Colonization of Māori Philoso-phy'. In Oddie, G. and Perrett, R. (eds.) *Justice, Ethics and New Zealand Society*. pp. 1–10. Oxford: Oxford University Press.

Keane, B. (2012). *Ngā rōpū tautohetohe – Māori Protest Movements – Rugby and South Africa*. Wellington: Te Ara – the Encyclopedia of New Zealand. Ngā rōpū tautohetohe – Māori protest movements – Te Ara Encyclopedia of New Zealand.

King, M. (1985). *Being Pākehā: An Encounter with New Zealand and the Māori Renaissance*. London: Hodder & Stoughton.

King, T. (2003). *The Truth About Stories: A Native Narrative*. Minneapolis: University of Minnesota Press.

Krzyzosiak, J. and Stewart, G.T. (2019). 'Can Culturally Responsive Policies Improve Māori Achievement? *Curriculum Matters*. 15: pp. 42–58. https://doi.org/10.18296/cm.0036

Māori Law Review. (2014). *Waitangi Tribunal finds Treaty of Waitangi Signatories Did Not Cede Sovereignty in February 1840*. Wellington: Māori Law Review. Waitangi Tribunal finds Treaty of Waitangi signatories did not cede sovereignty in February 1840 – Māori Law Review (maorilawreview.co.nz)

Marshall, J.D. (1987). *Positivism or Pragmatism: Philosophy of Education in New Zealand*. NZARE. nzare.org.nz

May, S. (2012). *Language & Minority Rights: Ethnicity, Nationalism and the Politics of Language*. 2nd Edition. London and New York: Routledge.

McAllister, T.G., Kidman, J., Rowley, O. and Theodore, R.F. (2019). 'Why isn't My Professor Māori? A Snapshot of the Academic Workforce in New Zealand Universities'. *MAI Journal*. 8(2): pp. 236–249. https://doi.org/10.20507/MAIJournal.2019.8.2.10

Ministry of Education. (2020). 'Pūtaiao'. www.tmoa.tki.org.nz/Te-Marautanga-o-Aotearoa/Nga-Wahanga-Ako/Putaiao

New Zealand Government. (1987). 'Māori Language Act'. www.legislation.govt.nz/act/public/1987/0176/latest/whole.html

Rath, J. (2012). 'Autoethnographic Layering: Recollections, Family Tales, and Dreams'. *Qualitative Inquiry*. 18(5): pp. 442–448. https://doi.org/10.1177/1077800412439529

Richardson, L. and St. Pierre, E.A. (2018). 'Writing: A Method of Inquiry'. In Denzin, N.K. and Lincoln, Y.S. (eds.) *The Sage Handbook of Qualitative Research*. 5th Edition. pp. 818–838. Thousand Oaks, CA: Sage Publications, Inc.

Roberts, P. (2015). 'It Was the Best of Times, it Was the Worst of Times . . .: Philosophy of Education in the Contemporary World'. *Studies in Philosophy and Education*. 34(6): pp. 623–634. http://dx.doi.org/10.1007/s11217-014-9438-z

Smith, G.H. (2003). 'Kaupapa Māori Theory: Theorizing Indigenous Transformation of Education and Schooling'. www.aare.edu.au/data/publications/2003/pih03342.pdf.

Smith, L.T. (1999). *Decolonizing Methodologies: Research and Indigenous Peoples*. Dunedin: Zed Books/University of Otago Press.

Smith, L.T. (2011). *Opening Keynote: Story-ing the Development of kaupapa Māori: A Review of Sorts*. Edited by Hutchings, J., Potter, H. and Taupo, K. NZCER. Hei Hauhake Whakaaro – A Resource for Kaupapa Māori Researchers (auckland.ac.nz) www.nzcer.org.nz/nzcerpress/kei-tua-o-te-pae-hui-proceedings

St. Pierre, E.A. (2018). 'Writing Post Qualitative Inquiry'. *Qualitative Inquiry*. 24(9): pp. 603–608. https://doi.org/10.1177/1077800417734567

Stewart, G.T. (2007). 'Kaupapa Māori Science [Unpublished EdD thesis]'. University of Waikato. https://researchcommons.waikato.ac.nz/handle/10289/2598

Stewart, G.T. (2019). 'Mātauranga and Pūtaiao: The Question of Māori Science'. *New Zealand Science Review.* 75(4): 65–68. https://scientists.org.nz/NZSR

Stewart, G.T. (2020). 'Māori Science Curriculum'. In Atwater, M.M. (ed.) *International Handbook of Research on Multicultural Science Education.* pp. 1–23. Springer International Publishing. https://doi.org/10.1007/978-3-030-37743-4_33-1

Stewart, G.T. (2021a). *Māori Philosophy: Indigenous Thinking from Aotearoa.* London: Bloomsbury.

Stewart, G.T. (2021b). 'Writing as a Māori/Indigenous Method of Inquiry'. In Stewart, G.T., Devine, N. and Benade, L. (eds.) *Writing for Publication: Liminal Reflections for Academics.* pp. 41–54. Singapore: Springer. https://doi.org/10.1007/978-981-33-4439-6_4

Stewart, G.T. (2022). 'Mātauranga Māori: A Philosophy from Aotearoa'. *Journal of the Royal Society of New Zealand.* 52(1): pp. 18–24. https://doi.org/10.1080/03036758.2020.1779757

Stewart, G.T. (2023). 'Kaupapa Māori Autoethnography'. In Anteliz, E.A., Mulligan, D.L. and Danaher, P.A. (eds.) *The Routledge International Handbook of Autoethnography in Educational Research.* pp. 326–336. Routledge. www.routledge.com/The-Routledge-International-Handbook-of-Autoethnography-in-Educational/Anteliz-Mulligan-Danaher/p/book/9781032119922

Stewart-Harawira, M. (1993). 'Māori, Who Owns the Definition?' *Te Pua.* 2(1&2): pp. 27–33. No doi.

Webster, S. (1998). *Patrons of Māori Culture: Power, Theory and Ideology in the Māori Renaissance.* Dunedin: University of Otago Press.

Willmott, B. (1989). 'Introduction: Culture and National Identity'. In Novitz, D. and Willmott, B. (eds.) *Culture and Identity in New Zealand.* pp. 1–20. GP Books. Culture and identity in New Zealand: David Novitz and Bill Willmott: 9780477014229: Amazon.com: Books.

14

CONCLUDING THOUGHTS

Selves, Cultures, Limitations, Futures

Alec Grant

> One must have chaos in one, to give birth to a dancing star.
> I tell you: you still have chaos in you.
>
> (Nietzsche, 1969, p. 46)

Introduction

I argued in my opening chapter that autoethnographers, while accepting their intercorporeality or embodiment among other bodies, may also claim non-enduring and disconnected self-identities. I also recognise that the relationship between bodies and selves is often disputed in philosophical debates. However, for pragmatic convenience, in this final chapter I take "bodies" to co-entail and co-imply contributing autoethnographers' claimed identities, or "selves," and will henceforth simply refer to "self," "selves," or "selfhood," as appropriate.

I discussed the interrelated concepts of *Selfhood* and *Culture* in Chapter 1 as having definitional importance in autoethnography, and thus in need of scrutiny and unpacking from a philosophical autoethnographic standpoint. I expand on this discussion here, while tacitly, sometimes explicitly, inviting you to join the conversation. My aim is not to give equal attention to all the contributors' chapters. Instead, I make – sometimes extended – selective reference to aspects of them as and when I feel appropriate in the context of my developing discussion. Along the way, while also giving relevant space to the work of and about Virginia Woolf, I suggest some

DOI: 10.4324/9781003274728-14

emerging implications for philosophical autoethnography. I finish the chapter by addressing the philosophical limitations of the volume and argue for a future text, needed to articulate the philosophical basis of image- and performance-based autoethnography.

Selfhood and Culture: Orienting Questions

While reading through the chapters, I kept the following four questions in mind. These arise from my introduction chapter, and I will go on to answer them in sub-sections:

- *What forms of selfhood do I see represented, and are these claimed as enduring over time or disconnected and non-enduring?*
- *What issues of selfhood and contested ownership of selfhood do I think have been raised?*
- *Are there tensions for me in the chapters among and between representations of agentic and constrained selves?*
- *When do I see culture/society explicitly queered across the chapters, in contrast with acceptance of culture/society as 'the space of the familiar'?*

***

What forms of selfhood do I see represented, and are these claimed as enduring over time or disconnected and non-enduring?

I read off from contributors' chapters an appealing range of tacit, implicit, and explicit representations of selfhood. I partially or wholly identify with most of these, while sympathetically rejecting some aspects of them – either, in one case, because of a universalising claim made, or because of a lack of felt relevance for my own life, times, and contextual circumstances.

I read the self-as-author, and sometimes selves more generally, variously described across this volume as: ontologically and dialectically, tragically happy (Art Bochner); postmodern, shifting, epistolary (Alex Brostoff); lesbian feminist, in-between (Elizabeth Ettorre); multiple, refracted, raced, gendered (Renata Ferdinand); inherited, shared, morally valued (Mark Freeman); fictive-enacted, sardonic, comedic (Alec Grant); symbiotic, extended, co-extensive (Andrew Herrmann); existential, liminal, becoming (Christopher N. Poulos); black, feminist, politicised (Menah Pratt); intersubjective, existential, dialogical (Shelley Rawlins); stigmatised, embodied, resisting (Julie-Ann Scott-Pollock); subjugated, political, postcolonial (Georgina Tuari Stewart).

I'll expand a little on these: from an onto-epistemological smorgasbord, I see you, dear reader, as having been invited to sample, digest, and perhaps identify with the idea of selves, and perhaps your own self, as:

- **enduring**, in terms of an assumed universal capacity for empathic responsiveness towards suffering, vulnerability, and striving towards meaningful happiness (**Art**);
- **non-enduring** and ideological interpellation-challenging, intersubjective, intertextual, aesthetically and playfully represented (**Alex**);
- **enduring** and developing, in the 'in between' of embodied intersubjective life, functioning as transitional spaces to negotiate relationships with others (**Betsy**);
- multiple, sometimes **enduring**, sometimes **disconnected**, submissive, assertive, motivated by gendered, racialised, and socialised double-consciousness (**Renata**);
- **enduring, developing,** shared and inherited, in an intellectual lineage necessary for moral development (**Mark**);
- storied, partly-fictional and **-disconnected**; retrospective across several situated lives, and real to the extent that they purportedly are or have been enacted (**Alec**);
- **enduring**, where self-organization is treated as a compound verb in bringing co-emergent webs or relational significance into meaningful life (**Andrew**);
- **enduring**, moving existentially across liminal space, with the hope of transcending human suffering and, ultimately, nothingness (**Christopher**);
- **enduring** and emerging in a lived experiential philosophical and political discourse, shaped by intergenerational history, gender, race, religion, and class (**Menah**);
- **enduring** and dialogically and existentially reflexive, where self-representation, by definition, must always be at pains to include the voices of others (**Shelley**);
- **enduring** and corporeal, where the disabled body is accorded power as a valuable lived-experiential tool in analysing and interpreting social life (**Julie-Ann**);
- **enduring**, while resisting the marginalisation and cultural and political erasure resulting from European colonisation and assumed assimilation (**Georgina**).

***

What issues of selfhood and of contested ownership of selfhood do I think have been raised?

Whoever really owns a self? The disabled self is often captured in a voyeuristic, patronizing, or judgemental optic; the black woman academic self is frequently traduced, trivialised, or forced to conform to their positioning by the white mainstream; and the ethnic, indigenous self can find its historical paradigms and traditions conveniently erased. The question of self-ownership, in the sense of self-governance that's not significantly interfered with or undermined, seems to me to be most starkly relevant and pressing in the chapters written by Julie-Ann, Renata, Menah, and Georgina. These chapters address, respectively, selves colonised and appropriated by prejudice, othering, and ableist discourse; by the gendered, racist, and micro-aggressive white academy; by malestream Western philosophy sitting alongside a broader gendered and racist US society; and by European cultural and epistemic colonisation and imperialism.

Self and selfhood need to be thought about in extended social, existential, and moral terms. My reading of Shelley's work is that she represents herself as consciously living *distributed* social and existential selfhood, in an ethical act against the lone-self solipsism which always threatens the inclusive, socially progressive agenda of autoethnography. Christopher and Art both link the self to human suffering: respectively, in terms of the existential importance of courageously combating and transcending human anxiety, and the moral need to write against superficial and banal aspects of affective selfhood.

Selfhood also moves outward in extended synchronic and diachronic directions, in ways that can be productive or destructive. I read selves for Andrew as co-developing and co-inscribed within organizing and the material world, and always governed by existential choice and dignified human meaning- and sensemaking. Betsy starkly describes the threats to the integrity of her selves. These are caused by discrimination against her sexual orientation and gender, and result in her feeling that she neither organisationally fits in nor is fit for purpose. Mark's shared and lineage-driven self values intellectual practice and inheritance as moral life work. I'm with Mark in believing this to be vitally important in the face of our increasingly intellectually debased and commodified academies, where in my experience "thinking with" and even just "thinking" are constantly devalued.

And there's the disappearing and non-positionable self. I wrote my own chapter in a deliberately satirical and narrative theory-informed way in large part to avoid claiming an enduring, solid identity. Because of this, I find it difficult to think about my "self" (if I really am, or if I constitute, a coherent self?) in any kind of substantial way. This makes threats to my self-integrity – real or imagined – equally difficult to think about. I seem to have a knack (or defensive vice?) for keeping threats to my selfhood at bay by lampooning them.

I also find Alex's take on the self and selfhood, and corresponding threats, difficult to think about clearly. No doubt because of my long immersion in autoethnography, this is I think because of the lack of clearly distinct and distinguishable "selves" (in the senses that I pragmatically defined the term earlier) in their chapter. However, I regard this in positive terms in two ways: first, in the compelling beauty, fun, and challenge of their work; second, in what we can learn from autoetheory – to my mind autoethnography's intellectually helpful, close narrative relative.

Turning to some general points: in the face of the range of understandings and utilisations across the chapters, I think it reasonable to suggest that it would be useful for narrative philosophical autoethnographers to be as clear as possible about what they mean by *the self* and *selfhood* in their work, whether writing about their own selves or the selves of others. I'm not necessarily suggesting that they *over-labour* such a display of clarity in their writing, although doing so might sometimes enhance it in critically reflexive terms. What do you think?

I think also that such clarity needs to be balanced with caution around making sweeping, totalising generalisations about the role and function of self in autoethnography. There are obvious cross-cultural transferability problems in writing as if "selfhood" had a clear, ubiquitous, and universal meaning. However, it seems to me that such universalising claims are widely, if often tacitly, held among the evocative autoethnographic community. Unless explicitly qualified as a culture-centric Western assumption, written from the standpoint of narrative autoethnography as therapy, I believe this to be specious.

Culturally taken-for-granted forms of narrative entrapment, colonialisation, and appropriation can also be read off across the volume: my own representations of entrapment in the military culture of the 1960s and 70s, and in the more recent culture of UK higher education, for example. I also read ideological entrapment for writers and readers and literary critics in Alex's work; and sexually exploitable, imposed heteronormative identity entrapment in Betsy's narrative.

And as an elderly man I'm struck by how my aging body promises to gradually relinquish ownership of itself (Small, 2007). From a metanarrative perspective, my editing this volume and my philosophical autoethnographic contribution within it might be read off by younger eyes as irrelevant and passé. I might be positioned as an autoethnographic dinosaur, extinction long overdue. In my younger days I took it for granted that – broadly speaking – social institutions, institutions, groups, and organisations were reliably and unconditionally supportive of me as a person of value and esteem. Now, in line with what Small describes as the "tolerable necessity" (p. 266) of thinking about my own mortality – recognising as true that "our well-being is at significant and increasing risk the longer we live on past our prime" (p. 59), I sadly realise that I'm generally more likely to be regarded as irrelevant, an irritation, surplus to advanced capitalist requirements except to the extent that I remain an exploitable commodity. Lanoix (2009) helps me understand and *feel* the ways in which old human bodies are expected to fit into organisational, institutional, and cultural time narratives, all of which advantage the young. And Overall (2019) is generally on the money in asserting that the current cultural main deal for the elderly is to fade away quietly and lose their social presence. To my chagrin, I'm probably already inscribed within several disappearance stories.

There is an obvious link here to the social justice function of autoethnography. It seems important to me that philosophical autoethnographers recognise and, when necessary, explicitly call out *all* forms of oppressive narrative entrapment, colonisation, and appropriation when they recognise these as occurring. In related terms, however, a less obvious and uncomfortable thought occurs to me. This is that autoethnographic selfhood positions, in and of themselves, can be colonising, appropriating, and entrapping.

Ideal and utopian forms of life writing are often blind to privilege. As an example of this, Virginia Woolf (1929) – to my mind a superb early feminist philosophical autoethnographer – expertly challenged the patriarchal narrative subjugation and suppression of creativity in women, while making important contributions to narrative theory. However, according to Light (2007, pp. 111–116), backed up in diary accounts over five volumes (Woolf, 1979, 1981, 1982, 1983, 1985), Woolf spent a lifetime deliberately knowing little about the lived-through experiences of poor women, and the poor more generally.

What she did know was gleaned in her early life from the – always socially distanced – poor-visiting and other forms of charity work conducted by her mother and others from her class (Light, 2007), and, later, from her own snobbery-imbued voyeuristic constructions of the motivations and social-psychological status of her servants:

> Of course, one is right about Nelly . . . she is in a state of nature; untrained; uneducated, to me almost incredibly without the power of analysis or logic; so that one sees a human mind wriggling undressed – which is interesting.
>
> *(Woolf, 1982, p. 241)*

Light (2007) argues with biographical authority, backed up by numerous such diary entries, that although feeling repelled by the spectacle of the poor, Woolf took for granted as natural the idea of domestic service as a cultural and social necessity. Finding it degrading to write about them except in the language of condescension familiar to her class, she kept her distance from, and accorded very little first-person narrative voice to, her poorly paid, housed, and treated domestic servants. Ironically, these were the women who made her creative life possible.

Are there lessons here for narrative philosophical autoethnography? At a general level, we perhaps shouldn't stop being concerned about the voices routinely excluded from autoethnographies. It seems to me that such exclusions are inevitable and may occur as a function of a sense of social superiority as in Woolf's case; related narrative habit and voice privilege biases; missed or unseen opportunities; restricted discursive repertoires; and cultural situatedness. They may also occur because of a neglect of non-Western philosophical traditions, which I will discuss at the end of this chapter.

I think it's therefore useful to press home and labour the rhetorical questions: what selves haunt the background of our work as absent presences? What is the opportunity cost and moral cost of the voices that escape the attention of our autoethnographic focus in any one piece of writing? I'm not talking here about the ethical issue of voice exclusion in the usual, single research study-situated way that's often rehearsed in qualitative inquiry texts. To return to points I made in my introduction chapter, I mean more by my question that perhaps much of my own work, and the work I often see emerging from the narrative autoethnographic world, functions in "gated community" terms (Chetty, 2018), regarding which stakeholder group voices are allowed in or routinely excluded.

I want to suggest that autoethnographic and life writing can sometimes function as an unconscious form of defensive narcissism to keep marginalised or *othered* communities out of the narrative frame. In 2022, I contributed to a journal special supplement celebrating autoethnography in mental health nursing (Grant, 2022). The point of the supplement was to promote what was perceived by its editors to be a relatively new methodology within mental health nursing research. Not having the chance to engage with the articles other than my own until the supplement was published, I was disappointed and disturbed by the complete absence of any narrative attention paid to the angry and betrayed voice of the mental health system survivor. I was also struck by the lack of critical reflexivity in the articles I read, the corresponding collective self-satisfied celebration of mental health nursing and psychiatric careers, and the positive 'Trip advisor' take on institutional psychiatric culture of the variety I mentioned in Chapter 1.

I can't speak about the levels of complacency that may or may not be felt about such narrative practices by senior, and other, members of our autoethnographic communities. However, there's a wider point at play here: it does seem to me that at a global level, narrative autoethnography in its conventionally understood sense can sometimes be disturbingly geopolitically time-bound and insular. This is unavoidable in many respects; I don't think it likely that in the foreseeable future we'll see many autoethnographies written by Buddhist monks in Chinese-colonised Lhasa, Tibet. That said, an open question for me is the extent to which the autoethnographic meta-community seriously aspires to extend its global and cultural reach and inclusion, and in what ways?

I should at this point mention a personal paradox that speaks to this issue. While I believe in the usefulness and power of autoethnography and continue to think it true that autoethnography saved my life (https://youtu.be/VXqCw-Tyq0E),[1] I could never be an enthusiastic member of any autoethnographic inner circle. Expanding macro-circles is something to be desired. Bud Goodall urged the widening of communities and cultures of ethnographic practice in the interests of progressive social justice. This was in line with his transformational vision of ethnographers "evolving to a higher state of scholarly consciousness," to connect with the "souls and hearts and minds – of other human beings." (Goodall, 2000, p. 198). Meso- and micro-circles, in contrast, always seem to me to threaten this vision, in their displays of insularity, inward-looking levels of group satisfaction, and "family" nepotism. The idea of meso- and micro-inner circles shouts "GATED COMMUNITY!" loudly to me. I don't think it rash to claim that some selves may be excluded and punitively *othered* if they challenge the integrity, assumptions, practices, modus operandi, or procedural rationality of these circles (Grant et al., 2022).

***

Are there tensions for me in the chapters among and between representations of agentic and constrained selves?

There seems to me to be an often hidden, or played down, or unacknowledged, tension between agency and constrained selfhood in many of the autoethnographies I've read over the years, including in my own work. Selves can often seem unconvincingly omnipotent and optimistic in their aspirations to rise above contingent selfhood. This is despite what Christopher and Art, and often I and many others, write about shaping selfhood in preferred directions.

Another, related, personal paradox: while I love my writing, when I'm (thankfully only occasionally these days) troubled by rational-realist thinking, I think that anything I might write about my selves is always semi-truthful: a farrago. From a rational-realist perspective, even the objectively verifiable bits don't really convey me qua *me* – either because of what I feel constrained to omit from my stories, or because of what I've forgotten. No surprises there. Rational-realist life always exceeds the tales we tell about it – to others and to ourselves. I argued in my philosophical autoethnographic chapter in this volume that *narrative smoothing* – papering over the cracks in a story purporting to be true – is inevitable for all of us. This in turn pulls on *narrative retrofit*: kitting old stories out with handy current decorative bits and pieces. However, given that memory functions as a kind of selective amnesia, much of what I've naturally or defensively forgotten about my past might well be more significant and interesting than what I remember, no matter how much I pretty this up.

Well! That's a wee bit disappointing! And what's more – to draw on a point that Mark Freeman makes in his chapter – my memory seems to me to be a narrative fictive resource for an equally fictive self. In rational-realist world, perhaps the best that can be said for the self I've crafted in my chapter is that it's "real" only insofar as it corresponds to the stories I've spun about my lived-through experiences, and the extent to which I really *did* live these stories. Fortunately, Mark reminds me, you, all of us, that the rational-realist, or literal, perspective is not the only one available. Aided by the creative imagination, the self can also be viewed as a literary, as a poetic, accomplishment.

But . . . even so . . . Woolf (1929) was still right, I believe, in thinking that much of the life writing she came across failed to the extent that in important respects it excluded the person:

> She was unravelling the premises of life-writing, the idea of plotting a life when a life has no plot, and the piling up of 'events,' which so often, she believed, left out the person to whom things happen.
>
> *(Light, 2007, p. 257)*

Descriptions of things happening tend to substitute for and conceal persons. From my increasing familiarity with her work, I'm pretty sure that Woolf meant the interior of personhood; the phenomenological picture of the inside of being a person; the 'what is it like to be' qualia of situated, lived-through, interior selfhood. Regarding my own autoethnographic writing, I'm not sure what can be done about Woolf's concern. Things happen to me, and those things conceal me and often take the place of me. Does this make my self-representation incoherent? I think that if I tried to describe the internal me to whom things happened in a detailed, qualia-rich way, I'd always fail. I can and do describe my shifting feelings, thoughts, and moods. But, valuable as those descriptions are for all autoethnographers – so beautifully deployed in her writing – it seems to me that these constituted "surface" issues for Woolf. In support of Art's take on storying happiness, which I'll move on to discuss momentarily, perhaps the interiority of selfhood and narrativisation shouldn't appear in the same sentence? What's your own position on this as an autoethnographer, or as someone who might want to become one?

Art's chapter stood out for me as triggering, intriguing, and thought-provoking. On one level, I read no incoherence in his writing: his narrative seems simply and honestly to be about mutually responsive suffering selves writing for suffering selves. All well and good from one perspective, with the caveat I made earlier that I read this as a universalising standpoint going well beyond its range of contingent convenience. It also seems to me to be beyond logical dispute that, in narrative theoretical terms, connection with 'suffering happiness' in Art's sense (a variant of a slogan shared among many in the evocative autoethnographic communities) is just one among many possible reader responses at the writer-reader interface (Grant, 2018).

I read Art arguing that incoherence is fundamentally built into selfhood at onto-epistemological levels. In an ideal normative sense, life *should* be happy, but he sees vulnerable selves constrained to suffer in lived-through experiential terms because life – presumably subsuming day to day culture – is unsatisfactory. If I've connected with his writing in the way he intended, I'm in full agreement with Art. He does indeed imitate life for me on this point, in being a responsible spokesperson for what life is always SHOUTING OUT LOUD AT US.

To complicate things, suffering becomes conflated with happiness. For Art, deep, worthwhile forms of happiness – of the kind we *really* strive for, but which become obscured by more trivial affective distractions – entail suffering, not its absence. I think this is an important point, well made. However, to compound this picture, selves are *representationally* constrained in conveying their suffering because – in my view, like the interior self in Woolf's sense – the happy self defies narrativisation. And even if it didn't, Art explains, agentic selves seeking happiness are further constrained in psychoanalytic terms, because happiness always eludes them.

Moreover, even when this appears not to be the case, Art argues that "Happiness (is) . . . is private and subjective, not public or communal" (my brackets). What do you think? Is situated happiness impossible to convey or connect with through evocative writing? At a surface – perhaps superficial and trivial – level, day-to-day life, novels, films, theatre performance, and many other life spectacles and experiences seem to give the lie to this viewpoint. But on a more profound level, I think that Art is on to something. Happiness as a "what it is like" qualia event seems an intensely difficult-to-articulate private-self experience, and we don't really need a Wittgenstein to remind us of this.

I think Art is correct in believing that most of us humans confuse the hedonistically superficial with happiness. The extent to which we plump for surface pleasures undermines our capacity for *tragic happiness* of the better-quality, life-affirming moral variety that Nietzsche wrote about. Thus, as I argue in my own philosophical autoethnographic chapter in this volume, the sufficiently self-aware self needs always to strive to overcome itself. This, I read Art as implying, is the moral purpose of autoethnography. I absolutely believe this to be the case and wrote as much in my MA Philosophy dissertation (Grant, 2020).

Picking up on a point I raised in Chapter 1, I extend Art's position here to the unconditional positive regard superlatives I see bandied about at conferences in response to mediocre work. I wonder if this phenomenon sometimes constitutes a kind of mass, vicarious therapy experience? Is it a form of Nietzschean ressentiment that's – ultimately ineffectually as ressentiment always is – perpetually victim- rather than life-affirming? Is it uncharitable of me to regard such conference happenings as embarrassing lightweight salves in the production of pseudo-happy selves?

Betsy Ettorre's reading of Butler as a means of managing the agentic vs. constrained gendered and sexualised binary, got me thinking about self-entrapment via gender essentialism, and the importance – in line with Ahmed (2006) and Sedgwick (1993) – of queering cultural life to sustain self-integrity. I was particularly taken with Betsy's "in between" concept, which I read off as a lived act of resistance to entrapment.

I made a connection from this concept to Woolf (1929) again, this time on the importance of androgynous writing:

A great mind is androgynous . . . the androgynous mind is resonant and porous . . . it transmits emotion without impediment . . . it is naturally creative, incandescent and undivided.

(p. 97)

it is fatal for anyone who writes to think of their sex. It is fatal to be a man or woman pure and simple; one must be a woman-manly or man-womanly.

(p. 103)

Notwithstanding the contemporary need to sometimes write from an explicit, situated, gendered, or gender-fluid position and choose from a range of personal pronouns, I find the idea and the ideal of androgynous writing in Woolf's work very appealing. Almost a century ago, in her man-womanly novel *Orlando: A Biography*, Woolf (1928) challenged the hegemony of patriarchal hierarchies and related modes of knowing, being, and writing. The hero of the novel is an Elizabethan nobleman who becomes a woman at about the age of 30 and lives for another three centuries without ageing perceptibly. According to de Groot (2010, p. 43), Orlando constituted a deliberate *queering* of historical novelistic culture, which managed "to upset the rational realism of the form and to bend it as far out of shape as possible" (de Groot, 2010, p. 43).

You, dear reader, might think that because Woolf was writing at a time when rigid gender binaries were culturally dominant, her work is no longer relevant. I disagree; androgynous writing still has, I believe, the capacity to subvert tacitly and implicitly gendered self-narrative entrapment for those of us autoethnographers who linger on in either of our traditional gender binary identities. I haven't reached the point in being even an early work-in-progress in androgynous writing, and perhaps I'm too long in the tooth and too obstinately unreconstructable for this to ever happen to any degree. And the – at this stage unanswered – big question arises for me about the possibilities for this to be carried off in narrative philosophical autoethnography. In addition to her exemplary *Orlando*, Woolf (1929) gives us some literary pointers:

> One must turn back to Shakespeare . . . for Shakespeare was androgynous; and so were Keats and Sterne and Cowper and Lamb and Coleridge. Shelley perhaps was sexless . . . Proust was wholly androgynous, if not perhaps a little too much of a woman.
>
> *(p. 102)*

***

When do I see culture/society explicitly queered across the chapters, in contrast with acceptance of culture/society as "the space of the familiar"?

It seems to me to be a nontrivial assertion that purposefully queering cultures results in the creation of new ones, and that the creation of new cultures is a critical function of autoethnography. The Nietzsche aphorism that I opened this chapter with signals for me the fragility and contingency of cultural life, and the importance of imaginatively writing or crafting new cultural worlds into existence. I think that the "dancing star" metaphor is significant in at least two ways: any form of cultural or organised social group is condemned to be time-bound, time-limited, and problematic, given its internal contradictions. Moreover, cultural and social groups exert a centripetal pull on members to conform, and this is often experienced as oppressive.

Sara Ahmed, Eve Sedgwick, Virginia Woolf, and Renata Ferdinand (in this volume) all directly reference or allude to straight and slanting lines in symbolising cultural adherence and resistance. Renata uses the metaphor of the "crooked room" to display her feelings of being out of kilter with white society; in critiquing heteronormative representations, Sedgwick (1993, pp. 73–103) draws on literature to ask the rhetorical question "Is the Rectum Straight"; Woolf (1929) rails against the straight patriarchal rigidity and androcentrism of Britain in the late 19th and early 20th centuries. And Ahmed (2006) writes:

> Spaces and bodies become straight as an effect of repetition . . . Given this, the work of ordinary perception, which straightens up anything queer or oblique, is not simply about correcting what is out of line . . . . Spaces as well as bodies are the effects of such straightening devices.
>
> *(p. 92)*

Spaces as well as bodies are made straight. But cultural spaces and bodies are never naturally or essentially straight. Nascent within them is the potential for spaces and bodies to slant off in all sorts of directions. I draw on Nietzsche in my belief that it's the moral duty of philosophical autoethnographers to welcome the chaos they have within them, and to see the space of the straight familiar in cultural life as strange and in constant need of queered, creative bending (see my discussion of this point in Chapter 1).

Woolf (1929, p. 95) beautifully describes seeing the queer in the familiar:

> At this moment, as so often happens in London, there was a complete lull and suspension of traffic. Nothing came down the street; nobody passed. A single leaf detached itself from the plane tree at the end of the street, and in that pause and suspension fell. Somehow it was like a signal failing, a signal pointing to a force in things which one had overlooked. It seemed to point to a river, which flowed past, invisibly . . . and took people and eddied them along . . . Now it was bringing from one side of the street diagonally a girl in patent leather boots, and then a young man in a maroon overcoat; it was also bringing a taxicab; and it brought all three together at a point directly beneath my window; where the taxi stopped; and the girl and the young man stopped and they got into the taxi; and then the cab glided off as if it were swept on by the current elsewhere. The sight was ordinary enough; what was strange was the rhythmical order with which my imagination had invested it.

In contrast, I read Art saying he sees life as culture in disappointingly familiar terms. Suffering subjectivities always obscure the tragic happiness agenda. At the risk of perhaps reading too much into them, I infer from Art's words that he's taking to task conventional, culturally sanctioned forms of – superficial – subjectivity. I'm reminded of what Ellis and Flaherty said in 1992:

> Subjectivity can be both unpleasant and dangerous: unpleasant because emotional, cognitive, and physical experiences frequently concern events that, in spite of their importance, are deemed *inappropriate topics* for polite society . . .; *dangerous* because the workings of subjectivity seem to contradict so much of the rational-actor world-view.
>
> *(Ellis and Flaherty, 1992, p. 1)*

Perhaps the rational-actor world view is only accepting of ultimately unsatisfactory, 'bread and circuses' forms of subjectivity. For Art, life that's deemed unsatisfactory in this sense is unavoidably linked to unhappiness. To recap, the argument is that happiness in the conventional cultural sense of the term can function as a toxic distraction that inhibits life affirmation.

However, Art's sense of life as the space of the disappointingly familiar – of a familiar that's never good enough – to which we can all empathically connect is, from my perspective, overly optimistic. When I read a text written from a space of un-queered, familiar cultural concern about an experience I haven't lived through myself, I can and frequently do feel some degree of sympathetic responsive connection, especially if I see this as implicitly invited. However, equally, I often find myself judging the person's plight as relatively trivial and, to my mind, represented in parochial and insular terms that I can't, or don't want to, empathically reach out to.

My thoughts at this point on an emerging general implication for philosophical autoethnography: I agree that life experienced as day-to-day culture isn't up to moral snuff in promoting good quality – life-affirming – happiness, and I think that in this regard autoethnography has a culturally critical calling-out duty. However, I sometimes worry that I maintain this standpoint defensively because of my chronic resistance to full cultural socialisation (see my autoethnographic chapter in this volume). Is my resistance an existentially authentic choice, or a failure of my early upbringing, or a bit of both? Whatever the case, is my resistance skewing my take on culture in both my autoethnographic work and what I regard the purpose of autoethnography to be vis-à-vis culture in a jaundiced, possibly unfair way? Some of you might think I'm simply projecting too much, and in need of remedial psychoanalytic treatment? I sometimes think this myself, thankfully not too often.

I read Alex Brostoff's chapter as constituting a sustained queering cultural critique. Queering takes place at postmodern and poststructural levels in constant identity-segueing, and at ironic, metanarrative and metametanarrative levels. In poststructuralist terms, there are no bodies. Just texts. Just words, expressed in letter exchanges. For me, these words violate predictable, familiar, and conventional human cultural experiences but fail spectacularly, in entertaining ways. In line with what I said earlier about the absence of palpably distinct selves in Alex's work, this was a reminder to me of the usefulness of writing about the self as text; of textually representing selves where agency, ontology, and epistemology are indeterminate, and ideology-busting.

Renata Ferdinand describes in her chapter the ways in which her cultural environment doubly violates her determined self. The space of the (disappointingly, in Art's terms) familiar is viewed through the lens of the crooked room, which, although unsatisfactory, has hitherto been predictable in its crookedness. Renata constantly tries to stand up straight in cultural worlds, but no matter what remedial steps she takes she's condemned to remain slanted. This seems to me to be the result of the compound paradox of Renata experiencing as crooked the familiar straight world, viewed from the familiar crooked room. Renata's vengeful agentic self is symbolised by her alter ego ideal. Her constrained self still plays by the tacitly deferential cultural rules of "professionalism" in straightworld. This marks a disconnect between Renata as professionally constrained academic/goodgirl, who constantly strives to meet the stereotypically normative demands of the white academy, and "Pinkie," the feisty, blinged-up sassy girl who takes no shit, and who's called upon as a culture queering ally in times of distress. Pinkie is an essential back-up self because goodgirl's attempts to live up to her professor script are constantly stymied by repeated gendered and racialised micro-abuses.

I'm left thinking that Renata needs to queer her cultural spaces more, as far as she possibly can. Fusing Professor Ferdinand with Pinkie would, I believe, enable her to live more comfortably in and with the goodness and beauty of her crooked rooms, without ever feeling the need to straighten them. I'm so pleased to see that she's made a great start in that regard (Ferdinand, 2022).

In my own autoethnographic chapter – the one I'm of course most familiar with – cultural events and situations are consistently queered. I'm slanted against the straight lines of all the cultural, social, and organisational circumstances represented in my stories, making specific queer moments stand out, punctum-like, through the deliberate performance of satire and magical realism. I seem in my chapter to be the performing midwife at the birth of little dancing stars functioning as antidotes to cultural-, social-, organisational-, and life-tedium.

And aren't we all performers? Andrew Herrmann reminds us that organisation is a verb. We perform "organisation." We're all unavoidably complicit in our co-shaped, co-emergent, co-constructed organisational selves and worlds. In this regard, performing self-culture seems to me to be more a case of perpetual dialectic compromise negotiation than individual free choice in a simplistic existential sense.

What do I take from this? In terms of emerging implications, there seems to me to be a clear set of choices open to philosophical narrative autoethnographers. These amount to respecting and justifying the culturally familiar, and familiar self within culture, or queering one, or the other, or both. A queered self might be viewed as an enduring or a discontinuous self, in either case with a more or less coherent identity. A familiar self in a familiar culture is, I think, perhaps more likely to be an enduring one. A discontinuous self may find itself in familiar, enduring cultures or societies, or in discontinuous ones. A queered culture is made purposefully, or strategically, or politically, or aesthetically, strange, dancing star-like. A familiar culture rolls on, relatively unchanged and indifferent.

There's a power issue underpinning this set of choices. In poststructural terms, Butler (1997, p. 382) argues that we're forever in danger of being over-familiar with our cultural selves. In general terms, this is because of our prolonged location in, and socialisation to, dominant discourses, our willingness to compliantly respond to constant hailing (or interpellation) by joining the discursive party, and constant rehearsal and repetition of our various selfhood performances. We are always simultaneously *enabled and violated* by our participation in cultural selfhood – violated by the affronts to our selves, which are an inevitable consequence of willing entrapment, or by the more or less conscious oppression we experience through unwilling participation. However, following Butler, we have the capacity to engage in counter-violation as an act of resistance. A self who knows itself in discourse, and who constantly rehearses, repeats, and replicates itself, can draw from discursive repertoires to make "enabling violations" to its performed cultural selfhood. In short, we can continually act on our familiar cultural selves, reifying and reinforcing them, or we can tweak them to make life more bearable and, through the creation of oppositional or counter-discourses, bring new worlds into being.

***

Limitations of This Volume, and the Future

It's time for me to end this volume by considering what's missing from it, and what I think needs to happen from this point on. With the notable exception of Georgina Tuari Stewart shining a light on Māori philosophy in her chapter (see also Stewart, 2021), this entire text is biased towards Western philosophical traditions in defining, making sense of, and writing philosophical narrative autoethnography. Van Norden (2017, p. xix) has recently issued a multicultural manifesto to redress the imbalance produced by the almost exclusive dominance of the Western philosophical traditions in the work of professional philosophers, and on university courses on philosophy. He regards the omission of the philosophies of Asia, India, Africa, and the Indigenous Americas as a form of *structural racism* to the extent that this omission constitutes the systematic denigration of people and races not represented.

What would sub-genres of philosophical autoethnography work look like if they were grounded in the philosophies of Japan, India, China, and the Muslim world, and the African, American, and Australian first peoples (Baggini, 2018)? What voices could then be included that had hitherto been neglected, gated out?

One challenge for narrative philosophical autoethnographers whose writing is informed by Eastern, particularly Buddhist, philosophy is in losing the *self* in their work. What would a "No Self" autoethnography look like (Garfield, 2022)? The puzzle implied in this question might perhaps be expressed as a Zen Koan:

What is autoethnography when it has no self?

The idea of no-self philosophical autoethnography might be seen to resonate with the posthuman and related post-qualitative turns in qualitative inquiry, including the need for what Ken Gale describes as "methodogenesis" (Gale, 2018, 2023, p. 71). This concept takes to task all forms of qualitative inquiry grounded in, necessarily anthropocentric, reason – in effect *all* forms of qualitative inquiry (Hein, 2021). In related terms, I read Ken as arguing across his work for the refusal of *auto*ethnography's implied anthropocentrism.

I think that Ken is to be congratulated for being a trailblazer in the, for me, hugely entertaining narrative representation of bodies – all bodies, inhuman, human, organic, inorganic – as co-immanent and co-becoming in relationally fluid flux and play (Gale, 2018, 2023). However, I read living human bodies as having lingering dominance in his work (not least Ken's living human body). Where there are such bodies, there are surely selves glued to subjectivities. Ken might take issue with me on this point, given that he rests his case on poststructural readings of "immanence," from which perspective there is no transcendence; nothing above or beyond, in Platonic, Kantian, or Cartesian terms; no external perfect driver (Hein, 2021). According to Deleuze (2001), in contrast to the metaphysics of transcendence, immanence, while occurring from within, paradoxically shouldn't be regarded as being *in* something, or depending on an object, or belonging to a subject.

As much as I respect some aspects of Deleuzian philosophy, particularly – in partial sympathy with Ken's methodogenesis concept – the need to use scholarly labour to write against the "Dogmatic Image of Thought"[2] (Deleuze, 1994, in Klevan and Grant, 2022), I do not buy the idea of immanence as a kind of free-floating metaphysical ghostly trickster phenomenon; a metaphysical, rhizomatic, ineffable will-o'-the-wisp whose spectral light escapes the attention of those of us who remain stuck in categories, binaries, methods, and methodologies. Nor do I buy, to paraphrase Hein (2021), immanence as the non-thought integral to thought; the source of all concepts, while exceeding them; the ultimate, ubiquitous pre-/post-/existent, independent of human intersubjectivity.

Since thinking selves are the locus, or point of emergence, of the supposed plane of – subsequently conceptualised and narrativised – immanence, it seems to me that if there are no selves (thus subjects), it logically follows that there can be no such immanence. Moreover, I'm with Garfield (2017) in his – shades of David Hume – implied rejection of the Deleuzian idea that immanence does not depend on an object:

> If you ask me what it is like to be me, *simpliciter*, you ask me to describe consciousness itself, apart from any object of consciousness. There is no such thing. Consciousness is always consciousness of something, and when the object is subtracted, nothing remains to be characterized.
>
> *(p. 75)*

I will labour and extend on my point: Contra Deleuze, even presupposing its usefulness as a metaphysical phenomenon to account for – among other things – the creation of new concepts and diffractive representation, I fail to see how immanence can give birth to itself, without entailing pre-existing selves united in their intersubjectivity. I'll go further: Despite verbal gymnastics to the contrary, 'immanence' in its poststructural sense seems to me to be an implausible form of the kind of transcendence Deleuze and his followers refuse – sneaked in, in obfuscating conceptual camouflage, through the metaphysical back door.

So again I ask rhetorically, what is autoethnography when it has no self?

These questions, challenges, provocations, and pointers to future directions seem important to me in moving philosophical autoethnography beyond the gated communities of Western philosophy. What about you? What do you think?

And what would a future nonnarrative, non-text-based philosophical autoethnographic volume have to say about increasingly emerging image- and performance-based research, with or without selves, in autoethnographic film, animation, anime, documentary, dance, sculpture, painting, photography, theatre, song, and more? Andrew Herrmann (2022) writes:

> We are often bound to the written word, but that has been changing . . . I love film, but I am not a film expert. I could not tell you if a documentary is autoethnographic . . . I cannot tell you if a beautiful photographic collage is autoethnographic . . . I can't tell you if a particular anime is autoethnographic. We need people who can.
>
> *(p. 130)*

I think that Andrew is right, with the qualifier that such people need also to be able to articulate the philosophical basis of their work. This is something I've been talking about with Susan Young, my esteemed animation autoethnographer colleague and friend over several years. We would love to see, participate in, and – fate willing – edit a follow-up companion volume. If this comes off, it might be titled something like *"Making Philosophical Sense of Image- and Performance-based Autoethnography."* This would be such a glorious and immense dancing star, well worth the labour of giving birth to.

Notes

1 International Conference of Autoethnography (ICAE)
  Inaugural Lifetime Contribution Award, 'in recognition of making a significant contribution to the development and nurturance of the field of autoethnography and those working within it'. Presented at the 7th conference, on the 21st July 2020.
2 *"**The Dogmatic Image of thought** (Deleuze, 1994) is a philosophical concept which proceeds from a distinction that can be made between a tacit human investment in either the ontology of sameness . . . or difference. While the former ontological position is conservative in valuing conformity and stability, the latter – in line with the post-structural project generally – values difference as instability, as unpredicted and unpredictable **becoming** into the not-yet-known."* (Klevan and Grant, 2022, p. 86).

References

Ahmed, S. (2006). *Queer Phenomenology: Orientations, Objects, Others*. Durham and London: Duke University Press.
Baggini, J. (2018). *How the World Thinks: A Global History of Philosophy*. London: Granta.
Butler, J. (1997). 'Gender is Burning: Questions of Appropriation and Subversion'. In McClintock, A., Mufti, A. and Shohat, E. (eds.) *Dangerous Liaisons: Gender, Nation, & Postcolonial Perspectives*. pp. 281–395. Minneapolis: University of Minnesota Press.

Chetty, D. (2018). 'Racism as "Reasonableness": Philosophy for Children and The Gated Community of Inquiry'. *Ethics and Education*. 13(1): 39–54. https://doi.org/10.1080/17449642.2018.1430933

de Groot, J. (2010). *The Historical Novel*. London and New York: Routledge.

Deleuze, G. (2001 [1995]). *Pure Immanence: Essays on a Life*. Translated by Boyman, A. Brooklyn: Zone Books.

Ellis, C. and Flaherty, M.G. (1992). *Investigating Subjectivity: Research on Lived Experience*. Newbury Park, CA: SAGE Publications, Inc.

Ferdinand, R. (2022). 'Pinkie Points it Out: Never Tell a Black Woman . . .' *The AutoEthnographer*. 3(1). editor@theautoethnographer.com https://theautoethnographer.com/

Gale, K. (2018). *Madness as Methodology: Bringing Concepts to Life in Contemporary Theorising and Inquiry*. London and New York: Routledge.

Gale, K. (2023). *Writing and Immanence: Concept Making and the Reorientation of Thought in Pedagogy and Inquiry*. London and New York: Routledge.

Garfield, J.L. (2017). 'Illusionism and Givenness'. In Frankish, K. (ed.) *Illusionism as a Theory of Consciousness*. pp. 73–82. Exeter: Imprint Academic Ltd.

Garfield, J.L. (2022). *Losing Ourselves: Learning to Live Without a Self*. Princeton and Oxford: Princeton University Press.

Goodall, H.L. (2000). *Writing the New Ethnography*. Lanham, MD: AltaMira Press.

Grant, A. (2018). 'Voice, Ethics, and the Best of Autoethnographic Intentions (or Writers, Readers, and the Spaces in-between'. In Turner, L., Short, N.P., Grant, A. and Adams, T.E. (eds.) *International Perspectives on Autoethnographic Research and Practice*. pp. 107–122. London and New York: Routledge.

Grant, A. (2020). 'How Does Nietzschean Self-Deceiving Moral Identity in a Modern Context Relate to Lukes Third Dimension of Power?' Unpublished MA in Philosophy Thesis. Open University.

Grant, A. (2022). 'What Has Autoethnography Got to Offer Mental Health Nursing?' *British Journal of Mental Health Nursing: Autoethnography and Mental Health Nursing Supplement:* pp. 4–11. https://doi.org/10.12968/bjmh.2022.0035

Grant, A., Barnes, J., Klevan, T. and Donaldson, A. (2022). 'Tensions in Managing the Online Network Development of Autoethnographers: A Four-Way Dialogue'. *Social Work & Social Sciences Review*. 18(1): pp. 15–30. https://miar.ub.edu/issn/0953-5225

Hein, S.F. (2021). 'Deleuze and Absolute Immanence: Achieving Fully Immanent Inquiry'. *Qualitative Inquiry*. 27(5): pp. 512–521. https://doi.org/10.1177/1077800420935929

Herrmann, A. (2022). 'The Future of Autoethnographic Criteria'. *International Review of Qualitative Research*. 15(1): 125–135. https://doi.org/10.1177/19408447211049513

Klevan, T. and Grant, A. (2022). *An Autoethnography of Becoming a Qualitative Researcher: A Dialogic View of Academic Development*. London and New York: Routledge.

Lanoix, M. (2009). 'A Body No Longer of One's Own'. In Campbell, S., Meynell, L. and Sherwin, S. (eds.) *Embodiment and Agency*. pp. 164–183. State College: PA: The Pennsylvania State University Press.

Light, A. (2007). *Mrs Woolf & the Servants*. London: Penguin Books.

Nietzsche, F. (1969 [1883–85]). *Thus Spoke Zarathustra: A Book For Everyone*. Translated by Hollingdale, R.J. London: Penguin Books.

Overall, C. (2019). 'Aging and the Loss of Social Presence'. In Apostolova, I. and Lanoix, M. (eds.) *Aging in an Aging Society*. pp. 65–81. Sheffield, UK and Bristol, CT: Equinox Publishing Ltd.

Sedgwick, E.K. (1993). *Tendencies*. Durham: Duke University Press.

Small, J. (2007). *The Long Life*. New York: Oxford University Press Inc.

Stewart, G.T. (2021). *Māori Philosophy: Indigenous Thinking from Aotearoa*. London: Bloomsbury Academic.

Van Norden, B.W. (2017). *Taking Back Philosophy: A Multicultural Manifesto*. New York: Columbia University Press.

Woolf, V. (1979). *The Diary of Virginia Woolf Volume 1: 1915–19*. Edited by Bell, A.O. Harmondsworth: Penguin Books Ltd.

Woolf, V. (1981). *The Diary of Virginia Woolf Volume 2: 1920–24*. Harmondsworth: Penguin Books Ltd.

Woolf, V. (1982). *The Diary of Virginia Woolf Volume 3: 1925–30*. Edited by Bell, A.O. assisted by McNeillie, A. Harmondsworth: Penguin Books Ltd.

Woolf, V. (1983). *The Diary of Virginia Woolf Volume 4: 1931–35*. Edited by Bell, A.O. assisted by McNeillie, A. Harmondsworth: Penguin Books Ltd.

Woolf, V. (1985). *The Diary of Virginia Woolf Volume 5: 1936–41*. Edited by Bell, A.O. assisted by McNeillie, A. Harmondsworth: Penguin Books Ltd.

Woolf, V. (2014 [1928]). *Orlando: A Biography*. London: William Collins.

Woolf, V. (2014 [1929]). 'A Room of One's Own'. In Woolf, V. (ed.) *A Room of One's Own and Three Guineas*. London: Harper Collins.

INDEX

Printed and bound by CPI Group (UK) Ltd, Croydon, CR0 4YY

12/07/2024

01018196-0005